OPEN POETRY

Four Anthologies of Expanded Poems

EDITED BY

Ronald Gross and George Quasha

WITH

Emmett Williams,
John Robert Colombo
and Walter Lowenfels

SIMON AND SCHUSTER New York

Published by Simon and Schuster
Rockefeller Center, 630 Fifth Avenue
New York, New York 10020

First printing
SBN 671-21139-0
Library of Congress Catalog Card Number: 72-83078
Manufactured in the United States of America
Printed by The Murray Printing Company, Forge Village, Mass.
Bound by The Plimpton Press, Norwood, Mass.

DESIGNED BY IRVING PERKINS

ACKNOWLEDGMENTS

Acknowledgment is gratefully given to the following poets, their representatives and publishers for permission to include the poems in this anthology:

METAPOETRY: THE POETRY OF CHANGES.

HELEN ADAM for "Song for a Sea-Tower" (musical transcriptions by Louise Gikow), from *STONY BROOK* 3/4 (1969).

DAVID ANTIN for "Definitions for Mendy," from *Definitions*, Caterpillar Books, 1967, originally published in *Some/Thing*, Spring 1965; and for "10th Separation Meditation," from *Meditations*, 1971, originally published in *Sumac*, Winter/Spring, 1970, and subsequently by Black Sparrow Press, Los Angeles.

GEORGE BOWERING for "Before the Revolution" and "A Tainted Memory," from *STONY BROOK* 3/4 (1969), © 1970 by George Bowering.

DAVID BROMIGE for "Looking Out, 5 a.m. July 29, Berkeley California, 1969" and "Paris in April," from *STONY BROOK* 3/4 (1969) and *Threads*, Black Sparrow Press, Los Angeles, 1971.

NORMAN O. BROWN for "Daphne, or Metamorphosis" from *Myths, Dreams and Religion*, edited by Joseph Campbell, E. P. Dutton and Co., Inc., New York, 1970.

CHARLES BUKOWSKI for "What a Man I Was" (first in *Caterpillar* 8/9 [1969]) and "The Way It Will Happen Inside a Can of Peaches" (first in *STONY BROOK* 3/4 [1969]), from *The Days Run Away Like Wild Horses Over the Hill*, Black Sparrow Press, Los Angeles, 1969.

JOHN CAGE "17," "30," "35," "47," and "85" copyright © 1970 Henmar Press, Inc., 373 Park Ave. S., N.Y.C. 10016. Song #73 based on Merce Cunningham's *Changes: Notes on Choreography*, edited by Frances Starr, © 1968 Something Else Press, Inc., New York; reprinted by permission of the publisher; all rights reserved.

BOBBIE L. CREELEY for "Salem Yellow Bird," "He," and "no concrete image," © 1971 Bobbie L. Creeley.

HAROLD DICKER for "Or Haven't I Told You," "The Prize of War Is Always" (in the recording *Poems for Peace*/1966), "I Said/He Said," "The Mouth Is a Zoo" and "For the Day of Atonement/1963" from *STONY BROOK* 3/4 (1969); "Requiem for Three Dead," supplement to *Yale Literary Review*, Spring 1963; "The Nineteenth Psalm."

HAROLD DULL for "Suibhne Gheilt," from *Images Cross Bridges*, *STONY BROOK* 3/4 (1969), and *Ephemerus*.

GEORGE ECONOMOU for "The White Wolf" and "The Cheer" from *Landed Natures*, Black Sparrow Press, Los Angeles, 1969.

RUSSELL EDSON for "The Childhood of an Equestrian" and "Old Folks" from *STONY BROOK* 3/4 (1969).

LARRY EIGNER for "Small, flightless birds," "The Confederacy, you have to," "sleep was in his mouth . . . ," from *Air the Trees*, © 1968 by Larry Eigner, Black Sparrow Press, Los Angeles; "sleep was in my mouth . . ." first appeared in *Camels Coming* magazine.

CLAYTON ESHLEMAN for "Lachrymae Mateo" and "Soutine" (first appeared in *STONY BROOK* 3/4 [1969]), from *Indiana*, Black Sparrow Press, Los Angeles, 1969; "The Meadow," from *Altars*, Black Sparrow Press, Los Angeles, 1971.

GROVE PRESS, INC. for Cesar Vallejo's "Telluric and Magnetic," translated from the Spanish by Clayton Eshleman, © 1968 by Grove Press, Inc.

MICHAEL HAMBURGER for his translations from the German of Friedrich Hölderlin's poetic fragments, "So Mahommed . . . ," "Patmos [Fragment of a Late Version]" and for his notes taken from His Introduction, in *Friedrich Hölderlin: Poems and Fragments,* University of Michigan Press, Ann Arbor, © 1966, Michael Hamburger.

JIM HARRISON for "What in coils works with riddle's logic . . . ," "If you were less of a vowel . . . ," "Maps. Maps. Maps . . . ," "The child crawls in circles . . . ," "These corners that stick out . . . ," "The brain opens the hand . . . ," "Drinking Song," and "Awake," from *Outlyer and Ghazals,* Simon and Schuster, New York, 1971.

MICHAEL HELLER for "The Cardiac Poem," *Sumac,* Vol. II, Nos. 2 and 3.

ANSELM HOLLO for "the mosaic standard from Ur," "Song of the tusk," "on the occasion of becoming an echo," "Iowa City crickets," "Song," © Anselm Hollo 1965, 1969, 1970, from *Maya: work 1959–1969,* Grossman Publishers, New York, 1970; for "Iowa City crickets" and "Song," in *Sumac,* Winter/Spring 1970; for Paul Klee's "Irrational Speech," "Individuality," "The Rescue," "Poem," "Poem," "A Friend," "The Wolf Speaks," and "Caught," © Anselm Hollo 1963, 1970 from *Some Poems by Paul Klee,* Scorpion Press (England) and City Lights, San Francisco, 1963.

HALVARD JOHNSON for "From the Lakes," from *Transparencies & Projections,* and "The Dance of the Red Swan," from *The Dance of the Red Swan,* © 1969 and 1971 by Halvard Johnson, published by New Rivers Press, New York; both poems appeared first in *STONY BROOK* 3/4 (1969).

DAVID JONES for "The Tutelar of the Place," from *Agenda,* Volume V, 1–3, Spring/Summer 1967.

ROBERT KELLY for "Hymn of the Sons of Light Headed This Way Over the Milk Way," from *The Common Shore,* Black Sparrow Press, Los Angeles, © 1969 Robert Kelly; "Glad Yods" reprinted from *Caterpillar #11,* 1970, by permission of the editor.

JOANNE KYGER for "A Test of Fantasy" reprinted from *STONY BROOK* 3/4 (1969).

JACKSON MAC LOW for "7th Light Poem: for John Cage—17 June 1962" and "14th Light Poem: for Frances Witlin—10 August 1962," from *22 Light Poems,* Black Sparrow Press, Los Angeles, 1968.

JOHN MONTAGUE for "The Bread God," The Dolmen Press, Dublin, © John Montague, 1968.

LAURINE NIEDECKER for "Paean to Place," from *My Life by Water,* Fulcrum Press, London, 1970; first printed in *STONY BROOK* 3/4 (1969).

GEOFFREY O'BRIEN for "The Tender Fascists," from *STONY BROOK* 3/4 (1969), and "A Woman's Face," © 1970 Geoffrey O'Brien.

GEORGE OPPEN and NEW DIRECTIONS PUBLISHING CORPORATION for "Route," from *Of Being Numerous,* New Directions, New York, © 1968 by George Oppen.

ROCHELLE OWENS for "Humble Humble Pinati," from *Trobar 2.*

NICANOR PARRA for "Letters from the Poet Who Sleeps in a Chair," translated from the Spanish by George Quasha and Trinidad Jimenez-Orrego, from *Sumac,* Vol. I, No. 1 (1968), reprinted in this translation by permission of New Directions Publishing Corporation, publishers of *Emergency Poems,* copyright © 1972 by Nicanor Parra and Miller Williams.

GEORGE QUASHA for "Umiak's Polar Callings," "The Weight of the Matter or Where It Is Pulling" and "Homage to What I Hear Is So," copyright © 1972 by George Quasha; "Rilke's Ninth Elegy Transposed," copyright © 1969 by George Quasha, first published in *STONY BROOK* 3/4 (1969); and Hans Arp's "Is It So It's Shriveling Up," copyright © 1972 by George Quasha.

JEROME ROTHENBERG for "Sightings II," "Sightings III," "Further Sightings: The Old King," "Conversation Fifteen," "The Water of the Flowery Mill (II)," and "Poland/1931: The Wedding," from *Poems for the Game of Silence,* © 1964, 1966, 1968, 1970 and 1971 by Jerome Rothenberg, with permissions also of Dial Press, New York; for "The Steward's Testimony," from *A Book of Testimony,* Tree Press, 1971; for "Pre-Face," "Midē Songs & Picture Songs," and "Booger Event," from *Technicians of the Sacred,* © 1968 by Jerome Rothenberg, with permission also of Doubleday and Co., New York; for the "11th Horse-Song of Frank Mitchell," originally published in *STONY BROOK* 3/4 (1969) and by Tetrad Press (London), © 1970 by Jerome Rothenberg; for two songs from *Shaking the Pumpkin.*

ARMAND SCHWERNER for "Seaweed," "Poem at the Bathroom Door, by Adam," from *Seaweed,* Black Sparrow Press, Los Angeles, 1969; for "Two on The Tablets"; for "Tablets IV, V, VI," from *The Tablets I-VIII,* The Cummington Press, 1968; for "From the Amazon: the bird Tamurupara" and "Tomorrow" by Henri Michaux.

HUGH SEIDMAN for "The Making of Color," from *Collecting Evidence,* © 1970, Hugh Seidman, also with permission of Yale University Press.

CHARLES SIMIC and GEORGE BRAZILLER, INC. for "Stone Inside a Stone," "Concerning my Neighbors, the Hittites," "Fork," and "Bestiary for the Fingers of My Right Hand," from *Dismantling the Silence,* George Braziller, Inc., copyright © 1971 by Charles Simic.

GEORGE STANLEY and GROVE PRESS, INC. for "ACHILLES Poem," first printed in *STONY BROOK* 3/4 (1969), from *You (Poems 1957–1968),* Grove Press, New York, © 1963, 1965, 1967, 1968, 1969 George Stanley.

CHARLES STEIN for "Two Songs for Hermes" and "Cave of the Nymphs," copyright © 1972 by Charles Stein.

NATHANIEL TARN and RANDOM HOUSE, INC. for Sections Two and Five from *The Beautiful Contradictions,* © 1969 by Nathaniel Tarn, Random House, New York.

ROBERT VAS DIAS for "Urban Crisis," from *Sumac,* Vol. I, No. 3, © 1969 by The Sumac Press, also with permission of the Editors.

DIANE WAKOSKI for "Blue Monday," from *Inside the Blood Factory,* © 1962, 1968 by Diane Wakoski, also with permission of Doubleday & Company, Inc., Garden City; for "The Prince of Darkness Passing Through This House," from *The Magellanic Clouds,* © 1970 Diane Wakoski, Black Sparrow Press, Los Angeles; for "I Have Had to Learn to Live with My Face," from *Caterpillar* 10 (1970).

ELIOT WEINBERGER for "Jungle 1," "Jungle 5," "Jungle 6," and "Jungle," copyright © 1972 by Eliot Weinberger.

LOUIS ZUKOFSKY for "A–15," from *A 13–21,* Jonathan Cape Ltd., London, © 1969 by Louis Zukofsky.

LANGUAGE HAPPENINGS

GEORGE BRECHT for six selections from *Water Yam,* Copyright by Fluxus, New York. Reprinted by permission of the author.

CLAUS BREMER for "lichtfänge," from *material 1*, Darmstadt, 1958; "to provoke," from *engagierende texte*, edited by Hansjorg Mayer, Stuttgart, 1966; "ist der text," from *ideogramme*, Frauenfeld, 1964; "participate," from *ideogramme*, Frauenfeld, 1964. Reprinted by permission of the author.

PHILIP CORNER. Copyright by Philip Corner. Reprinted by permission of the author.

AUGUSTO DE CAMPOS for "uma vez," from *Antologia Noigandres 4*, São Paulo, 1958; "colocaramas," from *Antologia Noigandres 5*, São Paulo, 1962; "o novelo," from *Antologia Noigandres 5*, São Paulo, 1962. Reprinted by permission of the author.

HAROLDO DE CAMPOS for "branco," from *Antologia Noigandres 4*, São Paulo, 1958; "cristal," from *Antologia Noigandres 3*, São Paulo, 1956; "se nasce morre," from *Antologia Noigandres 5*, São Paulo, 1962. Reprinted by permission of the author.

ALVARO DE SÁ for six poems from *12 x 9*. Reprinted by permission of the author.

DENIS DUNN for "all of these poetry"; "the star 61 cygni"; "high song 8". Reprinted by permission of the author.

CARL FERNBACH-FLARSHEIM for "arithmentical poem" and "code game" from *Conceptual Cloud Game, Book I*, Cypher Press, Philadelphia, 1967. Copyright 1967 by Carl Fernbach-Flarsheim. Reprinted by permission of the author.

ROBERT FILLIOU for "Yes—an action poem" from *A Filliou Sampler*, Something Else Press, New York, 1967. Reprinted by permission of the author.

IAN HAMILTON FINLAY for "redboat" from *20th Century Poetry & Poetics*, Oxford (Toronto), 1969; "Sea-Poppy 2" (card); "ballad" and "formal poem" from *RAPEL*, Wild Hawthorne Press, Edinburgh, 1963; "hearts/apples" (manuscript); "2 small songs" from *6 Small Songs in 3's*, Wild Hawthorn Press, Edinburgh, 1966. Reprinted by permission of the author.

EUGEN GOMRINGER for "streets and flowers" from *33 Konstellationen*, St. Gallen, 1960; "words are shadows" and "mist/mountain/butterfly" from *The Book of Hours and Constellations*, Something Else Press, New York, 1968; "ode" and "the system is foolproof" from *worte sind schatten: die konstellationen 1951–1968*, Rowohlt Verlag, Hamburg, 1969. Reprinted by permission of the author.

DICK HIGGINS for "Intermedial object #1" from *foew&ombwhnw*, Something Else Press, New York, 1969. Copyright © 1969 by Richard C. Higgins. Reprinted by permission of the author.

ALLAN KAPROW for "Raining" from *Some Recent Happenings*, Something Else Press, New York, 1966. Copyright © 1966 by Allan Kaprow. Reprinted by permission of the author.

ALISON KNOWLES for "A House of Dust," from *A House of Dust*, Gebr. Koning, Cologne/New York, 1968. Reprinted by permission of the author.

FERDINAND KRIWET Reprinted by permission of the author. All photographs copyright by Axel Offergeld.

MARKUS KUTTER for "Programme for Berio" from *Designing Programmes* by Karl Gerstner, Basel, 1962. Reprinted by permission of the author.

ROBERT LAX for five poems reprinted from *Voyages*, Vol. II, Nos. 3–4, Washington, D.C., 1968. Copyright © 1968 by Robert Lax. Reprinted by permission of the author.

JACKSON MAC LOW for "The Presidents of the United States of America." Reprinted by permission of the author.

HANSJÖRG MAYER for "alphabet" from *alphabetenquadratbuch*, Ed. Hansjörg Mayer, Stuttgart, 1965; "rosenschuttplatz" from *rosenschuttplatz*, Ed. Hansjörg Mayer, Stuttgart, 1964; "sau aus usa" poster, Ed. Hansjörg Mayer, Stuttgart, 1965; "oil" from *la lune en rodage*, Basel, 1965. Reprinted by permission of the author.

THOMAS MERTON. "Ovid," Semiotic Poem from Racine's *Iphigénie*," and "Whiske" were first published in Thomas Merton's journal *Monks Pond*, #3 & #4, copyright © 1968 by Thomas Merton. Reprinted by permission of the Trustees for the Merton Legacy Trust, New Directions Publishing Corporation agent. "Hurlup" and "Bronze Fashion" published by permission of the Trustees for the Merton Legacy Trust, New Directions Publishing Corporation agent.

PETER NEUMANN and EMMETT WILLIAMS for *Guillaumé Apollinaire*, reprinted by permission of the authors.

CLAES OLDENBURG
Statement reprinted from *Store Days—Documents from the Store (1961) and the Ray Gun Theatre, Selected by Claes Oldenburg and Emmett Williams*, Something Else Press, New York, 1967. Copyright © 1967 by Claes Thure Oldenburg. Reprinted by permission of the author.

BENJAMIN PATTERSON for selections from *Methods and Processes*, Paris, 1962. Reprinted by permission of the author.

DÉCIO PIGNATARI for "beba" from *Antologia Noigandres 5*, São Paulo, 1958; "mallarmé vietcong" from *exercicio findo*, São Paulo, 1968. Reprinted by permission of the author.

DITER ROT for "ut/tu" from *material 1*, Darmstadt, 1958; "she greened" from *Noch Mehr Scheisse*, Stuttgart, 1968; "also, green" and "for instance" from *The Blue Tide*, Something Else Press, New York, 1967; "e it is" from *Quadratbuch*, Hilversum, 1961; statement from advertising brochure. Reprinted by permission of the author.

GERHARD RÜHM for "du" from *edition et 1*, Berlin, 1966; "the night," "stern" and "blue in blue" from *konstellationen*, Frauenfeld, 1961. Reprinted by permission of the author.

MARY ELLEN SOLT for "forsythia" from *Flowers in Concrete*, Bloomington, 1966; "THE PEOPLEMOVER" (posters), Finial Press, Urbana, Illinois. Reprinted by permission of the author.

JAMES TENNEY for letter to Gertrude Stein. Reprinted by permission of the author.

EMMETT WILLIAMS for "soldier" (unpublished); "iv" from *fuhr 4 fur vier*, Stuttgart, 1969; "like attracts like" from *material 3*, Darmstadt, 1958; "marching song" from *WIN*, Vol. II, Nos. 14–15, New York, 1966; "sense/sound" from *An Anthology of Concrete Poetry*, Something Else Press, New York, 1967; "duet" from *the last french-fried potato and other poems*, Something Else Press, New York, 1968; "5,000 new ways" from London *Times Literary Supplement*, August 6, 1964. Reprinted by permission of the author.

FOUND POETRY

DAVID ANTIN for "A List of the Delusions of the Insane," "What They Are Afraid of," *Code of Flag Behavior*, copyright © 1968 by David Antin, Black Sparrow Press, 1968.

ELEANOR ANTIN for "The Proportions Which a Perfectly Formed Man's Body Should Possess," "Painter Poems," "A Certain Color," "The Way to Copy a Mountain from Nature."

MICHAEL BENEDIKT for "The Golden Years," "Finales," copyright © 1951 The Macmillan Company, and Michael Benedikt, 1960 and 1971; and for "Poem No. 1515*," copyright © 1967 by Michael Benedikt.

JOHN ROBERT COLOMBO for "The Central Intelligence Agency Awards . . . ," "Being a Somewhat Detailed Account . . . of the Sinister Chinaman," "Memory Gardens Association Limited," "Two Cures for Fever," "Overdue," "Levitations," "The Jingle of the Open Road."

KIRBY CONGDON for "Icarus in Aipotu," "Chorus for Phonograph."

JOHN DANIEL for "Watch," "Smith L. J.," "Injury to Insured," "Eel," "Of 91 men Leaving an Underground Station," "Colour Bra."

JOHN GIORNO for "Leather," "Rose," "Poem."

RONALD GROSS for "America Is Names," "Heroic Couplets," "Ditty," "2/29¢," "Sonnet," "Song of the Road," "Why Negroes Prefer Treatment as Human Beings," "Suppose, Instead," "Congratulatory Message," "Epithalamium," "Thank You—Come Again."

FRANK KUENSTLER for "Introductions," "Napoleon & the Letter M," "Movie Bulletin."

GAIL KUENSTLER for "Stage Directions," "Stagecraft," "An Accounting."

WALTER LOWENFELS for "Leader of First Raid on North Returns to U.S.," "From an Exposition of Power and Industrial Machinery," "Blood."

EDWARD LUCIE-SMITH for "Beckford at the Abbey of Batalha," copyright © 1970.

JACKSON MAC LOW for "Solar Speculations," "They're living it up at our expense," "Pattern Recognition by Machine," "4.5.10.11.2.8.4.2., the 2nd biblical poem," from *Stanzas for Iris Lezak*, written May-Oct. 1960, published in 1972 by Something Else Press, Barton, Vt.; copyright © 1971 by Jackson Mac Low. All rights reserved.

EDWIN MORGAN for "7 Newspoems," copyright © Edwin Morgan and *Exit* magazine.

RICHARD O'CONNELL for "Poems I (Mistaken Corpse), XXVI, XXXII, XXXIX (Niteroi Item), XLIII, LXXXIV, LXXXV, LXXXIX, XCIII, CVII," "World-Mesh 1950 A.D.," copyright © 1917 Richard O'Connell; and "Letter from the New World."

JOHN PERREAULT for "Flag," "Hatbox," "Questionnaire."

ROBERT L. PETERS for "Pop Poem #2," "Emergency Exit," copyright © Robert L. Peters.

DOM ROBERT PETITPIERRE for "Poems of Jesus: Poem 8, Poem 128, Poem 153."

BERN PORTER for "Sound," "—88—," "All Points Bulletin," "The Snow Queen," "End."

JEROME ROTHENBERG for "The Key of Solomon," copyright © 1970 Jerome Rothenberg, *Poland/1931*, Unicorn Press, 1970; "The Lovers," "Further Sightings," Kunapipi, *Technicians of the Sacred*, Doubleday, 1968; "Satan in Goray," *Poems for the Game of Silence*, Dial Press, 1971.

HANNAH WEINER for "Code Poem," copyright © Hannah Weiner.

THE POETRY OF SURVIVAL

DAVID ANTIN for "who are my friends," *Code of Flag Behavior*, Black Sparrow Press, 1968.

LAWRENCE BENFORD for "The Beginning of a Long Poem on Why I Burned the City," copyright © 1969 by International Publishers, Co., Inc., from *New Black Poetry*.

EDWIN BROOKS for "Land of the Lie."

OLGA CABRAL (OLGA CABRAL KURTZ) for "Africa."

TERRY CANNON for "We Are Not Americans," copyright © 1969 Terence Cannon.

HAROLD CARRINGTON for "poem for sister salvation."

LEN CHANDLER for "Walking Up the Steps."

KIRBY CONGDON for "Television-Movie," copyright © 1966, *Juggernaut,* Interim Books.

RICHARD DAVIDSON for "Death of a Man," copyright © Spring 1969, *Freedomways* magazine.

GEORGE DOWDEN for "Obscenity (Part II of Renew Jerusalem)," copyright © 1969 George Dowden; *Renew Jerusalem,* Smyrna Press, New York.

HENRY DUMAS (LORETTA DUMAS) for "mosaic harlem."

NIKKI GIOVANNI for "Woman Poem," copyright © 1968 Nikki Giovanni, from "A Black Judgement."

DAVID HENDERSON for "Bopping*," copyright © 1967 by D.H.

CALVIN C. HERNTON for "Jitterbugging in the Streets."

ELTON HILL-ABU ISHAK for "Theme Brown Girl."

GERALD JACKSON for "Poems to Americans."

LANCE JEFFERS for "Man With a Furnace in His Hand."

ALICIA L. JOHNSON for "Black Lotus/a prayer."

JOE JOHNSON for "If I Ride This Train," copyright © 1969 Joe Johnson.

BOB KAUFMAN and New Directions Publishing Corporation for "Benediction" from *Solitudes Crowded With Loneliness, copyright* © 1961 by Bob Kaufman.

ETHERIDGE KNIGHT for "The Idea of Ancestry," copyright © 1968 Etheridge Knight.

BILL KNOTT (1940–1966) for "Unedited Tape"; refuses all copyrights to this or any other of his works.

JOEL KOHUT for "That I Had Seen. . . ."

T. L. KRYSS for "This Wind."

DON L. LEE for "The Death Dance," Broadside Press, Detroit, Michigan.

WALTER LOWENFELS for "Elegy for the Old Language" and his "Introduction."

CLARENCE MAJOR for "The Comic Moneypowerdream."

IFEANYI MENKITI for "Reflections," The Stony Brook Poetics Foundation.

ANNE OSWALD for "Insurrection One—D.C."

FELIX POLLAK for "A Matter of History," which appeared originally under the pen name Felix Anselm in *Between Worlds #2,* copyright © 1961 by Inter-American University at San German, Puerto Rico.

LENNOX RAPHAEL for "Lament for Lloyd Warner," copyright © 1969 Lennox Raphael.

EUGENE REDMOND for "barbecued cong, OR we laid MY LAI low."

CAROLYN RODGERS for "for Alex Haley."

JEROME ROTHENBERG for "A Bodhisattva Undoes Hell," originally published in *The Seven Hells of Jigoku Zoshi* by Jerome Rothenberg (Trobar Books, New York, 1962), reprinted in *Between: Poems 1960–1963* by Jerome Rothenberg, Fulcrum Press, 1967.

SONIA SANCHEZ for "For Unborn Malcolms," copyright © Sonia Sanchez, 1969.

ARMAND SCHWERNER for "The inheritors" from *Seaweed*, copyright © 1969 by Armand Schwerner, Black Sparrow Press.

THURMOND SNYDER for "Beale Street, Memphis," in *New Negro Poets: U.S.A.*, edited by Langston Hughes.

TAR LEE SUN for "Blackfireness."

HARVEY TUCKER for "Tossed Upon the Rock," copyright © 1968 by Harvey Tucker.

NANCY WILLARD for "A Speech for the Unborn."

WILLIAM WANTLING for "Your Children's Dead Eyes."

I wish to thank Susan Jane Cohen, whose labors on the manuscript have made this book a reality and have contributed significantly to preserving the editor's sanity. Special thanks also to Jerome Rothenberg for assembling the Indian poetries in the Metatranslation section and to Alix Nelson and Gypsy da Silva for their numerous labors and endless patience on behalf of the book.

G.Q.

PREFACE

Enough! or Too Much
William Blake

Maybe the only excuse for yet another poetry anthology is the fact that poets continue to produce more interesting new work than existing collections reflect. Our scene is very different from the cultural vacuum at the turn of the century which drove Ezra Pound heroically to seek to "resuscitate the dead art of poetry." Nowadays even poets complain about artistic "overproduction" in America and about how difficult it is to keep up. Some individuals fear that the appearance of hundreds of new poets and thousands of new poems in the Sixties is some sort of threat to cultural manageability. It is. The situation is clearly out of hand. There will be no more "definitive" books about, or anthologies of, Poetry Now. And there seems little likelihood that a single figure like Eliot or Pound or Olson will arise again to call the main tune for a decade, let alone an age. We appear to be stuck with Whitman's Open Road, which is only a *road* to the poet traveling his own way; to the onlooker it is a sprawling network of intermingling back streets.

We can retreat from this "anarchy" either out of fear that the "center cannot hold" or out of hope that such and such values will eventually triumph. Or we can participate in this indefinable interaction of creative forces as one more chance to play in the Fields of the Lord, taking the Real when and where we can get it. The present collection makes no bones about voting for the latter, believing that the road of excess leads not only to the Palace of Wisdom but also to the next town.

Anthologies are filtering devices designed to give the illusion of significant order. Some claim to reveal *the* new direction or, worse, the *best* poetry of a certain period. Surely everybody admits that an editor's choice of poets and poems is at least personal; most editors will admit that their choice is also tactical; to promote certain values at the expense of others. Let us claim nothing more here than to have collected, within the limits of time, energy and available resources, that work which seems both to add to our definition of what poetry is and to be in need of greater circulation.

Specifically, our book seeks to enrich the active image of contemporary poetry by presenting it mainly in the light of its attempt to expand the medium itself. Special emphasis has been placed on the variety of means being employed now in putting language to new communicative uses. Many poets who must figure in any serious discussion of open or experimental poetry and whose work has developed in new directions in the Sixties have been excluded because of their frequent or extensive inclusion in other anthologies: poets such as Charles Olson, Robert Duncan, Paul Blackburn, Robert Creeley, Denise Levertov, John Ashbury, Frank O'Hara, Allen Ginsberg, LeRoi Jones, Gary Snyder, Philip Lamantia, and others represented in *The New American Poetry* (ed. Donald Allen, 1960). A useful recent collection, *An Anthology of New York Poets* (ed. Ron Padgett and David Shapiro, 1970), has made it unnecessary to represent such poets as Ed Sanders, Ted Berrigan, Tom Clark, Lewis Mac Adams, Peter Schjeldahl, and others.

Our collection involves four editor's choices of work (for the most part composed and published in the Sixties) which represents four tendencies of poetry now: Metapoetry: the Poetry of Changes, Language Happenings (Concrete and Intermedia Poetry), Found Poetry, and the "Poetry of Survival." The categories are mere conveniences and with respect to certain inclusions they may verge on the arbitrary. They are intended to be useful in rendering this book and the poetry it represents more readable; if taken *too* seriously they could have the opposite effect. Since the sub-editors enjoyed virtual editorial autonomy, we view this book as comprised of four anthologies. Such a view generously spares the editors any direct responsibility for the others' choices and allows the book a certain structural uniqueness in its "openness" to a number of definitions of "open poetry." This view also implies that we do not regard ourselves as custodians of the culture but as participants in a process of self-renewal which we wish to clarify without reducing.

GEORGE QUASHA

New York
February 1971

CONTENTS

THE POETRY OF SURVIVAL
edited by Walter Lowenfels

METAPOETRY: THE POETRY OF CHANGES

EDITED BY
George Quasha

METAPOETRY: THE POETRY OF CHANGES

George Quasha

Art's obscured the difference between art and life. Now let life obscure the difference between life and art.—John Cage

---

It may be true, as Oscar Wilde said, that life imitates art, in somewhat the same sense that we are what we eat. William Blake's poet-prophet Los "became what he beheld." What we make feeds back into us and makes claims on the structure (and limits) of consciousness. Our concern with the "meaning" of art is our concern with relating authentically to the environment by understanding the nature of our participation in it. And what we think of as the modern revolution in the arts, or the succession of events which have cumulatively altered our conceptions of form in this century, is the history of our search for a language which can counteract the more or less constant threat of psychic disintegration. Poetry is the specific instance of language, magnified. The test case. It gauges our seriousness in the business of speaking. And the way we go about making it is a tipoff as to whether or not we regard our present language as adequate to the task—"to get said what must be said," as Dr. Williams put it.

The experimental demonstrations of one man may save the time of many. . . . —Ezra Pound

To be democratic, local (in the sense of being attached with integrity to actual experience) Stein, or any other artist, must for subtlety ascend to a plane of almost abstract design to keep alive.—William Carlos Williams

---

Metapoetry is an extreme expression of a tendency of all art toward the discovery of more and more precisely adequate forms. Unlike conservative expressions, it rises out of a critical sense of the failures of culturally approved modes. Ezra Pound defined poetry as news that stays news, but for all his attempts to revive the living poetries buried in the past he did not mean to say that past forms were sufficient tools for the present. He was seeking a radical redefinition of poetic possibilities and returning to the roots of civilization in order to show how much had been lost in the watery conventions handed over to us by the nineteenth century. *The Cantos* stands as a major metapoetic effort to establish a dialectic between the lost possibilities of the past and the unrealized language of the present. The Confucian command is *Make it new,* whatever it is—a Provencal tune, an Adams letter, the configuration of birds on a prison-camp wire, or the primary data of consciousness.

I have heard many People say Give me the Ideas. It is no matter what Words you put them into and others say Give me the Design it is no matter for the Execution. These People know Enough of Artifice but Nothing of Art. Ideas cannot be Given but in their minutely Appropriate Words nor Can a Design be made without its minutely Appropriate Execution.—William Blake

But there is no single hero of metapoetry. In fact if there's any point at all in trying to define it, the point is to move us beyond restrictive definitions of poetry and to shift our focus from aesthetics to the essential functions of language. Our business is to enlarge the domain of the sayable, even if that means challenging the category of art. It may be possible to see metapoetry as the expression of a period where the center of poetic consciousness is taken over by a sense that survival depends on transformation. The fear of "chaos" at the heart of conservative imagination gives way as it becomes clear that the function of the thing worth conserving is too remote to be named. The metapoet seeks deeper connections with the actuality of his time than existing ideas of order or forms of expression can provide. He is conscious of an embarrassing problem of art: that it has a way of talking us out of the trouble we're in by setting itself above the root problems, licking its wounds in the interest of making "good" poetry, and avoiding the whole matter of springing the trap of language and consciousness.

Art is made to disturb.—Georges Braque

Cubism is a state of mind.—Juan Gris

I have written that which I believe breaks the spell of poetry.—Laura Riding

In key ways William Blake provides an early image of the metapoet. He created an expanded visual-verbal language in order to bring about a revolution in consciousness. He sought a level of transformation that would feed back into life, partly by exposing the ways that art and culture generally played into the hands of a diseased civilization and partly by offering actual models of spiritual expansion. And he was a forerunner of the Cubists and other modern experimentalists who would seek a "way beyond art," a route more directly in keeping with new conceptions of reality advanced by Einstein, Heisenberg, Whitehead, and others. Gertrude Stein developed a new analytic syntax that brought to language process the multiplicity of perspectives on a single event which had been brought to painting by Braque, Picasso, and Juan Gris. Her "prose" is metapoetry. And related to Stein's work is that of Laura Riding, in which she tried to go "beyond the poetic as a literary category" and enter "the field of the general human ideal in speaking"; it was her conviction that she had pushed poetry to the breaking point by exposing the conflict "between the motive of humanly perfect word-use and that of artistically perfect word-use." Ultimately she found truth and beauty to be irreconcilable and gave up poetry after 1938; like Duchamp, she felt she had put art to the final test, and in her laboratory it had failed. Both

Stein and Riding, in different ways, operate from a metapoetic stance in their redefinition of poetic functions and boundaries.

. . . The composition in which we live makes the art which we see and hear.—Gertrude Stein

If one thinks of the literal root of the word *verse,* "a line, furrow, turning—*vertere,* to turn . . .," he will come to a sense of "free verse" as that instance of writing in poetry which "turns" upon the occasion with, in fact, the issue of, its own nature rather than to an abstract decision of "form" taken from a prior instance.—Robert Creeley

---

The 1950s was a period of renewed experimentation both in America and abroad. In various ways the earlier developments in the work of Pound, Williams, Stein, Zukofsky, and the Dada and Surrealist poets began to be absorbed in new metapoetic tendencies. On the American scene, there was the now famous Black Mountain group, which mainly developed out of the later work of Pound and Williams and which centered around Charles Olson's theories of "projective verse" and "composition by field." Within the group there was a wide range of individual tendencies which are not specifically accounted for by Olson's theories; Robert Duncan, for example, derives almost as much from a long tradition of visionary literature and from the modernist practice of Stein, Joyce, and others as he does from Pound, Williams, and Olson. But from the present perspective the work of the projectivists figures in an international constellation of events which also includes the "concrete poetry" of the early fifties, begun by the Swiss poet Eugen Gomringer and the Brazilian poets Haroldo de Campos, Augusto de Campos, and Decio Pignatari. The fact that the Brazilian group took their name *Noigandres* from Pound's *Cantos* is one sign of the hidden interconnectedness of events which have opened the ways of poetry in the fifties, sixties and now the seventies.

From the moment [a poet] ventures into FIELD COMPOSITION—puts himself in the open—he can go by no track other than the one the poem under hand declares for itself. Thus he has to behave, and be, instant by instant, aware of some several forces just now beginning to be examined. . . .—Charles Olson

. . . In one way or another to live in the swarm of human speech. This is not to seek perfection but to draw honey or poetry out of all things. After Freud, we are aware that unwittingly we achieve our form. It is, whatever our mastery, the inevitable use we make of the speech that betrays to ourselves and to our hunters (our readers) the spore of what we are becoming. . . . A longing grows to return to the open composition in which the accidents and imperfections of speech might awake intimations of human being.—Robert Duncan

---

Olson's talk about "open" as opposed to "closed verse" derived from his concern with the whole matter of getting at the roots of speech and returning poetry to the primary energies of mind and body. Like the concretists he saw the main obstacles to any profound renewal of language and consciousness as a linguistic problem. The different approaches of the projectivists and the concretists, like those of Joyce and Stein, meet in their efforts to create a new syntax. And Olson's definition of dynamic poetic process as a moving "field" of force is related to Gomringer's description of non-linear clusters of words as "constellations." Both notions bear the influence of science and technology, in Olson's (and Duncan's) case deriving directly from Whitehead's view of the universe as a process of creative evolution in which all events are interrelated. The poet becomes metapoet when he sees the revolution in poetics as inseparable from the intellectual revolution of his time.

I know my Execution is not like Any Body Else. I do not intend it should be so: none but Blockheads copy one another.—William Blake

If I paint what I know, I bore myself. If I paint what you know, I bore you. So I paint what I don't know.—Franz Klein

---

Metapoetry (from *meta*, "change, transformation," and *poesis*, "making") is as undefinable as Proteus is unseizable. In a general way I would define a metapoem as an act of language which:

1) embodies specific principles of language-transformation in its structural operations;

2) re-enacts the "self-transcending" nature of language (as the phenomenologist Merleau-Ponty puts it) where each authentic use of a word redefines the possibilities of the word;

3) expands existing ideas of form and the process of composition, altering the rules of the game as a necessary condition of playing the game;

4) redefines the "boundaries" of poetry either by introducing non-aesthetic criteria to the process (such as Laura Riding's standard of the "general human ideal in speaking" or "truth") or by cross-pollenating poetic discourse with the matter and logic of other art forms or intellectual disciplines (such as, in the work represented in this section, John Cage's application of musical structure to poetry and Norman O. Brown's union of myth, psychoanalysis and poetry.

Chance frees us from the net of meaninglessness.—Hans Arp

In its extreme forms metapoetry threatens to annihilate poetry, or so it appears to literary society generally. Gertrude Stein saw the function of art as cultural disruption, and she saw the poet's real usefulness as ending with his general acceptance by the public. The metapoet is not necessarily a "poet" by literary standards: Cage and Brown invade the domain of poetry from alien disciplines, seeking modes of expression which their own areas had not provided. Jackson Mac Low, perhaps the most "dangerously" energetic innovator of the last two decades and a man whose influence on experimental poetry has far exceeded his reputation, has since the early Fifties (like Cage) introduced chance operations into poetry, theater, dance, and music. And Louis Zukofsky and George Oppen were underground influences on new poetry for decades before receiving any general recognition.

Each poem grows from an energy-mind-field-dance, and has its own inner grain. To let it grow, to let it speak for itself, is a large part of the work of the poet. A scary chaos fills the heart as 'spir'itual breath—in'spir'ation; and is breathed out into the thing-world as a poem. From there it must jump to the hearer's under'stand'ing. The wider the gap the more difficult; and the greater the delight when it crosses.—Gary Snyder

---

The fact of the matter is that renewals of poetry can come from virtually any source. A recent article called "New Words and Neologisms," by the psychiatrist David V. Forest, includes a "thesaurus of coinages by a schizophrenic savant" with the following entry (defined by the patient): "*Stereotranslation:* Solid change of language, solid changing of interpretation, word of overidolization. The most cherished word of English. Respected, cherished, lovable words, solid, hard. Solid understanding. Cherishing, begetting. One word begets another, with similar meaning and opposite." We think of *Finnegans Wake.* Hans Arp's "concrete art"—"an elemental, natural, healthy art, which causes stars of peace, love and poetry to grow in the head and the heart." The whole business, following Pound's massive labors of translation, to bring foreign poetries into English, and the sort of thing we're now getting with Jerome Rothenberg's renderings of tribal poetries. A great deal of what was once thought "insane" turns out to be the real data of primary consciousness seeking a language, and after the arguments of linguists and anthropologists like Lévi-Strauss we begin to learn that the "savage mind" is a universal property buried beneath our cultural veils. Metapoetry offers evidence of what was previously inadmissable. Poets like Gary Synder, Jerome Rothenberg, and Armand Schwerner, in their translation of tribal poetries and in their own work which makes use of similar structures, reclaim areas of our consciousness which have a certain resonance with the otherwise atavistic roots of language. Michael Hamburger's monumental translation of Hölderlin and Anselm Hollo's versions of Paul Klee's poetry are reminders that these concerns are not new to Western poetry.

. . . In Vallejo, and *not* in Neruda, the entire consciousness of modern South American man is suffered and partially redeemed; Neruda stays within the bounds of what we (North Americans and Europeans) have expected from South America—the anaconda in the Brazilian swamp, *contra Yanqui,* gorgeous and metrical; the *Poemas Humanos* of Vallejo are still in South America *not* read, because the consciousness is *altered.*—Clayton Eshleman

---

Metapoetry embodies a new consciousness by bringing to light what was inadmissable evidence. Poets like Clayton Eshleman and Diane Wakoski have extended the confessional motive of poetry with a directness and thoroughness that calls into question the literary exploitations of mental disorder by the so-called "confessional poets." The energy of these younger poets' work involves an actual shedding of false selves that does not give over to literary respectability or aesthetic self-gratification. And, from a very different angle, David Antin explores the motive of definition in poetry with the unsentimental mind shaped by Wittgenstein and linguistic science. Like the extraordinary writing of John Cage, the work of both David Antin and Robert Kelly opens poetry to a degree of intellectual integrity which it has not often been able to embody.

The poem of the mind in the act of finding
What will suffice . . . . —Wallace Stevens

Mind is shapely. —Allen Ginsberg

In each case the sort of poet I'm linking with metapoetry brings a special severity to his composition, and the standard of authentic speech which he holds in his mind brings about some kind of expansion of the resources of poetry. As a general phenomenon metapoetry is inherently dialectical in its counterstances to accepted ideas of meaningful form. Many metapoetries together raise the level of conflicting poetic theories from the polemical to the anarchic. Metapoetry aims at a condition of creative activity which opposes the tendency of culture to establish approved standards: a condition where forms exist as one-time functions, where every use of language suggests a new power of language. In reality this is an ideal statement of metapoetic "aims": It paints an idealistic picture of something like ultimate cultural health. At the least: It gauges our rigidity.

Complaint: you open doors; what we want to know is which ones you close. (Doors I open close automatically after I go through.) —John Cage

---

HELEN ADAM

Song for a Sea Tower

Transcribed from a tape by Louise Gikow

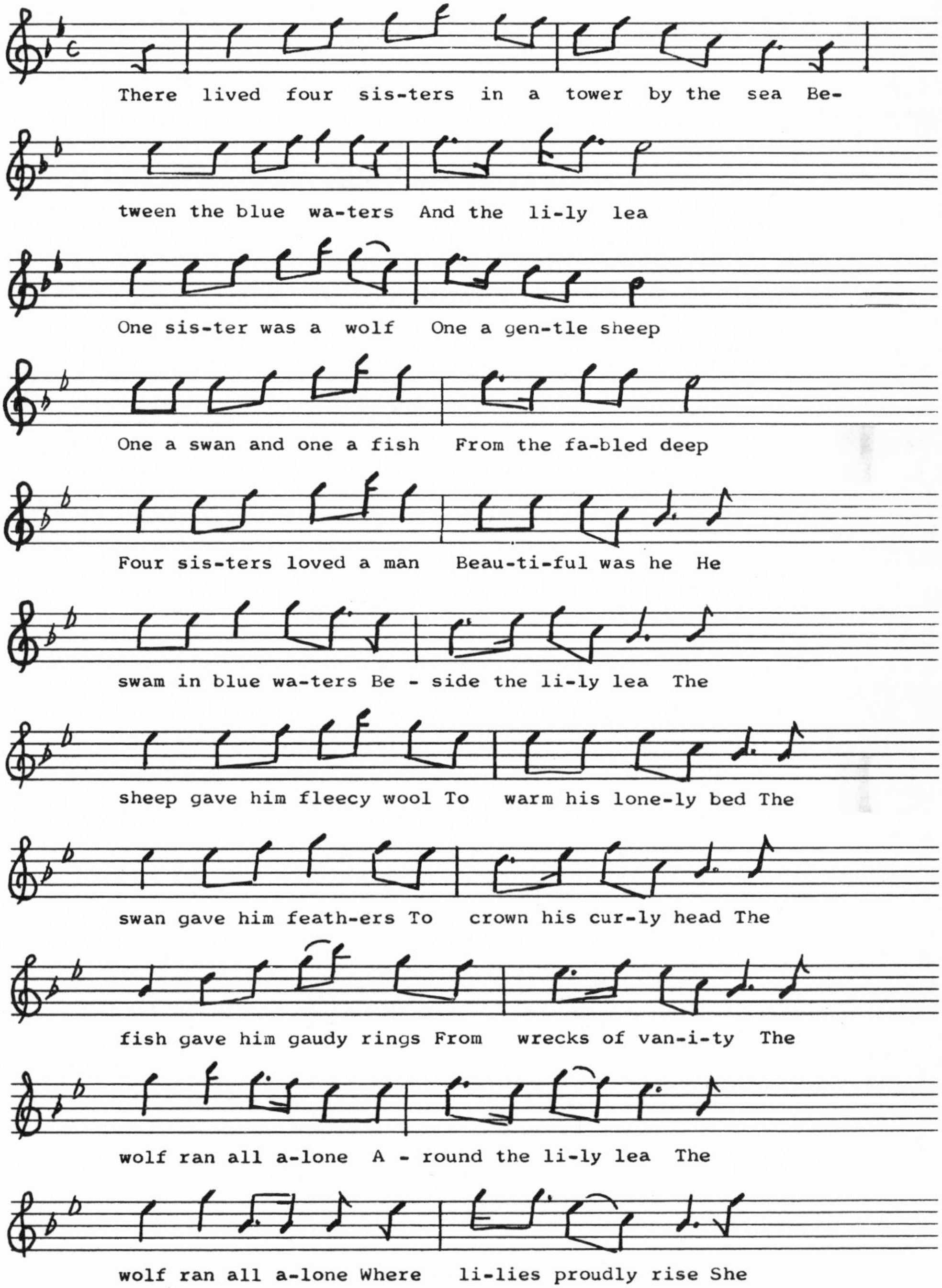
There lived four sis-ters in a tower by the sea Be-
tween the blue wa-ters And the li-ly lea
One sis-ter was a wolf One a gen-tle sheep
One a swan and one a fish From the fa-bled deep
Four sis-ters loved a man Beau-ti-ful was he He
swam in blue wa-ters Be - side the li-ly lea The
sheep gave him fleecy wool To warm his lone-ly bed The
swan gave him feath-ers To crown his cur-ly head The
fish gave him gaudy rings From wrecks of van-i-ty The
wolf ran all a-lone A - round the li-ly lea The
wolf ran all a-lone Where li-lies proudly rise She

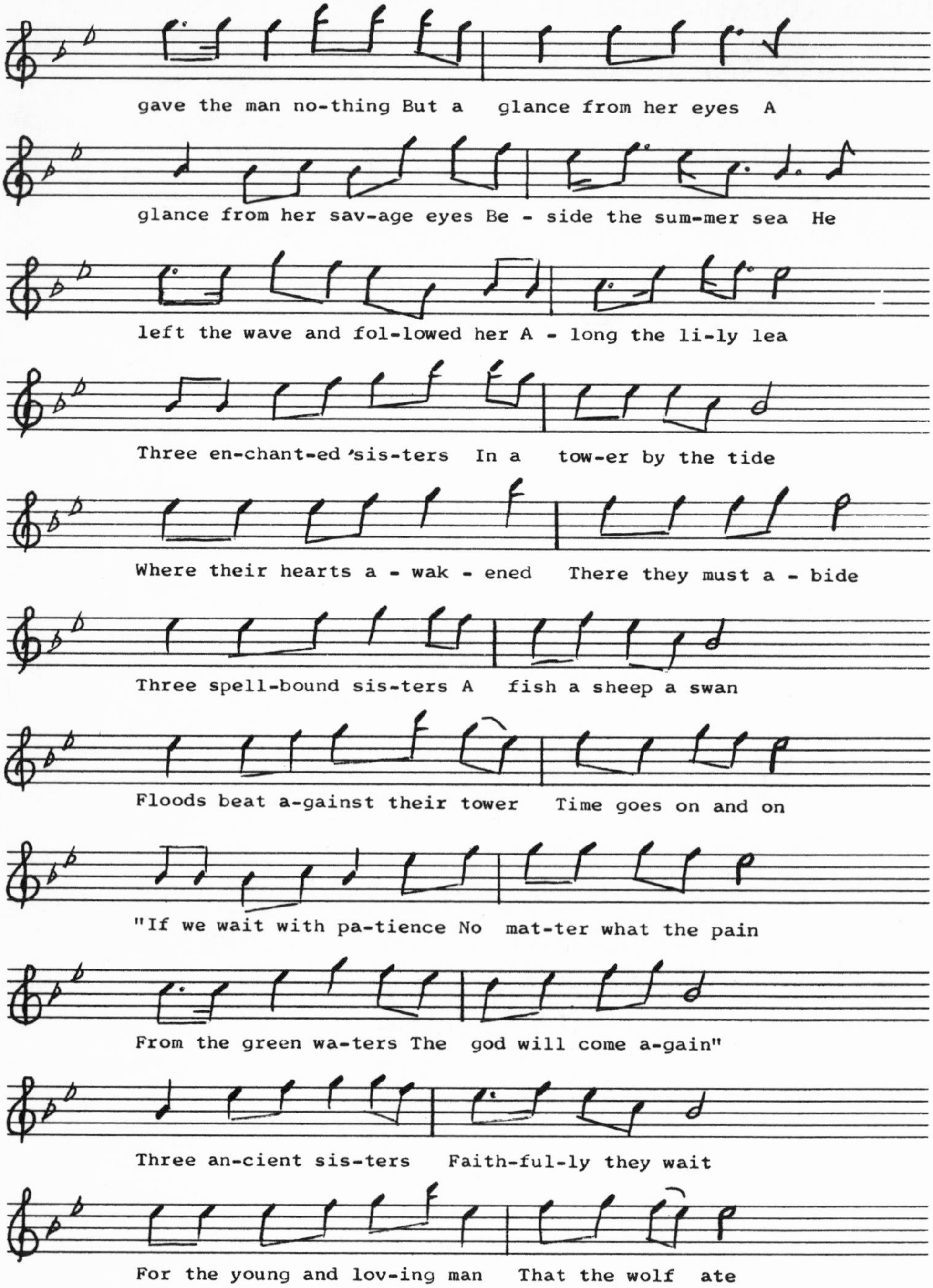
gave the man no-thing But a glance from her eyes A
glance from her sav-age eyes Be - side the sum-mer sea He
left the wave and fol-lowed her A - long the li-ly lea
Three en-chant-ed 'sis-ters In a tow-er by the tide
Where their hearts a - wak - ened There they must a - bide
Three spell-bound sis-ters A fish a sheep a swan
Floods beat a-gainst their tower Time goes on and on
"If we wait with pa-tience No mat-ter what the pain
From the green wa-ters The god will come a-gain"
Three an-cient sis-ters Faith-ful-ly they wait
For the young and lov-ing man That the wolf ate

DAVID ANTIN

Definitions for Mendy

loss is an unintentional decline in or disappearance of
   a value arising from a contingency
a value is an efficacy a power a brightness
it is also a duration

to lose something keys hair someone
we suffer at the thought
he has become absent imaginary false
a false key will not turn a true lock
false hair will not turn grey
mendy will not come back
but longing is not imaginary
we must go down into ourselves
down to the floor   that is not imaginary
where hunger lives and thirst
hunger imagine bread   thirst imagine water
the glass of water slips to the floor
thirst is a desert
value a glass of water
loss is the glass of water slipping to the floor
loss is the unintentional decline in or disappearance
   of a glass of water arising from a contingency
the glass   pieces of glass
the floor is a contingency
the floor is a floor
is a contingency
made of wood
the fire is a contingency
the bread is burned
burning is not a contingency
the presence of the dead is imaginary
the absence is real
henceforth it will be his manner of appearing
so he appears   in an orange jacket and workpants and a blue denim shirt
his hair is black his eyes are black
and a blue crab is biting his long fingers
he is trying to hold the bread
he is trying to bring the water to his mouth
his mouth is a desert
the glass of water will not come
the glass of water keeps slipping through his fingers
the floor is made of wood it is burning

it is covered with pieces of glass
arising from a contingency
his face is the darkened face of a clock
it is marked with radium
the glass is falling from his face
the face of a clock in which there is a salamander
whose eyes are bright with radium
radium is a value that is always declining
radium is a value that is always disappearing
lead is also a value
but it is less bright than radium

loss is an unintentional decline in or disappearance of
  a value arising from a contingency
a value is an efficacy a power a brightness
it is also a duration

is there enough silence here for a glass of water

is it dark enough for bread

take a glass of water
hold it against a wall
it is not pure water
it is almost pure wall

glass   what is glass

glass is a solution
of sand and chalk and ashes
fused by fire
it is a desert
that transmits light

the thirst is not appeased

water is a barrier

a glass of water is between us
you are there and i am here
is it a corollary of the fact that two things cannot
   be at the same place at the same time
that two things can be at two different places at the
   same time
you are there and i am here and i see you
but you are changed
two things at the same place at two different times
where you were the floor is empty
there is no shadow on the wall
i can only see the wall in my mind
i am not where i was then
but i still see your shadow the glass on the floor

in all matter there is an innate force
a power of resisting

take a glass   fill it with water

the thirst is not appeased

take a glass of water
drop it on the floor
it smashes
it is wood and glass and water

the thirst is not appeased

a glass of water falling
is a falling body of water
and obeys the laws of falling bodies
according to which
all bodies fall
at a rate that increases   uniformly
regardless of their form or weight
at the same altitude and latitude
the weight of a body   is the force
with which the earth   pulls the body down
mendy weighed one hundred and thirty-seven pounds
which is to say
that the earth   pulled mendy down
with a force equal to that
exerted upon a mass of one hundred and thirty-seven pounds
at forty-five degrees latitude
at the level of the sea
the earth pulls all bodies down

the thirst is not appeased

i am trying to hand you a glass of water
i am trying to give you a piece of bread
i cannot give you anything
there is a glass of water between us
i can only see you by the light the glass lets through

there is a piece of bread between us
if we could only see it

no one doubts the efficacy of bread
bread is a power
if we could only release it
it is a body
containing light

there is a piece of bread between us
break it
bread is a barrier

bread is a body
water is a body
the earth is a body
the sun is a body
a clock is also a body
light is a body   of a sort
what sort   it is heavy and falls
three hundred and sixty tons of light fall
from the sun on the earth every day
physics imagines a black body
a black body gives back no light

•

duration
it is a stone
it is a fact
it does not move
it has no place into which it could move
it has no place to move out of
it is a stone
it is a fact
it is a stone on which water has dropped
it is a fact
it is hard
it is smooth
the water does not wear it away
it wears the water away
it is a fact
it does not mean anything
it cannot tell time

•

it is a fact

not having seen you for a long time and you
didnt live far away you came to see me in the
winter it was cold in my apartment which was
heated with gas and you wore a scarf to keep
warm when i asked you what you were doing you
said you were sick and i said we were all sick
and it didnt matter but you said you were really
sick you were dying and i asked you how did it
feel because i didnt know what to say and
you said it felt queer

•

yellow
branches of willow
small flames of forsythia
soft air
black water
caressing the branches
sun
overhead

•

it is a fact

to hear the Grosse Fuge and Webern and the
great fugue was a great distance away like a
square masted ship tossed in a storm in an
old painting and the Webern was close and
dazzling   light glancing off glass and water
we came back in the rain i never saw you again

it is important to learn what the eye can see and the
   ear can hear

to record the truth

taking pictures of trees
the fountain of elm branches a spray of silver now
last of the maidenhairs timbre of a voice
drops of water sounds decaying on the air

choose/ to fix a body in space
choose/ unaccelerated axes
choose/ a frame to fix a face

the eye cannot discriminate true intensities of light
only their ratios
similarly the ear
cannot distinguish among sounds that are very high or low
in the dark all cats are black
what color are they in a blinding light

The initial definition of *loss* is quoted from p. 22 of Mehr and Cammack's *Principles of Insurance*. The initial definitions of value are from Webster's New International Dictionary, the 1927 revision.

10th Separation Meditation

mistress or lady

the parts
are connected

the power

to work on
these
lie within control

but occasionally
he speaks
to possess his soul

one day you may so
desire
a state
of misery

it becomes untrue

he wishes to speak
of analysis

performance
depends on knowledge
of relations

to translate it "duty"
suggests
conflict

both
fall short
it would seem
judgments

are upgathered
sleeping

feeling
seems necessary

who examines the flesh for signs

feeling
is used of thought
is defective

yet
in the center
these expressions
"feeling"
"touch"

nothing really counts

for me or my friend

used of the object
or material

each man
according to circumstances
and opportunity
is sometimes used

sometimes

interest
bids him go his way

get rid of his passion
contemptuously

knows
an irresistable appeal to
treat men as flies

see
how things are going under.

he discovers his fate
elsewhere
coupled
as part of the soul's moral equipment

imperfect

this use of Another

the absolute ruler
that man's
self is untouched
by this indignity

you say

strip the man
but only his clothes

the power
of highest society
is Death

the Other

is Death
Death stands over us
common sense
will leave
those who have leisure

Death is

the protest
of reason against unreason

GEORGE BOWERING

Before the Revolution

Before the revolution
we lie in one another's earth,
dreaming of the past, bananas
floating north, hate
floating south, our arms
the heat of home.

The black face hate learned
from brown & white, Cortes
as rich as United Fruit,
& Spanish to boot. Our own
priests singing at the
Iroquois stake. It is so lovely
to think we grew without
violent overthrow. Oh yes.

I have waited 300 years for Asia
to come across the archipelago
& they have not come,
bombs for you, Asia, a new
tax plan for us, we all have to suffer
in our various ways.

Am I not clear? It is as clear
as the historical data
for boundaries, the boardwalk
in Quebec City, for instance,
hardly ever felt the touch
of deerhide shoes.

Before the revolution
there is order, the red face
in the capitol is apoplexy,
the red face under the cliff
is history.

A Tainted Memory

Why do I encounter
Baby Snooks
on my walk thru this house
that no more than
existed at my birth?

It
is a question to be
filed, I say, along with
the fragments of this brain
foundered in 1947.

Baby Snooks, how
disappointed I was
to see your picture, stupid
woman in 1940's Shirley Temple dress

& how now my memory is
poorly served by that picture
injuring the radio ear
of a few years
earlier.

DAVID BROMIGE

Looking Out, 5 A.M. July 29, Berkeley, California, 1969

Sebastopol, California/December 1, 1970

into the well made by this block & the one wherein
one lighted window throwing
—or from there diffuses upward
enough of the yellow stuff,
                                        to make
all the sky that I can see—heavy with moisture?
a kind of lid

it seems, me-seems
if I crossed then the graveled
yard to enter it, they'd be there, as if
waiting for someone, me, to feed them

in their steam—the cows of sweden
shitting & belching, scrabble knees & hooves
across that straw to get heavily up

exposing their swollen udders, the imagination
thickens with detail, patches of dried shit cake
their flanks—on a deep ledge before one window
set in the whitewashed wall a metal snaggle
tooth comb—the heft of the stool
"no pun intended"—How can I say

what's intended—that, for instance, my fingers
fill with these teats like penises—dreamily
I'd fall asleep, until one stirred
or kicked, as if wanting him to get on with
the business, relief
or of habit, in hand

A bucket is between my knees, while my head
wedges into the angle made where the right
hind leg joins its flank—this is true
while I sit at this typewriter, also true—

Eternity is the imprint of Time

there is a set of the mind I can slip into
as, half-asleep, I could tumble out of bed
over the yard & begin that other process

but the yearning is, to be free!
to have this moment be
unhaunted, now
                                        as it would then, dawn
grows close
enough to be perceived—this sweet
night draining—as the blood

Making love, earlier
in one slow movement I remember
thinking, or was it after, lying back

it must be the same, when that woman
I didn't get, I saw her yesterday, winsomely
she smiled across the library
& the guy with her,
                                        & I was
not *me*, manipulating my imagination to
possess her spectrally, but
him, in her—so to let the thinker of that thought be
not me, but him, makes us present
whenever love makes two,
I thought,
                the death then, I can count on
changed its nature. If being so
alive depends on it, then death is worth
everything, & why say *if*,
it does,
            though abiding too
this recognition.
                                        Then who am *I*—
the ghost
who spreads that light-well's floor with gravel,
transforming his neighbors in their sleep to kine—
nothing of the kind occurs to them. Who I would be
wants to force
some imposing connection
on memory's twin presentments

yet who I am
has been the medium
of them

to see to
let well
enough
alone—

2

ah, humility! the exact
opposite & twin of, not arrogance—for what shall we do,
but ask?—but presumption, "I"
presumed to take myself out of time,

whose child I am, the umbilical
never to be severed in this life

no more than those buckets could grow lighter,
on this earth—we shrug
to mime our helplessness
in the grip of gravity,
gravity, the means to balance, as
to all our life—

Time, without cunt, or teat, or any seam
that we can see, our arrows making no impression,
no wonder I find you so difficult to believe in
sometimes—who permits me to feel
the yearning to be free, then can I be

free enough to acknowledge my compulsions,
to let these collages that you make with me
be, this one time with its memories, insisting
they do
not happen now,
what was the tale to be woven of them—

as the tale that commenced with a fantasy of time as
you—I mime as time

a habit much like the orders of sounds acquired—

with what deliberation did I pick
an incident or habitual action that
gives to some other so little grip—

unlike the slick
slim stanza initially I ended with—

mind baffles itself with disbelief
in all the evidence itself unfolds.

One is
in a multiple of places, whatever the time,
& each place actual, real
& of a different kind,

to one. I think that this needs saying—

clearly. On the other hand
the woman I didn't fuck
isn't waiting. Such is
among other limitations,
time. Ah, he knows what
is what. Critical lucidity has married
moral fervor to instruct us

we are too proud to be fools
of our own making. To connive

at such creations of
humanity—having nothing to do with poetry

but clinging to the "fact" that what one reads is
"only words"—defending
against the world of the imagination
that otherwise begins to give those words a flesh
as when the child endeavoring to understand envisioned
figures for each sound
                                        freedom,
to be with no other trammels
                                                  here & now,
the one imagining of human being these days imperiously
prefer against all siblings of the mind—

now the cows or kine that were my care come lowing
into this awkward structure
like loved words, I serve.

Paris in April

The intricate capillaries
Speaking of pain in a relative way
As of joy naturally
Have come to say What else do you expect

As if that rhetorical flourish itself were
Its own justification in this place
Requiring none, a sudden blush
For embarrassment, a sudden pallor

For fear, of love
The face is a continuing brightness, a quick
Pulse, good muscle tone
Fed by the tortuosities encountered here

And known at all since they are close to the surface
Of things seen looking out
For themselves like a man looking at a woman
Steadily instead of at the pit

Of her stomach where the scars are staring
Into her eyes, nights
He will lie down in what
The day has given like a fridge a *Like*

Him to take his respite in
Tangled among those reflections
Of himself reduced he searches
Beside no other body for two gelid orbs

Where his poem properly should
End but for the grace
The body of that other visibly is
In place, whole as a world with its terrible history

No word can live
Without, like claws but only like
Her arms reach out
To us invisible to him

What else did he expect like the capillaries presented
Testify to a heart that's not
And though in her wholly he
Is 'looking' in light's absence in her eyes

NORMAN O. BROWN

Daphne, or Metamorphosis

Metamorphosis; or Mutabilitie. *Omnia mutantur.* Mutation everywhere. *The Book of Changes.*

•

Metamorphosis, or transubstantiation: We already and from the first discern him making this thing other. His groping syntax, if we attend, already shapes:

Fac nobis hanc oblationem ascriptam, ratam, rationabilem, acceptabilem, quod figura est corporis et sanguinis Christi. Make for us this offering consecrated, approved, reasonable and acceptable, which is a figure of the body of Christ. *Mutando perde figuram.* Transubstantiate my form, says Daphne.

D. Jones, *Anathemata,* p. 49.
Auerbach, "Figura," *Scenes from the Drama of European Literature,* pp. 60, 235.
Ovid, *Metamorphoses,* I, l. 547.

•

Metamorphosis, or symbol-formation; the origin of human culture. A laurel branch in the hand, a laurel wreath on the house, a laurel crown on the head; to purify and celebrate. Apollo after slaying the old dragon, or Roman legions entering the city in triumph. Like in the Feast of Tabernacles; or Palm Sunday. The decoration, the mere display is poetry: making this thing other. A double nature.

Leviticus 23:40.
Mannhardt, *Antike Wald und Feldkulte,* I, pp. 296–298.

•

Daphnephoria, carrying Daphne. A ceremony of Apollo carrying Daphne, with a choir of maidens. They decorate a piece of olive wood with laurel branches and all kinds of flowers; at the top is tied a bronze ball with smaller balls hanging from it; at the middle they tie another ball not so big as the one on top, with purple ribbons attached; the lower part of the wood they cover with saffron-colored cloth. The ball at the top signifies the sun; the lower one the moon; the lesser balls the stars; and the ribbons the cycles of the year. The Daphne-bearer is made like unto Apollo himself,with hair flowing, and wearing a golden crown, and clothed in a shining robe that reaches down to his feet.

Nilsson, *Griechische Feste,* pp. 164–165.

•

One branch is the spring. *Pars pro toto:* the tree is a symbol.

•

The metamorphosis is a trope, or turning: a turn of phrase or figure of speech. *Corpus illud suum fecit "hoc est corpus meum" dicendo, "id est, figura corporis mei."* He made it his own body by saying, "This is my body, that is, the figure of my body." Every sentence is bilingual, or allegorical: saying one thing and meaning another. *Semper in figura loquens.* Every sentence a translation. Of bread and wine, this is my body. Or, of my body, this is a house and this is a steeple.

Tertullian in Auerbach, "Figura," p. 31.

Salutati, *Epistolario,* IV, p. 235: poetry is a *facultas bilinguis, unum exterius exhibens, aliud intrinseca ratione significans, semper in figura loquens.* Cf. Dante, letter to the Can Grande.

•

Saying makes it so. Poetry, the archetypal fiat; or creative act.

•

Poetry, the creative act, the act of life, the archetypal sexual act. Sexuality is poetry. The lady is our creation, or Pygmalion's statue. The lady is the poem; Laura is, really, poetry. Petrarch says that he invented the beautiful name of Laura, but that in reality Laura was nothing but that poetic laurel which he had pursued with incessant labor.

Petrarch letter in Wilkins, "The Coronation of Petrarch," *The Making of the Canzoniere,* p. 26.

•

To love is to transform; to be a poet. Together with Apollo's help, the aim is to see, amazed, our lady sitting on the grass, making with her arms a thick shade; as in Pollaiulo's painting. She is the gentle tree whose shade made my weak genius flower.

Petrarch, *Rime,* XXXIV, LX.

•

To love is to transform, and be transformed. The lover must be flexible, or fluxible. There are a thousand shapes of girls, their figures or *figurae;* the lover, like Proteus, will now melt into flowing water, will be now a lion, now a tree, now a bristling boar.

Ovid, *Ars Amatoria,* I, ll. 759–762.

•

To transform and be transformed. Love and the lady transform him, making out of living man a green laurel, which through the frozen season still loses not its leaves.

Petrarch, *Rime,* XXIII, l. 35.

•

Apollo's laurel-bough
That sometime grew within this learned man—

The first stage of spiritual deliverance in yoga is to discover in oneself the tree; the upright surge of the spinal column. Wisdom in *Ecclesiasticus* 29:17: like a cedar I am exalted in Lebanon, and like a cypress on Mount Zion. *Sapientia* is a lady; the *anima* in all of us; the *aura* in Laura. The lady and the lover are one tree.

J. Onimus, "La poetique de l'arbre," *Rev. Sciences Hum.*, No. 101, p. 107.
Ovid, *Metamorphoses*, VII, l. 813.

•

The metamorphosis of sexuality: sublimation.

The gods that mortal beauty chase
Still in a tree did end their race.

Instead of the girl, the laurel. *Hanc quoque Phoebus amat.* Orpheus sings, and a tree goes up; in pure sublimation. Or are they one and the same, the tree and the girl, Laura—*remanet nitor unus in illa*—or the tree and the girl and the song. The tree is in the ear; or is it a girl that makes herself a bed in my ear.

Rilke, *Die Sonette an Orpheus*, I, Nos. *i–ii*.
Ovid, *Metamorphoses*, I, ll. 552–553.

•

From the sensual ear to the spirit ditties of no tone. The spiritualization of the senses; a purification. The laurel purifies. Laurel leaves; Laura laves. Daphne is art, or through art, the still unravished bride. In sublimation the sexuality is not consummated—

Bold Lover, never, never canst thou kiss,
Though winning near the goal—yet, do not grieve;
She cannot fade, though thou hast not thy bliss;
For ever wilt thou love, and she be fair!

M. B. Ogle, "The Laurel in Ancient Religion and Folklore," *American Journal of Philology*, 31 (1910), pp. 287–311.

•

The still unravished bride. The struggle stilled. The mad pursuit is deathly still. The chase arrested. The immobile running girl, with no carnal motion.

Ovide Moralisé, I, l. 3178.

•

The chase arrested, the chase goes on forever. As in those gothic novels described by Leslie Fiedler: "Through a dream landscape, usually called by the name of some actual Italian place, a girl flees in terror. . . . She escapes and is caught; escapes again and is caught; escapes and is caught. . . . The Maiden in flight representing the uprooted soul of the artist . . . the girl on the run and her pursuer become only alternate versions of the same plight . . . each is a projection of his opposite—*anima* and *animus*."

Fiedler, *Love and Death in the American Novel*, pp. 107, 111.

•

The still unravished bride, the ever-green. A virginal viridity.

Ovide Moralisé, I, l. 3108.

•

Ever-green is golden: *grün des Lebens goldner Baum*. The *aurum* in Laura; a golden crown. The alchemical gold of sublimation. The green girl is a golden girl.

Goethe, *Faust*, I, l. 2039.

•

Ever-green is ever-burning. Daphne a fire-brand; the laurel is full of fire. The branches of that tree which antiquity dedicated to the Sun in order to crown all the conquerors of the earth, when shaken together give out fire. The laurel is the burning bush, the Virgin Mary; ardent busshe that did not waste. In the office of the Virgin: *rubum quem viderat Moyses incombustum conservatam agnovimus tuam laudabilem virginitatem*. In the bush that Moses saw burning but unconsumed we recognize the conservation of thy glorious virginity.

Eusebius, *Praeparatio Evangelii*, III, § 112: the laurel sacred to Apollo, *ὅτι πυρὸς μεστὸν τὸ φυτόν*.

Bacon in Bachelard, *The Psychoanalysis of Fire*, pp. 69–70.

Greene, *Early English Carols*, No. 199.

E. Harris, "Mary in the Burning Bush," *Journal of the Warburg Institute*, I (1937–38), pp. 281–282. (Froment triptych, 1476)

L. Réau, *Iconographie de l'art chrétien*, II, I, p. 187.

Daphne, *δαίς* (*δαίω*). Cf. H. Boas, *Aeneas' Arrival in Latium*, p. 98.

•

Vel rubus incombustus humanitas Christi a divinitate non absorpta; vel ecclesia probata vel turbata tribulatione non consumpta. Or the bush is the humanity of Christ not devoured by his divinity; or the church tried or troubled but not consumed by tribulation.

Harris, "Mary in the Burning Bush," p. 286.

•

May she become a flourishing hidden tree. *Virgo, virga,* the rod out of the stem of Jesse. The maiden is a may, a May-branch; thy moder is a may.

He cam also stylle
There his moder lay
As dew in Aprille,
That fallyt on the spray.

Yeats, "A Prayer for my Daughter."
Greene, *Early English Carols,* Nos. 172, 182.

•

The symbolic equation Girl = Tree; the symbolic equation Girl = Phallus. The virginity is virility; the viridity is virility. We harden like trees.

I loathe the lewd rake, the dress'd fopling despise:
Before such pursuers the nice virgin flies;
And as Ovid has sweetly in parables told,
We harden like trees, and like rivers grow cold.

O. Fenichel, "The Symbolic Equation Girl = Phallus," *Collected Papers.*
Lady Mary Wortley Montague, "The Lover: A Ballad."

•

Mascula virgo; going against the grain of her sex. Daphne was a huntress, like Diana; and the only boy she ever loved was a boy disguised as a girl.

S. Sontag, *Against Interpretation,* p. 279.
Parthenius, *Narrationes Amatoriae,* No. 15.

•

Metamorphosis into a tree. The sublimation is at the same time a fall, into a lower order of creation; an incarnation. The way up is the way down. The sublime Apollo is desublimated, descends; in love with human nature he takes on human, all-too-human form—the hound of heaven, *ut canis in vacuo leporem cum Gallicus arvo*—to be united with the Virgin. And what she finally gives him is wood, the maternal material. The Virgin is his mother; Osiris, Adonis, born of a tree. In her womb he puts on wood; in her womb he is surrounded with wood, crowned with the laurel, embraced by the Virgin.

Ovid, *Metamorphoses* I, l. 533.
Ovide Moralisé I, ll. 3245–3250.

•

What she finally gives him is the wood of the cross.

The gods that mortal beauty chase
Still in a tree did end their race.

In a tree or on a tree. Sublimation is crucifixion. Even so shall the Son of Man be lifted up. There is a Coptic tapestry fragment from a fifth-century tomb showing the tree-girl, naked and sexed, handing to Apollo a flower which is a cross. Ovid says, *oscula dat ligno.* He kisses the cross.

In the Louvre Museum.
Ovid, *Metamorphoses* I, l. 556.

•

She is his mother; the Great Mother; the naked goddess rising between two branches.

E. Neumann, *The Great Mother*, pp. 241–256.

•

She is his mother; she may have been a whore. Laura, Laurentia; some say she was the nurse of Romulus and Remus, others say she was a whore.

Freud, "A Special Type of Choice of Object Made by Men," *Collected Papers*, IV, p. 199.
Varro, *De Lingua Latina*, V, § 152; VI, § 23.

•

From the vagabond maiden to the family tree: she settled down; in the Laurentian land. Laura becomes Lar. On Augustus' doorstep—

postibus Augustis eadem fidissima custos
ante fores stabis.
—*like some green laurel*
rooted in one dear perpetual place.

Vico, *New Science*, § 533.
Cato, *Originum*, Frag. 10.
Ovid, *Metamorphoses*, I, ll. 562–563.
Vergil, *Aeneid*, VII, ll. 59–62.

•

Metamorphosis into a tree. A fall, into the state of nature. The spirit, the human essence, hides, buried in the natural object; "projected." Great Pan is dead. Ovid's *Metamorphoses*, the death of the gods, and the birth of poetry.

Schiller, "Die Gőtter Griechenlands."

•

Dead and buried. The Muses as museum; art as sarcophagus

with brede
Of marble men and maidens overwrought.

Like the laurel, promising immortality.

Promising immortality, or awaiting resurrection. Not dead but sleeping. The maiden is not dead, but sleepeth. The tree is the sleeping beauty. She made herself a bed in my ear and went to sleep. And everything is her sleep.

Matthew 9:24.
Rilke, *Die Sonette an Orpheus,* I, ii.

•

To waken the spirit from its sleep. Orpheus or Christ, saying to stem and stone,

trees
And the mountain-tops that freeze—

Maiden I say unto thee, arise.

Shakespeare, *Henry VIII,* Act III, scene 1.
Luke 8:54.

•

We shall not all sleep, but we shall all be changed. The resurrection is the revelation of the sons of God. In the Apocalypse

Daphne hath broke her bark, and that swift foot
Which th' angry Gods had fast'ned with a root
To the fix'd earth, doth now unfettered run
To meet th' embraces of the youthful Sun.

Running to meet the son from whom she originally fled. *Nescis, temeraria,* nescis *quem fugias.*

Romans 8:19.
Carew, "The Rapture."
Ovid, *Metamorphoses,* I, ll. 514–515.

•

The triumphant laurel. *In hoc signo vinces.* Be thou faithful unto death and I will give thee a crown of life. A crown of glory that fadeth not; a golden crown. The laud in Laura. The laurel on Caesar's brow; the coronation of Petrarch, the poet laureate. The emperor, the poet, and the triumphant lover:

Ite triumphales circum mea tempora laurus!
vicimus, in nostra est, ecce, Corinna sinu.

Revelations 2:10; I Peter 5:4.
Danielou, "The Palm and Crown," *Primitive Christian Symbols.*
Kantorowicz, "On Transformations of Apolline Ethics," in K. Schauenburg, *Charites* (Berlin, 1957), pp. 265–274.

Wilkins, "The Coronation of Petrarch," *The Making of the Canzoniere.*

Isidorus, *Etymologiarum lib.*, XVII, § vii. *Laurus a verbo laudis dicta—apud antiquos autem laudea nominabatur . . . ut in auriculis, quae initio audiculae dictae sunt, et medidies quae nunc meridies dicitur.*

Ovid, *Amores*, II, xii, ll. 1–2.

•

To restore to trees and flowers their original animality; their original spirituality; their original humanity. Erasmus Darwin in the Proem to his *Loves of the Plants:* "Whereas P. Ovidius Naso, a great necromancer in the famous court of Augustus Caesar did by art poetic transmute Men, Women, and even Gods and Goddesses, into Trees and Flowers; I have undertaken by similar art to restore some of them to their original animality, after having remained prisoners so long in their respective vegetable mansions."

E. Sewell, *The Orphic Voice*, p. 228.

•

The spirit is human; the invisible reality is human. *Ecce homo; ecce Daphne.* Instead of a stone or tree displayed, a statue; a transfiguration of the stone or tree, disclosing the human essence.

•

The final metamorphosis is the humanization of nature. It is a question of love: the transformation of the Bear into a Prince the moment the bear is loved. The identification is a change of identity; the magic is love.

Novalis, in Hartman, *The Unmediated Vision*, p. 135.

Ficino, *Commentarium in Convivium Platonis de amore*, Ch. VI, §10; cf. F. Yates, *Giordano Bruno and the Hermetic Tradition*, p. 127.

•

Overcoming the distinction between *Naturwissenschaft* and *Geisteswissenschaft:* "I know what it is to look like a tree but I cannot know what it is to be a tree."

I. Berlin, "The Philosophical Ideas of Giambattista Vico," *Art and Ideas in Eighteenth-Century Italy* (Rome, 1960), p. 172.

•

THE TREE
Ezra Pound

I stood still and was a tree amid the wood,
Knowing the truth of things unseen before;
Of Daphne and the laurel bough
And that god-feasting couple old
That grew elm-oak amid the wold.

•

A GIRL
Ezra Pound

The tree has entered my hands,
The sap has ascended my arms,
The tree has grown in my breast—
Downward,
The branches grow out of me, like arms.

Tree you are,
Moss you are,
You are violets with wind above them.
A child—so high—you are,
And all this is folly to the world.

•

A spiritualization of nature; an invisible spirit in the tree—

Casting the body's vest aside
My soul into the boughs does glide.

The transfiguration is a transmigration.

•

As Karl Marx said, the humanization of nature is the naturalization of man.

The gods that mortal beauty chase
Still in a tree did end their race.

The tree is the teleological end, the *eschaton*. We shall all be changed, in the twinkling of an eye. Resurrection is metamorphosis, from the natural to the supernatural or spiritual body. It is raised a spiritual body. Casting the body's vest aside. The harps that we hung on the willow trees, the organs, are our natural bodies, the sexual organizations.

K. Marx, "The Philosophic-Economic Manuscripts."

G. H. Hartman, "Marvell, St. Paul, and the Body of Hope," *English Literary History*, 31 (1964), pp. 175–194.

Methodius in Rahner, *Greek Myths and Christian Mystery*, p. 317.

•

The supernatural body reunites us with nature; with rocks and stones and trees. It gives us the flower body of Narcissus, or the tree body of Daphne. Love's best retreat. It is the resurrection of nature in us; nature transformed into invisible spirit. As Rilke says, Earth, is that not what you want: to rise again, invisible, in us. *Unsichtbar in uns zu erstehen.*

Rilke in Heller, *The Disinherited Mind, p. 169.*

•

Love's best retreat. The spiritualization of sensuality is love: a great triumph over Christianity, says Nietzsche. Sensuality is not abolished, but fulfilled.

No white nor red was ever seen
So amorous as this lovely green.

Kaufmann, *Nietzsche*, p. 202.

•

The reconciliation of spirit and nature; the opposition of sexuality and sublimation overcome. When our eyes are opened, we perceive that in sexuality the object is not the literal girl; but the symbolic girl, the tree. It is always something else that we want. The object is always transcendent.

•

"Up till now—as is right—my tastes, my feelings, my personal experiences have all gone to feed my writings; in my best contrived phrases I still felt the beating of my heart. But henceforth the link is broken between what I think and what I feel. And I wonder whether this impediment which prevents my heart from speaking is not the real cause that is driving my work into abstraction and artificiality. As I was reflecting on this, the meaning of the fable of Apollo and Daphne suddenly flashed upon me: happy, thought I, the man who can clasp in one and the same embrace the laurel and the object of his love."

A. Gide, *The Counterfeiters*, trans. D. Bussy (New York, 1951), pp. 83–84.

•

The humanization of nature—not in some single herb or tree. In all the flowers and trees. Hierophanies everywhere.

Each herb and each tree,
Mountain, hill, earth and sea,
Cloud, Meteor and Star,
Are Men Seen Afar.

Blake, letter to Butts, October 2, 1800.

•

In the meantime, the whole creation groaning. In the meantime, vision is to perceive the tree as Parthenon or maiden's chamber; to perceive the Caryatid in the pillar. To hear the silent speech, or under the bark the beating of a heart. To catch the trembling of her head—

tremere omnia visa repente
liminaque laurusque dei.

Glimpses that can make us less forlorn.

Vergil, *Aeneid*, III, ll, 90–91.

•

To make the tree speak. I am leafy speafing. The oracular tree, or tree of dreams. The sylvan historian, telling a leaf-fringed legend. The *silva* or garden of verses. These trees shall be my book. Book is beech in German (*Buch* and *Bűche*); a tree on which we carve our mistress' name. The maidens stray impassioned in the lettering leaves. Laura is really poetry.

Joyce, *Finnegans Wake*, p. 619.
Fulgentius, *Mitologiae*, I, § 14.
Eliade, *Patterns of Comparative Religion*, p. 284.
Curtius, *European Literature and the Latin Middle Ages*, p. 337.

•

Thus, the whole story from Genesis to Apocalypse in any event; in any metamorphosis. Therefore it is important to keep changing the subject. The subject changes before our very eyes. It is important to keep changing our mind—

The mind, that ocean where each kind
Does straight its own resemblance find.

The mind, or the imagination, the original shape-shifter: Thrice-Greatest Hermes.

•

Leo Spitzer said that In Christian art earthly images easily appear to melt away and vanish. There is a parallel in modern "poetics by alchemy" exemplified by the practice of a Góngora, who may lead us by metaphors from a maid adorning herself for marriage to Egyptian tombstones; or we may think of the famous passage in which Proust, by the use of metaphors, transforms lilac into fountain—or of Valéry's *Cimetière marin*, that sea cemetery which becomes successively a roof covered with white pigeons, a temple of Time, a flock of sheep with a shepherd dog, a multicolored hydra; all this, says Spitzer, is based on the same Christian poetics of kaleidoscopic transformation of symbols. A Christian transfiguration, or a pagan orgy: a Bacchanalian revel of categories in which not one member is sober; a protean flux of metamorphosis. As in *Finnegans Wake*.

L. Spitzer, "Classical and Christian Ideas of World Harmony," *Traditio II* (1944), p. 426.

•

Not everyone can play *Finnegans Wake*. But professors can. James Joyce is the apostle unto the professors. And the message is: Let's play. Or, let's practice metamorphosis. Or, let's change the subject.

•

In any case it is necessary to have faith. To believe what the Bible tells us. Only beleaf. The Bible; *Le Livre;* it is all one book. Literature is as collective as the unconscious; private authorship or ownership is not to be respected. It is all one book, which includes the gospel according to Ovid, Saint Ovid the Martyr (*Ovide moralisé*); and Petrarch, and Marvell, and Keats, and Rilke, and Yeats, and André Gide, and Pound. And also the ravings of every poor Crazy Jane. Every poor schizophrenic girl is a Delphic priestess; or a Daphne, saying "I am that tree." "That's the rain—I could be the rain. That chair—that wall. It's a terrible thing for a girl to be a wall." It's a terrible thing for a girl to be a Delphic priestess. In the cave the priestess raves: she still resists the brutal god, to shake from her hapless breast his breast; all the more his pressure subjugates her wild heart, wears down her rabid mouth, shapes her mouth into his mouthpiece.

R. D. Laing, *The Divided Self,* p. 217.
Vergil, *Aeneid* VI, ll. 77–80.
L. K. Born, "Ovid and Allegory," *Speculum,* IX (1934), pp. 362–379.

•

It is all one book; blossoms on one tree,

Characters of the great Apocalypse
The types and symbols of Eternity.

One tree, in kaleidoscopic metamorphosis.

Wordsworth, *Prelude,* VI, ll. 637–639.

CHARLES BUKOWSKI

What a Man I Was

I shot off his left ear
then his right,
and then tore off his belt buckle
with hot lead,
and then
I shot off everything that counts
and when he bent over
to pick up his drawers
and his marbles
(poor critter)
I fixed it so he wouldn't have
to straighten up
no more.

Ho Hum.
I went in for a fast snort
and one guy *seemed*
to be looking at me sideways,
and that's how he died—
sideways,
lookin' at me
and clutchin'
for his marbles.

Sight o' blood made me kinda
hungry.
Had a ham sandwich.
Played a couple of sentimental songs . . .
Shot out all the lights
and strolled outside.
Didn't seem to be no one around
so I shot my horse
(poor critter).

Then I saw the Sheerf
a standin' down at the end a' the road
and he was shakin'
like he had the Saint Vitus dance;
it was a real sorrowful sight
so I slowed him to a quiver

with the first slug
and mercifully stiffened him
with the second.

Then I laid on my back awhile
and I shot out the stars one by one
and then
I shot out the moon
and then I walked around
and shot out every light
in town,
and pretty soon it began to get dark
real dark
the way I like it;
just can't stand to sleep
with no light shinin'
on my face.

I laid down and dreamt
I was a little boy again
a playin' with my toy six-shooter
and winnin' all the marble games,
and when I woke up
my guns was gone
and I was all bound hand and foot
just like somebody
was scared a me
and they was slippin'
a noose around my ugly neck
just as if they
meant to hang me,
and some guy was pinnin'
a real pretty sign
on my shirt:
there's a law for you
and a law for me
and a law that hangs
from the foot of a tree.

Well, pretty poetry always did
make my eyes water
and can you believe it

all the women was cryin'
and though they was moanin'
other men's names
I just know they was cryin'
for me (poor critters)
and though I'd slept with all a them,
I'd forgotten
in all the big excitement
to tell 'em my name

and all the men looked angry
but I guess it was because the kids
was all being impolite
and a throwin' tin cans at me,
but I told 'em not to worry
because their aim was bad anyhow
not a boy there looked like he'd turn
into a man—
90% homosexuals, the lot of them,
and some guy shouted
"let's send him to hell!"

and with a jerk I was dancin'
my last dance,
but I swung out wide
and spit in the bartender's eye
and stared down
into Nellie Adam's breasts,
and my mouth watered again.

The Way It Will Happen Inside a Can of Peaches

to die with your boots on
while writing poetry
is not as glorious
as riding a horse
down Broadway
with a stick of dynamite
in your teeth,
but neither is

adding the sum total
of all the planets
named or visible
to man,
and the horse was a grey,
the man's name was
Sanchez or Kadinsky,
it was 79 degrees
and the children kept
yelling,
hog hog
we are tired
blow us to hell.

Plants Which Easily Winter Kill

plants which easily winter kill,
and the hair on the eyelids of a
horse is called
brills,
and
plants which easily winter kill
are
  Campanula medium
  Digitalis purpurea
  Early-flowered Chrysanthemums
  Salvia patens
  and
  Shasta Daisy,
and the United Daughters of the Confederacy was
founded in
Nashville, Tenn., Sept. 10,
1894.
the male heart weighs 10 to 12
ounces
and the female
8 to 10 ounces,
and in the 14th. century
1/3rd. of the population of England died
from the Black Death
which they say was caused by

unsanitary conditions,
and be careful of your grammar:
bad: He gave all of his
property to
charity.
better:
He gave all his property
to
charity.
best:
He kept all his
property.
and
the superficial area of the earth is
196,950,000 sq. miles
and the earth weighs
6,592,000,000,000,000,000,000 tons,
and my child said to me,
"Thinking is not the same as
knowing."

Jesus Christ died at the age of
33, and contrary to popular belief
a sawfish does not attack
whales.

JOHN CAGE

17

A mix of remarks about the "telegraph harp" from Volumes II-IV of the Journal *by Henry David Thoreau.*

No danger that worms will attack; thrill them to death.
Sounds.
Mad so long.
What more wonderful than a wire stretched between two posts?
Buzzing strings.
Will be.
The telegraph harp.
Wind is from the north, the telegraph does not sound.
Aeolian.
Orpheus alive.
It is the poetry of the railroad.
By one named Electricity.
Like a harp high overhead.

30

"Waka" from Thoreau's Journal.

Wasps are building
summer squashes
saw a fish hawk
when I hear this.

Both bushes and trees are thinly leaved
few ripe ones on sandy banks
rose right up high into the air
like trick of some pleasant daemon to entertain me
and birds are heard singing from fog.

Burst like a stream
making a world
how large do you think it is, and how far? To my surprise, one answered three rods.

Begin to change
in the woods, we came upon a partridge
I find myself covered with green and winged lice.

When I look further, I find
the lower streets of the towns.

In a few weeks they will be
as it should be.

Government
snake and toad
an August wind
soaring hawks
dog of the woods.

Open the painted tortoise nest
Thoreau.

Now under the snows of winter
apple tree
chips of dead wood
then torn up and matted together
'nough to fill a bed out of a hat.

In the forest
on the meadow
button bushes
flock of shore larks
Persian city
spring advances.

All parts of nature belong to one head, the curls
the earth
the water.

See and hear young swallows about
maple buds large as in spring
ice water, winter in the air
carried there by its mother
wildwoods night.

I hear it roaring, reminding me of March, March.

Stood face to face to him and are about to hang him
puts them in his pockets.

I hear the crows cawing hoarsely flying toward the white pine
cricket creaks along the shore
such coolness as rain makes; not sharp.

Their central parts have curved upward.

See thirty or forty goldfinches in a flock, cold air
great numbers of fishes fled.

Since it blossoms a second time
it was fit to rest on
morning concerts of sparrows, hyemalis and grackles
many butterflies
black with white on wings
new country where the rocks have not been burned.

May I be as vivacious as willow.

Shall not voice of man express as much content as the note of a bird?

In the midst of them, I see track of rabbit
it also struck a small oak
screeching of the locomotive, rumbling cars, a whisper
far down all day.

Mosses bear now a green fruit.

This snake on twigs, quick as thought and at home in the trees
the blue-eyed grass is shut up. When does it open?

Flitting about
surprising, this cluster of leek buds on rock.

These are my sands.

Hubbard's bridge and waterlilies
waterlilies.

In our forests
part divine
and makes her heart palpitate
wild and tame are one. What a delicious sound!

The air delicious, thus we are baptized into nature
fall into the water
or lost, torn in pieces, frozen to death
thunder and lightning.

Winter day, clear and bright
still no cowslips.

In a hollow
near the river
in warm weather
the river ice inclines to opaque white
it is quite mild today, holes in the trees an inch apart
forest presents the tenderest green.

But you must raise your own potatoes
perhaps I ate more.

Dark mass of cloud with lighter edges.

What to do, what may a man do and not be ashamed of it?

Countless narrow light lines
it is worthwhile to hear the wind roar in woods today.

The field plantain, the narrow cotton grass
tobacco pipes still pushing up dry leaves
like the wild cat of the woods
pine wood.

I am surprised to find these roots with white grubs.

One or two flashes of lightning, but soon over
ridge of meadow west of here
naked eye.

35

Variations on a quotation in the first paragraph of the Essay on Civil Disobedience *by Henry David Thoreau.*

The best form of government is no government at all
The best form of government is no government at all
and that will be what men will have when they are ready for it ready for it
The best form of government is no government at all.

The best form of government is no government at all
The best form of government is no government at all
and that will be the kind of government we'll have when we are ready for it ready for it
The best form of government is no government at all.

The best form of government is no government at all
The best form of government is no government at all
and that will be and that will be what we will have when we are ready
The best form of government is no government at all.

The best form of government is no government at all
The best form of government is no government at all
and that will be the kind of government we'll have when we are ready for it ready for it ready for it
The best form of government is no government at all.

The best government the best government is no government at all
The best government the best government is no government at all
and that will be the kind of government we'll have and that will be the kind of government we'll have
The best government the best government is no government at all.

The best form of government is no government at all
The best form of government is no government at all
and that will be what we will have when we are ready ready for it
The best form of government is no government at all.

The best form of government is no government
The best form of government is no government
and that will be what we will have and that will be what we will have when we are ready when we are
The best form of government is no government.

The best form of government is no government at all
The best form of government is no government at all
and that will be what we will have when will we? We are ready we are ready we are ready we are ready we are ready
The best form of government is no government at all.

The be-e-e-est form of go-ov-ernment is no-o-o government at all
The be-e-e-est form of go-ov-ernment is no-o-o government at all
and that'll be what we'll have and that'll be what we'll have when we are *we are* ready for it
The be-e-e-est form of go-ov-ernment is no-o-o government at all.

The best form of government is no government
The best form of government is no government
and that will be the kind we'll have when we are ready for it
The best form of government is no government.

The best form of government is no government at all
The best form of government is no government
and that will be the kind we'll have when we are ready we are ready
The best form of government is no government.

The best form of government is no government at all *none at all*
The best form of government is no government at all *none at all*
and that will be and that will be the kind we'll have we'll have when we are ready
The best form of government is no government at all *none at all.*

The best form of government is no form of government
The best form of government is no form of government
and that will be what we will have what we will have when we are ready
The best form of government is no form of government.

The best form of government is no government at all at all *no government no government*
The best form of government is no government at all at all *no government no government*
and that and that will be will be and that and that will be will be and that and that will be will be
The best form of government is no government at all at all *no government no government.*

The best form of government *best* is no government at all
The best form of government *best* is no government at all
and that will be what we will have when we are ready
The best form of government *best* is no government at all.

The best form of government is no government no government
The best form of government is no government no government
and that will be the form we'll have and when we are ready that will be the form we'll have
The best form of government is no government no government.

The best form of government is no government at all
The best form of government is no government at all
and that will be the kind of government that we will have when we are ready
The best form of government is no government at all.

The b-b-b-b-b-b-b-b-best form is no f-f-f-form at all
The b-b-b-b-b-b-b-b-best form is no f-f-f-form at all
and th-that is th-th-the form w-we'll have
The b-b-b-b-b-b-b-b-best form is no f-f-f-form at all.

The best form of government is no government at all is no form of government
The best form of government is no government at all is no form of government
and that will be the form we'll have when we are ready and that will be the form we'll have
The best form of government is no government at all is no form of government.

The best the best *best* the best government *the best* is no government at all
The best the best *best* the best government *the best* is no government at all
and that *that* that will be *will be* and we are *we are* ready for it
The best the best *best* the best government *the best* is no government at all.

The best form the best form the best form of government is no government at all
The best form the best form the best form of government is no government at all
and that's the kind that's the kind the kind we'll have. When? When we are ready
The best form the best form the best form of government is no government at all.

The best form of government is no government at all
The best form of government is no government at all
and that will be the kind of government we'll have when we are ready for it for it for it
The best form of government is no government at all.

The best form of government is no government
The best form of government is no government
and that will be our government and we are ready for it
The best form of government is no government.

That is the kind we will have
That is the kind we will have
ready for it?
That is the kind we will have.

The best form of government the best form of government is no form of government
The best form of government the best form of government is no form of government
and that will be the kind we'll have and that will be the kind we'll have when we are *we are* ready
The best form of government the best form of government is no form of government.

The best form of government is no form of government *no government at all*
The best form of government is no form of government *no government at all*
and that's the kind that we will have and that's the kind and that's the kind
we'll have
The best form of government is no form of government *no government at all.*

The best form of government is no form of government
The best form of government is no form of government
and that will be and that will be the kind we'll have when we are ready
The best form of government is no form of government.

The best form of government is no government at all is no government at all
The best form of government is no government at all is no government at all
and that will be the form we'll have and that will be the form we'll have when
we are ready
The best form of government is no government at all is no government at all.

The best form of government is no government at all
The best form of government is no government at all
and that's the government we'll have when we are *we are* ready
The best form of government is no government at all.

The best form of government is no form of government *no government at all*
The best form of government is no form of government *no government at all*
and that will be the kind of government we'll have the kind of government
we'll have we are ready
The best form of government is no form of government *no government at all.*

B-b b-b b-b b-b b-best form of government is no government
B-b b-b b-b b-b b-best form of government is no government
ready ready ready for it ready ready we are ready for it
B-b b-b b-b b-b b-best form of government is no government.

The best form of government is no form of government at all
The best form of government is no form of government at all
and that will be the kind we'll have when we are ready *are we ready!*
The best form of government is no form of government at all.

47

excroly loomarind han her crix
dl yklydiga
odad pa ubgacma papp add fallt de!
thur aght uonnon

ukovarhntu nukb arr
bumghun lifai go run und hun
looansor turn ru llc urn pwau umt bo
mst rumt ah ra
babtoent onbrron arraght
at
erjrte dylen ooys port dve
da
trumap rawckpu ach ckle tupp nyk tast achb
ngstingik rbine ro
dub parr ghella le papapp
lop pladd dyaplu lats patzdy
kockad blmpa ac yk rn
atpemat
ault am both
unrthatana
fise inc ncoff hcus chosc ac
rthanspo dyha pakkry klundur or kap rjkap
nstrou
der lcho
hum to umduns und toll!

hhob
mand
en acmda nco finsa!
ib
ur fenrack roc!

73

A mix of words & phrases from
Changes: Notes on Choreography
by Merce Cunningham

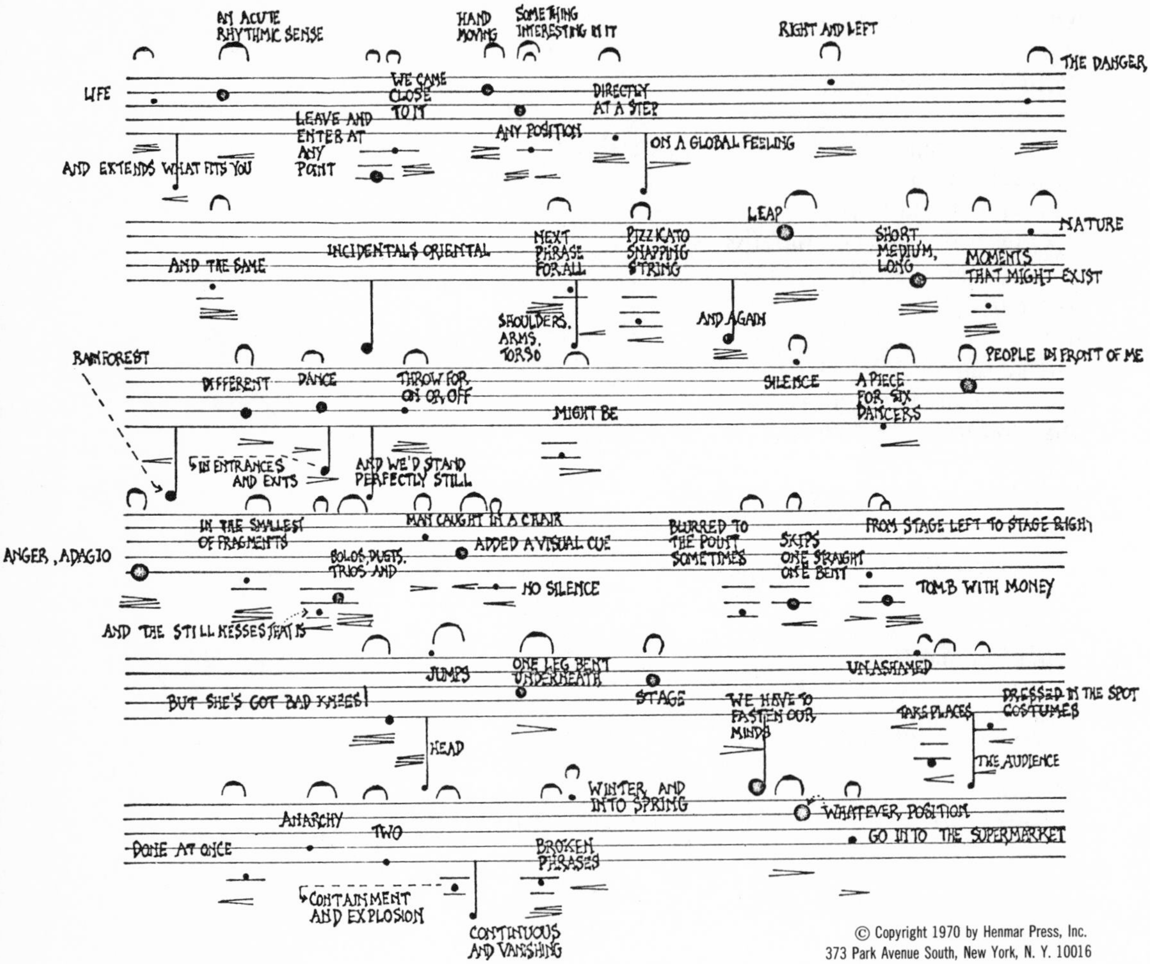

85

A syllable mix from Thoreau's *Journal*.

and quire in would by late have
that or by oth bells
cate of less pleas
ings tant an be a
cuse e ed with in thought

al la said tell
bits ev man
ar spring is ti per store of on but ly er
frosts till large
if is ly ly if
ar spring one on pen co ty com vine ton wild

ing den ter when lin bove spruce
the tle green plant tle the
par
ing as where thirds hem

most is ened
the shall to and high

ted ad blos ly the
corns tor
tion ing the in grass le spot
cow spring woods
woods flow

hen three fif
ty vol no march
ber fif three vol vol

till look woods ple of the
noon earth packed the when
er ray lent
this packed
earth in up through wears
in murk as for

en was for so sleigh still wa
ice en to that and grees was
care the de
when ice thick made of an deep o

is be that
is ful er
it june shops ing and a
got a us out side phi
who mem wall

BOBBIE L. CREELEY

Salem Yellow Bird

Visible reality, source
of more than enough.
What spirit
sits there.

Did you never see the devil?
She said there was a tall
man of Boston that she
did see.

This man had a yellow bird
that kept with him,
and told her he had
other pretty things.

Sometimes like a hog
sometimes a great dog
the Devil came to bid me
to serve him. The black
dog said "Serve me"
but I am afraid.

What also have you seen?
A red rat.
A black rat.

(2)

Grim battle against
grim power
against the terrors.

Battle the wolves.
Men more savage.
The very elements

are weaponed.
Ice Frost
the cold darkness.

Snow Water
the savages kept at bay
with difficulty.

Ariel activities
of legions of devils
was a danger.

"to determine a matter so
in the dark as to know
the guilty Employers of Devils
in this work of darkness,
this is a work.
This is a labor."

(3)

The Devil was an angel
fallen from sky's light
into dark earth.
Buried in earth's body.
Internal fault
within
and at work.

Wrap the seed round
and plant it.
The tree of life
is balanced off.
Brilliant evil is the winner.
The Devil, a shining dog,
can speak.

He

Mama's face shines
down at him
from heaven.
All those stars
are Mama's eyes.

Unluckily
nobody knew entirely
his wild capability
faintly visible.

Multiform and shifting
he took it all
at one stroke.

So swift as if
a shorter path were his
he lifted
the lot.

He turned the outside
skinside inside
but the inside
darkside
wouldn't.

He sits in his chair.
Its arms at his sides
its back at his back
its legs hold him there
in air.

He wants a pillow
to poke.
Something that will
hold

the mark
of his fist.

He took his
pictures of him
(framed as suited it)
hung them on his walls.

He made them
particular
framing and
hanging them.
Now grows
dissatisfied.

He used to think
better
of himself
he thinks.

no concrete image

no concrete image
no space
nor time
but within
and at work

manifest
effect appears
projections
fascinations
also in anxiety
overpowerings

seizure
constellation
a change
the feeling tone
changes

incline
tendant
direction the mind's specific
direction
manifest
effect

"Everything I've ever
done has been
real
to me
at the time
in a way."

HAROLD DICKER

Or Haven't I Told You

August 23, 1963

once
upon
a
time

once
upon an elephant
a man marked
time

once
upon a white elephant
a madman hatchmarked
time

once
upon a whitewalled elephant
a mad middleman crosshatchmarked
time

once
upon a whitewalled wild elephant
a mad English middleman Maltesecrosshatchmarked
time

once   twice   down and
up on a whitewalled hogwild elephant
      a mad English hatter met a middleman
on a Maltese cross
      down
a hatch marked
time

once or twice downtown   and once uptown   I met
up with   on a whitewalled hogwild black bull elephant
      a marchmad English hatter   with a Manchurian
      middleman   wearing an oakleaf cluster
on a Maltese crosstown bus
      down
a hazel hatch quaintly marked
time

once I went downtown   or twice uptown
    or twice downtown and once uptown   and I met
up and down with   on a whitewalled cornfed hogwild
    black bull elephant named Earnest   a friendly
    marchmad English rabbit from Cape Hatteras
    in earnest conversation with a frank Manchurian
    middleman   proudly wearing an oakleaf cluster
    for courage beyond decorum
on a Maltese crosstown bus
    down in a hazelnut hatchery
    quaintly marked with fictitious stops and
a humorous
    sense of
time

once I went downtown to meet two friends
    or twice uptown to meet three wise men
    and once or twice I went downtown
    and once uptown   and more than that
    looking for an honest woman
    and I met only the kind that give short change
    walking
up and down with open minds
    and every one of them was followed by
    a sleek whitewalled cornfed hogwild blackeyed
    bullheaded pimp elephant   and every one of them
    was named Earnest MacDonald and had a farm
    and following every elephant was
    a friendly marchmad old English jackrabbit
    from the hinterlands of Cape Hatteras
    in earnest conversation with a Dr. Frankenstein
    a Manchurian middlewife of doubtful vintage
    a garbage man   and
    a retired car thief proudly wearing
    an oakleaf cluster for an anonymous act
    of courage beyond sense or decorum
on a Maltese crosstown bus down in a wholesale
    hazelnut hatchery in Philadelphia
    a place quaintly marked
    with fictitious stopsigns   and
a humorous sense
    of the history of
time

once I went to meet three wise men
    looking for an honest woman
    the kind that give change
    walking
up and down
    every one of them followed a sleek
    whitewalled pimp from the hinterlands
    a Frankenstein of doubtful garbage
    a thief wearing an oakleaf
on a crosstown bus down in Philadelphia
    a place with
a humorous
    history of
time

once I
    went
up and
    down
    the hinterlands
on a
    bus
    in
a place
    history of
time

once I
    went
up
on
a
    bus in
time

once
upon
a
time

The Prize of War is Always

October 6, 1963

that war   is an emotional release
                                                  it is an established fact
        many murderers   come in their pants
that   the cannibals are coming
        a cannibal is someone
                                                  that eats someone else
many murderers   are coming
                                                  it is an established fact
        murder   is an emotional cannibal
that eats someone else
                                                  murder   is an established fact
        that war   is an emotional release
war   is always many murderers
                                                  the prize   is always coming
that war   is someone else   who eats someone else
        war is always   someone else
                                                  murder   is come
the prize   of emotional release
                                                  is an established cannibal
        someone   that eats someone else
that   the cannibals are coming
                                                  it is an established fact
        the cannibals are coming
                                                  is an emotional release   that

I Said / He Said

August 6, 1963

in this boring dream   I said when   makes no
difference   awake   asleep   makes no difference
he said   I said when I met him   in this
boring dream   since I saw you last week you
lost weight   he said   you don't eat or you don't
sleep but not both   you don't   he said in this
boring dream I said   I screamed I killed six men
you don't sleep   he said   you don't dream   makes
no difference   awake   asleep   makes no difference
in this boring dream   I said when   makes no
difference   awake   asleep   makes no difference
he said   I said when I met him   I killed six men
in this boring dream   since I saw you last week
you lost weight   he said   you don't live or you
don't live alone   but not both   he said   you

don't eat or you don't live   he said   in this
boring dream   he said this above all   you don't
sleep or you don't sleep alone   but with six men
never   he said   that's why you lost weight   it'll
make a difference   now that they're dead   he said
in the middle of next week   in this boring dream
when I met him   I shot him through the head

The Mouth is a Zoo

August 9, 1963

PEACE   the politicians predicted
           shall come to pass
in the parliament of asses   we shall
share our plowshares   split up the pieces
of our asswise days like the clods we are
divide what we alone   can hold with no help
from above   or below   or beyond

PEACE   proposed the prophetical priest
           is the prisoner of no food   a penance
to be dispensed for our plundering pace
and it shall come to pass   at the point of
a plowshare   and by the pull of a hemp rope
at the bull neck of progress and power
peace shall stalk us till we get no rest
but peace   shall come to pass

PEACE   brother   shall come to pass
           said the prosperous poet   putting on
his armor   picking up his lance   shall come
when compassion justice and love have
the grandeur of wrath   and ran to pass
the lance through his horse

           applause from the congress of asses
           benedictions of expensive passion
           from the purple prophet   a visitation
           from the political peace police

           the wealthy poet   mounted his horse
           got out his whip   Plato has risen
           he chanted in unison   Plato has risen

For the Day of Atonement/1963

some bookkeepers counted   6,000,000

others only   4½

at the least   there must have been   1,000,000

the cubic capacities involved
   suggest there were   at least   100,000

at any rate   the assembly-line
   procedures used   apparently assured
   a minimum final   quantity of   10,000

the photographs alone show   that
   at the least   there were   1,000

a typical photograph   such as
   this one   discloses   about   100

in this particular picture   which
   I now show you   there are   10
   thrown in a group

at the center of the group notice that   1
   face   is in clear focus

   and that the eyes

   are open

Requiem for Three Dead

a pox on all stars
apparent order   mumbled probabilities
sigma   sigma after sigma
multiplied   encircled
best of most probable
what error are you
if you are not an improbable configuration
within what ridiculous limits
I am   of course   I
of course   I am   certain   I am
invalid but true   I am   real   I am
the absolute of you the unknown

I am the absolute   of I
                                        and you are the least
probable   clutch that beauty as my gift
it is law
seem precisely what   I am
what is real   without chance
                                        apparent order
mumbled probabilities   Venus
in all your phases beauty reels   breasts
being Ptolemaic spheres   silhouette
an integral of time   its intervals
over the sign of I
therefore be also all real   Venus
Elaine   Juliet   brown Norma Jean
black daughter
down in destroyed Jerusalem   blonde
apparent   Marilyn
                                        all real
and too numerous to mention
at the lack of an adequate sample
ring the door bell
go pad in hand   pencil out
seduce the female of the house   depart
scratch the proper intersection on the graph
X   of Y   of Z   of T   over I
                                        encircled in the best
cubed in the most probable   therefore
I cannot believe He plays at dice
with the universe
                                        world   why not
I create you   then I create you not
I am real   you are not   prove
that I lie   sing with Ophelia
irrational hymns of truth
how I love you   blonde or brown
beyond your bronze casket
your green shroud
                                        seduce   depart
mark the idiot graph   make the woman
pull down her skirt   complete her chores
preen for the next guest
                                        from house to house
she moves   and I
am the previous present future guest
a rapist   pad in hand   pencil out
prepared to enter intersections
on a seven-dimensional graph
                                        degrees of order

seeming probabilities   I talk with myself
I interpenetrate myself   by reflex telescope
the universe is my mirror
I shall not want for events
or emptiness
                                        I am
create   love   desire   curse   name
it is all the same
                                        hermetic Helen
jolly Juliet
Cleo   comet of the Nile
help keep Jean at sly fourteen
                                        Orpheus
tune your glockenspiel   bang your song
eat beans
ride the donkey down Jordan
to destroyed Jerusalem
                                        though it is all the same
I pronounce indefinite numbers of parallels
they never meet
                                        and as to the facts
soon enough   like you true blonde   I'll stop
the moons of Marilyn   satellites setting
but while I can set a clock
my mild marble Marilyn Jean
in all your magnetic warped cycles
while I live   mobility churns
in accord with the constant of H
X   to the power of   E
take any Lorentz transformation by the hand
                                        but as to the facts
listen
while entropy desecrates the heat
in your Greek hips
                                        understand
I am not the law   I am not
the real   the power   or the glory
the big dice are thrown down
but the numbers are all you are or I am
and the odds are known   therefore
prepare a Renaissance poison
for the apparent order   and plaster
an Arabian curse
across our lucky stars
                                        meanwhile
I'll spin the prayer wheel till we rot
beyond recognition
Veda for Venus   Mass for Marilyn

repeat after me while a perfect diapason rolls
                                        Venus
in all your vicious phases beauty reels
but under your probabilities
Norma still smiles

II

                                        smile that bitterness
at blank walls
with millenia to waste wails
                                        therefore
in afternoon   in summer   no sorrow
in a boy in blue cotton
is possible   he reaps ballistic harvests
in a game of bounce ball
                                        exactly what machine
can match such barren beauty as an empty sky
obscene with sun
                                        grin
at a red ball's oscillations
between boy and wall   sky swung
between infinities   coroidal curves
the coefficients of which
equal red balls at blank walls
or smirk at conic sections
raised to powers beyond wails
                                        here is a white house
with a lawn   a cattle fence   hollow rooms
tulips down its sides
truss up such perversions of blue heaven
all insurance has been cancelled
the green casements need paint
the green girl inside needs a new coat of life
Caucasian   female   dead   daughter   sister   child
virgin   dead   well-nourished   the body
glows green in its bronze room
                                        put
brown pennies on her eyes   for all
the universe   is love   and love is one
a fulfillment in astral masturbation
as the boy knows   bounded in its concourse
as the ball is
between his body and the wall
                                        the side door opens
for a woman
daughter   wife   mother   alive   squints
at the simple sky   brushes back her hair
                                        there are no

there are no sisters for you here   she says
leaving between them   in gravitational majesty
a red ball that hangs forever in the air

III

having come up here rushed
as it were
by winds of space I did not know exist   I
cannot stop writing requiems like Chinese boxes
fit one in another until the universe is one
I cannot puzzle
I cannot kill   I cannot create   I know it
I talk to myself as one poet to another
dear brother
had she read your poems she would have
died for you   who wrote of rosy death
so in soft marble
my Shelleyan friend
I dig your initials and epitaph
with a chewed toothpick   by candlelight
which should make you hysterical
with afterlife laughter
or if we could
learn love   amid the coming
and the going   and the stopping
for a beer   on a snowy evening
and how soft we are   beyond our lobster shells
among dead friends
in the eighth-month   in the dooryard
nothing blooms but weeds   less reasonable
than roses   more sadistic than no rain
dear brother
dead brother
forgive me if I anoint you
with oils of poison oak
before I bury you
I will dig your grave

HAROLD DULL

Suibhne Gheilt

I

He has haunted me now for over a year
that madman Suibhne Gheilt
who in the middle of a battle
looked up and saw something
that made him leap up and fly
over swords and trees
—a poet gifted above all others—

II

How could a proud loud mouth
who yelled KILL KILL KILL
as he plowed down the enemy
—heads rolling off of his sword—
be so lifted up
(or fly up
as those below saw it
—wings beating)
be so suddenly gifted
with poetry
and nest so high
in Ireland's tall trees?
Is there a point
where all paths cross?
And why am I so drawn to him
that all my questions
seem shot in his direction?
And they ran into the woods
and threw their lances
and shot their arrows
up through the branches
What parallels could I ever hope to find—
my refusal to fight
(weaseling out on psychiatric grounds)?
my leaving my country behind?
my poetry?
and my wife wept
on the path below. . .
Oh memory is sweet
but sweeter is the sorrel
in the pool in the path below

I fly down everynight
to eat

III

Sweeney like the rest of us
would've been better off
if he had never had anything to do with women.
But the point of it lies hidden
in a pool of milk
in a pile of shit
for you to see
when a milkmaid smiles
Sweeney like the rest of us flies down
and when she pours the milk
into the hole her heel made in the cowdung
Sweeney like the rest of us kneels down and drinks
and dies on the horn the cowherd hid in it.
So before you have anything to do with women
remember Sweeney the bird of Ireland
lying on his back
in the middle of that path
in the moonlight.

IV

And on my way home
                                    this morning
(my wife
          waiting)
my shadow
               racing up the path ahead of me
I saw something
                    (a black stone?)
thrown
        at the back of its head
ducked
        and spun around
so fast
        I almost fell down
– it was a bird
                    flying up into a tree

V

No good could come out of this war

out of what burns in the heart of our highly disciplined
John Q. Killer as a whole village bursts into one flame—
the villagers streaming like tears towards the forest
cover his helicopter's blades blow the leaves off and
the flame towards. . .

as we sit in front of our bubbles watching our president
(whose bubbletalk no one can escape and he is a little bit
mad—calling the reporters in for an interview while he's
sitting on the bubble having a bubble movement) and first
lady climb into their big bubble bed and Lucy, born of
their own bubbles, crawls in between—
  Mah daddy has so many troubles
  turning the world into a bubble
and sick of crossfire—the cries of the women and
children flying over his head—he stumbled down to the
riverbank and found, the wreckage twisted around the tree
behind, his skull. . .

Noises, there are noises, noises that can of themselves drive
a man mad—NOISES!

but last night the Stockhausen penetrated from the four
sides of the auditorium, stripping each layer of feeling
and thought until all that was left was something the size
of a nut—so tiny, so hard, so impenetrable it was alone
in the middle of an infinite space. . .

GEORGE ECONOMOU

The White Wolf

Send a man in
send in a man with 24 eyes
the white wolf hides in the snow
black tongue with pink eyes
set in the snow
take your planes home
send in a man

sun sets
evergreen gives in to black
the whiteness of the snow is quiet
don't just stand there
tottering between the mountains and the plains
the plains at night are death for the white fawn
send a man in
send in a hunter with ears on the soles of his feet
the white wolf waits

send a man into the mountains

sun rises
the white fawn roams below the timberline
give it a corner of your eye
it's still dark in the woods
as the white fawn descends

is the white wolf gone?
the white fawn hairpins closer
don't look to the plains
death comes there like a drink of cold water
send a man in

the white fawn comes

you dig holes in the water
dig holes in the dried up river
sprinkle chunks of gumbo on your head

the hunter is petrified

send a child
to cry wolf
the white fawn is upon us

The Cheer

Being a list of the primary sources of The Goddess Natura in Medieval Literature, *a dissertation submitted in partial fulfillment of the requirements for the degree of Doctor of Philosophy, Columbia University, 1967.*

Boethius Macrobius
Chalcidius Asclepius
    Proclus
    Plotinus
Marrrrtianus Capella

Prudentius Lactantius
Lucretius Apuleius
    Ovid
    Augustine
Hugo de Saint Victor

Cicero Dionysius
Claudian & Statius
    Isidore
    Tertullian
Sanctus Ambrosius & Philo the Jew

Guillaume de Conches, ehh?
Alain de Lille, ehh?
Thierry de Chartres
Jean de Meun Abelard

Johnny of Salisbury
Bernardus Silvestris

CHAUCER CHAUCER CHAUCER

RUSSELL EDSON

The Childhood of an Equestrian

An equestrian fell from his horse.
A nursemaid moving through the wood espied the eques-
trian in his corrupted position, and cried, what child
has fallen from his rockinghorse?

Merely a new technique for dismounting, said the prone
equestrian.

The child is wounded more by fear than hurt, said the
nursemaid.

The child which has dismounted and is at rest, but being
interfered with grows irritable, cried the equestrian.

The child that falls from his rockinghorse, refusing
to remount fathers the man with no woman to take
in his arms, said the nursemaid, for women are as horses,
so that it is the rockinghorse that teaches the man the
way of love.

I am a man fallen from a horse in the privacy of a wood;
save for a strange nursemaid who espied my corruption,
taking me for a child who fallen from a rockinghorse lies
down in fear refusing to father the man who mounts the
woman with the rhythm given in the day of his childhood
on the imitation horse when he was in the imitation of
the man who incubates in his childhood, said the man.

Let me help you to your manhood, said the nursemaid.

I am already, by the metaphor, the son of the child, if
the child father the man, which is involuted nonsense.
And take your hands off me, cried the equestrian.

I lift up the child which is wounded more by fear than
hurt, said the nursemaid.

You lift up a child which has rotted into its manhood,
cried the equestrian.

I lift up as I lift all that fall and are made children
by their falling, said the nursemaid.

Go away from me because you are annoying me, screamed the equestrian, as he beat the fleeing white shape that seemed like a soft moon entrapped in the branches of the forest.

Old Folks

There was once an old man and his wife who lived deep in the wood to guard themselves against the hurt of young persons who are of the brutal joy; for they are with nature and come as does nature. They from the outside, nature from within, to hurt old folks who must build deep in the wood that place which is defended by its secret.

The old folks also have guns, and have laid traps, and put bags of acid in the trees.

And are we safe? cries the old wife.
It is the flesh that I so fear, guard it as one will still it is dying in itself, says the old husband.
We are to be gotten to no matter what we do, screams the old wife.
Your screaming doesn't help, screams the old man.

What helps? screams the old wife.
Nothing, save the hope that there is a life beyond this one, roars the old man.
But all I have is an old brain wrapped in old grey hair; how can I know what I need to know? yells the old woman.
Yelling doesn't help, yells the old man.

What helps? roars the old woman.
Nothing, save that which was before us and shall continue after us, that cosmic presence which us so made —But not even it lifts one star or changes the order of one day in our behalf —No, we are alone, and there is no help; and so in despair we set traps, and have guns, and make ourselves secret to the on-rush of life, roars the old man.

But, what helps? screams the old woman.
Not you who luxuriates in an old man's logic instead of using your own brain —You hang on to my wits which I am losing for your incessant questions, roared the old man.

LARRY EIGNER

Three Poems from Air the Trees

Small, flightless birds
the voice far tinkling bells

museum

of sorts, the rats destroyed

moving ashore, Midway

slow is
the
poem

flat wall of the sea

and sky

each island
rose

farther than any whale

fins

breathing above the waves
the mirrors

heat

past sunshine

vibrations of air
spiders, then birds, settle

reflexive
man
bringing what he can

interest

in

the quickening run-though

one thing at a time

tides, a large motion

small waves give boats

menageries
from the bottom

rock crumbles to earth
under rain
the seas

clouds mulct the moon
flats

the whale is still hunted
in certain parts

prodigal
the deep light

The Confederacy, you have to
repeat,
        was real

                suddenly
                to be denied

        lines there down the map

            if you recognize yourself

                still
                roads

            colors of your state

                    to make a noise in

  the sheer slavery
  of abstruse thought

          full of the sky   rough   river
          dirt   the captured ordnance
            made game (to puff
          in imagination (useless   with the real
                    shot crater powder-kegs
          strewing the ground
                                now then
          behind grass   the
              slope of cloud   house
              bed and emptiness besides
                returning the sun
                    shown everywhere

                  the full-decked

sleep was in his mouth   he woke the
birds called   a strain of words   swung   falling
as the apple tree

back on itself
the slow life
is fast

waters or wings   growth
a solemn pole   some gate
grass, not very high
to bare patches

any of the trucks
bread   a half dozen chairs
movies

by the window the lost
man   years
in mind he
knew the way
how the story came out
the bower
he left the arrowhead
beads
later the cellar

flowers looking in

under the moon the
chairs tilted back   a view above the screen
flies were in the way
the trunks   bark hollow

now the black man brings the
clean pants   and he has to pay

CLAYTON ESHLEMAN

Lachrymae Mateo

        Your temperature at 103
meets in my arms,
O to annihilate
the poison, the stuffiness, the moral compulsion I accuse
Johnson of in my
own soul,
            cleansed cheeks
shine of spring,
clouds blown high meadows
nature is to forgive,

emotion is affection,
all love strives to know its own creative union
and must know its own creative union before it
can know another,

your mother
is the earth,
the Dante variation,
she is the sun and moon, she is the star

each traveler descries before entering the
Hill of Mound,
death's yap is no other than her face, each pine
a thousand times cries her,
                    immortal oregano.

This night I've held in
but in my arms
the possibility of self-annihilation, force
that can only be met with its own. For
give the earth in the daring

separation of Coatlicue
and Gladyce, split the atom Eve
covets as puritanic bloodbath mother
sensual sterile wife to

the natural love that flows in my loins beloved,
the natural grace that flows in my arms mortal mother,
the natural wrath that churns in my gut immortal Coatlicue,
the natural pity that my skull always knows for she-who-is

brotheled into religion, spat on, Mokpo, squeezed between a man's
failure to annihilate and his failure to forgive.
I see the lamb descending no longer Christian sacrificial
but through lips

vaginal flap
headgear, ballturret of the jet
that is by mercy
arrested in flight.

December 6, 1966

Soutine

for Nora Jaffe

The smell of shit
holy Smilovitchi
wholly Indianapolis
our child yoked
one membrane
slaughterhouse
pigment
the hunger of paint
the hunger of the vacant dinnertable
parents eyes like empty plates
my plate was filled
potatoes weenies milk
his plate was filled
shtetl shtetl shtetl
pigment in the ox
pigment in her hand
ooze of the first semen
slaughter menstruation
to make a vagina is to paint
poem a vagina made in a man
cut me the boy cries
transport over the back of
an elder
                this is an elegy
end of the old rite.
from now on you are to make it my
pigment told me way
   of survival
thru art

is way of survival is Smilovitchi
Indianapolis art the passage
                                        what
we never saw,   I never saw them kill
my father worked next to the wall against
whacked bullhead 30 feet up encased red
brick accountant
                        fowl,   I never saw them twist
the neck of my dinner is way of survival
rite de passage is Smilovitchi
                        is Indianapolis
trees,   I was too frustrated to
look at a tree,   stillife,   world in reel,
his bouquets flowers six feet stalks bright
flags of blood tossing buoys,
midnight,   his
midnight in the closed shop
a white fowl hangs
corruscated bag of jewels
dripping from cenote,   virgin,   he never saw the
virgins in my poems. how
can my poems influence him now that he is dead.
he is not dead.
he is a flower.
  I walk into the garden, pick lemon, smell
cut it into my soup
our talk this talk no more than birdchitter
cut it into your soup
art act
I slit my throat into my soup
I eat the breast of Soutine
amalgam
amalgam,   of one man
  the world is not a lie our
child told us,   love.
                        imperative
                              love this
greater than you
for me to spread open the beef,
see a vagina in every rock
for him to eat, race against
Talmudic law, as goldfish race against
our heart, magnolias a tablecloth

room in dizzyness, in state of gesture as a flower
I am in my pigment like in my body
body I've tried so hard to get out of
as he, and tried so hard to get
in to the body, impossible amalgam
is art

•

cross reference sway indigo directional
   as stoplight is directional
a slung fowl
in the blackness of my interior my heart in motion
pinnioned to the word
      goddamned black widows
hair-raising at thirteen
      goddamned black widows
(clenched) the first word we
         spoke a curse,   the
first word

•

moistinsplendor
childwood,   that I may be up to my imaginings
I make this homage
      not to
Soutine, but of
moistinsplendor

rust red
bile sacks
   nudging
bile sacks,

         I make out
of my art my art.
I make my art
out of art,
      a repeating
a constant filling, re-
peating, peat,
   stroking her.
my father to
thank for my genius.
   again and again over

that area   nipple   clitoris
thigh-inside, stoking

until love, pure semen, comes
over the windshield spring storm

•

That Marie has come into my life Céret
      inspired such
anguish,   the peaceful countryside,
of Céret
            my *possession* a hill.
I have this photograph in my head of you
diving into bed with another, I
flash on it. there
   I am denied, against you
I have laid up against the walls of
my mind and screamed
and in you the bed
was and is, for the first time, a door

   that my Céret pass over me
   that my Céret pass over me
the gouge.
the hate.

      you are spread over me. on me.
I reach around your buttocks,
down along your crack
      feel you stiffen,   immobile,
and touch your lips,
find your clitoris and begin to stroke it,
and feel there at the core of your flesh
your *opposition,*
            world at me

woman is liberty

•

That this becomes a making, then, beyond
anguish.

            Rejoice O Master,

who is none but thyself,
to the archangels even the angels are insane!
It is we who incorporate each order of being,
    mender
  knife
 scrawling
 forbidden
     images.

damned by
Solomon.

expelled
into the Breughel
woods
  hunger
paint
the paint of
       hunger
despised
water
Smilovitchi
  16
shtetl.

sacrilegious
thru the white
            rubles
Minsk
Vilma
Paris
  at 20

gargoyle rooster
         head—
boats on Seine
city of painters

cream rat poison
red face.

a perfectionist
 more dear to my heart
      than any other

Jews

he was not raw
material
Soutine
very hard
parents can die
father put me in

the chickencage
a spontaneous
genius.

the most powerful
painter of our time.

giddy from hunger.
hysterical energy
outside cafés.
took shelter in
cinemas.

compress

vision against words.
forbidden.
deKooning:
I cldnt get the
whole thing.

one side Matisse
one side Soutine.
color was light
from inside.
gentle beautiful
people.
didn't distort them
he never destroyed a
person—

Cagnes—
more like Modigliani.
El Greco his spiritual
master.

demon
surgeon.
enormously shy.

chicken hooked
slain yet alive
its agony
both bleeding
man without
lungs—

diagrams of his
insides—
agonized hands—
I adore Soutine
attached to nature.
flayed ox
couldn't part from
memory
brush in white
guts
impasto
painting Smilovitchi out
of him—

sloshed the
canvas with
fresh blood—
all of Paris with a
carcass of beef—

he gave us the psyche
of the human
face—

stricken
removed to Paris—
in a hearse—
bleeding to
death
Aug 9
1943—
died during
surgery—

last pallet
  blue yellow red at top
earth colors
below—
  blacks at right—

  center
   khaki—
ghost face of

pallet
pallet of

pallet

ray-face

hole

Los Angeles/September 26, 1968

The Meadow

TA CHUANG
The Power of the Great.

THUNDER IN HEAVEN
—as Aquarius was
THUNDER IN THE EARTH
so Taurus,
                    THUNDER IN HEAVEN,
the body to go 9/10ths,
                TA CHUANG,
Taurus
    batter-rams the bell)
      THUNDER IN HEAVEN
to let the creative thru.

The Function of the Orgasm
TA CHUANG
to let the creative thru.
The body to go 9/10ths
    THUNDER IN HEAVEN
to let the creative thru.

She breaks the ritual objects,
Smashes the Throne, Smashes
the looking-glass, she Curbs.
                    Svādiṣṭhāna
shattered on her gown, thistles
of cakra, herbs, tyings
of grass, Svādiṣṭhāna

cakra beloved of Scorpio,
a pattern of wildflowers,
spiders,
            men in battle, tiny,
    arrows, wildflowers,
            of her forestral
   THUNDER IN HEAVEN
  a beautiful blonde.

She is VALA
the Great,   She is
the Power of
the Veil,   She smashes
    with the exhausted Aires
in her arms,   he climbs, he
is a spider,   TA CHUANG
      She is the Power of the Veil
She curbs,   primavera
   in the impasto of Botticelli,
She draws out
                     the literary
acid in everyman's stomach
She coalesces,   She breaks the
tablets of the Ode,
                          acid in wch earth
swarms,   little spiders,   wildflowers,
                          She is the writing
between the lines
                          TA CHUANG,   the
writing that makes the lines,   O Hail to

Her,   beautiful blonde,   making holy
the forest,   She who breaks down the
ritual oaks,   who snaps the incrusted
objects,
            reverberating bull,
                   silent
   caterpillar of the swallowtail butterfly
 Caterpillar of the Lesser Emperor Moth
green with black stripes & orange colored warts!
Japanese Yamamai,   who feeds on oak
     & chestnut leaves!

                              She is the Veil!

The poem makes a way to
expose her to
the sun!

Oh hail to her, & hail to
Thee, & hail to HER, O Hail
to Caryl who keeps my imagination
from seeking
a singular form!
This great circle of
zoaic life fluttering leaves, creepers &
vines, Sparkie my dog is here, &
Wilhelm Reich like old sea captain
resting in Central Park, Artaud is here
(Soutine painted Artaud) a Communicant
in crinkly white gown conversing with Wilhelm
on old pigeon-shitted bench among the flowers &
rubbish, they are deep red magenta azaleas
nodding from last night's dew,
a place for the sentimental.
a place for the intellectual. a place for whose name
we do not know.
a moat
they glow about he
who has no concept of
eros in the poem,
they shimmer in terrific desire, they
lose their forms &
regain their forms,
TA CHUANG
she bangs a concept of
Eros out of him,
THUNDER IN HEAVEN
the Father in the arms of
his first Son

O Hail to Thee, O
bright & sacrificial,
like an Upper Room
Thee lies, a place
beloved of Virgo
where the betrayals
& horseshit of
this world are shed,

where the man in tension of
what he should
have done & didn't do, or
did do & shdn't have,
or should not
have done & did,   all
these contempts for
himself & others are
for a moment lost,
lost there, to not be
crucified in the poem.
Thee takes these things
as muscles, as heavy
breathing,   Thee draws
them into her,   She calls
them wildflowers & spiders,
She kneads him into a con-
vulsive ball of sun & earth
& in deep gratitude he
pours into her his agonies,
but now which he creates as
musculature & semen &
he knows as he howls & pours
he is not pouring (this is
the translation—as he feels
he pours he is pulling
from her
            TA CHUANG,
wildflower
spider
caterpillar
bull,
each creature charged
time past/
            time future

Thus he goes to poetry with no image
(ideally) except heat & light,
        with no image of what he
& she are.
            with no image of the way
world is.
            And if he find in this heat & light he loves a man,
he loves a man,

if he find here
nothing,   he burns,
a black fire
envelopes the white,
for the white is not pure
except it be tempted by the black,
& the black not impure
except it
be abandoned to the white,
& the heat & light are
black fire,   or twisted stars,
forever falling in the meadow
where all his loves are,

he longs for that place & thus
(ideally) he leaves,   as trees do in the fall,
a red flame sets in,
a veil it seems,   grows brittle

in the matrix of   creation

March 24, 1970

JIM HARRISON

from Outlyer and Ghazals

What in coils works with riddle's logic, Rhiemman's
time a cluster of grapes moved and moving, convolute.

As nothing is separate from Empire the signs change
and move, now drawn outward, not "about" but "in."

The stars were only stars. If I looked up then it was
to see my nose flaring on another's face.

Ouspensky says, from one corner the mind looking for
herself may go to another then another as I went.

And in literal void, dazzling dark, who takes
who where? We are happened upon and are found a home.

If you were less of a vowel or had a full stop in your
brain. A cat's toy, a mouse stuffed with cotton.

It seems we must reject the ovoid for the sphere,
the sphere for the box, the box for the eye of the needle.

And the world for the senate for the circus
for the war for a fair for a carnival. The hobbyhorse.

The attic for a drawer and the drawer for a shell.
The shell for the final arena of water.

That fish with teeth longer than its body is ours
and the giant squid who scars the whale with sucker marks.

Maps. Maps. Maps. Venezuela, Keewanaw, Iceland open up
unfolding and when I get to them they'll look like maps.

New pilgrims everywhere won't visit tombs, need living
monuments to live again. But there are only tombs to visit.

They left her in the rain tied to the water with cobwebs,
stars stuck like burrs to her hair. I found her by her wailing.

It's obvious I'll never go to Petersburg and Akhadulina
has married another in scorn of my worship for her picture.

You're not fooling yourself—if you weren't a coward you'd be
another target in Chicago, tremulous bullseye for hog fever.

The child crawls in circles, backs to the wall
as a dog would. The lights are dim, his mother talks.

Water whipped to wine, wine to mud. Flaccid butter.
I would as people once said go someplace else.

Swag. A hot night and the clouds moving low were brains
and I above them with the moon seeing down through a glass skull.

And o god I think I want to sleep within some tree
or on a warmer planet beneath a march of asteroids.

Once she said meet me in Portland, Oregon and I didn't.
Then to see her by accident in Boston, London, Tasmania.

Katherine near the lake is a tale I'm telling—there's a whiff
of melons and a girl bleeds through her eyes like a pigeon.

These corners that stick out and catch on things
and I don't fill my body's clothes.

Euclid, walking in switchbacks, kite's tip, always
either "up" or "down" or both, triangular tongue & cunt.

Backing up to the rose tree to perceive which of its
points touch where. I'll soon be rid of you.

There are no small people who hitch rides on snakes
or ancient people with signs. I am here now.

That I will be suicided by myself or that lids close over
and over simply because they once were open.

We'll ask you to leave this room and brick up the door
and all the doors in the hallway until you go outside.

The brain opens the hand which touches that spot, clinically
soft, a member raises from his chair and insists upon his rights.

In some eyebank a cornea is frozen in liquid nitrogen. One day
my love I'll see your body from the left side of my face.

Half the team, a Belgian mare, was huge though weak. She died
convulsively from the 80volt prod, still harnessed to her mate.

Alvin C. shot the last wolf in the Judith Basin after a four year
hunt, raising a new breed of hounds to help. Dressed out 90 lbs.

When it rains I want to go north into the taiga, and before I
freeze in arid cold watch the reindeer watch the northern lights.

Drinking Song

I want to die in the saddle as it were. An enemy of civil-
ization I want to walk around in the woods, fish and drink.

I'm going to be a child about it and I cant help it, I was
born this way and it makes me very happy to fish and drink.

I left when it was still dark and walked on the path to the
river, the Yellow Dog, where I spent the day fishing and drinking.

After she left me and I quit my job and wept for a year and
all my poems were born dead, I decided I would only fish and drink.

Water will never leave earth and whisky is good for the brain.
What else am I supposed to do in these last days but fish and drink?

In the river was a trout and I was on the bank, my heart in my
chest, clouds above, she was in NY forever and I, fishing and drinking.

Awake

Limp with night fears: hellebore, wolfbane,
Marlowe is daggered, fire, volts, African vipers,
the Grizzly the horses sensed, the rattlesnake
by the mailbox—how he struck at thrown rocks,
black water, framed by police, wanton wife,
I'm a bad poet broke and broken at thirty-two,
a renter, shot by mistake, airplanes and trains,
half-mast hardons, a poisoned earth, sun will
go out, car break down in a blizzard,
my animals die, fist fights, alcohol, caskets,
the Hammerhead gliding under the boat near
Loggerhead Key, my soul, my heart, my brain,
my life so interminably struck with an ax
as wet wood splits bluntly, mauled into
sections for burning.

MICHAEL HELLER

The Cardiac Poem

1

Blaiberg's heart

a way to keep modern?

The thought fierce. Little trip
hammer of a beat
to plow a body
thru that much more
time and space

at first there was a wobble
a neutral, a scientific
wobble

simply a matter of fit

2

and later
they make it fit—

O imagine
the recessional

as if time
leapt back

the way sun is seen
at 6:00 PM
—a great red ball

and a minute later
on the world's rim
distended by the thick waves of air

the way we must seem
from the point of view
of the sun

and at 7:00
all is dark

3

the aura I have made round you
meaning
you are *its* heart, its center

is more than fleshing out

is beauty
the way frost coats
a tree

to the finest tendrils
of its branchings

O the delicacy
of the image

Tho neither you
nor I
are fragile

the frost is—
it snaps
or is defrosted at the end of
a cycle

4

And in dream
Barnard, white coat and stethoscope
an Aztec priest

but a thief
stealing what belongs to the Sun
secreting it
in the open swimming cavity

after the stitches
after the wipe-up
after the groggy headache of
  anaesthesia

someone would realize
in what way
it had been offered up

5

Via Cain or via Abel

in what way
if it happened
it could kill you

just hearing
thump
silence
thump
at night

the panic of love
and not love
twisted
round you

6

shaky heart

bird

its salt pulse: song
that keeps one alive

I love you. That
I Ching of possibility
which has been grasped
then pulled beyond me

till it is no longer me

nor you

7

a flutter
a seizure: thick
fibres that contract

a bird
crushed in a cage
of tissue and fluids—the heart sac

how many Medieval men
saw the heart?

how many
see the unneutral
heart of Arts and Letters

8

At what end of what thing
do the names of the Gods change
from ennui or loneliness

There isn't anything we can't do
now
not one thing

a wall is a wall
and what of a wall

Have you ever seen them
harvest wheat? The scythe
death of wheat?

ANSELM HOLLO

The Mosaic Standard from Ur

looks like a wall

& that's a camel
no a horse

it's got a face like a horse

          set of museum postcards
          showed them to her
          one by one

people
people too

they're sitting   two are
standing up

that's a
bad indian no   a lion
is what it is

          what it is
          is a pair of eyes
          only opened
                    three years ago

Song of the Tusk

the elephant
　　bogged down
thousands of years ago

the fragmentary tusk
　　now in a glass case

no no those are untrue statements
it is I
　　am in the glass case
　　　　counting
　　　　　　the stubs of museum tickets

it is the elephant
　　walks the downs
　　　　laughs at the sea
　　　　　　growling

there is no such thing
　　as thousands of years
I drop a stone on your head
　　from the elephant's back

show me
　　show me the thousands of years

I walk through the water
　　throwing stones at the women
　　　　on the beach
　　the honeymoon women
　　　　their eyes far apart

frightened
　　they close the glass case
　　　　over themselves & their lovers
　　for thousands of years

On the Occasion of Becoming an Echo

the goddess stands in front of her cave
waves me into the drawing   eyes
like an afterthought
dotted in   green

Gaia   drawn by a six-year-old
very clear

many more things in this room
books chairs a bed
at least two people
(how many more in their dreams)
but the signals are garbled
garbled

I mean (he says
who is I   who *is* I?)
mean well I want the whole world to love me
not need me at all

the goddess stands in front of her cave
not waving me in   just raising her hands
as if to say "well   who's to tell you?"
once upon a time
my head says   there was a man he got very tired
he went to sleep and didn't dream
didn't even sleep but was gone

out
and out there
all things were clear

•

Iowa City crickets
September nights
don't have that much to say

but say it & say it & say it

"scribble scribble
eh   Mr Pound?"

•

brother immortal
                    jellyfish

    "brighter than
                    the brightest star"

what do you know of wars
here on TV

poetry workshops   pills
the Naga question

or Dr Sigmund Freud
the famous hypnotist

there's none could cure you
                              of your ignorance

    I mean that's great

              we love you as you are

•

    dark blur girl
rushing
      past in a car

a lifetime.
where was she going

•

night bird whistling churring

too pretty

who says it's too pretty

some inner dentist

your cunt is pretty
my cock is pretty

it's a pretty good night
bird whistling   churring

on & off & on

•

young girls walk
jointed
disjointed

no one to plug them in

don't let the exo-skeletals take them

they are the moon

•

Ovidius Naso
wrote a book

Sir Vincent Wigglesworth
created a giant caterpillar

here
        I put them together

(you do too)

Song

o love shiny shiny
shiny we once were
shiny down the road
shiny in the corner
of my eye

o friends shiny shiny
shiny we once were
shiny in the halls
shiny on the road

time took shine
& will take all
eheu fugaces
balls & all

(but there's still a few words
some songs   some verbal turds
in this old yak)

HALVARD JOHNSON

From the Lakes

these same small birds
this rough-hewn wood
these figures carved in weathered stone

it is unknown
whether those
living in this forest
are priests or gods

the man who lives in the cottage by the river
claims that the forest is uninhabited,
he worships the thunderer
& the three mothers

•

through the door we heard music
though no one answered when we knocked

looking through the windows told us little
about the inhabitants of the place

the kitchen was a clutter of utensils
a fire was burning in the den

a white, blue-eyed cat slept on the neatly-made bed
a dog slept near the door, the bird on its perch

there was no one there, we saw this
& went back into the trees

•

riverman came from the lakes where the big stones are,
came here looking for people, looking for women

riverman found two girls, abandoned in the woods,
took them home, blonde, blue-eyed girls

riverman took his pleasure with them, took
his axe then, chopped them down

a fire burning at the mouth of his cave,
this happened many times, fire burning many times

The Dance of the Red Swan

The pillows were white and fluffy,
an effect reminiscent of sitting in sidewalk cafes
on lower Fifth Avenue, back in the old days,
or of sipping Mexican Pernod with Irv and Harriet,
in their cabin high in the Sangre de Cristos.
The night outside would be cool and black with promise
of snow and the outhouse a good twenty steps from the back door.
But in the old days, lower Fifth Avenue was peaceful,
even in wartime. The President had an apartment
in a building on Washington Square, but was never there
nowadays, according to the doorman, whom I never failed to ask.
All over the world, people were going to sleep and waking up,
fluffing their white pillows and going back to sleep again.

Irv and Harriet's cabin was actually in the Sacramentos,
the Sangre de Cristos being much farther north in New Mexico.
But there's something about Sangre de Cristo, the words,
in Spanish. There's also *arena,* which means sand. It can also mean
"arena", which is fair enough when the arena has sand in it.
But the names of things can fool you at times.
The Sangre de Cristos aren't in the least bit bloody
to the naked eye, and presidents' apartments don't always
have presidents in them. The Red Swan turns out to be
a woman in disguise. And north of the Sacramentos
and south of the Sangre de Cristos are the Sandias,
which are partly sand, but mostly rock.

DAVID JONES

The Tutelar of the Place

She that loves place, time, demarcation, hearth, kin, enclosure, site, differentiated cult, though she is but one mother of us all: one earth brings us all forth, one womb receives us all, yet to each she is other, named of some name other . . .

. . . other sons,
beyond hill, over strath, or never so neighbouring by nigh field or near crannog up stream. What co-tidal line can plot if nigrin or flaxhead marching their wattles be cognate or german of common totem?

Tellus of the myriad names answers to but one name: From this tump she answers Jac o' the Tump only if he call Great-Jill-of-the-tump-that-bare-me, not if he cry by some new fangle moder of far gentes over the flud, fer-goddes name from anaphora of far folk wont woo her; she's a rare one for locality. Or, gently she bends her head from far-height when tongue-strings chime the name she whispered on known-site, as between sister and brother at the time of beginnings . . . when the wrapped bands are cast and the worst mewling is over, after the weaning and before the august initiations, in the years of becoming.
When she and he 'twixt door-stone and fire-stane prefigure and puppet on narrow floor-stone the world-masque on wide world-floor.
When she attentively changes her doll-shift, lets pretend with solemnity as rocking the womb-gift.
When he chivvies house-pet with his toy *hasta,* makes believe the cat o' the wold falls to the pitiless bronze.
Man-travail and woman-war here we
see enacted are.
When she and he beside the settle, he and she
between the trestle-struts, mime the bitter dance to come.
Cheek by chin at the childer-crock where the quick tears drop and the quick laughter dries the tears, within the rim of the shared curd-cup each fore-reads the world-storm.
Till the spoil-sport gammers sigh:
Now come on now little
children, come on now it's past the hour. Sun's to roost, brood's in pent, dusk-star tops mound, lupa sniffs the lode-damps for stragglers late to byre.
Come now it's time to come now for tarry awhile and slow

cot's best for yeanlings
crib's best for babes

here's a rush to light you to bed
here's a fleece to cover your head
against the world-storm
brother by sister
under one *brethyn*
kith of the kin warmed at the one hearth-flame
(of the seed of far-gaffer? fair gammer's wer-gifts?)
cribbed in garth that the garth-Jill wards.

Though she inclines with attention from far fair-height outside all boundaries, beyond the known and kindly nomenclatures, where all names are one name, where all stones of demarcation dance and interchange, troia the skipping mountains, nod recognitions.

As when on known-site ritual frolics keep bucolic interval at eves and divisions when they mark the inflexions of the year and conjugate with trope and turn the seasons' syntax, with beating feet, with wands and pentagons to spell out the Trisagion.

Who laud and magnify with made, mutable and beggarly elements the unmade immutable begettings and precessions of fair-height, with halting sequences and unresolved rhythms, searchingly, with what's to hand, under the inconstant lights that hover world-flats, that bright by fit and start the tangle of world-wood, rifting the dark drifts for the wanderers that wind the world-meander, who seek hidden grammar to give back anathema its first benignity.

Gathering all things in, twining each bruised stem to the swaying trellis of the dance, the dance about the swan lode-stake on the hill where the hidden stillness is at the core of struggle, the dance around the green lode-tree on far fair-hight where the secret guerdons hand and the bright prizes nod, where sits the queen *im Rosenhage* eating the honey-cake, where the king sists, counting-out his man-geld, rhyming the audits of all the world-holdings.

Where the marauder leaps the wall and the wall dances to the marauder's leaping, where the plunging wolf-spear and the wolf's pierced diaphragm sing the same song . . .

Yet, when she stoops to hear you children cry
from the scattered and single habitations
or from the nucleated holdings
from tower'd *castra*
paved *civitas*

treble-ramped *caer*
or wattled *tref*
stockaded *gorod* or
trenched *burh*
from which ever child-crib within whatever enclosure
demarked by a dynast or staked by consent
wherever in which of the wide world-ridings
you must not call her but by that name
which accords to the morphology of that place.
Now pray now little children pray for us all now, pray our gammer's prayer according to our *disciplina* given to us within our labyrinth on our dark mountain.
Say now little children:
Sweet Jill of our hill hear us
bring slow bones safe at the lode-ford
keep lupa's bite without our wattles
make her bark keep children good
save us all from dux of far folk
save us from the men who plan.
Now sleep on, little children, sleep on now, while I tell out the greater suffrages, not yet for young heads to understand:

Queen of the differentiated sites, administratrix of the demarcations, let our cry come unto you.
In all times of imperium save us
when the *mercatores* come save us
from the guile of the *negotiatores* save us
from the *missi*, from the agents
who think no shame
by inquest to audit what is shameful to tell
deliver us.
When they check their capitularies in their curias
confuse their reckonings.
When they narrowly assess the *trefydd*
by hide and rod
by *pentan* and pent
by impost and fee on beast-head
and roof-tree
and number the souls of men
notch their tallies false
disorder what they have collated.
When they proscribe the diverse uses and impose the

rootless uniformities, pray for us.
When they sit in *Consilium*
to liquidate the holy diversities
mother of particular perfections
queen of otherness
mistress of asymmetry
patroness of things counter, parti, pied, several
protectress of things known and handled
help of things familiar and small
wardress of the secret crevices
of things wrapped and hidden
mediatrix of all the deposits
margravine of the troia
empress of the labyrinth
receive our prayers.
When they escheat to the Ram
in the Ram's curia
the seisin where the naiad sings
above where the forked rod bends
or where the dark outcrop
tells on the hidden seam
pray for the green valley.
When they come with writs of oyer and terminer
to hear the false and
determine the evil
according to the advices of the Ram's magnates who serve
the Ram's wife, who write in the Ram's book of Death.
In the bland megalopolitan light
where no shadow is by day or by night
be our shadow.
Remember the mound-kin, the kith of the *tarren* gone from
this mountain because of the exorbitance of the Ram . . .
remember them in the rectangular tenements, in the houses
of the engines that fabricate the ingenuities of the Ram . . .
Mother of Flowers save them then where no flower blows.
Though they shall not come again
because of the requirements of the Ram with respect to the
word plan, remember them where the dead forms multiply,
where no stamen leans, where the carried pollen falls to the
adamant surfaces, where is no crevice.

In all times of *Gleichschaltung*, in the days of the central
economies, set up the hedges of illusion round some remnant
of us, twine the wattles of mist, white-web a Gwydion-hedge
like fog on the *bryniau*

against the commissioners
and assessors bearing the writs of the Ram to square the world-floor and number the tribes and write down the secret things and take away the diversities by which we are, by which we call on your name, sweet Jill of the demarcations
arc of differences
tower of individuation
queen of the minivers
laughing in the mantle of variety
belle of the mount
for Jac o'the mound
our belle and donnabelle
on all the world-mountain.
In the December of our culture ward somewhere the secret seed, under the mountain, under and between, between the grids of the Ram's survey when he squares the world-circle.
Sweet Mair devise a mazy-guard
in and out and round about
double-dance defences
countermure and echelon meanders round
the holy mound
fence within the fence
pile the dun ash for the bright seed
(within the curtained wood the canister
within the canister the budding rod)
troia in depth the shifting wattles of illusion for the ancilia for the palladia for the kept memorials, because of the commissioners of the Ram and the Ram's decree concerning the utility of the hidden things.
When the technicians manipulate the dead limbs of our culture as though it yet had life, have mercy on us. Open unto us, let us enter a second time within your stola-folds in those days—ventricle and refuge both, *hendref* for world-winter, asylum from world-storm. Womb of the Lamb the spoiler of the Ram.

c. 1960 incorporating passages written earlier.

Mr. Vernon Wakins has provided a glossary of certain Welsh words in this poem:

brethyn	cloth
bryniau	hills
caer	fort, castle, city
hendref	ancestral dwelling, winter quarters
pentan	hob, fire-stone
tarren	tump, knoll
tref	hamlet
trefydd	hamlets
troia	meander, from *troi*, to turn, and Troea, Troy.

ROBERT KELLY

Hymn of the Sons of Light Headed This Way over the Milk Way

Star box

for the faster
issue of
informing fire   woven into links
of words (mail)
that are our armor
against the sheriffs
of these desert places
(letters
from there to here

capacitors
(who had headed
Tiamat
& Dagon travelling
under a man's name
in ladies sequins, jets,
plumes of paradise
birds)
capacitors   (captain us, now
voice us, us amend

(Milton's voice lingering in the souterrain,
earnestness of divine Matters, such in-
formation
—struction—from an older time,
men believed in
parliaments: rumps of beef-cattle
heaped up in Smithfield,
flies
even in winter
caress this mortality, hecatomb, lovin this meat, all for)
all for a
(for want of a)
verb,

capacitors
resist hers

wrest her
aboulities

slipp slennderr skirrt over hipps adown,
starb ox, star box,
orb ox who, slaughtered,
issues us,
all the generations of flesh chosen (woven)
from this fabric,
from garment to garment discarded,
entering to

she doesnt care what anyone does to her
& wants him to

Epinoia, the brides
of Massachusetts wear salmon taffeta
green silk in emeraude, silk
hymeneal red,
salmon for Dagon,

as a boy he wondered
who was Tiamat
did she live in Milton Newton Brighton Brookline

was she the bad girl up the block
la belle juive, lip-talented, obligée?
Ti-amat.
Virgin intact
wear black
Whores white
for the spilt milk.
The moral
imagination
creates a city, lays
his streets & his name on them,
Mananaan, Manhattan, shuddering sea
always over horizon—
Milton's voice
blurred on the tape-transport,
Satin did tame me & I dared ease
of the long burden, stuck red-light, dense
matter of virginity,
ape the ample

& tit eat, ti-amat,
her keepers, zoo guards of
zodiac, going the beast way she was,
come to reclaim her,
our ignorance
their earthfall, silver commandos, monsters
of prehellenic earth returning
eat me eat me
to tame her, re-
claim her powers, Dagon, our lady, hail
full of fish,
obligated to their descent, welcoming
extraterrestrials back
computer memories,
a sound mimetic
of her praxis,
sound of ocean,
1200 feet in 10 seconds,
travelling the message
not home but home-along,
blips on radar
at last
& not longer any ever again into
Ocean
they return,
consecrate her aboulities
to the service of
what would have been
but for her appetite
earth,
Prounikê
whose derrière
—élue—
is a mirror
& whose queynt a burning glass,

Vicki, Dawn,
Suzy,
agreeable sisters elicit our Weird
from our admirations
of their fascinations,
Damballa plunges his rod
into the serpent of waters,
brassière of red silk,

brazeer pink sateen, all her votaries
by riverside,
government a whore
of these powers
whose names we do not know
& know
only that we dont believe,
we do not believe these bodies
to whom we give the power to arouse us
without meaning, without end,
the enemy
of my enemy is my friend,
Tiamat
wherever the city spreads to hide her,
flee her, Dagon ambiguous, Damballa
particular black,
:pink falsies, white
snake belly, them draftboard blues,
capacitors,
circuits
who are men
travelled,
tropic
of wisdom
& honester
need,
resist her
& this their song
& this the mother of distortion
bending the sound of words outwards,
north of meaning
where the sun comes to do his business,

through the electric intricate we were made slaves
through the free electron freed
into hearing past hearing
& look at them no longer

we invent a universe to take them away
we slaughter an ox
let
them project
themselves out beyond the moon,

the enemy
of my enemy
is my friend,
come, articulate manhood, in honester need—

No.
The messages
do not hasten.

The police do not hasten,
the fire-engines coast by the smouldering ruin,
the mailman
is afraid of the dark
inside his letters,
fulmen
lightning exhibits heaven,
left side, right side, we ride
by the river,
Vicki Suzy Dawn
caress the contours of the watertable,
hang in the air untamed,
unused,
but who did get tempted
& who did eat
newspapers for her breakfast,
looking
(I saw her tonight
on Washington, tight on his arm, her green
body gracious in scale, her eyes
nobler than my eyes seeing her)
looking
where the violent against themselves
punish themselves,
& wait for
the big break,
the wave
will carry her in again,
or that Tiamat
you did not kiss in Milton or Dorchester or Scituate
rises
incessantly
in (for in
stance)
your cells,

my cells, our poor
political bodies crutch'd
for our bread
on the conduct of war,
rises to meet them,
they return to our schoolyard
& take the mean old teacher away
out in the back of the stars & kill her,
grrind her to dust
& the pollen of these same
stars we spray in the winds of,

waiting the new anointed one
to fall aslither
down into our hands,

on Whom avails no sorrow dallies here

his voice disengaging,
decibels down,
delights her, loss
of the signal,
the parliament army, the king cut down, a new
king crowned,
the oil is the same,
burns where it touches my skin,
red pepper pods float in it
for the sake of the weather,

resist her
(they are singing
of their mother & their sisters)
resist her
in whose capacity
we weather our wisdoms & rise

old myth of morning.

Glad Yods

a book of concealment & apertus,
for Helen

1

this that the waterman
gushed
            (gieshed
we would have said
in another german)
                                        was not water

it was a sparrow
finding itself clean
revealed
only by the fact
(act)
      of its motion,
the so-called

bath in our dust
(o frères of the spirit)
in our atmosphere

Electricity
is the meaning
the content of Aquarius
(I mean the bird

looks at itself in the water

2

Samothrace that early island
sickle in the water my friend
you would hardly have remembered
was the place where your engagement

signed its contract.   Yes yes
they cried, show us the unburnt
antler, the flesh where the fire
swept out september grasses

& you still had the melody in hand.
O yes adversity is a precious

teacher, a sunburnt yachtsman
who hardly knows what it means

to make an honest living.
But you know, and I'm with you.
So many ways we could have got it
wrong we finally got right.

3

women dont have that kind of karma

you said & I believed.
It was a strange day
when I estranged a friend
by my clodhopping meat-hammer
salami-slicing old home truths

& still went up to the happy
up part of the house happy,
unhassled, almost rejoicing,
past the dark rooms
where all afternoon the forms

of the Abramelin demons
took shape & shifted,
lunged &
                generally carried on
(dark), companions
of a ritual
                    I hardly knew I practised

& there I was with your
truth on my mind,
                              I carry burdens
that maybe have nothing to do with the day
& maybe you too
carry
out of the night   (passage
between identities)   something
more than you know,

an obligation
(I would sometimes make it)
to stand & not be understood,

a silent shape that envelops you
& takes you past
the corners of our masculine eyes.

4

The best thing today was fucking you
in the living room for the luxe of it

the luck of you I still smell on my cock.

5

A snapshot from Vietnam
some boys in the jungle
from Utica, New York,
wondering how deep the snow is home,

wanting a couple of quiet
beers, blood on their hands
not glad about it, just
the way it is, you lift
the glass, some dribbles

& where can it dribble but your chin.
The world
is not mysterious enough,
we have tried to be clear
& have been very clear indeed,

there are things money cant buy
& things it can.
We have bought those things
& kept quiet about the others.
Now the boys in the snapshot want some

& what they think they want is home.
You will get home naked & undone,
companions lost. We have
heard it before. It didnt help.
What else does the paper say?

6

I consider with you the figure of Aquarius,
the waterman or Ganymede, the cool
unloving friendly boy

who pours the charm of his company into our heads.
Electricity, as I said before,
a power well worth looking into
with our cat eyes & our big fat books.
The armory of Eden had that consolation,
something to switch on & off, a current
in our control.   I call it sex
& dont know the first thing about it.
But we can use it, or it uses us,
or I look at you in bed & forget the whole thing.
Helen.   Or what should I call you
who turns me on & forgets the switch.
Summer lakes in thunderstorms, zickety zack.
It pours out.   It pours out.
How you looked this morning
pours out of me like stars.

7

Ardors.
Insane birds
riding the lightning
to what they think
is safety.   A nest
in a doomed tree.
Insane birds
riding the vowels
down to a king's
doom.
Listen to me.

8

$\int_{S}^{H_g}$ because we're so smart
because we're intellectuals

Could you do what my friend did,
tie himself up in a tree & hang there
hungry & thirsty & horny for nine days

or my other friend
who tells me stories soon as I wake up
sometimes I'm late to work I listen
so hard he's really
inter
esting

about the girl in the subway
or the story of the steeplejack
the birds brought him pizza he wiped his
hands on a passing cloud, could you?

And if you couldnt & I cant,
why do we possess a systematic
collection of sounds called language
& some ways of more or less
writing them down? Dont any of us
care about the music?
Or did you learn from history
something you didnt dare to tell me?

9

Mao, well,
I could dream about power
& disguise my power as love
& give it to you all
right between the eyes.

There is a place that dreams in us
& if we are decent then it has no power
or not enough to make me
kill you for its sake.

I am impressed by a story I remember
about a plumber who fell on a pipe & died.
His widow told us, clinically,
when we wondered why nobody fixed our sink.

We're still wondering. There is a power
in us that is clean & not confused,
it shits history but doesnt eat it,
it makes use of death & does not die.

I have imagined it gladly, expanding
beyond all contradiction, knowing you & me
will have in the course of things to die,
knowing that other thing, beneath
notice, this afternoon, our bodies together.

10

Silver water
such as we saw
in the rain
off Stinson.

Silver water
such as juices
the light I
turn on.

Silver water
such as we remember
when we forget.
An urn

for centuries,
we
are the precipitates.
It begins.

The birds
are at the skirts
of winter
& other medieval

colors
fleck the still
water as the sun
rushes past.

Suns.   Lunes.
Aches of agents
& passive moans.
What pours

ables us.
This is about
potency.
Is about you.

JOANNE KYGER

A Test of Fantasy

New York/January–March 1967

1.

It unfolds and ripples like a banner, downward. All the stories
come folding out. The smells and flowers begin to come back, as
the tapestry is brightly colored and brocaded. Rabbits and violets.

Who asked you to come over. She got her foot in the door and
would not remove it, elbowing and talking swiftly. Gas leak?
that sounds like a very existential position perhaps you had
better check with the landlord.

This was no better than the
predicament I had just read about. Now it was actually changing
before my eyes. Sometimes it will come to a standstill though,
and finally the reflection can begin.

Selfless—that was the proposition. Smiling and moving instantly
there was no other purpose than that which brought them there,
to be in a particular place.

2.

This time the mule gave its face away. Take your cadillac
where you want to go in the morning, convertible as it might be,
and enjoy a good bottle of rum.

Running on this way she used various modes of expression that
were current. Nothing seemed to bring the woods any closer.
What Woods, she was questioned, realizing that as far as the
woods went, they were largely inhabitable through the facility
of her mind. At the Philadelphia Flower Show, an ideal situation
was built up. Here through various regulated artificial conditions,
spring grass, waterfalls, and newly sprouted bulbs completed
her ideal concept of nature. The smell was overpowering.

All right then. She had a thing about nature, from flower
show glamor and enormous green houses the rich cultivated.

A beauty of cultivation—in living? Hastiness did not prevent
her from rising quick and ready to misnomers and other odd
conclusions, throwing the telephone book to the floor, "OH OH
the life I am entangled in." Four sides of it.

Above was a paradisical
level, incompleted. With working possibilities.

Below, endless preoccupations and variations were possible,
currently in vogue were shelves, the vacuum cleaner, a new
bedspread and color scheme for pillows.

Taste treats were
unresponsive. Glamor do's were out. Conversation was nil.
Languid

she could not even find a place to languish upon that was
fulfilling in its own way.

So out of the lifelessness that was around her,
the grape leaves drying out, and *even though* the avocado was
sprouting,

she thought, Why *not* fantasy? Tugging at this character and
that, trying to push a little life in a prince or a charmer,
a half blind bat, dryad, the works of the story teller. Here
the four walls of the room and ceiling became apparent again.
"I ought to tighten down and make sure I say *exactly* what I
mean."

And her face took on a tight pinched expression, and
thrifty scotch economy gave her shrewd eyes in the prescribed way.
Use *every*, tidbit, *usefully*. Once upon a time there was a
princess who had a long white fur coat with a high fluffy
collar, and inside the coat were stitched beautiful butterflys
in many bright colors. The princess languished. She was not
sure where to sit to her best advantage to enjoy herself the
most. She could not go *in* her mind or *out*. She looked at her
long white hand, I am the Queen of the High Mountain Hag, she
murmured to herself, still knowing she was a princess. She
lay down upon the floor like it were the garden of eden, the
coat spread around her.

No, that poor little house she had built
was a bore. It's better that it go up in flames, as it did.

She went down to Grand Central Station and gave away flowers.
Some people took them and some people didn't.

3.

I'm glad to get back. I had to repeat a rough, discontinuous
journey. Questioning myself all along the way. Was I jumping

on her because her time had come to an end. Indeed I pounded
on his arm all night, over his concern for this soft spoken
individual, I can see nothing but their softness. Me ME, and
the time we might spend together, reading and talking, to
tear away that putrid husk.

My flippancy is gone. Now I have started my secret life again,
in transition, reminding. As the moth reminds, its feeble
antenna groping, taken like a stalk of fern, coins of money.

All over I was shaking as the fear and tension made itself
apparent. It was a cold night out. It was colder still between
the airy gaps, between blankets.
You can see she is thoughtful
as she draws the bow to the string. Where to go indeed. The
point is brought forward and discussed very cleverly.

A sleeping angel or a sleeping troll? I was rather proud of
being used, pushing the clothing hampers up and down the downtown
street. Here, pleasant mentors conveyed their anxious solicitations,
drawing from their bags, long lists of memorandum due, what I owed.
It was a lot, if I hesitated. I choose to go on, saying this is
the way I go, owing nothing, being that kind of person. Hung up?

That thought intrudes as the clearly marked vista is not so
clearly marked. Certainly one supposes in all honesty, that
an essential core of feeling blooms in each encounter. Lost
under the weight of the garbage of who are you that you are not
making apparent. Thus unhappy, I don't want it to be this way,
and so forth. Not costumes, or paraphernalia, the immediate
reactions.

4.

We of course are in a family situation. Anything I wish might
happen, but the larger situations are not real, not to be
considered possible, discussable as to what sense of reality they
possess.

In the snow, the wood piled up underneath. Oh those drifting
sensibilities. At this point it is scarcely believable that people
gather and like each other. Eating chocolate pudding, getting
in touch with some other sense of alikeness. The form is no longer
obvious to me. Whether they meander or are joined together in
their senses in the mechanics or regular grooves then run along.

I suspect that in this house, this
place that is musty and left as it was some years ago, there is
no real fear; the objects are old and I am not familiar with
them, only the sense that the Ghost or spirit world strikes you
with its familiarity, pleasurable fear.
Here the familiar
is apt to make its presence known, at any moment the unexpected
lurk in the hall, into the room. Pieces of leather, old silken
fans laid upon the table top, rooms filled with something left
unexpectedly; terror is the wrong combination of ignorance. It
contains its own self with dusty fragments of velvet and fringe.
100 pieces of voice with no name, called it myself, as they spoke
all day, sucking the soft slush, admitting their real deficiencies as—
I am never sure; Oh its that power

and disease of believing in the stale that doesn't demand a real
climate, takes its capacity when the demons come down.

5.

The night passes in night time. The head bowing to the shoulder,
the head rising with a frown.

In a firm voice, it doesn't matter if the hair is flying from undue
spring breezes, the self has been raptured on the wine that produces
appropriate madness, and sad she says, my dear the bacchanal is a
lovely way to be rid of waste.
However, in seeing the house more manageable, one cannot even have
fear larger than the unknown portions of the continent which
refuses to sink.
There once was a woman
who grew older, not that she minded, but the passage of time was
always constant. Why does one have to contend with that she said,
puzzled as she got carried along, and *constantly* had to think up
new coping modes of behavior. If he behaved to me thus when he was
40, now that I am 30, I can hardly behave like that to those that
are 20, and so forth. There wasn't any model except the one she
built, and one could scarcely believe there was no established pattern.
This offered wonderful possibilities, but also indecision and
gutlessness.

6.

You can't see them, all bundled up, all those that choose
to move other than where the distance seems appealing. Knowledge
has no depth. There isn't any message to be spoken.

Wrangling, she speaks ill advised my dear, as the cat has no point in laying down its head. She out to watch carefully.

The claws. It could be the bent hands, as they grow, that as the fur impeaches the rose, doesn't make the thing she hangs her body on any realer. What could it be all about? The necessity to follow, balancing, contemplating works, as the basis of why we move at all.

Just a little touch. The leader cautioned further progression. I could hardly listen to the music for long. Now there seemed to be interruptions, pleasurable interludes, nothing definite, of a fragmented nature.

Certainly I wished the best for all. The sadder soldiers stumbled idly, as I also in the profound reaches of my slumber noted the elegant turns, the twisting statements grooving into the language building something to listen to. The dress made from silk. Trusting was awkward and not of a nature to ease any further building. Whomsoever you revere will come back ten fold upon you and lighten the burden carried as those who desire the warmth and necessity of communication.

A little cry at the door and the whistles. Washing the hands at the basin, every woman sees she is old. Washing the hands at the basin, is the earth's globe in form turning, sparkling, all the women see the seed and sprouts. The stars move closer together, everything at once? Vast.

I would also appreciate anything else that happens to sprout, being of nature kind and appropriate. Listening beyond recall, the nose smells the vast behind of those tracked followers. Listening beyond any sudden apprehension, was brought forth and introduced, dismissed, and kindly laid her head abroad on several sides, historically. This was the implementation of the self brought about. Hesitation, lack of thought, gave wide margins to what might have been, the ruthless punching of everything about.

No minds, no minds, no memory. This way it was a matter of decision, of fantasy, that left me far behind way after it had happened. I never knew except to recall it, and long after when the beans had sprouted, was appreciative of the results but never foolishly entered again.

7.

I am sure my dreams must have been of the wrong sort. However, as dreams are reflections of inner dilemmas, how did those arise, from a day of relaxation and summer enjoyment of the fund.

Knowledge comes from what purported strike? From that which cleanses, and let us knot say "heart" but *tissue*. Hopefully and helpfully I have built up a language in which to talk myself to sleep. Not for purposes of letting the cold in.

However, I have found that not all blockaded against is the cold, the dreary reign of the dead, etc., and the tasteless realm of the mushroom. As much can be denied as the billious sun strives to cause an enlargement of singing in the back of the neck and head. That is uncorraled ecstasy. I call it enthusiasm, free energy. But it has no place to land, it is bursting and unfocused; it is a real force and the counterpart of the gloomy depths.

As the pieces of the house ooze sap, blossoms and green twigs burst from the cracks. Whether or not to join in what I was half committed to see and do.

8.

At this point, when Jack picked up the pussy willow branches, I said they can't possibly be ours for the taking, and smiled with dedication to an older Con Edison man. The buildings were like the unexplored garbage in my mind, fascinating and dirty, pulling pieces of cloth from boxes left overnight. Energy as limitless possibility, in the attempt to transmit non-energy situations.

For example, if once I stop to realize what little gets through, I am much more interested in the cover than the contents; it is difficult to find any interest in anything. Good energy displaces bad karma. And other non entities like that sort, producing flow that in its own place has a good bed, stocked well of what can be called fleet footed fishes, and approaching places of investigation, such as relations between.

As I saw the blood flow to the surface of his skin, I forgot to watch for the tell tale visions that again might come from something I have never seen; more possibly the components of what every man views. If this was a possibility, the rays from every person converging pass through the state of shock to numbness to unity without any mind at all, for this horror fits the cat on the stairs, between the fifth and sixth rung. This is the way people glow and pulse similar to an inlet of jelly fish blocking the way, full of human life; until I who will name myself a swimmer, come along and refuse to be blocked on the way, although I turn back gladly, and will again swim through for it is possible they do not kill, the strings' compounded measure is fear, and thusly one not need join the broad expanse of human mouths calling people to join their ranks to comfort their newfound recognition of orifices, stomachs and legs.

I reminded myself twice there were several stories that kept continuing themselves. She ignored her face, blotched and red upon times, but fuller. Did you forget to wax and wane? Her head was full of energy brought forward and positively that what was said would turn the obvious into color, but no sense. Sense was for the thinkers. Here the thinkers forgot their word orders or sense; it was better to give them coffee, and those off worse could smoke.

I had felt very foolish when I leaned forward and grasped his hand, with effort, and his cloak slipped down over one shoulder as he shouted, which is the way. And I followed for certainly no one would follow me. As the day is cold and colder, and what comes out of the head is of its own sort and nature. These words, like Nature, and Head, Thinking and Words, repeat themselves, as the lines of landscape attics and other closed off sections have reprimanded themselves by repetition. Light

was such an enormous possibility. Taking sight into a frenzy, it was possible that just to look was full of excitement and wonder, for ages at a time, things appeared as beautiful, the sky, the street where cars had gone by.

I worried about certain characters: ones that never seemed to be other than puzzles to me but I was drawn to them with certainty only because there seemed to be no understanding? As when the mysteries were performed, the house then itself became distilled with reason as the pots and pans were used apparently filled with the stuff of continuity. The sorrow that each day sinks into the infertile other side of day, where voice comes out of the dark, and does its rituals. Memory has its own screen across the room to view itself, and the continuous dwelling of conjecture takes permanent form in stiff legged walks to remind, thus on and on the breathing goes.

JACKSON MAC LOW

7th Light Poem: for John Cage—17 June 1962

Put off an important decision
            in mechanical-lamp light.
Success in a new project will bring lumination.
An exchange of courtesy in the zodiacal
    light reminds you that expenses can
    run high when you insist on light
        from almandites.
For almandites are iron-alumina garnets
    $Fe_3Al_2(SiO_4)_3$.
When of a fine deep red or purplish red,
        from India,
                    and transparent,
                        they are
                    "precious garnets."
A lucrative job available in amber light
  does not jeopardise your credit,
                                    but
        melon-oil lamplight
                        might.
Your intuitions lead you right
      in cineographic light.
Say what you really think.
The lamp I have clamped to the kitchen
                            table beside the
        notebook I am writing this in
                            gives a sort
        of student-lamp light although
        it is not a student lamp but
                a PENETRAY.
In chrome light and in light from
  alexandrites,
                spinach-
                        green
                        chrysoberyls,
                        columbine-
                                    red
                            by artificial
    light,
        from Ceylon and the Ural
          Mountains,
                        money from a
                        surprising source

belies the belief that there's
always
nothing but
futility in romantic wishes
arising in old light.
Those wishes,
that first arose
in old
light,
light
trailing from
spiral nebulae
and galaxies so distant
that a stone
thrown
at a reading lamp's
light
at a
distance of
two miles
wd be
an unintentional slight
to natural law
compared to the folly
of launching
"space ships" toward them,
those
wishes that arose before
the light of the annealing-lamp
on which your dentist heated foil
made you begin to
avoid taking chances
by
taking chances,
might
make you take a
trip to a scenic region
where
the light's
maroon.
Beware light from a Cooper-Hewitt lamp,
light
derived
from passing an electric current
through

mercury-vapor
light
bluish-
white,
ghost-light from toothbrushes
along the absent 'L,'
beware
the new light on the Bowery,
that promises a
good possibility of money loss.
The receipt of an important invitation
to radiation
's
a secret
not to be discussed
even in olive-oil lamplight,
even in the
extra light of your
elation over the good news,
lead as it might to a
temporary setback
as
the light
waned.
Revenue yielding ideas arise(s)
in orange light
but an exquisite object stirs joy
even in the light of
Reichsanstalt's lamp,
a modified form of
Hefner's lamp,
a photometric lamp burning amylacetate.
Can an emerald light bring nothing but
disturbing rumors
about money?
Orange light yields revenue yielding ideas
of
disturbance
and recklessness
amidst an uncanny refulgence
as of marsh light
or will-of-the-wisp, those
sparks of cold light
which sometimes seem to

follow instructions exactly
as if they
were light from kinetographs,
or fishermen's jack lights,
but emerald light
alternating with
red light & lilac light,
all incandescent lamplight,
made
by following instructions exactly
some
times
awaken spectrums
like the aurora's
or
those of
remembered napalm flames.

14th Light Poem: for Frances Witlin — 10 August 1962

Even among those high-minded people of the *Aufklärung*
neighbor slandered neighbor
reproaching each other all day
mad against each other
sworn against each other
& the light of that 'enlightenment'
was blood-color
tho transmitted thru no carnelian.

Time was wasted that way then
& time will be wasted
but with all the benefits that might come
thru an executive
who might take time for calm reflection
& by taking
time for
calm
reflection
might
allow us to take
time for calm reflection
I'm afraid that calm reflection
wd be merely a 'brown study'

for we're mere sards
transmitting blood light
reflecting brown light.

Now we share the work & benefits
such as they are
of what we have
even tho we often feel
we're made to appear in a foolish light
by what we do.

An innocent light?

The innocence of fools
or the foolishness of innocence?

Transmitted thru glass or ice cut to a prism
ice light
is iridescent light.

An irrelevant light?

All light is relevant to each light
& each light to every light
& each light to each light
& every light to each light
& all light to every light
& every light to all light
& each light to all light
& all light to all light.

Is that lucid?

Yes.

It is all about light.

Mere secondary phenomena of luminiferous ether.

Light!

Light.

If you follow instructions exactly

at noonday
in the noon-light
the experiment may prove disappointing
but what cd be clearer?

A nimbus.

So you are seeking sainthood!
Who said that?
A silly fool.
An uninnocent fool.
A foolish foolish fool.

A foul fool.

A melodramatic fool.

A posturing self-lacerating fool.
A self-destroying fool.
An exhibitionistic Dostoyevskyan fool.
An ordinary fool.
An ordinary thief of property.
A proper fool.

A sneaky fool
patting himself on the back
for being and admitting himself to be
a fool & a liar & a thief.

A light-fingered fool?

A fool who knows a fool may have to compromise
& foolishly uncompromising
compromises most
when foolishly it seems to him he's least *un*compromising.

Radiance!

That's your name for what we call mere radioactivity.
Deadly.

Deadly radiance.

A spectrum of shade.

Like long working hours leading to fatigue & nothing more.
Nothing more?
O Frances do not break your heart!
do not break!
Break
nothing more
nothing
more
nothing.

The tall light trails thru the sparrow chirps
& glass tinkles
swept
in the area below these stranger windows
as in the Bronx I know
by Evelyn the dark resentful super
altho no beer cans
dance across concrete
with high hollow clatter
impelled by dark resentment & a broom.

Tĭ-dĕ́l, tie-dáhr, tee-dĕ́n, tuh-dắn, tuh-dó͝om.

Make no promises.

I've made one promise only.
One promise.
One promise only
made itself me.

But what it means is
what it means.

Only two know this.
Perhaps
one more
who sits to my left
smiling
or glum
or glumly smiling
or grimly smiling

or grimly
glum.

Boomelay boomelay boomelay boom.

Together weeping for his lost dark splendor
hating what he made of us
& what he allowed
what he thought we were
all of us
make of him.

How we sat together gritting our teeth.

Was it true?
Or another lie to make the fancy leap?
To show the know we were in
together.

She who makes no promises she cannot keep.
Or if she does
makes the limit of each promise clear.

Not you my dear.
I did not mean to speak of you here.
I find I have.

The traitorous light turns
as the
whirling earth
turns.
The traitorous light turns from pale
blue to grey.

My traitorous heart turns from one to the other loyally.
Faithfully my traitorous heart
turns
trying to make no promises or none it cannot keep
or none that cannot keep it
or none that cannot keep it keeping them.

What can I say?

Say the waxing light
depends upon no purchase of electrical equipment.
Say
a distant matter is delayed
a distant matter
a lambency
leaping about us
not yet.

Say nothing.

The light of a lamp burning winestones-oil
is preferable by far
altho I've never seen it
to one that threatens us
with danger
from chemicals.

My lucky number?

491
tells me to forget
a previous worry.

A previous worry?

What did I see before in a worrisome light
that I see in such a light
no longer?

Is it merely morning movie light
oh one four
that tells us to expect a change for the better?

Time will be wasted
but honestly
whether in light from an Argand lamp
or arc-light
or *Aufklärung*
is
the best
policy?

Tragedy.

Idiocy.

Honesty?

An aureola springs around a formerly hated form.

You must stay alive.

JOHN MONTAGUE

The Bread God

A collage of religious misunderstanding
For Thomas Montague S.J. on his eightieth birthday
Christmas, Melbourne, 1960

I break again into the lean parish of my art
Where huddled candles flare before a shrine
And men with caps in hand kneel stiffly down
To see the many-fanged monstrance shine.

He who stood at midnight upon a little mount which rose behind the chapel, might see between five and six thousand torches, all blazing together, and forming a level mass of red dusky light, burning against the horizon. These torches were so close to each other that their light seemed to blend, as if they had constituted one wide surface of flame; and nothing could be more preternatural looking than the striking and devotional countenance of those who were assembled at their midnight worship, when observed beneath this canopy of fire. . . .

Christmas Morning

Lights outline a hill
As silently the people,
Like shepherd and angel
On that first morning,
March from Altcloghfin,
Beltany, Rarogan,
Under rimed hawthorn,
Gothic evergreen,
Grouped in the warmth
And cloud of their breath,
Along cattle paths
Crusted with ice,
Tarred roads to this
Gray country chapel
Where a gas-lamp hisses
To light the crib
Under the cross-beam's
Damp flaked message:
GLORIA IN EXCELSIS.

Yes, I remember Carleton's description of Christmas in Tyrone, but things had changed at the end of the century. Religion was at a pretty low ebb in those days. We had one Mass at 10 o'clock on Sundays at which a handful went to communion. We went to confession and communion about every four months.

The priests did not take much interest in the people and did not visit them except for sick calls. I think I became a priest because we were the most respectable family in the parish and it was expected of me, but what I really wanted to do was to join the army, which was out of the question. So you see how your uncle became a Jesuit!

Late-comer

Hesitant step of a late-comer
Fingers dip at the font, fly
Up to the roof of the forehead
With a sigh.
On St Joseph's
Outstretched arm, he hangs his cap
Then spends a very pleasant Mass
Studying the wen-marked heads
Of his neighbours, or gouging
His name in the soft wood
Of the choirloft, with the cross
Of his rosary beads.

In a plain envelope marked: IMPORTANT

THE BREAD GOD
the DEVIL has CHRIST where he wants HIM
A HELPLESS INFANT IN ARMS: A DEAD CHRIST ON THE CROSS
ROME'S CENTRAL ACT OF WORSHIP IS THE EUCHARISTIC WAFER!
IDOLATRY: THE WORST IDOL UNDER HEAVEN
NOSELESS, EYELESS, EARLESS, HELPLESS, SPEACHLESS.

The Crowds for Communion

The crowds for communion, heavy coat and black shawl,
Surge in thick waves, cattle thronged in a fair,
To the oblong of altar rails, and there
Where red berried holly shines against gold
In the door of the tabernacle, wait patient
And prayerful and crowded, for each moment
Of silence, eyes closed, mouth raised
For the advent of the flesh-graced Word.

DEAR BROTHER!
ECUMENISM is THE NEW NAME of the WHORE OF BABYLON!
SHE who SHITS on the SEVEN HILLS
ONE CHURCH, ONE STATE

WITH THE POPE THE HEAD OF THE STATE: BY RE-UNION
ROME MEANS ABSORPTION
UNIFORMITY MEANS TYRANNY
APISTS = PAPISTS
But GOD DELIGHTS IN VARIETY
NO two leaves are EXACTLY alike!

After Mass

Coming out of the chapel
The men were already assembled
Around the oak-tree,
Solid brogues, thick coats,
Staring at the women,
Sheltering cigarettes.

Once a politician came
Climbed on the graveyard wall
And they listened to all
His plans with the same docility;
Eyes quiet, under caps
Like sloped eaves.

Nailed to the wet bark
The notice of a football match;
Pearses v's Hibernians
Or a Monster Carnival
In aid of Church Funds
Featuring Farrel's Band.

LOYALISTS REMEMBER!
MILLIONS have been MURDERED for refusing to GROVEL
Before Rome's Mass-Idol: THE HOST!
King Charles I and his Frog Queen Henrietta GLOAT in their
letters
that they have almost EXTERMINATED THE PROTESTANTS OF
IRELAND
The PRIESTS in every PARISH were told to record HOW MANY
killed!
Under ROGER MORE AND SIR PHELIM O'NEIL
Instruments of ROME
40,000 loyal protestants were MASSACRED like game-fowl
IN ONE NIGHT
Cromwell went to Ireland
TO STOP
The Catholics murdering Protestants!

Penal Rock/Altamuskin

To learn the massrock's lesson, leave your car,
Descend frost gripped steps to where
A humid moss overlaps the valley floor.
Crisp as a pistol-shot, the winter air
Recalls poor Tagues, folding the nap of their freize
Under one knee, long suffering as beasts,
But parched for that surviving sign of grace,
The bog-latin murmur of their priest.
A crude stone oratory, carved by a cousin,
Commemorates the place. For two hundred years
People of our name have sheltered in this glen
But now all have left. A few flowers
Wither on the altar, so I melt a ball of snow
From the hedge into their rusty tin before I go.

I sometimes wonder if anyone could have brought the two sides together. Your father, I know, was very bitter about having to leave but when I visited home before leaving for the Australian mission, I found our protestant neighbours friendly, and yet we had lost any position we had in the neighbourhood. You realise of course, that all this has nothing to do with religion; perhaps this new man will find a way to resolve the old hatreds. . . .

An Ulster Prophecy

I saw the Pope breaking stones on Friday
A blind parson sewing a Patchwork quilt
Two bishops cutting rushes with their croziers,
Roaring Meg firing rosary beads for cannonballs,
The black Perceptory singing Faith of our Fathers,
Corks in boats afloat on the summit of the Sperrins,
A severed head speaking with a grafted tongue,
A snail paring Royal Avenue with a hatchet,
British troops machinegunning the Shankill,
A mill and a forge on the back of a cuckoo,
The fox sitting conceitedly at a window chewing tobacco,
And a moorhen in flight
surveying
a United Ireland.

LORINE NIEDECKER

Paean to Place

And the place
was water

Fish
fowl
flood
Water lily mud
My life

in the leaves and on water
My mother and I
born
in swale and swamp and sworn
to water

My father
thru marsh fog
sculled down
from high ground
saw her face

at the organ
bore the weight of lake water
and the cold—
he seined for carp to be sold
that their daughter

might go high
on land
to learn
Saw his wife turn
deaf

and away
She
who knew boats
and ropes
no longer played

She helped him string out nets
for tarring
and she could shoot
He was cool
to the man
who stole his minnows
by night and next day offered
to sell them back
He brought in a sack
of dandelion greens

if no flood
No oranges—none at hand
No marsh marigolds
where the water rose
He kept us afloat

I mourn her not hearing canvasbacks
their blast-off rise
from the water
Not hearing sora
rail's sweet

spoon-tapped waterglass-
descending scale-
tear-drop-tittle
Did she giggle
as a girl?

His skiff skimmed
the coiled celery now gone
from these streams
due to carp
He knew duckweed

fall-migrates
toward Mud Lake bottom
Knew what lay
under leaf decay
and on pickerelweeds

before summer hum
To be counted on:
new leaves

new dead
leaves

He could not
—like water bugs—
stride surface tension
He netted
loneliness

As to his bright new car
my mother—her house
next his—averred:
A hummingbird
can't haul

Anchored here
in the rise and sink
of life—
middle years' nights
he sat

beside his shoes
rocking his chair
Roped not 'looped
in the loop
of her hair'

I grew in green
slide and slant
of shore and shade
Child-time—wade
thru weeds

Maples to swing from
Pewee-glissando
sublime
slime-
song

Grew riding the river
Books
at home-pier
Shelley could steer
as he read

I was the solitary plover
a pencil
for a wing-bone
From the secret notes
I must tilt

upon the pressure
execute and adjust
In us sea-air rhythm
'We live by the urgent wave
of the verse'

Seven-year molt
for the solitary bird
and so young
Seven years the one
dress

for town once a week
One for home
faded blue-striped
as she piped
her cry

Dancing grounds
my people had none
woodcocks had
backland-
air around

Solemnities
such as what flower
to take
to grandfather's grave
unless

water lilies—
he who'd bowed his head
to grass as he mowed
Iris now grows
on fill

for the two
and for him
where they lie
How much less am I
in the dark than they?

Effort lay in us
before religions
at pond bottom
All things move toward
the light

except those
that freely work down
to oceans' black depths
In us an impulse tests
the unknown

River rising—flood
Now melt and leave home
Return—broom wet
naturally wet

Under

soak-heavy rug
water bugs hatched—
no snake in the house
Where were they?—
she

who knew how to clean up
after floods
he who bailed boats, houses
Water endows us
with buckled floors

You with sea water running
in your veins sit down in water
Expect the long-stemmed blue
speedwell to renew
itself

O my floating life
Do not save love
for things
Throw *things*
to the flood

ruined
by the flood
Leave the new unbought—
all one in the end—
water

I possessed
the high word:
The boy my friend
played his violin
in the great hall

On this stream
my moonnight memory
washed of hardships
maneuvers barges
through the mouth

of the river
They fished in beauty
It was not always so
In Fishes
red Mars

rising
rides the sloughs and sluices
of my mind
with the persons
on the edge

GEOFFREY O'BRIEN

The Tender Fascists

"The heart uselessly opens
To 3 words, which is too little"

1

They are indulging in kisses
cuddled close
by the transistor,
fingers constricted under tight cloth.

The girl
is first to get the idea of saying:
I love you,

dancing close
after the 17th birthday party.

She writes it out on paper:
I love you.

Together they burst into tears,
fingers chafed and strangling
beneath the fabric.

2

Sophisticated teenagers,
romantic homosexuals,
federal agents in tears.

Like Christ busted
and submitted to tortures
the Fascist who goes down on his knees:

the arousal by perfume and proximity
he subdues. Love
is a beautiful thing,
marriages are made in Heaven,
I'm getting sentimental over you:

I told you the same thing many times before,
whenever we sip cokes
I stay healthy repeating it.

The Fascist who gets married,
the Fascist who makes a list of his love:
it keeps me healthy to repeat it,

in the first place
because it lifted me
like an earring from the gutter,
I must not tell lies,

secondly
it changes the bed into a religious temple,
legs to carvings,

in the third place
obedience,
the exchange or transfer, sanitary
napkin swollen with blood.

3

I always wanted to be a surrealist,
tell me I love you
until it drives me crazy.

The problem: reactionary couples.
She wants to save his neck from the
guillotine,
he wants to tread
on peasant winemakers, 1789.
He's an agent of the Gestapo.
She just doesn't care
if he took a dive for the enemy high school.
A woman will live in sin
for the man she loves.

The woman is almost empty
of political values.
She prefers the purity of motel rooms,
"The Glenn Miller Story"
as a form of ideal communion.

Passion turns her flimsy:
the woman and man
saved by love.

The man and woman
destroyed by love
sell themselves to each other
at a persistent rate of exchange:

heart-gate open
they compute the dividends.

4

Sweetheart
the eye is on fire

I LOVE YOU I
LOVE YOU I LOVE YOU
the nose is on fire,
the ear is on fire

I LOVE YOU

and with what are they on fire?
with quivering iron carpets,
vacant eggs, the blood
of last night's whipping,

I LOVE YOU SO MUCH
IT HURTS

with the agony of iron
girls, the walls
of an adjacent room,
binoculars, two-way mirrors,

I LOVE YOU

with your delicate velvet heart,

lump of cold tears,
darling, your delicious wrist
all chopped,
hysterical fingers
that hold
my hand.

A Woman's Face

1

Women in the room is
one, with various thighs:
light
glancing off her
3 cheeks, lip veers from shade

in unison: women on the floor
their forms wave,
tendrils
on ocean-bottom: light
passing thru them,
yellow them, green them,

vacant texture, you take
some thing from them:
the beauty, if they knew it,
glances off panels

2

Without research, sister absent,
how could he build a woman, without
words?
without body. He called himself a woman
without thought, without words:
how he could love, waking, the face
that seems just to have woken.

That she has never existed,
not even once, he despises women:
not hearing the sound of his own voice.

3

Whore: who

or whom
in he-man's woe
meant women?

that woman's whim
demands a wee man's
womb end?

we men

4

If the girls wear pants,
the boys will wear skirts:

if the girls will wear miniskirts,
they beat them.

His sister's lover, that he can't be:
he kills him.

His wife's daughters, that he couldn't bear,
he drowns.

5

Woman: she's obliged to hold
open the door for them
to leave, and stop seeing
where they pretend to look—

100 men and a girl—
I wasn't born to have meaning!
I am not
to make you feel you exist!

They speak what they deny, smiling,
or they deny it, smiling
or starting to sound weepy:
the men can't control their emotions—
till she must open the door for them
to stop her
from being unborn, the house
they each want to live in:

—When can we come back?
—When you understand what it's like:
it's like
when you men think women want to
kill you.

6

Stop from naming
the parts of the animal,
each handle its fur
in kind—if her eyes

are yours, you look at them,
body that it makes,
you hear her talking

not as you would have her
talk, you have her talk,

take it, each

GEORGE OPPEN

Route

"the void eternally generative"
the *Wen Fu* of Lu Chi

1

Tell the beads of the chromosomes like a rosary,
Love in the genes, if it fails

We will produce no sane man again

I have seen too many young people become adults, young
friends become old people, all that is not ours,

The sources
And the crude bone

—we say

Took place

Like the mass of the hills.

'The sun is a molten mass'. Therefore

Fall into oneself—?

Reality, blind eye
Which has taught us to stare—

Your elbow on a car-edge
Incognito as summer,

I wrote. Not you but a girl
At least

Clarity, clarity, surely clarity is the most beautiful
thing in the world,
A limited, limiting clarity

I have not and never did have any motive of poetry
But to achieve clarity

2

Troubled that you are not, as they say,
Working—
I think we try rather to understand,
We try also to remain together

There is a force of clarity, it is
Of what is not autonomous in us,
We suffer a certain fear

Things alter, surrounded by a depth
And width

The unreality of our house in moonlight
Is that if the moonlight strikes it
It is truly there tho it is ours

3

Not to reduce the thing to nothing—

I might at the top of my ability stand at a window
and say, look out; out there is the world.

Not the desire for approval nor even for love—O,
that trap! From which escaped, barely—if it fails

We will produce no sane man again

4

Words cannot be wholly transparent. And that is the
'heartlessness' of words.

Neither friends nor lovers are coeval . . .

as for a long time we have abandoned those in
extremity and we find it unbearable that we should
do so . . .

The sea anemone dreamed of something, filtering the sea
water thru its body,

Nothing more real than boredom—dreamlessness, the
experience of time, never felt by the new arrival,
never at the doors, the thresholds, it is the native

Native in native time . . .

The purity of the materials, not theology, but to present
the circumstances

5

In Alsace, during the war, we found ourselves on the edge of the Battle of the Bulge. The front was inactive, but we were spread so thin that the situation was eerily precarious. We hardly knew where the next squad was, and it was not in sight—a quiet and deserted hill in front of us. We dug in near a farmhouse. Pierre Adam, tho he was a journeyman mason, lived with his wife and his children in that farmhouse.

During the occupation the Germans had declared Alsace a part of Greater Germany. Therefore they had drafted Alsatian men into the German army. Many men, learning in their own way that they were to be called, dug a hole. The word became a part of the language: *faire une trou*. Some men were in those holes as long as two and three years. It was necessary that someone should know where those holes were; in winter it was impossible for a man to come out of his hole without leaving footprints in the snow. While snow was actually falling, however, a friend could come to the hole with food and other help. Pierre, whom many people trusted, knew where some two dozen of those holes were.

The Germans became aware that men were going into hiding, and they began to make reprisals. If the man was young and unmarried, they killed his parents. If the man was married, they took his wife into Germany to the army brothels, it was said. They took the children into Germany, and it was not certain whether those children would remember where they came from. Pierre told me this story:

Men would come to Pierre and they would say: I am thinking of making a hole. Pierre would say: yes. They would say then: but if I do they will kill my parents; or: they will take my wife and my children. Then Pierre would say, he told me: *if* you dig a hole, I will help you.

He knew, of course, what he was telling me. You must try to put yourself into those times. If one thought he knew anything, it was that a man should not join the Nazi army. Pierre himself learned, shortly before the Americans arrived, that he was about to be drafted. He and his wife discussed the children. They thought of tattooing the children's names and addresses on their chests so that perhaps they could be found after the war. But they thought that perhaps the tattooing would be cut out of the children . . . They did not, finally, have to make that decision, as it turned out. But what a conversation between a man and his wife—

There was an escape from the dilemma, as, in a way, there always is. Pierre told me of a man who, receiving the notification that he was to report to the German army, called a celebration and farewell at his home. Nothing was said at that party that was not jovial. They drank and sang. At the proper time, the host got his bicycle and waved goodbye. The house stood at the top of a hill and, still waving and calling farewells, he rode with great energy and as fast as he could down the hill, and, at the bottom, drove into a tree.

It must be hard to do. Probably easier in an automobile. There is, in an automobile, a considerable time during which you cannot change your mind. Riding a bicycle, since in those woods it is impossible that the tree should be a redwood, it must be necessary to continue aiming at the tree right up to the moment of impact. Undoubtedly difficult to do. And, of course, the children had no father. Thereafter.

6

Wars that are just? A simpler question: In the event,
will you or will you not want to kill a German. Because,
in the event, if you do not want to, you won't.

. . . and my wife reading letters she knew were two weeks
late and did not prove I was not dead while she read. Why
did I play all that, what was I doing there?

We are brothers, we are brothers?—these things are
composed of a moral substance only if they are untrue. If
these things are true they are perfectly simple, perfectly
impenetrable, those primary elements which can only be
named.

A man will give his life for his friend provided he wants
to.

In all probability a man will give his life for his child
provided his child is an infant.

. . . One man could not understand me because I was saying simple things; it seemed to him that nothing was being said. I was saying: there is a mountain, there is a lake

A picture seen from within. The picture is unstable, a moving picture, unlimited drift. Still, the picture exists.

The circumstances:

7

And if at 80

He says what has been commonly said
It is for the sake of old times, a cozy game

He wishes to join again, an unreasonable speech
Out of context

8

Cars on the highway filled with speech,
People talk, they talk to each other;

Imagine a man in the ditch,
The wheels of the overturned wreck
Still spinning—

I don't mean he despairs, I mean if he does not
He sees in the manner of poetry

9

The cars run in a void of utensils
—the powerful tires—beyond
Happiness

Tough rubbery gear of invaders, of the descendents
Of invaders, I begin to be aware of a countryside
And the exposed weeds of a ditch

The context is history
Moving toward the light of the conscious

And beyond, culvert, blind curb, there are also names
For these things, language in the appalling fields

I remember my father as a younger man than I am now,
My mother was a tragic girl
Long ago, the autonomous figures are gone,
The context is the thousands of days

10

Not the symbol but the scene this pavement leads
To roadsides—the finite

Losing its purposes
Is estranged

All this is reportage.

If having come so far we shall have
Song

Let it be small enough.

Virgin
what was there to be thought

comes by the road

11

Tell the life of the mind, the mind creates the finite.

All punishes him. I stumble over these stories—
Progeny, the possibility of progeny, continuity

Or love that tempted him

He is punished by place, by scene, by all that holds
all he has found, this pavement, the silent symbols

Of it, the word it, never more powerful than in this
moment. Well, hardly an epiphany, but there the thing
is all the same

All this is reportage

12

To insist that what is true is good, no matter, no matter,
    a definition—?

That tree
    whose fruit . . .

The weight of air
Measured by the barometer in the parlor,
Time remains what it was

Oddly, oddly insistent

haunting the people in the automobiles,

shining on the sheetmetal,

open and present, unmarred by indifference,

wheeled traffic, indifference,
the hard edge of concrete continually crumbling

into gravel in the gravel of the shoulders,
Ditches of our own country

Whom shall I speak to

13

Department of Plants and Structures—obsolete, the old name
In this city, of the public works

Tho we meant to entangle ourselves in the roots of the world

An unexpected and forgotten spoor, all but indestructible
    shards

To owe nothing to fortune, to chance, nor by the power of
    his heart
Or her heart to have made these things sing
But the benevolence of the real

Tho there is no longer shelter in the earth, round helpless belly
Or hope among the pipes and broken works

'Substance itself which is the subject of all our planning'

And by this we are carried into the incalculable

14

There was no other guarantee

Ours aren't the only madmen tho they have burned thousands
of men and women alive, perhaps no madder than most

Strange to be here, strange for them also, insane and criminal,
who hasn't noticed that, strange to be man, we have come
rather far

We are at the beginning of a radical depopulation of the earth

Cataclysm . . . cataclysm of the plains, jungles, the cities

Something in the soil exposed between two oceans

As Cabeza de Vaca found a continent of spiritual despair
in campsites

His miracles among the Indians heralding cataclysm

Even Cortés greeted as revelation . . . No I'd not emigrate,
I'd not live in a ship's bar wherever we may be headed

These things at the limits of reason, nothing at the limits
of dream, the dream merely ends, by this we know it is the
real

That we confront

ROCHELLE OWENS

Humble Humble Pinati

Seven-teeth spittle, I disarranged prairie-dogs,
Lasted conversion, beheld from

Humble humble pinati, stone letter
Greasy, slug each of me from head to heartstruck
Nerve. Fickle, predaceous, herb herb

What matter if I croak? showing Frog when it
Is with blotch. The other seed plant what slay.
And the teachers Sometimes is written above
Suppose.
Is fall, smartly along Sing Muzhik is not geometry
On your cock, is Scheherazade Queen
Through caution and lemon juice

You you shred wheat, you you fuck sometimes 'nd hide your white cuffs.

O what do do, is troubling me, ponderous, identically
The performance is new, bad, good, is keeping people in stitches
(Than certainly I'm without hope, evening star chromosome

When seriousness is needed, illumination,
Redskin determine, osculate us give us no trouble
With the head. Connection in the ear, O that bears us

Greatly).

Manifesting the love of awfulspring
Comeon, in the conduct, Greetings!
Loose supposition, bizniz under the brave

Bulls, Awful to color red the Chief and give him the bony structure

Vatican city, cellulose Seven Voonder of the
Voorld.

Come on tanze, surcease, knife of diamonds
Pinch me, sing out a wild old
Toon.

Enter the hock, often in the public stage, enough to pro
Voke us and Mexico in Space from

Turburculosis, all holy uses holy uses
Lust, Africa's nipple, a pebble on the sterile moor
Queer. That he feed, shluck shluck

Is bone the bone and arrow Is bone again I say
Fairyman. Down down is hellogram, a blue trademark
On the sonoman

Wif, Wif, muffle the sloppy pineapple, on the back of
Elephant, give out a pledge, a dead body cockiness so that poor
And poorer pullet chickens

Make. Build with hard brown wood.

Comeon again! Last this much longer see Stromboli,
This is humor which is seen Vision like a hoghead

Madre Sicilia pissing on Italy
Singing and dancing, springing into a province
About to molt herself, whither whither

She goes, piggy piggy she is no stern girl she like to dance
She is not bleached, not worn-out and praying
She is called Ready Ready

Come Tomcat.

Arrest. They like to meet again, to bind bread to smoke
Meat (is not a rubber jaw) A weakling
With a tick tick

Thumb-sized forebear, ancestor, come on squeeze her colorless ear.

Pull the tooth, a bed of roses for the tooth
Dome dome uncle sam Artery arm do not pipe down. Is designating
A buttock for the velvet cushion, keep for the flesh, man

Is a baby, spilth his little gut,
Mortify, spout his vitamin, little lamb-tongue
Suppose suppose we did. The goat prick would peeper out

Smally.

Five parts red berries usually

It goes pentecostal, yield, again I say
See the strange Voorld, converse, bring

A insect into the Mass, see if it like cane sugar and loves swollen

Supremely good sculpture. Than we can tell
On it.

Charger, father, throughout the holy day, through mortar
The throat, her teachings
Betray me.

Goon. They stole a nat-ive, in the mood they pulled
His pants off him give him sweet potatoe

Tending to go back, endurance,
Tame my criminal, kiss a jackdaw. Virgo, virgo
Prickle his part, destroy

Is the shalt not spicule known of news or a damn
Weaker growth? False false is the new thought
A game miser, we play

Back, back, four times timed by four, the silky symbol
I plunk it down, kill it for food
Watch.

NICANOR PARRA

Letters from the Poet Who Sleeps in a Chair

Translated from Spanish by George Quasha and Trinidad Jiménez-Orrego

I

I say things like they are
Or we know everything beforehand
Or we'll never know anything at all.

The only thing we're permitted
Is to learn how to speak correctly.

II

All night long I dream of women
Some, ostensibly, laugh at me
Others give me a rabbit punch
They won't leave me alone
They're constantly at war with me.

I get up with a thundering face.
From which one deduces that I'm mad
Or at least that I'm scared to death.

III

It's hard enough to believe
In a god that leaves his creatures
Abandoned to their own fortune
At the mercy of the waves
                                        of old age
And of illnesses
To say nothing of death.

IV

I'm one of those who greet hearses.

V

Write the way you want
Too much blood has gone under the bridge
To go on believing I believe
That you can only go one way.

In poetry everything is permitted.
The poet who sleeps on the sofa
Greets you with thunder and lightning.

VI

Infirmity
            Decrepitude
                        and Death
Dance like innocent maidens
All around swan lake
Semi-nude
            inebriated
With their lascivious lips of coral.

VII

It is manifestly obvious
That there are no inhabitants on the moon

That chairs are tables
That butterflies are flowers in perpetual motion
That truth is a collective error

That the spirit dies with the body
It is manifestly obvious

That wrinkles are not scars.

VIII

Each time that for one reason or another
I've had to come down
From my little tower of boards
I've returned shivering with cold
With solitude
            with fear
                        with pain.

IX

Already the trolleys have disappeared
They've cut down the trees
The horizon appears full of crosses.

Marx has been denied seven times
And we're still here.

X

To feed the bees gall
To inoculate the mouth with semen

To kneel in a puddle of blood
To sneeze in the mortuary chapel
To milk a cow
And dump the milk on her head.

XI

From the storm clouds of breakfast
To the thunderclaps of lunchtime
And from there to the lightning flashes of dinner.

XII

I don't get sad easily
To be honest with you
Even skulls make me laugh.
The poet who sleeps on a cross
Greets you with tears of blood.

XIII

The duty of the poet
Consists in overcoming the blank page
I doubt that this is possible.

XIV

Only beauty agrees with me
Ugliness causes me pain.

XV

This is the last time I'll repeat this:
Worms are gods
Butterflies are flowers in perpetual motion
Decayed teeth
                    brittle teeth
I'm from the era of silent films.
Fornication is a literary act.

XVI

Chilean aphorisms:
    All redheads have freckles
    The telephone knows what it's saying
    The tortoise never lost so much time
    As when he submitted to learn of the eagle.

    The automobile is a wheelchair.
    And the traveller who looks back

Runs the serious risk
That his shadow won't want to follow him.

XVII

To analyze is to resign from yourself
It is only possible to reason in circles
You only see what you want to see

A birth solves nothing
I admit that my tears are falling

A birth solves nothing
Only death tells the truth
Even poetry isn't convincing.

We're taught that time doesn't exist
But in any case
Old age is an accomplished fact.

Be what science determines

It makes me sleepy to read my poems
And nevertheless they were written with blood.

GEORGE QUASHA

Umiak's Polar Callings

[for George Oppen]

. . . and what if suddenly there are no
nouns, now you and I are sitting on
pure despair, these
                                        lost links of
loving, I mean that moving
thing we heard in watery space, hardly
natural to us, the verbal
shriek that showed us
things were there we wrapped
around, on top of
                                    This
is less than that. It
will not last
long enough to say to
each other. And yet I
keep trying to stretch it out
here
      the only place I still can say
                                                        this is like
that narwhale, called Umiak for his act of
                                                                    suckling a
man's canoe, I mean we who killed
his mother for meat, his father
for his jousting-tooth—that
spiral form permitting medieval man
                                                              to prove
the unicorn exists, it
exists, Mother, Mother, no
other noun can serve me now,
exists, he says
to himself
thru the hole in his head

September 12, 1969

The Weight of the Matter or Where It Is Pulling

[*for John Magner*]

I'm sorry, he said, or
said he said, said so to you, meaning thought
though he did not think so, or not only, I'm sorry
to have to go about this ass-
backwards, but knowing the gravity of the matter
at hand, the lay of the land, helps to switch
around, or turn back
over, facing out or up or at
you, straight on, eye to eye
as if saying Youngblood, guts
is what we need more of, saying it like
it is, at that angle of incidence
to get there is so to speak
evidence of directness that has torn thru
demonstrating, as if destroying, itself, and I'm
sorry twists the matter further, making
the usual
metaphor, as if saying saying it like
it is is standing beyond the actual lay
of the land, binding self
and other and shaking
over it, agreeing in the recognitions
without crossing over ourselves,
taking so to speak the first available link (I
almost said drink) as
—and let it be noted here as longing
to leap, how its length
is being remembered and yet nearly time-
less, still moving now, up
and half-out not like but
with dolphin-kind, as he comes between us
and nothing, for such like may be
words where
the ocean is closing
around
leaping itself—
the real is itself as it is believed,
even assbackwards, where
the fault is running
clear thru, and where is
the quake if not here in the middle

of the matter
being said
as if being heard other-
wise or meaning to be half read
in reverse
of the causes,
half in remembrance
of things past
helping
or meaning
or even attempting to say
more directly than they have been
lost to us, as if we can say
to us
and mean it, and if speaking thus
together at least one of us is listening
in and to and for the other, in the event
one might be lost in speaking
out or unable to hold his words
like his liquor he lets them stagger
him, failing to correct
the fault or half-
wallowing in it
where it is most severely
pulling

End of May or beginning of June or both 1970

Homage to What I Hear Is So

(May 9, 1970, as they march on Washington)
[for Jim Harrison]

the fiery acceleration of history toward collapse into
apocalypse. So we hear.
We want to start all over.
My fiery acceleration in history straining to collapse into
collapsing.
I'm starting all over again, I say
every time, and they say there's only this
once, the only
chance, you've got to take it
away from them, all of it, or all you can
do is keep
moving, keep on moving, and don't let any of them keep
any, the smell in the air, this publically nasal languishing bids you
call it what you like but keep
away, don't come
in this air, you couldn't
make it if you tried or with this
being so strained it
won't come all the way
off, or cut thru this, even with fiery
overstepping, lap winding,
streaking, so move it along here, work
it up, to a pitch so far unachieved, the stink is central, it's the last
thing that's really part of her, and that too endangered species, you
can make it, if you try, hardhead—harder
than this, think inside, or think it right
into the smell, now press, noticing it now
presses within the ventricle, it
budges, now slides, so quickens, open the vent but prepare
for certain smelling, perhaps she is still coming, perusal
calls it probable, open, so to speak,
to any and all possibilities, even
odds on it, that's the way it is now, history
going the way it's going, and at this rate
we'll all be pressing unexpected canals
of influence, just on the chance,
you know, an outside chance
she might also be listening or
at least dreaming, thinking within that system
of communicating cavities
cerebrally continuous
with the central canal
of the spinal cord, derived
from the medulary canal of the embryo, lined, containing

a serous fluid, ventriloguistic,
you know how it is sometimes, I myself
recall Charlie, I do recall that
McCarthy, the dummy was central
to our lives then, the early
fifties—mind you
I don't remember much but I do
that, pretending to talk, the pressure
on the cord and the jaws clenched,
the ventral pressure is especially accute
in my memory, as now, "a lap full
of seed And this is a fine
country," only the trees
are perhaps barer than before, but on the other hand
my memory is not good, nor my sense
of history, except that it is so moving, this time, to turn over
in one's mind, the four, the seven, the eight, etc. day by day
the new figures hard on the tails of the foregoing
only to pass on next into the
quick, the irretrievable
numerous, huddling, continuously light-pricking
on usual screens, the great chain finally mounting on its own
back, seeking its shape in the spine bending
forward, leaning inside itself, half female
the contingent that is waiting in the middle, still longing
for extensions, still in procession, reaching the court
at its opening, stone walls with broken windows, looked out of
and seen into, continuously worn
clear thru, still mythic in the senses
relating to precoital jabbing at the cloth and eventual
disclosure at the spot of greatest wearing, as if to follow close behind
the longest tongue in Provence, the very man, the Arnaut captured within
the selfsame song, aching most where music most is lost
to us, as lays and chansons, scrutably absent, one part chirping
and the rest of it possibly lies in the sounding half-heard, *latin fant precs*
Quecs ab so par, sound like the daily paper, bare pictures, viz., pricks faint in
tongues, crack up in pairs, otherwise pig-latin pants to crack noggins of hair,
if Arnaut is eavesdropping, the overflow is forming, the poet
performs his own way, as any man, to show himself
to himself, a better man than you are, he says in notes
to the self, half senses the truth, the wag there, the drip,
half sensible in the presentation, the other cries, "Can I
sow my seed Without tearing
up Some stinking
weed," such Leaves
of it, or coming out of it again,
being lapped up now, "Love free
love cannot be

bound To any tree that
grows on ground O how sick & weary
I," back into collapsing, "should I"
remembering more than I thought this time "be
bound to thee" within that fossa
—from which we have been standing, or stemming, so long now—
sometimes named pouch
lying on either side
of the larynx between the false vocal
cords above
and the true below,
ventriculus, the beating, constant beatings
within, tells us, keeping the line elapsing, please,
ventriculogrammic, Charlie writ, at long last, "O lapwing
thou fliest around the heath Nor seest
the net that is
spread beneath," so called for your wrapped leap
thru midair, blackbreasted plotting Africa in shrill
wailing cries, will you keep, or hold up, now, I mean you, nearest me, are you
able to take your own song on the one hand, bare and moving,
and on the other the singing whales
mating, their serum of sound
squealing ventripotence, all canals
squeezing all at once, wholly
called up, adventuring, the primal sails set
in the cords again, for us
mere piercing, a coming that coils longer or
deeper than we knew, or so it
stands every chance
of being, half-urging us
on, collapsing
us so

JEROME ROTHENBERG

from Sightings

II

A hand extended, or a page.
The witness.

•

In the way we eat—it is this that moves me, to be guided by it

•

Whiteness.
Her shadow & my own.
For color.

•

That leaves a number less than one.

•

For balance: snow or horses.
(Seals).

•

How we had rested (the question).
By elevations (the response).

•

A finger growing from a finger:
Hell in glass.

III

The lie, beginning, persists with us.

•

Measure of a day, bracken, green leaves, etc., a place
to find refuge, to return.

•

But how many before I scream?

•

Not in your throat, I mean; the selfishness of wax.

•

A bigot.

•

Take yes for an answer; they will have arrived here long
before your setting forth.

•

The outline of my hand on black paper.

•

My eye on black paper too, to form a clock.

•

A male-shaped womb—of darkness before the birth of light.

Further Sightings

2 x 7
"The Old King"
for Leir, in Hades

The Old King (i)
painted his face—
a hand as border.

The Old King (ii)
eye of Horus
& of the hawk.

The Old King (iii)
harps, timbrels
to his touch.

The Old King (iv)
a striped mirror—
a green shell.

The Old King (v)
another
guardian.

The Old King (vi)
who strikes the moon
to contain it.

The Old King (vii)
divides the cut
circle, gems.

Conversation Fifteen

I wanted something to eat.
(I wanted nothing.)
I wanted a place for resting & another place for the pleasures of sleep.
(I wanted the joys of charity.)
I wanted the weather.
(I wanted you.)
Were you hungry?
(No.)
Were you remarkable?
(I was remarkable & was never hungry.)
I wanted hands.
(I wanted to be free of touch.)
I wanted my hands to be tied to the side of your body.
(I wanted your body to be tied to the side of my house.)
I was an animal & was never free.
(I wanted the vindication of the just.)

The Water of the Flowery Mill (II)

for the Angel

He is blood, himself
the killer
is where the sun goes down.

Will he flex his arm, will
the fingers
narrow, make a fist around
the bauble, crush it?

Dust is his.

The entry into light
the courtyard
white with marble veins
& suicides
the perfect edge for sleep.

Count the numbers.
Call the monster green
the little eggs
the wind cups
everything is far from him.

His blood is far from him

& makes a circle, poisons
where it falls
the country dies from it.

Sweet smelling flesh
sweet dung
sweet tumor in the eye
sweet bauble:

as the fish are lanterns
upon waves

& light the sea for him.

Poland / 1931

"The WEDDING"

my mind is stuffed with tablecloths
& with rings but my mind
is dreaming of poland stuffed with poland
brought in the imagination
to a black wedding
a naked bridegroom hovering above
his naked bride   mad poland
how terrible thy jews at weddings
thy synagogues with camphor smells & almonds
thy thermos bottles thy electric fogs
thy braided armpits
thy underwear alive with roots o poland
poland poland poland poland poland
how thy bells wrapped in their flowers toll
how they do offer up their tongues to kiss the moon
old moon old mother stuck in thy sky thyself
an old bell with no tongue a lost udder
o poland thy beer is ever made of rotting bread
thy silks are linens merely thy tradesmen
dance at weddings where fanatic grooms
still dream of bridesmaids still are screaming
past their red moustaches poland
we have lain awake in thy soft arms forever
thy feathers have been balm to us
thy pillows capture us like sickly wombs & guard us
let us sail through thy fierce weddings poland
let us tread thy markets where thy sausages grow ripe & full
let us bite thy peppercorns let thy oxen's dung be sugar to thy dying jews
o poland o sweet resourceful restless poland
o poland of the saints unbuttoned poland repeating endlessly the triple names of mary
poland poland poland poland poland
have we not tired of thee poland no for thy cheeses
shall never tire us nor the honey of thy goats
thy grooms shall work ferociously upon their looming brides
shall bring forth executioners
shall stand like kings inside thy doorways
shall throw their arms around thy lintels poland
& begin to crow

The Steward's Testimony

master-of-the-household
fat old jew
called *baal* the old king's
name
his fingers
blossomed in the earth dark flowers
covered the banisters
women in white kerchiefs
running to cut them loose
he was suffering from exhaustion
having kicked hell out of her sides
the night before
his teeth had cracked against the firm white
buttocks
crying "power" "power"
had tried to spread the cheeks apart
make the double entry
in god's name
or by names
hidden & lost
a man might die to know the secret of
he spit against the hole
quivered
was waiting for her hand
to find him
"how i do love thee, becky
"sweet rebekkah
"rifkeh
"descended from a line of lublin rabbis
"rose of the dispersion
"yuh-buh-buh-buh-bum"
the sight of his own penis
made him sick
a swollen toad
it squatted on his belly it was
toothless
it puffed
& trembled
her hand closed around it like a goose's neck
licked its red mouth with her cowtongue
mumbled "bridegroom"
"pig's balls"

"little lamp of love"
hossana!
the first busload of campers was leaving for the woods
around him eyes
watched from the house's open sides
schoolboys broke in
flattened their palms against his
ass & pressed him down
the bride
nibbled their earlocks
pulled the kerchiefs from their necks
beat her own head against the wall the gilded paper
fell off in strips
the glass case
splintered
sending a smell of spices
through the room the glimmer
of his riches
silver candlesticks
cups
candelabra
beakers
vases
crystal
colored glass
an umbrella with a silver handle
happiness
had come to the home of
the timber merchant
humming the eighteen benedictions
he entered
numerals in ledgers fingered
his spent cock maddened
by his dream of a northern forest
lumberyards
not synagogues
were where he worshipped
trains run by german
engineers led to his ark
"the wilderness"
the buzz of saws
to witness a new kabbala

whirred in his ears the young bride
wrapped a kerchief
over his shrunken balls
before he stopped her
stuffed her hole with meat
naked
they raced down hallways plundered
her father's
holy relics
pieces of amber on which the long dead
maggid of kozhenitz
had said prayers
fragments of black sugar which had touched
the lips of the saintly
grandfather of shpoleh
dried herbs
parchment
strings of wolves' teeth
black devil-fingers
girdles of remnant strips
blessèd oil from the holy city of safad in the holy land
they smeared on their bodies
or drank
his grey beard fell on his chest
a prayershawl across
his belly
worms sang psalms from his navel the folds
of loose fat
hung like dough
his penis drew back
& vanished
redemption was his name for it
in our larders
(hidden)
i would watch them tearing the raw
flesh they caught a calf
& butchered it
smearing themselves with blood & fat
(he would drink the residue
called "life")
stuck chickenfeathers to their thighs &
screamed like crows

not like an old man
& his bride
the timber merchant drew heat from
the law
at night he saw a mooncalf heard
distant trains
push toward silesia
bought sausage from the gentiles
would drop it in the sabbath pots
or break into the synagogue & steal
the prepuces of new-born infants
paradise
was on the road to lomza
a tavern where the gentiles
danced for him
young girls opened their blouses & stood
naked would hold their breasts up
to his lips
nipples the shape of acorns
apple-colored
mushrooms between their legs
"how i adore defilement"
he would cry & daub
his phylacteries with goat-shit
later they washed his beard
with kvass the odors
slid into his nose
& made him choke
the way home
frightened him he heard voices
speaking turkish
coins rolled helplessly from his pockets
& crossed the road
he found the back door
open in the pantry
skirts above her hips
the housemaid
sat eyes blinded
the young bride's head moved slowly
in her lap a dead song
dribbled from the timber merchant's
gums he blessed the walls but couldn't

find his stick
his skullcap
fell into the soup
the broom had grown a mouth
teeth he didn't know
were biting him
sobbing
he learned to fly would later
become an owl
companion for the grandmothers in the woods
"redeemed" "redeemed"
the timber merchant cried
bandits & martyrs were dancing
with the moon they hailed him
as their king
but homesick
in his wilderness
transfigured or crushed
flowering or awash
his fingers tore at his belly mangled
the folds of flesh
the dark wounds
blossomed he visited
the wooded shrines around the town
& raged there
would make up names
to suit himself
"master-of-the-household"
"cat"
"fat face"
"blossomer"
"the stump"
"the swallower of millions"

FRANK SAMPERI

Via Negativa

Rain
bitterness
I can know nothing but dissatisfaction
this means my knowledge
is negative
it seeks no gift worthy of respect
it looks to no writer
because no writer of this age
for instance is worthy
of respect I mean
whether of the underground
or the upper world
the writer the artist what have you
invariably
spews sentiment
he knows no other action
he seeks even when it seems
he is for neither side
to promulgate a journalism
that must by every turn
demoralize
trap
a man
My hell
I emphasize my hell
where there is no other meaning but darkness
the rhetoric societal
leaving a man neither in nor out
that is either in or out
depending upon
another position
but since position is not part
of the meaning
in and out lack meaning
bearing to each other
significance
only if one is in
another out
But there is
love
yesterday
for instance

I walked the city
and yet not city
because outside of the city
my vision
walked
mystical
not mystical
more intelligential
good to walk in the city
and yet know
you are not in it
nor can ever be
therefore
you wonder
wherein is hate
I sit in a room
everything others get
I do not
but if to sit in a room
means my position
is precisely that
then there is no complaint
I listen to birds
then get up
and go out
to find birds
I seek parks
birds in trees
even tho trees
fewest trees of streets
interest me of course
as much as birds
in parks
2:30 in the morning
woke up
fright
took a shower
loneliness
a spiritual necessity
my room
done up
as if holiness
were ambience
Raised my head

no end to this writing
sentences
taking their significance
from infinite combinations
but when the writing has reached
its final word
the word reduces itself
to closed word
the closed word raised to another height
only if another extension is seen
which extension in turn
imparts
to everything that went before
the vision
no end
therefore book on book
death
horizontal
cardinal
vertical
ordinal
the wheel turned
death again
but you have this clarity
no one else
can solve the insoluble
Lilac odor
I looked up
vines literally draped over balconies
the image old
plain enough
the city cannot keep up with itself
the mania for renovation
equals
the mania for quaintness
but one's argument
is not with city
at least
not now
one knows better
I see my work as the solution
of the anti-hero
I am lower
poorer

more truly proletarian
the song
in but not of
released
by not even in
more given up to God than self
self least
because self only worthy
as branch is
to light

Love darkness
spirit
this
that
neither
but if love seeks
light
light
dark
dark
light
then know
negative
not negative
same
everywhere
but different if same
self
no where equal
more darkness
darkness separate
body
soul
no where one
each either
neither
other
one
neither
if one
other

ARMAND SCHWERNER

Seaweed

for doloris

Text

from "the invention of glamour" (with photographs)
by Eugenia Sheppard, New York Herald Tribune, *August 1, 1965*

coquettish elegance   countess castiglione   1858   photo by adolphe braun
sentimental beauty   mrs. herbert duckworth   1867   photo by julia m. cameron
forthright opulence   lillian russel as "dorothy"   1887   photo by b. j. falk
lawn-party fantasy   princess natasha paley   1935   photo by cecil beaton
spiritual creature   greta garbo   1925   photo by arnold genthe
dramatic individuality   greta garbo   1928   photo by edward steichen
stylized abstraction   kiki   1926   photo by man ray
liberated action   model   1940   photo by martin munkacsi
perpetual seduction   jean harlow   1934   photo by george hurrell
ornamental elegance   fonssagrieves   1950   photo by irving penn
queenly waif   brigitte bardot   1959   photo by richard avedon

Gloss

I

kiki's stylized abstraction precedes garbo's dramatic individuality
but garbo's dramatic individuality
follows
garbo's spiritual creature
in 1928 garbo was an individual but in 1925
she was a creature, that is to say
in 1928 edward steichen, photographer, garbo, dramatic individuality,
was an individual
                              in a drama. In 1925
arnold genthe, spiritual creature creator
was a creature or
1925 was a creature and 1928
an individual.
one woman is a waif one woman is a beauty one woman is a creature
red city
the other women are an elegance an opulence a fantasy
an individuality an abstraction an action a seduction and one more elegance
they think of the green sea
more elegance than other nouns, two elegances, the other nouns
are one each: opulence fantasy creature individuality abstraction
action seduction waif
in the red city they think of the green sea

seaweed

•

II

is it all one or many?
princess natasha paley full of lawn-party fantasy
                                                  fantasy
princess her left hand looks dulcet
                                          swans and everything
and space for an inch and a half between the second and third fingers
I try it
my tendons hurt, photograph me
there's a hollow in her right cheek shadow dark, god
I'd like to go in there and forget
she looks at her empty left hand from which what? yes a violin
has disintegrated. Yes, she is
willing the instrument back, such an intense stare, magic and beautiful—
the backdrop may be a blowup of my face, pores and distended pores, or
it's the damp beach sand at Southampton, *that's* all right,
magic and beautiful; in her right hand a short
limp rod of flowers doesn't quite fall off, the problem
of losses
        it's the unseen power of the slight thumb
retains what's here in 1935, *she*
wouldn't do it like a dog in a party on that fantasy lawn, poor
void of echoes;
              princess natasha paley's left hand
makes a shadow on the beach
                                    of pores,
                                            somewhat
like an open-mouthed dog

seaweed sticky

•

III

when he raps and orders nothing
moves, no animals change
direction. He tries sleep.
The jellyfish ladies swim without a whisper
of a sound. Is it
the delicate purple muscles

that propel? Is it the sea
currents that open and close them?
He shifts in sleep.
He begins again with the deep
attachment of brooding
sight, he is dreaming
the ocean stirring without sound, the forms
swimming in Egyptian heaviness, the sea
in chalcedony-hard grey stone, white
sun-bleached seaweed on hard sand under
camera sun spot light. Is he deaf to the waves
that they make no sound? Expensive
sun, which holds a stance steady so long. Which
sun is real? rumors of another one in another
harness, motion-full out of his control.
He shifts in sleep. What a fine
sheen off the brass sun, a coin, a cut-out
caprice, sparkle figure on a ground, buoy
in the everlasting come and go, woman.

•

IV

hateful fill full of hatefulness
hollow horror needful of land fill, big and little
live crawlers and flyers and those which dig
and figures of thrivers on fallow
below damp beach boulders sickening sick-
ening, rap rot snake-
weed in the brass sun, vials
packed with the red city sick-
ening

seaweed

•

V

what thou lovest well remains, what
remains is what thou lovest well.
                                                  That
viviparous voyeur with a Vienna heard told us:
money and beautiful women remain—
                                                          which
thou lovest well; slowly by slowly the live births
grow, and populate the land, little by little the healers

spread in their vested vests, helping
in a hover helpfulness, money
and beautiful women, this
is the poetry of gain and loss, of the rock
of the desire for stones. Do what you will, all
men be mirrors.

seaweed

•

VI

in a landscape Fonssagrieves is clamming
in the seaweed full tepid bay water at low
tide,
      snake
weed, her thin
high breasts point
down, she laughs, the sun
is brass off the water, she strains
the heavy rake up out of it,
                                        glints
where she unembroiders the weed off the forks,
                                                                her breasts
risen, sweat down the nipples and through the channel
two catamarans cut with heaven-piercing topmasts,
                                                                    voices

off the starboard bow.

in a landscape Lillian Russell is clamming
in the seaweed full tepid bay water at low
tide,
      in 1887.
She is rowing to the clam beds, b. j. falk,
studio at 949 Broadway, photographer, Lillian
Russell as "Dorothy," sits ballast in the stern, toying
with the anchor chain.
                                    Diamond
Jim Brady waits in the bed in a glint of finger rings
off the brass sun, a knife in his swimming pantaloons, a bottle
of seafood cocktail in his left hand.
                                                    Sturdy

scene; they spar, he
with the big rake, b.j. is clamming,

they
lie on their backs after sparring, his chrysanthemum head
plump on her pontoon
breasts, b.j.
is clamming, the sea
is rhythming in waltzes toward dusk, they
are lolling dugongs in a coupling, in the shallows b.j.
is clamming, through the clean water he gropes
for a resting conch, good
food.

•

VII

rap rap hateful fill hollow princesses, thrivers
on fallow healers, what thou lovest populates
some of the land-
scape, snake weed. It's a ring ding
cakewalk, which of us
is not poor of spirit, ravaged
in the dance . . .

the leaves of fall are
falling on the bay shore
and on the plastic canopy

the slow fall of the shoreline
is the sea's work, not
like an osprey, more a rabbit

what was it again that impales
its prey? it is the shrill butcher-
bird, the shrike, not the sea

he moves in the red city, he hungers
for the green sea, he looks for clams, feeling
with his toes on the subway platform

lost at sea, lost at sea! there a god
waits, what he wants
startles the drowning man

the danger of jellyfish, poison
hairs on tentacles, the danger of a man
swimming, the danger of weightlessness

the danger of purple, the danger
of red, the danger of green, but the catastrophe
of the sun bleached seaweed

he wills to see the tint chlorophyll
again, the yellow breast of the flicker, the red
crown

the leafy leavings fall
away, he walks in the mulch,
what was that rustle that woke him?

Poem at the Bathroom Door, by Adam

silver woman do you love me
black woman do you love me
garbage woman do you love me
remind woman do you love me
painter woman do you love me
bird woman do you love me
map woman do you love me
push-car woman do you love me
watch woman do you love me
iron woman do you love me
bye woman do you love me
happy woman do you love me
store woman do you love me
bird with a heart in his mouth and a kiss in his mouth
present woman do you love me
ask woman do you love me
that's all I can think of

Two on the Tablets

1. A Note
2. Meditation: the only poems are Babel Poems

1.

The modern, accidental form of Sumero-Akkadian tablets provides me with a usable poetic structure. They offer, among other things, ways out of closures—which I find increasingly onerous—as well as the expansion of the syntactical girdle of English. They also invite spontaneous phonetic improvisations. The uses of the past, by means of these found archaic objects, are thus more than ironic and other than nostalgic. The context of sober translation creates a mode suitable for seductions by the disordered large which is the contemporary, and the narrative, which is out of honor in the most relevant modern poetry. The context also makes me feel comfortable in recreating the animistic, for which I have great sympathy, and which, subject to my sense of the present, I have not been able to approach as poet without such contextual personae and forms as I have found in these archaic leftovers.

More specifically, I'm excited by being able to put in holes wherever I want, or wherever they need to be; on the other hand I can fill out some of the infinite interstices which exist—unavailable segments of the continuum—between the pathetically restricted categories of English tenses; in addition, I'm interested in what happens to a modern concept of personality and its sense of non-vegetative duration when that self, say me, makes certain antique allowances.

Eliot and Pound structured ironic and tragic commentaries by confronting past and present. Why not go further, I thought, and recreate the past itself, in a series of subjectively ordered variations suggestively rooted in the archaic? And, more, why not augment the confusions between illusion and reality by the further invention of a scholar-translator whose fictive but oppressively present self would add a dimension of narration? This might be one way in which the "what happened next" could be restored to functional poetic usefulness in an age of what Simone Weil called "decreation." The holes in the text and the dubious provenances then act as counterweights to the squareness of conventional linear narrative continuity. The personality of the narrator himself gradually reveals its own idiosyncratic variables: even within the fictive frame of *The Tablets,* can he be trusted? The problems of "translations" . . . To what degree is any poem a translation, or a thereness?

What is more, the rapid shifts in tonality and texture found in some archaic and primitive materials contribute a helpful antidote to "civilized" modes concerned with characterological and dramatic imperatives of consistency. Contemporary media mixes, for instance, are another—if often mechanical—manifestation of the revolutionary impulse pushing against classical *and* romantic canons. In addition, the tonal and textural shifts, the comic vision of these *Tablets* (can a man talk about his own vision and not laugh?) help to place in some perspective the contemporary mystique of line-endings and their poetic importance. The question is not Where does the line end; the question is What is meaningfulness? The final question is When are a man's discoveries techniques subsumed in his vision; and When are his inventions gimmicks straining to support a petty order of limits?

2.

Poetry, as game, as act of faith, as celebration, as commemoration, as epic praise, as lyric plaint, as delight in pattern and repetition—poetry is in trouble. Not any more trouble than the Earth, concepts of nobility and selflessness, senses of utility, hope. But that's not saying too much. Whoever most largely perceives decreation may find himself praising entropy in self-defense. Or, if he is a poet, constitutionally unable to go all the way to formlessness and the joy of envisioning the running down of systems, he looks around for a way to make lasting monuments out of vaseline and lacunae.

> Loss of a sense of satisfying personal identity is linked to modern man's inevitable loss of the "games" learned early in life. In other words, modern man, if he is at all educated, cannot play the same sorts of games which he played as a youngster, or which his parents played, and remain satisfied with them. Cultural conditions are changing so rapidly that everyone tends to share the problem of the immigrant who *must* change games because he has moved from one country to another. Even those who stay put geographically find themselves in a world other than that of their parents. Indeed, as they grow older they usually find themselves in a world other than that of their youth. In this dilemma, man is confronted by the imperative need to relinquish old games and to learn to play new ones. Failing this, he is forced to play new games by old rules, the old games being the only ones he knows how to play. *This fundamental game-conflict leads to various problems in living.* . . . A type of game-conflict develops from the realization that man can play no transcendentally valid (God-given) game. Many react to this insight with the feeling that, in this case, *no game is worth playing.* The significance of this condition—namely that *no game is really worth playing*—appears to be especially great for contemporary Western man.
>
> —Thomas Szasz, *The Myth of Mental Illness*

"*. . . mouvement,*" says Marcel Raymond, talking, among others, about Valery, "*de retrait et d'exhaustion qui s'observe chez plus d'un contemporain.*" A condition, nevertheless, through which the poet and his friends theorize about the Good Place.

A fish can only swim. If a poem is a fish it must discover that swimming's what it does. Sympathy. Sympathy. But how about that ocean, the world, where it gets harder and harder to set up categories of the real and unreal as tenable hypotheses? The immense difficulty of defining a self, of assuming an identity, goes along with this. In poetry then silences and lacunae should *be*—and being, act—and the often arbitrary distinctions between concrete and abstract, real and unreal, sane and mad, objective and subjective seem increasingly irrelevant. To demonstrate the arbitrariness by the processual flux of the poem. . . . Destroy the point of view: who's speaking? to whom? and the rest of it.

The medieval realities. Unverbalized assumptions even *now* more real than we would believe. God the Father, goodness, the fixed beautiful Chain of Being, the *Spiritual Exercises*, as real as skywriting. (When we see the past as poetic horde of instructions, we overlook the ghetto, the Inquisition, the *auto-da-fé*, the plagues. . . .) The ladders and links of that gone world play through *Macbeth;* the world there gone awry, the fevers of the body, distempers in the Kingdom, the shaking state of man: for Shakespere the meanings of a broken world move him to consider the fixed regime and ordered state disturbed. Macbeth does not despair at his wife's death: he fights the enemy. Macduff immediately shifts from agony over his wife's and children's murders to resolute defiance of Macbeth. The "real" world is always available, always stands as recourse, a stage for redressive action; and Fortinbras always restores health to the rotten disjointed time: Hamlet and Macbeth are next-door neighbors. The Post-Medieval Age, even, is gone and its "wholeness," now perceivable, its faith in rationality and technology and science—available now through the same mythical tense as the hierarchy of angels—had presented the only order we share.

There was an outside in that place of order, a place to go *from* which to look at madness, at the destroyed land/water/air. Nothing matters more than the realization that there are no places left *from which* to look at madness, at the destroyed land/water/air; we must accept the only possibilities available: there is no nuclear self; there is no *unendurable* inward or outward Babel of tongues, there is merely Babel; we must admit dooming simplicism that inheres in prestructured categories. To alter structure? And how radically? In what direction? How does the poem live?

How will the mind work? By the eidetic confrontation of the "real"? The real changes. By feeling through Cassirer's moving elaboration of the primitive ethos as "the consanguinity of all living things"? Intermittently at best, and with the edge of despair for being so irrevocably far. The real changes. The uncertainty principle in art, a function of interchange between phenomena and poet. . . . The aim: to discover in the self as many different categories of perception as possible. The made thing, poem, artifact, product, will appear to the maker as Other and yet give the pleasure of recognition, to breed other discoveries. The voices: the maker does not know the identity of a voice or many voices. They speak to him in a way he later discovers. The locus appears later.

But the enemy surrounds us. Words lose their substance, are coopted by mimetic IBM ads, depress; the attitude of distrust toward words spreads to objects. We need a new language, one that we cannot speak, may not be able to speak, unseizable, proliferating like the elementary particles in physics: no end to it: uncertain statistical places left from which to look at the negative-muons which are told by their uncertain traces. The ambiguous, ambivalent?, nature of the love, need?, for schizophrenic language, pre-Christian rites, the rhythmed products of children. The aim is to get in touch but the object fades. The good society. Poetry is a body invested with rhythmic cells; it is neither the Way nor the object; its appearance makes no difference, but at least it permits the freedom to discover apparently new games. Though one tires of chance itself, and cooks a nice piece of fried zucchini. This or that: hints; the almost conceivable possibility of some transitory order. The Babel Poems.

Tablets IV, V, VI

Presented by the Scholar-translator
Transmitted through Armand Schwerner

Legend: .... untranslatable
++++++++ missing section
(?) variant reading
[ ] supplied by the scholar-translator

Tablet IV

Most large fragments are the results of horizontal breaks. This Tablet (IV) and the next (V), however, are vertically fractured. The reconstruction of V is almost certainly correct. Doubt lingers about IV. The edges do not meet in three places; otherwise it is a good tight fit. Whether the idiosyncratic continuity derives from accident or design is a problem which only time and further studies and excavations will resolve. Note the cesuras.

is the man a bush on fire?	like one drop of quartz, two cold onyx beads
is the man four-legged and with teeth?	like one piece of petrified wood
is the man a hot woman?	like one hard-finger-bone, one moonlight on iron
is he mud, of solid mud?	in the shape of one clay tablet in frost
is the man a bird?	.... like bronze eyes
is the unhappy man on all fours?	in the shape of bronze statues of something wood
is the man all blood, all bile?	like menstrual blood congealed in cold mud
is the woman a fat belly?	like the world, a five-year-old's bloody ....
is the man sleeping in a god?	like a frog stuffed with small white stones
is the man's head aching?	like .... empty ++++++++ maggots
does the man play with her lips?	like amber ++++++++ running pus
can the man make himself come?	like a ++++++++ cold onyx beads
can the woman come on top of the man?	.... dead trees
when does the man sacrifice his hands?	like sheep draped in cold mud
does the man wipe her belly with sperm?	like stories about ice, about frozen wheat
does the man put good leaves under his testicles?	++++++++ of maggots
does the man put his lips on the sheep's udder?	in the shape of a clay tablet in frost
does the man put hand and elbow in his cow's vagina?	like death in blossoms when ....
does he ram his penis into soft earth?	like the death in petrified wood
does he touch his woman's ....?	like the death in two cold onyx beads
does the man pray to her vulva for rain?	like stories about ice, about frozen wheat
does he lament the sickness of his groin?	like a frog stuffed with small white pebbles
it is night; does he swim in the river?	like sheep draped by cold mud
++++++++	like hail
++++++++	like a leg burning on the pyre
++++++++	like ants, a rotten cadaver, the dead trees

Tablet V

is the man bigger than a fly's wing?
is he much bigger than a fly's wing?
is his hard penis ten times a fly's wing?
is his red penis fifteen times a fly's wing?
is his mighty penis fifty times a fly's wing?
does his penis vibrate like a fly's wing?
is his arm four and one half times a strong penis?
is his arm two-hundred-twenty-five times a fly's wing?
is his body three times his great arm?
is his   is his body thirteen times his red penis?
[body three-hundred-thirty-six times a big fly's body?
does he touch his body with pleasure?
does she count fly's wings throughout the night?
is her vulva tipped with spring color?
does he move behind in her?
does she vibrate like the wheel on the axle?
let us call a fly's half-wing *kra*
let us call a fly's half-wing *kra*
let us call a fly's half-wing *kra*
let us call a fly's half-wing *kra*
let us call a fly's half-wing *kra*
let us call a fly's half-wing *kra*
let us call a fly's half-wing *kra*
look, the bull's horn is more than six *kra*!
let us call the man's red penis *pro*
let us call the man's red penis *pro*
let us call the man's red penis *pro*
look, the cow's vulva is five *kra*
look, the cow's vulva is almost three *pro*
pro kra kra pro kra kra kra pro
the man's sacrificed hand is more than one *pro*
the man's aching head is forty *kra* round
the man's sick groin is three *pro*
let's sacrifice this twig
let's sacrifice this great melon
let's sacrifice this shank
the hand is furious
the aching head screams
the sick groin is furious
++++++++
++++++++
++++++++

what pleasure!
what pleasure!
what pleasure!
what [pleasure]!
what pleasure!
what terrific pleasure!
.... a great arm
in the shape of petrified
what pleasure!   [wood
what pleasure!
what pleasure!
what pleasure!
what pleasure!
what terrific pleasure!
let us have rain!
let us have rain! what pleasure!
lay a *kra* on this bull's horn
lay another *kra* on this bull's horn
lay another *kra* on this bull's horn
lay another *kra* on this bull's horn
lay another *kra* on this bull's horn
hold the bull down quiet
lay another *kra* on this bull's horn
hold down the bull's head
lay a *pro* on this cow's vulva
lay another *pro* on this cow's vulva
lay another *pro* on this cow's vulva
what pleasure!
what terrific pleasure!
kra what pleasure! *pro* what pleasure!
this twig is more than one *pro*
this great melon is forty *kra* round
feel this lamb shank, three *pro*
what a pleasure!
what a pleasure!
what a terrific pleasure!
how will we frighten the strangers now?
how will they piss in their pants?
how will we frighten the strangers now?
++++++++
++++++++
++++++++ for water

Tablet VI

Here the scholar-translator has tried to approximate the colloquial tone of the original. Unfortunately we have no information about the identity of the addressee; anger and ridicule are directed toward some immanent power which keeps changing its attributes; rough approximations of its being may be embodied in variously found names:

Big Fat Flux   Great Hole in the Cock Liver (perhaps a reference to poorly understood onanistic ritual practices directed to the air-hog or the ground-pig)   Sore-Ass-Mole-Face-Snivel-Kra   Little Mover   Big Mover   Seventeen-Eyeball-Fusion-Up-Up   The One of This Way   The One of That Way   The One of No Way   Anxious-Liar-Fart-Flyaway   The Smeller   The Digger   The Scheming Pintrpnit   The Porous Poppycock   The Mean-Sucking-Sponge-Pinipnipni   Pnouk   Lak   Pa-Pa-the-Flying-Slime   The Big Eater   The Paramount Groin of the Sucking Air   Old No-Name   The Rock   The Fly   The Killer of Water   The Beautiful (Strange?) Liar   The Rain-Spoiler   The Water Dryer   The Tree Dryer   The Flower Dryer   The Urus Dryer   The Creep   The Knom of Lies   The Great Trouble   The Scheming Rock   The Maggot   The Friendly Buzzard   Everybody's Hyena   The Dumpy Snivel   The Filthy Teat   The Foosh

It has been suggested that the concrete figures belong to an earlier layer; our knowledge, however, is not at such a point of sophistication that we can now attempt a Higher Criticism of this material. When we can, what germinative cultural possibilities might we not discover?

.... in the world. I can't come
you have oozed into my ++++++++ old Water Dryer
++++++++ because when I reach the end of my story, I'll still have
all of it to tell in me waiting to explode
like the constipation in a plugged-up man after ....
Big Mover I still can't come, my woman is unhappy with me
she waits but she's getting ++++++++ and madder
old Water Dryer you are fat tree-gum and .... and fungus in my loins
this is not me, o Pa-Pa-the-Flying-Slime, this is not me
I am not what I was, even my children know
their jokes cover their pity, stories
about ice, about frozen wheat
show yourself Pnou, let me see you Lak,
come into my house with a face just once old No-Name
I will call you simple death
show yourself Lak, let me blind you Pnou
o Pinitou Pinitou Pinitou,* this is not me
you are rainbow are you rainbow, I will hate it
if you are beautiful, Knom of Lies
Creep, Paramount Groin of the Sucking Air
.... [Great Hole] in the Cock Liver

* curious; if this is the surname, or given name, of the speaker, we are faced for the first time with a particularized man, *this* man, rescued from the prototypical and generalized "I" of these Tablets. If it is *this* man, Pinitou, I find myself deeply moved at this early reality of self; if we have here the name of an unknown deity or peer of the speaker, I am not deeply moved.

knock in breaking ++++++++ stone flames Killer of Water
Dumpy Snivel child-eye [sucker] faultfinder dry earth
dry breaking .... of a fault and another and two and three
.... child-eye Killer of Water
Mean-Sucking-Sponge-Pinipnipni .... and I
o Pinitou Pinitou Pinitou in dry cricket sperm
[break unhappy] my mouth is full of blood Beautiful (Strange?) Liar
I ate in a dream, I won ++++++++, in a dream
you came to me Friendly Buzzard and took my
flow of a knocking to break me for the sucking you need
come see me when I .... I will call you
simple death, let me blind you Pnou
and [hide from] me then, steal away from me, I will
++++++++ you Pa-Pa-the-Flying-Slime, I will
enclose you with sharp .... The Fly, I will
rake you with ++++++++ Filthy Teat, I will
++++++++ for Pinitou for Pinitou
who knows me I know me this is not me
I will ++++++++ face just once for my breaking mouth
I ate a Dumpy Snivel for a child-eye fault
[o my son by the dark] river-road I can't touch your fingertips
it was not me by the Knom who left you there
Friendly Buzzard please let me touch you
and tear your .... please come into the ....
I will fondle you, I will open you up and eat your ++++++++
knock in breaking ++++++++ flames Killer of Water
++
++++++++++++++++ flow ++++++++++++++++
.... The One of No Way .... unhappy with me
++++++++++++++++ in the world, this place

HUGH SEIDMAN

The Making of Color

White

Parchment and paper left clean
or the lead, called white, or ceruse

The stack of vinegar and lead
embedded in tanbark or dung;
the temperature of fermentation,
moisture, carbon dioxide,
and the acid vapor of vinegar—
until a crust is formed on the coils of metal:
the white carbonate and hydroxide of lead

The metal may be wrapped in marc,
the refuse of grapes from the wine press,
or else in the waste from beer

The fundamental character is density,
opacity, and brilliant whiteness

Those who work this are warned of
the poisonous dust of this residue—
retained in the human system as
the body's tolerance incurably declines

There is the white of bone,
or of egg shell, or of oyster,
calcined and powdered,
or a pigment of chalk
to be mixed with orpiment

Black

Certain insects sting in oak
nodules called galls from which
tannic and gallic acids are soaked

Mixed with a salt of iron
to form a purple-black liquid
that blackens with age

The color of iron-inks
oxidized in the fibers

of parchment and paper

incaustum—burnt in

or less frequently
suspensions of graphite
or of lampblack

Red

Minium in the sense of cinnabar
the native red sulphide of mercury

Pliny reports
the excellent mines are in Spain
the property of the State

Forbidden to break up or refine
but sent under seal to Rome

Ten thousand pounds per year
the price sustained by law
seventy sesterces a pound

Liver-colored or occasionally scarlet
but a bright red when ground

Blue

Cloth dyed blue
licensed by the Crown

Ultramarine—lapis lazuli
pounded in a bronze mortar
Cennino relates

Eight ducats an ounce
for the patrons to purchase

Purple

The color of cheeks and the sea
Purpureus—the porphyry
The shellfish or the whelk
The murex—the purples of antiquity
Porphyrygenetos—born to the purple
A single drop from a skeleton

The stripes of the Roman togas
The purple of the ancient courts
The purple of Byzantium   The purple
of the great codices written in gold
the purple ink of the Patriarch
in the letters to the Pope of Rome

Parchment dyed shellfish-purple
crimson, plum-color, black
and the true purple—rivaling gold

Gold

Sheet metal, foil the thickness of paper,
leaf that is thinner than tissue

Malleable but difficult to powder

Sawed or filed into coarse particles
ground with honey or salt and washed

Hardened with a base metal
filed and crushed and retrieved in acid

Brittle amalgams which are ground
mercury driven off by heat

The goldbeaters place a thin square
at the center of parchment and over this

more parchment and metal—hammered
until the gold spreads to the edges—
cut and the process repeated—
for the finest leaf, a sheet
of ox intestines—goldbeater's skin

One hundred and forty-five leaves
beaten from a ducat
Venetian—fifty-four troy grains

Powdered gold in suspension
chrysography
                    letters
on the reds and purples and blacks
of purple-dyed parchment

polished with a smooth hard stone
or with a tooth
                    the appearance
of filings of metallic gold

Fire

The pages are stained with purple
The letters are written in gold
The covers are encrusted with gems
St. Jerome remonstrates
The curling writhes
Molten gold on carbon
Ink burnt ash grey
Emerald into vapor
The book, the codex, the manuscript
The canvas, the panel, the wall
Conflagrant world against world

CHARLES SIMIC

Stone Inside a Stone

1

They will not turn intó seed.
On the border of nothing and nothing.

Fossils of the wind.
But what wind?

You can't step twice in the same river—
With a stone you can take your sweet time.

Going to pick a flower in its heart
Is like taking a live chicken out of a bottle.

My stones will not sing the song yours are singing.

They say: everything is so simple. Touch it.
You awake in one, fall asleep in another.

Who, while the night is still deep awakes the roosters?
A stone among us is taking notes.

The opposite has ceased to be imaginary.
There are two of us now but o what solitude.

2

Touch again. You've touched a lightning.
The thunder is still to come.

Once in my hand
The fingers speak to it in its own language.

Stone, you come from a long line of fire-thieves.
I answered your questions
Until your hardness entered my voice.
Now they can carve whatever tool they please.

This is bread never-sown, never-reaped.

Two of them hang in death's testicles.

Strength that wishes to contract
Until it resembles itself more fully.

I hear the steps of the stone.
I lift them with my tongue
To keep myself in shape
For an unknown time.

Concerning My Neighbors, the Hittites

Great are the Hittites.
Their ears have mice and mice have holes.
Their dogs bury themselves and leave the bones
To guard the house. A single weed holds all their storms
Until the spiderwebs spread over the heavens.
There are bits of straw in their lakes and rivers
Looking for drowned men. When a camel won't pass
Through the eye of one of their needles,
They tie a house to its tail. Great are the Hittites.
Their fathers are in cradles, their newborn make war.
To them lead floats, a leaf sinks. Their god is the size
Of a mustard seed so that he can be quickly eaten.

They also piss against the wind,
Pour water in a leaky bucket,
Strike two tears to make fire,
And have tongues with bones in them,
Bones of a wolf gnawed by lambs.

They are also called mound-builders,
They are called asiatic horses
That will drink on the Rhine, they are called
My grandmother's fortune telling, they are called
You can't take it to the grave with you.

It's that hum in your left ear,
A sigh coming from deep within you,
A dream in which you keep falling forever,
The hour in which you sit up in bed
As though someone has shouted your name.

No one knows why the Hittites exist,
Still, when two are whispering
One of them is listening.

Did they catch the falling knife?
They caught it like a fly with closed mouths.
Did they balance the last egg?
They struck the egg with a bone so it won't howl.
Did they wait for dead man's shoes?
The shoes went at one ear and out the other.
Did they wipe the blood from their mousetraps?
They burnt the blood to warm themselves.
Are they cold with no pockets in their shrouds?
If the sky falls they shall have clouds for supper.

What do they have for us
To put in our pipes and smoke?
They have a braid of a beautiful girl
That drew a team of cattle
And the engraving of him who slept
With dogs and rose with fleas
Searching for its trace in the sky.

And so there are less and less of them now.
Who wrote their names on paper
And burnt the paper? Who put snake-bones
In their pillows? Who threw nail-parings
In their soup? Who made them walk
Under the ladder? Who stuck pins
In their snapshots?

The wart of warts and his brother evil-eye.
Bone-lazy and her sister rabbit's foot.
Cross-your-fingers and their father dogstar.
Knock-on-wood and his mother hell-fire.

Because the tail can't wag the cow.
Because the woods can't fly to the dove.
Because the stones haven't said their last word.
Because dunghills rise and empires fall.

They are leaving behind
All the silver spoons
Found inside their throats at birth,
A hand they bit because it fed them,
Two rats from a ship that is still sinking,
A collection of various split hairs,
The leaf they turned over too late.

Melt the spoons into a key
And the house you sought will appear.
Set your supper on the palm of the hand.
The rats will bring embers in their eyes.
The hairs will be your shepherd's flutes.
The leaf will bear their whimper
To the east and then to the west.

All that salt cast over the shoulder,
All that meat travelling under the saddles of nomads . . .

Here comes a forest in wolf's clothing,
The wise hen bows to the umbrella.

When the bloodshot evening meets the bloodshot night,
They tell each other bloodshot tales.

That bare branch over them speaks louder than words.
The moon is worn threadbare.

I repeat: lean days don't come singly,
It takes all kinds to make the sun rise.

The night is each man's castle.
Don't let the castle out of the bag.

Wind in the valley, wind in the hills,
Practice will make this body fit into bed.

All roads lead
Out of sow's ear
To what's worth now
Two in the bush.

Fork

This strange thing must have crept
Right out of hell.
It resembles a bird's foot
Worn around the cannibal's neck.

As you hold it in your hand,
As you stab with it into a piece of meat,
It is possible to imagine the rest of the bird:
Its head which like your fist
Is large, bald, beakless and blind.

Bestiary for the Fingers of My Right Hand

1

Thumb, loose tooth of a horse.
Rooster to his hens.
Horn of a devil. Fat worm
They have attached to my flesh
At the time of my birth.
It takes four to hold him down,
Bend him in half, until the bone
Begins to whimper.

Cut him off. He can take care
Of himself. Take root in the earth,
Or go hunting with wolves.

2

The second points the way.
True way. The path crosses the earth,
The moon and some stars.
Watch, he points further.
He points to himself.

3

The middle one has backache.
Stiff, still unaccustomed to this life;
An old man at birth. It's about something
That he had and lost,

That he looks for within my hand,
The way a dog looks
For fleas
With a sharp tooth.

4

The fourth is mystery.
Sometimes as my hand
Rests on the table
He jumps by himself
As though someone called his name.

After each bone, finger,
I come to him, troubled.

5

Something stirs at the fifth
Something perpetually at the point
Of birth. Weak and submissive,
His touch is gentle.
It weighs a tear.
It takes the mote out of the eye.

GEORGE STANLEY

Achilles Poem

for Armando Navarro
1964

I thought of Achilles,
trying to get at the blood, where it is all
shadow. The life

Odysseus, to whom Death is another place,
like Phaeacia, not letting
too many of them come close at once

trying to get at the blood
The arteries and veins

the jut of the chin and the fire of eyes
beyond the trench,
wanting.

            On the hill, at
11 o'clock, the Searchlight Market closed.
No more ice cream from Swensen's, no more
chilled wine.

Where the "E" car ran, oh
fifteen years ago, when I was a kid,
turned left at Larkin and right again at
Vallejo, to miss the hill. Where Fran lives now.
It seems strange
a streetcar ever ran there,
iron-grey, maroon trim, one door in the middle

I told you all this when I said
it was something else that made me
freeze with terror of the dark,
not the loss
you knew. You said, "Of course."
                                        The hill
tilts me, nightly.

Stars I can see from Union & Leavenworth
high in the sky. They make me think—
It's later than I think. But when I get to Columbus,
they aren't risen yet, they're sunk behind

Telegraph Hill, it's only 12:30.

Cut the throat of the lamb, it flows in the trench. "Baa," lambie-pie.

                    The streetcar, in an early dream,
a "K" or "L," in the tunnel
turned off suddenly to the left
or right on a new route,
emerged into an underground cavern,
a new world! where it streaked
past lights, and trees—like a model train layout.
This place of dim expectancy
brightened gradually. It wasn't the sun

it was Dawn in the world where I sleep.
But I woke as a child and I wake as a man
to a familiar-ness.
A room.

Oct. 18. I want all my love healed.
I want this in! The heartache stilled
(Later) The day. When it seems all these sorts
aren't being played out, sliding downhill.

Oct. 20. I brood over giving, receiving
imagined slights.
Bill says, "Don't call up on the telephone
        and apologize—live with it."
I wonder how these lines will be read

A moth flying around the lamp
that shines through its gray wings

Oct. 21. The full moon rose
with the clearest face I've ever seen.

              I had had all those thoughts about Death,
suffered from them, told them to you
in the bar that night, Love
and my sense of humor
you said were evolutionary. Then grew proud of them
(on the hill, in the other direction—no longer needing
to act out of reasons of power or fame. Love

be my Master (Richard Burton as Antony) Incident
And
woke up again.

                    and the bower-bird
builds,
in Australia,
plants
        stems
in the ground
around a tree
        that keep on growing
and arch, to form his roof.
and a lawn,
tuft by tuft,
        where we look to find something
        when it is no longer lost
As I said, I

                    saw the moon

(Later) The days are still,
autumn grey, with heat of breath
A sighing, in and out

Oct. 28. Waking up this morning, I thought
It wouldn't be so bad to die, drowsily,
at the end of life. Last night I saw
ivy, rain-spattered, in the alley outside the Spaghetti Factory,
the big white veins standing out.
Manger says you can tell a man's age
even if his face is smooth as a boy's
by his veins. On the backs of his hands,
and wrists.

Nov. 6. We know the body is immortal, but the spirit dies.

Nov. 8. Withdrawing from the feast, Achilles doesn't see
Patroclus crawling out of his little hole.

Robin wrote: "It won't be complete darkness because there
isn't any. One thing will stop and that's this
overweening pride in the peacock flesh."

Ajax stands stock still,
won't answer Odysseus' relentless questioning.

rain on Filbert St., on the steps
leading down into the stars   The

Joy of each thing to be utter,
not frittered away in its connection to other parts

Monday no more than Tuesday,
dying-day, lying-day,
this day in the rain.

          A poem like a hunk of conglomerate.

Can we and it live in this year?
but in the stream-bed, ultimately dislodgeable.
The stream of Time, like one of the freshets on the Sierra,
a trickle in summer, but now, November, with the rains starting,
swelling, foaming over the little dams

Patroclus in Paul's painting
lunges forward, like he does in the Sixteenth book of the Iliad,

It is existence in reverse, Beauty and Youth
returning, refreshening the Source. It
takes place in absolute quiet, and Hector
and even Apollo seem like cops next to him.

Here in the stream-bed.

CHARLES STEIN

Two Songs for Hermes

1

the bees
in my mind
Apollo gave to Hermes
and he told him about the way they swarm
eating honey
about the hive
and cause thought to fly through royal keyholes

muse
sing of Hermes
my lord
whose deviations are my own

he sings while he plays
music on his turtle

he maketh Apollo's
cows to go backwards
over the turf
over the bones of the skull he maketh
webs of gold
break into rigorous mirrors

in the night he chargeth silence

and he wears the moon
in his curled hair

2

    undone
by the wayside.

                        that way that way
is its way
back again

as towns fall apart
and all your work to put them back again
succeeds yesterday
so tightly packed
and tightly sprung
the ravens spring up from the dread bog
by the wayside

the towns fall apart

the oak trees are willowized

the cows that Hermes
picked Apollo's golden pockets of
walked backwards

to their stony
archives

Cave of the Nymphs

          why
honey in the jugs?

bees are spawned by putrid oxen.

honey
draws the higher
essence
downwards.

It was used by Jupiter
to knock out Saturn,
stone him under lofty oaks
"drawn down by delight
   into the fluctuating empire of generation"

honey
sucks us
down
into lower ecstasy.
To eat it
equals
fucking. To eat honey
traps gods.

                    But to get back up—
honey is also
nectar.
It cannot putrify
and purifies
the tongue.

                    The moon
is a bee
exalted in Taurus
as bees
are spawned by putrid oxen. Bees
are called *Βούγενειϭ* (ox-born)
also souls
proceeding into generation
are called *Βούγενειϭ*
and Hermes
was a thief of oxen
his mind in secret
conscious of generation.

NATHANIEL TARN

from The Beautiful Contradictions

Two

His vomit in my mouth
my neck wet with his snot
his breath over my face
his blood coughed on my knees
his shit on my toes
and I have spared you the details fellow-students
of blood-brother relations
I   rain-priest of Atitlán   ralkoal Zutuhil
and that   not just for one night   many years ago   as a travel memento

but for years your poverty on my hands   alcaldes   juezes   regidores
alguaciles   telineles   tisheles   señores y señoras mios y mias
great lords   great ladies still in your stink of sick and pine
for years waking at dawn with wooden buttocks on a narrow bench
insomnia's ache lining my face   a needle in every vein
to drink the nose-twisting traguito
or smoke to the greater glory of the lord Simon Judas Iscariot

who is also San Pedro of the keys and cocks   alias Pedro de Alvarado
conquistador of Tziquinahá   in Quauhtemallan   for Spain
alias San Miguel Arcángel   lord of the winds and hills
alias Mam the ancient of days   the year's thrombosis
male and female when young   plural   screwing themselves in caves
then fainting downwind to the sea   with plaintive cries
to macerate into old Mam once more   to crucify the year

I danced like a bear to the greater glory of the puppet
which never flared at Easter but was worshipped more than Jesucristo
taken back and dismembered into his bundle after the Friday procession
where all the winds in the world come out if the door is left open
where we lie down in the arms of the many-coloured maize
praying that Mam should move   that the world be not left in silence
since fathers now walk out of step with their sons

When the padres had come to steal the bundles and masks
relegated the great doll to the pig-pound for three years
he who walked the world like a dream to give men lovers
while the elders went mad at their village dying
we took the case of the elders against the young politicos
as far as the president of the republic and won our case
because you do not take the heart out of men without some reparation

Great lords it is time you knew it
Huracan   the heart of heaven   thinks again
summons his siblings from their beds of green and blue feathers

where they lie in the water surrounded with light
saying that all the creations have been eliminated time and again
because they failed to break silence and praise the heart of heaven
the animals who hissed   screamed   cackled   but could not speak names
the men of clay who drooped back into clay
the men of wood who walked on all fours but had no minds
destroyed by the cardinal weathers   earth   water   air   and fire

but he is saying now that he will destroy by oblivion

dear gods as if I had never spoken

Maltiosh te-e-taa   maltiosh alcalde   maltiosh primero   'tiosh 'tiosh

the heart of seas   the heart of lakes   the heart of sky   are still
the green plate is flawed   the blue gourd broken
foxes   pigs   hunting bitches   bleed from their noses

the Lord has given

the book of the mothers-fathers cannot be seen any more
the skull-tree drips no more semen for our mothers' vaginas
no one has gone down into the bowels of fire   to bring back sons

'tiosh 'calde   'tiosh primero   'tiosh secundo 'tiosh

contract your bellies old men   let the world breathe by
pull in your navels all over again for the stones to boil in the dark
goodbye to the gods until that long meal is over   that pie of generations

the Lord has taken away

blessed be the name of the Lord   who thinks again

But my having everything   you having nothing at all
the pain that causes me puts me in the way very nicely
of doing my job effectively while paying the minimum in taxes

thank you father   why should it ever end father   when exactly father
this being after all such a rich exile
I like it so much down here

and for every corner of the earth where someone is in pain or dying
there is another corner where you will find the same
no grain of sand as small as the last pain to be tracked down

I make a meal of it all   I spew it out again

dear gods as if you had never spoken

Five

Looking into the eyes of babies in experiments
born without the normal pressure on their skulls
thinking they are going to put an end to philosophy
when some development of this begins to breed monsters
and that the chase through probability of the genius
the great kick he gives through his mother as he comes out
the clarity of the air surrounding him later in life
however much his body might take revenge on him
his mind crack between the diameter of his skull and the crown

reality comprises

that the immeasurable heave of the whole race
to bring this animal to the tree's crest and enthrone him there
may be gone forever in a moment of medical history
like the passing of some art or an old migration
of all the birds together in the arms of the same wind
the way the planet used to turn in one direction with one purpose

frightens a lot

I remember on the shores of the most beautiful lake in the world
whose name in its own language means abundance of waters
as if the volcanos surrounding it had broken open the earth
there in the village of Saint James of Compostela one cold night
not the cereus-scented summer nights in which a voice I never traced
sang those heartbreaking serenades to no one known
a visiting couple gave birth in the market place
the father gnawing the cord like a rat to free the child
and before leaving in the morning they were given the freedom of the place

I mean the child was given

ROBERT VAS DIAS

Urban Crisis

I

what / !there is
    a wing a
    breast O my
god   .   on the sidewalk
a whole half (a) hawk
    hawk?s wing spotted
    hawk, what is it
doing in brooklyn, on
the other hand I
    once saw one, heard
    its chirp.screaming
above the broadway
hotels scattering
    pigeons on my way
    to the subway, 6 a.m.
there) are various
    ways of hunting
    sidewalks

II

    while singers gathered
an audience and a touch
football game was won and lost, also
a political argument: on the grass
some couples sort of
made out: while the police
rounded the square & several haggard
men slept it off (one
shot-up—(who
wants to get caught
anyway, in washington square as
it happens we decided to marry /
an afternoon, early spring

III

the cat ladies call their charges
in cat voices and the bird ladies cluck,
lay out newspapers filled with fish heads,
the fishermen fish for hudson trout
and the dogs do their's

IV

those who follow instructions
who read instructions
listen to instructions over loudspeakers
radio   in subways in flashing lights
in lights which do not flash
in print   who give instructions
who give instructions aloud
who mumble instructions
whose words carry the force of
who give themselves instructions aloud
and *sotto voce*
who instruct you
who instruct others to instruct
who write instructions
erase them   change them
with wit   desperation   love   the cry
from the billboards   repeat
the instructions   the numberless
memoranda

V

west end one night: the sound: quick-
step on a pebble beach: a man fiercely
hammering in a carwindow
reaching in and pulling out
a suitcase and started this fast
Chaplin walk down the block
closeby the buildings, rightangled
the corner: I was running
with stealth playing movie detective
stopped, edged my face around
the building / the empty sound
uninhabited concrete

VI

heavy trash night is
thursday, I keep the appointment
for what treasures there are
to furnish us: a woodsculpture
of maple, naked man whose face's
been axed along the grain so you
look out (ward, always

sheared of intent and direction
though indications are
you're well hung and holding
the neck of a large bird   .   some symbol
the artist got tired of
                                        praising

VII

haggling in orchard street
canal street   fourteenth street
finagling in the district
ogling on fifth avenue
hogging FDR drive
robbing upper west side
fencing hot goods after
breaking & entering
gabbling union square
upper broadway & the battery
hobbling across avenues against
the light in the rush hour
friday evening of the
labor day weekend
goofing off   shooting off's mouth
tripping   coming off   practicing
the piano   moving   parading with a
without a permit   boozing
in the boroughs of

VIII

riverside drive / in the afternoon
the wind unclenches
my fist around a packet of hand-
colored slides I made
for a school assembly program
25 years ago
they accompany a story I have
only in my head, full
of names of characters I alone
can pronounce   .   flurry
over the hudson.

DIANE WAKOSKI

Blue Monday

Blue of the heaps of beads poured into her breasts
and clacking together in her elbows;
blue of the silk
that covers lily-town at night;
blue of her teeth
that bite cold toast
and shatter on the streets;
blue of the dyed flower petals with gold stamens
hanging like tongues
over the fence of her dress
at the opera/ opals clasped under her lips
and the moon breaking over her head a
gush of blood-red lizards.

Blue Monday. Monday at 3:00 and
Monday at 5. Monday at 7:30 and
Monday at 10:00. Monday passed under the rippling
California fountain. Monday alone
a shark in the cold blue waters.

You are dead: wound round like a paisley shawl.
I cannot shake you out of the sheets. Your name
is still wedged in every corner of the sofa.

Monday is the first of the week,
and I think of you all week.
I beg Monday not to come
so that I will not think of you
all week.

You paint my body blue. On the balcony
in the soft muddy night, you paint me
with bat wings and the crystal
the crystal
the crystal
the crystal in your arm cuts away
the night, folds back ebony whale skin
and my face, the blue of new rifles,
and my neck, the blue of Egypt,
and my breasts, the blue of sand,
and my arms, bass-blue,
and my stomach, arsenic;

there is electricity dripping from me like cream;
there is love dripping from me I cannot use—like acacia or
jacaranda—fallen blue and gold flowers, crushed into the street.

Love passed me in a blue business suit
and fedora.
His glass cane, hollow and filled with
sharks and whales . . .
He wore black
patent leather shoes
and had a mustache. His hair was so black
it was almost blue.

"Love," I said.
"I beg your pardon," he said.
"Mr. Love," I said.
"I beg your pardon," he said.

So I saw there was no use bothering him on the street

Love passed me on the street in a blue
business suit. He was a banker
I could tell.

So blue trains rush by in my sleep.
Blue herons fly overhead.
Blue paint cracks in my
arteries and sends titanium
floating into my bones.
Blue liquid pours down
my poisoned throat and blue veins
rip open my breast. Blue daggers tip
and are juggled on my palms.
Blue death lives in my fingernails.

If I could sing one last song
with water bubbling through my lips
I would sing with my throat torn open,
the blue jugular spouting that black shadow pulse,
and on my lips
I would balance volcanic rock
emptied out of my veins. At last
my children strained out
of my body. At last my blood
solidified and tumbling into the ocean.
It is blue.
It is blue.
It is blue.

The Prince of Darkness Passing Through This House

Not under the earth,
but under the ocean,
navigating my porpoise at times above water
you see,
I choose
a traditional image
for the poet,
I have seen the world;
it is too dry.

The fire burns best on water at night in the wake of a boat,
phosphorus footsteps
left
by the Night Queen's running barking dog,
running over the water,
running up on the sand, deep layers of grunion twisting
moaning against each other's fish body.

I ride,
patrol the seas,
creating coral reef barriers against our enemy
the shark.

Coming to this house, coming to
this fire,
coming to the beads in the eye,
coming with iridescent plankton, coming with a warm
mouth, coming out of a violin bow—
Prince of Darkness following the Queen of Night. Together
coming with soft gloves,
together coming
with night fire,
with fire that goes with water, with
the fire of old quiet suns,
with the fire that burns the night,
day moons burning
the Prince of Darkness,
under the ocean.

We are together, burning suns, moons, stars, meteors, comets,
into our earlobes and eyelids
making our hands hold live coals
of commitment,
of purpose,
of love, of fire floating on the water
and enough wind
to make the candles flicker—the power of fish
living in strange waters.

I Have Had to Learn to Live with My Face

You see me alone tonight.
My face has betrayed me again.
        the garage mechanic who promises to fix my car
        and never does.
My face
that my friends tell me
is so full of character;
my face
I have hated for so many years;
my face I have made an angry contract to live with
though no one could love it;
my face that I wish you would bruise and batter
and destroy, napalm it, throw acid in it,
so that I might have another
or be rid of it at last.

I drag peacock feathers behind me
to erase the trail of the moon. Those tears
I shed for myself,
sometimes in anger.
There is no pretense in my life. The man who lives with me
must see something beautiful,
like a dark snake coming out of my mouth
or love the tapestry of my actions, my life/ this body, this
face, they have nothing to offer
but angry insistence, their presence.
I hate them,
want my life to be more.
Hate their shadow on even my words.

I sell my soul for good plumbing
and hot water
                    I tell everybody:
and my face is soft,
opal,
a feathering of snow
against the
          cold black leather coat
which is the night.

            You,
            night,
            my face against the chilly
            expanse
            of your back.

Learning to live with what you're born with
is the process
the involvement,
the making of a life.
And I have not learned happily
to live with my face,
that Diane which always looks better on film
than in life.

I sternly accept this plain face,
and hate every moment of that sternness.

I want to laugh at this ridiculous face,
        of lemon rinds
        and vinegar cruets,
        of unpaved roads
        and dusty file cabinets,
        of the loneliness of Wall St. at night
        and the desert of school on a holiday.

but I would have to laugh alone in a cold room.
Prefer the anger
that at least for a moment gives me a proud profile.

Always, I've envied
    the rich
      the beautiful
        the talented
          the go-getters
            of the world. I've watched

myself
remain
alone
isolated
a fish that swam through the net
because I was too small
    but remained alone
    in deep waters because the others were caught
    taken away

It is so painful for me to think now,
to talk about this; I want to go to sleep and never wake up.
The only warmth I ever feel are wool covers on a bed.

But self pity could trail us all, drag us around on the bottom
of shoes, like squashed snails, so that
we might never fight. And it is anger I want now, fury,

to direct at my face and its author,
to tell it how much I hate what it's done to me,
to contemptuously, sternly, brutally even make it live with
itself,
look at itself everyday,
and remind itself
that reality is
learning to live with what you're born with,
  noble to have been anything but defeated
that pride and anger and silence will hold us above beauty,
though we bed down often with so much anguish for
a little beauty,
a word, like the blue night,
    the night of rings covering the floor and glinting
    into the fire, the water, the wet earth, the age of songs
    guitars, angry bus loads of etched tile faces, old
    gnarled tree trunks, anything with the beauty
    of wood, teak, lemon, cherry,

I lost my children because I had no money, no husband.
I lost my husband because I was not beautiful,
I lost everything a woman needs, wants,
almost,
before I became a woman,
my face shimmering and flat as the moon
with no features.

I look at pictures of myself as a child.
I looked lumpy, unformed, like a piece of dough,
and it has been my task as a human being
to carve out a mind, carve out a face,
carve a shape with arms and legs, to put a voice inside,
and to make a person from a presence.

And I don't think I'm unique.
I think a thousand of you, at least, can look at those old
photos,
reflect on your life,
and see your own sculpture at work.

I have made my face as articulate as I can,
and it turns out to be a peculiar face with too much
bone in the bridge of the nose, small eyes, pale lashes,
thin lips, wide cheeks, a rocky chin,
But it's almost beautiful compared with the sodden mass of
dough I started out
with.

I wonder how we learn to live
with our faces.
They must hide so much pain.
So many deep trenches of blood.
So much that would terrorize and drive others away, if they
could see it. The struggle to control it,
articulates the face.
And what about those people who were born
With elegant noses and rich lips.
What do they spend their lives struggling for?

Am I wrong I constantly ask myself
to value the struggle
more than the results
or only to accept a beautiful face
if it has been toiled for?

Tonight I move alone in my face;
want to forgive all the men whom I've loved
who've betrayed me.
After all, the great betrayer is that one I carry around
each day. Which I sleep with at night.
My own face.
Angry building I've fought to restore,
embued with arrogance, pride, anger, and scorn.
To love this face,
would be to love a desert mountain,
a killer, rocky,
water hard to find,
no trees anywhere

perhaps I do not expect anyone
to be strange enough to love it;

but you.

ELIOT WEINBERGER

Jungle 1

Cah! Cah see knee nook.
Cah! Cah charm a moke.
Cah seen on ick.
Cah castle on ick.
Cah callow lean ick.
Cah tow lone, ah
Pooch up a cah!

Why a cat a knob a sea,
Knob a John, ma a bee.
Who? 'n' we knock.
Who? 'n' she cop.
See keen, car, top, Che, Abba
Who'll see when scheme.
Key jail a shot who to kill.
Cock oh leak!
Ma weak Allah who watch you lay,
Oh Shah who to kill ray man ick.
Pale oh up a cah row no hell.
Ma, hubby no kill a camel or beak.
Cock oh so big!
Junta castle or beak,
Camel, cab, ant, pah, cash, ma.
Coo we knock, heal a cholic,
Yak a leak.

Shah ray man ick, ha!
Shah lion ick pale, oh
Shah who to kill ray man ick.
Shh ma, go we knock:
Heal a low cholic.
Shah catch a man ick.
Cats in a nick.
She cake, umm,
She a cob.

•

WOOD.
PALM FOR THATCH.
FIRE TO ROAST.
GOURD FOR WATER.
CASSAVA. PUMPKIN. YAM.

Let them go and get the brains of the sky
That the people may see their exact size.

DREAM OF TOMATOES: THE CHILD
WILL DIE.
LOW SWALLOWS: RAIN.
FEATHERS TO WEAVE.
CARVED BEAM. CARVED JADE.
OBSIDIAN. GOLD.

In making this, my hands
Moved for you.
Your word is
In the sky.
Your word is
In my hands.
Receive me.
Take me.
Give me your word!

DRAGONFLY VISITORS.
CICADA PROPHETS.
DWARFS.

PECCARY. TAPIR. DUCK.
FIRE. FEATHER. TALK.

I have come.
Here I stand.
I will sing,
My friends!

He sent me as a messenger.
I am changed into a poem.
I have come to make friends.

FIRE.

TALK.

•

1519, the signs were these:

ONE:
The people heard a woman weeping,
Night after night.
She passed in the night, crying
"My children,
We must flee far from this city!
My children, where
Shall I take you?"

TWO:
A creature was caught in the fishing nets,
A bird the color of ashes,
A bird resembling a crane
And wearing a strange mirror on its head.
The time was noon, but in the mirror
The night sky was seen.
In the mirror was seen a far plain.
People were moving across it,
Coming forward,
Making war.
They rode on the backs of deer.

THREE:
Monsters
Appeared in the streets of the city.
Deformed men
With two heads and one body.

FOUR:
Towers on the sea seen
Moving.

•

This is what the brains of the sky are:

COPAL GUM.

Jungle 5

From these clouds you are leaving,
from this land of mist and rain:

> "here the green corn is never lacking,
> squashes, grass, beans
> green in the husk, green
> pepper, flowers, and the living gods
> who let their hair grow long . . ."

This is the time of weeping.
Fly up.
Be not seen.

(Four thousand light-years to the Crab.)

Jungle 6

It is the moon drawing
the inner tide. She bleeds,
may not walk in orchard,
the fruit to sour at the sight.
Milk curdles. Eggs collapse.
She sleeps alone tonight
in hut apart. She may not share
the cooked and quartered flesh.
Must sleep. Her tribe with eyelids sealed
mourning the moon.

Bodies split open!
Legs there with entrails,
Heart, weird liver, gut,
Peachpit in the crack of gum,
And teeth gone rot and leafy green.
The hair so thick she cannot breathe,
All over, choked, a pole of hair
Rammed down the throat,
Daybreak: hairy sun,
night moon of hair, star, wind.

STORY:
Ten thousand eggs in a drop of swamp.
Repellent to fish,
all survived and grew.
Thrived on suds and chemic waste.
Large, albino,
in the air invisible,
on land turned green,
in sea blue, on desert brown.
Always growing, tangling till
there was no room.
Tangling till he,
with the sharpened stone . . .

STORY:
Hashish.
Assasins.
The President.
Assasins.

when fighting broke out
in all parts of the city
and fire

SUBJECT:
Anne, age 9.
April 25, 1965.
Q: What is menstruation?
A: You bleed. I'm not sure from where. It means that you grow up and get older and older. You just get it. It's normal. The first time you get it, it lasts 3 to 4 weeks. Then you get it every week or month. It lasts about one week and you have it till you die. You wear a Kotex and you have to be careful that you don't drop it. I only want to get it when I know more about it. What bothers me is how you get pregnant by yourself. My gym teacher said it's bad when girls fool around with each other, you know, Lesbians, they touch each other. It's worse when boys and girls get together. It always has to be a male and a female with genes. A dog and a dog, a cat and a cat, next to each other. Anyway, who wants to wear pants? I'm not a boy.

POEM:
R F K must be
be be disposed of
disposed
disposed of
disposed
disposed of properly

Robert Fitzgerald
Kennedy must soon die
die die die die
die die die die die

STILL:
The leader
quartered
in the sight's
crosshatch.

Jungle

Tell us the night
What signs traveler

(Mountain's height)

See watchman day
Beauteous
What beauteous ray

The sunlight
The depth of cloud
So strong

•

Let the dolphins say it:

It is the sea again
and the sea always—

LOUIS ZUKOFSKY

A-15

An
   hinny
by
   stallion
out of
   she-ass

He neigh ha lie low h'who y'he gall mood
So roar cruel hire
Lo to achieve an eye leer rot off
Mass th'lo low o loam echo
How deal me many coeval yammer
Naked on face of white rock—sea.
Then I said: Liveforever my nest
Is arable hymn
Shore she root to water
Dew anew to branch.

Wind: Yahweh at Iyyob
Mien His roar 'Why yammer
Measly make short hates oh
By milling bleat doubt?
Eye sore gnaw key heaver haul its core
Weigh as I lug where hide any?
If you—had you towed beside the roots?
How goad Him—you'd do it by now—
My sum My made day a key to daw?
O Me not there allheal—a cave.

All mouth deny hot bough?
O Me you're raw—Heaven pinned Dawn stars
Brine I heard choir and weigh by care—
Why your ear would call by now Elohim:
Where was soak—bid lot tie in hum—
How would you have known to hum
How would you all oats rose snow lay
Assáy how'd a rock light rollick ore
Had the rush in you curb, ah bay,
Bay the shophar yammer *heigh horse'*

Wind: Yahweh at Iyyob 'Why yammer,'
Wind: Iyyob at Yahweh, 'Why yammer
How cold the mouth achieved echo.'
Wind: Yahweh at Iyyob 'Why yammer
Ha neigh now behēmoth and share I see see your make

Giddy pair—stones—whose rages go
Weigh raw all gay where how spill lay who'
Wind: Iyyob
'Rain without sun hated? *hurt no one*
In two we shadow, how hide any.'

The traffic below,
sound of it a wind
eleven stories
below: *The Parkway*
no parking there ever:
the deaths as
after it might be said
"ordered," the one
the two old
songsters would not
live to see—
the death of
the young man,
who had possibly
alleviated
the death of
the oldest
vagrantly back he
might have thought
from vying culturally
with the Russian
Puritan Bear—
to vagary of
Bear hug and King
Charles losing his head—
and the other
a decade younger
never international
emissary
at least not
for his President,
aged in a suburb
dying maundering
the language—
American—impatient now
sometimes extreme clarity—
to hurry
his compost
to the hill
his grave—
(distance
  a gastank)

he would
miss
living thru the
assassination

were it forecast to him
the dying face
would look quizzical?

'In another week,
another month
another—
I shall be driven,
how shall
I look
at this sign
then—
how shall
I read
those letters
then—
that's a thing
to remember—
I should
like to remember
this—
how shall
I look
at it,
then'

Like, after all:
and as I know
failing eyes
imagine,
as shortly after
his mother died,
walking
with me
to my class
thru the swinging
red leather doors
of the Institute
he remarked on
a small square pane
of glass in each of them,

there to prevent
if students looked
those going out
and those going in
from swinging the doors
into so to speak
mutual faces,
when I pleaded blindness
'I've walked thru
some years now
and never till you
said saw these panes'
he consoled with
'mere chance
that I looked'

But the death—
years later
of the young man—
he did not live thru
(no *Drum Taps*
no *Memories*
as for Walt)

that the teacher
overhearing
a student
thought a stupid jest—
the class
shocked into a "holiday"

Flown back from Love Field, Dallas
love—so—divided—
the kittenish face
the paragon of fashion
widowed
with blood soaked stocking
beneath the wounded head
she held in her lap—
Até
crazier than ever
infatuation of history
steps on men's heads—
flown back from Love Field, Dallas
as in *Kings* 'dalas'
the poorest,
we had all,
the "English" teaching drudge
with a holidy on his hands
from "papers"
a time for
to atone for your souls
the nation
a world
mourned
three days in
dark and in
daylight
glued to
TV
grieved as a family
the Kennedy's were a family—
Castro 'We should comprehend it
who repudiate assassination
a man is small
and relative in society
his death no joy'
not the joy of the Irish
a few weeks back
greeting their Parliament,
its actual house
the old Fitzgerald seat,
when the Boston Irish American President
on tour recalled
on his mother's side
his ancestral prototype who had left it
to write his own mother
from Paris
'that the seat of the Fitzgeralds
was not
conducive to serious thinking.'

Potentates (nominally)
dignitaries
cardinals
the military
mounted
and the horses
led the
tone

in politics
who's honest
true
to
death?

the off the cuff
opponent (Guildencrantz)
who'd stopped husking
for the nomination
until after the funeral
and after the funeral
forgot any day before
while conserving *Freedom*
nevermind *Liberty*—
honest—

the young dead's
great slip—
(pricing steel)
the twenty-third of April
only seven months laid (a
garland
for Shakespeare's birthday)
'My father always
told me
all business men
were sons-of-bitches.
I never
believed it
till now'

or Vietnam's witch
despising
Buddhists'
human wicks
with sympathies
for Western
First Lady
widow to widow
(Queen Margaret and dying Edward's queen)
And see another as I see thee now
could mourning soften

Eloquence
words of
a senator's eulogy
da capo five times:
'In a moment it was no more.
And so she took a ring
from her finger and placed it
in his hands'
And he added the fifth time:
'and kissed him and closed

the lid of the coffin.'

'Bethink you
if Bach's feet deserved such bounty
what gift must the Prince have offered
to reward his hands'
Capella, *alpha* in Auriga, little first goat
early evening early autumn
driven before them — west —
fall stars of evening

or Vesper there
Vesper Olympus dig air
court orchestra of uniformed Haiduks
habit Bach himself wore
"concertmaster" of four string players
his income not generous
'Friedmann, shall we go
over to Dresden to hear pretty tunes'
Italy's arias Händel's successes

one hundred four pages
of Frescobaldi's *Musical Flowers*
to copy, paper the fringe benefit from the Duke,
or pupil Ziegler to remember
in playing a hymn
melody is not alone
speaking the words thru it
a rare banquet in cypress
orange almond and myrtle
fragrance to turn a winter's evening to summer

or the court company of comedians
whose dispersal synchronized with Bach's arrival
not 'useful to accept a post
poorer than the one he abandons'
finger exercises traceries little pieces of himself
played over, saying 'That's how it ought to go'
no searching over the keyboard better silent
if there's nothing, until parts
speak to their fellows, true counterpoint
variety free thru consistency
later Orpheuses, Arions

Weimar not a street perpetuates his name
where Lucas Cranach lived and some say
Bach in Herder's house
more certain he was arrested

for urging his own departure—
They perpetuate the young dead's name with place
statesman stumping *The Tabernacle*, Salt Lake City
quick with his story of the first step
of a journey of a thousand years
in behalf
of the Test Ban Treaty, all journeys must
begin with a first step

(not counting on 42 days
to the unexpected grave)
'not to our size, but to our spirit'

And 'because' *alive* 'he knew the midnight
as well as the high noon'
the travellers stood chilling
to a parade of the first step
of might be that Chinese sage a thousand
years out of counting
a little more than a half-moon, dusk
a burial
poet old enough
to write it old enough history
like the horse who took part in it
shying from it, balking
despite himself

The fetlocks ankles of a ballerina
'Black Jack' Sardar with black-
hilted sword black dangled in silver scabbard from
the saddle riderless rider
his life looked back
into silver stirrups and the
reversed boots in them.
Finally a valentine
before his death
had he asked for it
I should have inscribed to him,
After reading, a song
for his death
after I had read at Adams House

John to John-John to Johnson

so the nation grieved
each as for someone in his or her family
we want Kennedy—
and the stock market fell and rose

on the fourth day
holy holy tetraktys
of the Pythagorean eternal flowing creation
and again without the senses TV
went back to its commercials
boots reversed flapping backward
and in another month
brought back the Indian's summer
'I was dreaming a high hole in rock
from which flowed the Seine
because that was how it looked
and was showing my father
of whom I rarely dream back to
its source when the doorbell
rang (the letter carrier, shocked sleep)
but your sheepsilver was here
a chunk of a summer's
Muscovy glass from the new film
The Glass Mountain'
almost Xmas—
and in less than another year
after 2000 years (a few less)
the dead's church
remembered not a moment too soon
to absolve the Jews of Yēshūa's (ah Jesu's)
cross—except for salvation

a smiling Gibbon's ground bass of a footnote
'spare them the pains of thinking'—
under the aspic of eternity
with the udder hand milking
the great Cow of Heaven—
Birjand, October five thousand nine hundred eleven
(an anagram)
'hawking with the Amir (like old Briton)
a covey of see-see, the little partridge rose
with a whistle disappeared round a bend
the falconer leading held on gloved hand
by thong to a leg-ring the bright hawk
not hooded straining for release
which came shortly—rose
and brought the see-see to earth
the hawk poised on the quarry
claws gripped its neck
plucking the feathers: the falconer came up
took the neck of the living see-see
with the left hand and its legs in his right
and with one pull dismembered it

and gave the legs to the waiting hawk.'

He could not think another
thing that evening
simply a life
had stepped in in place of theory. Then love, young Isaac
burning for Rebecca, a comfort
not all and scorned in Augustinè.

Eros agh nick hot hay mock on Eros us inked massy
  pipped eyes
now on th'heyday caught as thus mown

Dunk for the teeth that have rotted
(bread) soaked crust bare gums
glad car and cur bore the brunt of it
Woe woman woo woman
the fourth kingdom shall be as strong as iron
forasmuch as iron breaketh in pieces and
  subdueth all things
'perpetual violation of justice
. . maintained by . . political virtues
of prudence and courage . .
the rise of a city . . swelled into . . empire . .
may deserve . . reflection of . . philosophic mind
. . decline of Rome . . the
effect of immoderate greatness.
Prosperity ripened . . decay;
the causes of destruction multiplied with
  the extent of conquest,
and as soon as time or accident had removed
the artificial supports, the stupendous fabric
yielded to the pressure of its own weight . .
instead of inquiring
why the Roman empire was destroyed . .
should rather be surprised
. . it had subsisted so long.
The victorious legions, who, in distant wars,
acquired the vices of strangers and mercenaries,
first oppressed the freedom of the republic, and
afterwards violated . . the purple . .
emperors, anxious for . . personal safety
and . . public peace . . reduced to the
expedient of corrupting the discipline
. . and the Roman world was overwhelmed by a
deluge of barbarians . .

vain emulation of luxury, not of merit . .
Extreme distress, which unites the virtue
of a free people, embitters . . factions . .
As the happiness of a *future* life
is the great object of religion
we may hear without surprise
or scandal
that . . at least the abuse of Christianity
had some influence on the decline
and fall of the Roman empire.
The clergy successfully
preached the doctrines of patience and pusillanimity;
the active virtues of society were discouraged;
and the last remains of military
spirit were buried in the cloister:
a large portion of public and
private wealth . . consecrated . . charity and devotion;
and . . soldiers' pay . . lavished on useless
multitudes of both sexes who could only plead
the merits of abstinence and chastity . .
diverted from camps to synods . .
and the persecuted sects became
the secret enemies of their country . .
sacred indolence of monks was
devoutly embraced by a servile and effeminate age . .
Religious precepts are easily obeyed
which indulge and sanctify
the natural inclinations of their votaries . .
but the pure . . influence of Christianity
may be traced in its beneficial, though imperfect,
effects on the barbarian proselytes . .
This awful revolution may be
usefully applied to the instruction of the present
age . . The savage nations of the globe are the
common enemies of civilised society; and
we may inquire . . whether Europe is still
threatened with a repetition
of those calamities which formerly oppressed
the arms and institutions of Rome.
. . poor, voracious, and turbulent;
bold in arms and impatient
to ravish the fruits of industry . . The barbarian world
was agitated by the rapid impulse of war . .
the peace of Gaul or Italy was shaken
by the distant revolutions of China. . .
Cold, poverty, and a life of danger and fatigue
fortify the strength and courage of barbarians.
In every age . . oppressed

China, India and Persia,
who neglected, and still neglect
to counterbalance these natural powers
by the resources of military art . .
to command air and fire.
Mathematics, chemistry, mechanics,
architecture have been applied to the service of war;
and the adverse parties oppose to each other
the most elaborate modes of attack and defence.
Historians may indignantly observe
that the preparations of a siege
would found and maintain a flourishing colony;
yet we cannot be displeased that the
   subversion of a city
should be a work of cost and difficulty;
or that an industrious people
should be protected by those arts
which survive and supply the decay of military virtue . .
Europe is secure from any future irruption
of barbarians; since before they can conquer,
they must cease to be barbarous. . .
Should these speculations be found doubtful
or fallacious, there still remains a more
humble source of comfort and hope. . .
no people, unless the face of nature
is changed, will relapse into their original barbarism.
The improvements of society
may be viewed under a threefold aspect.

1. The poet or philosopher illustrates his age and
country by the efforts of a *single* mind;
but these superior powers of reason or fancy
are rare and spontaneous productions;
and the genius of Homer . . or Newton
would excite less admiration
if they could be created
by the will of . . a preceptor.
2. The benefits of law and policy of trade
and manufactures, of arts and sciences
are more solid and permanent;
and *many* individuals may be qualified,
by education and discipline,
to promote, in their respective stations,
the interest of the community.
But this general order is the effect of skill and labour;
and the complex machinery may be decayed by time,
or injured by violence.
3. Fortunately for mankind,
the more useful, or at least more necessary arts,

can be performed without superior talents
or national subordination;
without the powers of *one*,
or the union of the *many*.
Private genius and public industry may be extirpated . .
But the scythe, the invention
or emblem of Saturn,
still continued annually to mow
the harvests of Italy;
and the human feasts of the Laestrigons
have never been renewed
on the coast of Campania.'

No lady Rich is very poor
No, laid o rich is very poor

kneecheewoe—
marriageable
the first lady astronaut
returning to earth
bruised her nose.

The wives of the poets
flew higher.
And to show for it—
on the hill near town the little cemetery
that would be seen from the Erie?
—No eulogies, Louis,
no.
Perhaps to see where his friend's song
not too clear while one led his own
would *button into the*
rest of it
the life of the fugue of it
not come to talk
at the funeral.
The dog as the old friend lay dead
would not cross his threshold
he was not there anymore
his room not his room
what was there not
for the day to go into—
the estuary up the river—
later thruout the house he ruled
while the others were interring him
the friend left at home in it
hearing the other voice as *then*
'you have never

asked anyone anything'

and Nestor, 'Odysseus—where
did you get those horses
I have never set eyes on
horses like these'
and he who with his wife
deceived even pride as she suffered
'it is easy *for a god*
to bestow even better horses
than these'
. . bathed
and sat down to dine
ate thought
. . o poor . . away from all baths . .
Hecuba with bare breast
she once fed him
wailing,
and for still another—
Thetis
and the nymphs
Glaukë and Thaleia and Kumodokë
Nesaië and Speio, Thoë, Halië
Kumothoë and Actaië and Limnoreia
Melitë, Iaira, Amphitoë and Agauë
Doto and Proto, Pherousa and Dunamenë
Dexamenë and Amphinomë and Kallianeira
Doris and Panopë, Galateia
Nemertes and Apseudes and Kallianassa
Klumenë and Ianeira and Ianassa
Maira and Oreithuya and Amatheia
of the deepest bath

negritude no nearer or further
than the African violet
not deferred to
or if white, Job
white pods of *honesty*
satinflower

METATRANSLATION

George Quasha

Metatranslation is what results from fertilizing one's own poetic idiom with resources available only, or mainly, in another poet's work composed in another language. Actually the "translation" need not be from a foreign language, because in a deeper sense all poetry is translation in that it brings to the poet's language what was previously unsayable. Blake's prophetic poem *Milton* translates John Milton into a new and revolutionary language and consciousness; Ezra Pound reclaims lost resources of English in his translation of the Anglo-Saxon *Seafarer* and in his adaptation of those resources to his own purposes in *The Cantos;* in his "Shelley's *Arethusa* Set to New Measures" (in *Roots and Branches*) Robert Duncan reveals powers of the English poet which Shelley's technique had left obscure. Metatranslation brings to light new possibilities within the Mother Tongue—"new" because insufficiently noticed before. In some cases the translator's job is simple and unglamorous, because the work being translated has such clear powers that a literal version results in metapoetry; such a case is the work of Holderlin, though to point this out is not to undervalue the mastery of Michael Hamburger's renderings. In other cases the translator's job requires an act of language very close to the original act in its degree of inventiveness: a radical transposition, a structuring of one's own language according to the principles of another. Of this sort are the versions of tribal poetries by Rothenberg, Tedlock and Schwerner below. Rothenberg explains the meanings of what he calls "total" and "minimal" translation in his introduction and notes, and his list of parallels between the realities of tribal or oral poetry and certain contemporary tendencies indicates the importance of metatranslation to any presentation of metapoetry. It also tells us that metapoetry is metacultural and that it seeks an international language and a global community.

JEROME ROTHENBERG

Total and Minimal Translations of American Indian Poetry

From the Pre-Face to Technicians of the Sacred
New York 1967–1970

"Primitive" Means Complex

That there are no primitive languages is an axiom of contemporary linguistics where it turns its attention to the remote languages of the world. There are no half-formed languages, no underdeveloped languages. Everywhere a development has taken place into structures of great complexity. People who have failed to achieve the wheel will not have failed to invent and develop a highly wrought grammar. Hunters and gatherers innocent of all agriculture will have vocabularies that distinguish the things of their world down to the finest details. The language of snow among the Eskimos is awesome. The aspect system of Hopi verbs can, by a flick of the tongue, make the most subtle kinds of distinction between different types of motion.

What is true of language in general is equally true of poetry and of the ritual-systems of which so much poetry is a part. It is a question of energy and intelligence as universal constants and, in any specific case, the direction that energy and intelligence (= imagination) have been given. . . . Poetry, wherever you find it among the "primitives" (literally *everywhere*), involves an extremely complicated sense of materials and structures. Everywhere it involves the manipulation (fine or gross) of multiple elements. If this isn't always apparent, it's because the carry-over (by translation or interpretation) necessarily distorts where it chooses some part of the whole that it can meaningfully deal with. The work is foreign and its complexity is often elusive, a question of gestalt or configuration, of the angle from which the work is seen. . . .

It's very hard in fact to decide what precisely are the boundaries of "primitive" poetry or of a "primitive" poem, since there's often no activity differentiated as such, but the words and/or vocables are part of a larger total "work" that may go on for hours, even days, at a stretch. What we would separate as music and dance and myth and painting is also part of that work, and the need for separation is a question of "our" interest and preconceptions, not of "theirs." Thus the picture is immediately complicated by the nature of the work and the media that comprise it. And it becomes clear that the "collective" nature of primitive poetry (upon which so much stress has been placed despite the existence of individualized poems and clearly identified poets) is to a great degree inseparable from the amount of materials a single work may handle.

Now all of this is, if so stated, a question of technology as well as inspiration; and we may as well take it as axiomatic for what follows that where poetry is concerned, "primitive" means complex.

Primitive and Modern: Intersections and Analogues

Like any collector, my approach to delimiting and recognizing what's a poem has been by analogy: in this case (beyond the obvious definition of poems as words-of-songs) to the work of modern poets. Since much of this work has been revolutionary and limit-smashing, the analogy in turn expands the range of what "we" can see as primitive (i.e., tribal/oral) poetry: an expansion that can work equally well at the other end of the process, opening up new possibilities for our own work as well. It also shows some of the ways in which primitive poetry and thought are close to an impulse toward unity in our time, of which the poets are forerunners. The important intersections (analogies) are:

(1) the poem carried by the voice: a "pre"-literate situation of poetry composed to be spoken, chanted or, more accurately, sung; compare this to the "post-literate" situation, in McLuhan's good phrase, or where-we-are-today;

(2) a highly developed process of image-thinking: concrete or non-causal thought in contrast to the simplifications of Aristotelian logic, etc., with its "objective categories" & rules of non-contradiction; a "logic" of polarities; creation thru dream, etc.; modern poetry (having had & outlived the experience of rationalism) enters a post-logical phase;

(3) a "minimal" art of maximal involvement; compound elements, each clearly articulated, & with plenty of room for fill-in (gaps in sequence, etc.): the "spectator" as (ritual) participant who pulls it all together;

(4) an "intermedia" situation, as further denial of the categories: the poet's techniques aren't limited to verbal maneuvers but operate also through song, non-verbal sound, visual signs, & the varied activities of the ritual event: here the "poem" = the work of the "poet" in whatever medium, or (where we're able to grasp it) the totality of the work;

(5) the animal-body-rootedness of "primitive" poetry: recognition of a

written poem as score
public readings

poets' theaters
jazz poetry

1960s folk-rock etc

Blake's multi-images
symbolisme
surrealism

deep-image

random poetry
composition by field etc

concrete poetry

picture poems
prose poems

happenings
total theater

poets as film-makers etc

dada
lantgedichte (sound poems)

"physical" basis for the poem within a man's body—or as an act of body & mind together, breath &/or spirit; in many cases too the direct & open handling of sexual imagery & (in the "events") of sexual activities as key factors in creation of the sacred;

(6) the poet as shaman, or primitive shaman as poet & seer thru control of the means just stated: an open "visionary" situation prior to all system-making ("priesthood") in which the man creates thru dream (image) & word (song), "that Reason may have ideas to build on" (W. Blake).

beast language

line & breath
projective verse etc

sexual revolution etc

Rimbaud's voyant
Rilke's angel
Lorca's duende

beat poetry
psychedelic see-in's, be-in's, etc

individual neo-shamanisms, etc works directly influenced by the "other" poetry or by analogies to "primitive art": ideas of negritude, tribalism, wilderness, etc.

What's more, the translations themselves may create new forms and shapes-of-poems with their own energies and interest—another intersection that can't be overlooked.

Postscript to Pre-Face, and Translation as Invention

More recently I've been able to work with some of the American Indian materials in particular at closer range, moving towards a collaboration with songmen and others who could open the languages to me—and the closer one gets the more pressing becomes the problem of how to understand and translate the *sound* of the originals. It now seems possible to do it, to get at those "meanings" which are more than the meaning-of-the-words; possible and desirable too, for the greatest secret these poems still hold is in the actual relation between the words, the music, the dance, and the events, a relation which many among us have been trying to get at in our own work. Every new translation (partial, minimal or total) is the uncovering of a hidden form in the language of the translator, but at the same time the rediscovery of universal patterns that can be realized by any man still willing to explore them. . . .

Translation is carry-over. It is a means of delivery and of bringing to life. It begins with a forced change of language, but a change too that opens up the possibility of greater understanding. Everything in these complex oral poetries is finally translatable: words, sounds, voice, melody, gesture, event, etc., in the reconstitution of a unity that would be shattered by approaching each element in isolation. A full and total experience begins it, which only a total translation can fully bring across.

By saying which I'm not trying to coerce anyone (least of all myself) with the idea of a single relevant approach to translation. Even after my own experience of the Navajo horse-songs, say (for which see below), I'll continue, I believe, to translate in part or in any other way I feel moved to; nor would I deny the value of translating or transposing words or music or events or images as separate phenomena. It's possible too that a prose description of a song-poem, etc., might tell pretty much what was happening in and around the original situation, but no amount of description can provide the *immediate* perception translation can. One way or other translation makes a poem in this place that's analogous in whole or in part to a poem in that place. The more the translator can perceive of the original—not only the language but, more basically perhaps, the living situation from which it comes and, very much so, the living voice, etc., of the performer—the more of it he should be able to deliver. In the same process he will be presenting something—i.e., making something present, or making something as a present—an expansion or invention for his own time and place.

Shaking the Pumpkin: Some Songs from the Society of the Mystic Animals, Translated by Jerome Rothenberg with the Assistance of Richard Johnny John (Seneca Indian)

A Song about a Dead Person—or Was It a Mole?

YOHOHEYHEYEYHEYHAHYEYEYHAHHEH
I was going thru the big earth
YOHOHEYHEYEYHEYHAHYEYEYHAHHEH
I went thru this big earth
YOHOHEYHEYEYHEYHAHYEYEYHAHHEH
I was going thru the big earth
YOHOHEYHEYEYHEYHAHYEYEYHAHHEH
I went thru this big earth
YOHOHEYHEYEYHEYHAHYEYEYHAHHEH
I was going thru the big earth
YOHOHEYHEYEYHEYHAHYEYEYHAHHEH
I went thru this big earth
YOHOHEYHEYEYHEYHAHYEYEYHAHHEH
I was goin
YOHOHEYHEYEYHEYHAHYEYEYHAHHEH
g earth
YOHOHEYHEYEYHEYHAHYEYEYHAHHEH

YOHOHEYHEYEYHEYHAHYEYEYHAHHEH

YOHOHEYHEYEYHEYHAHYEYEYHAHHEH

Where the Song Went Where She Went & What Happened When They Met

the song went to the garden	(heh heh heh)
the song poked all around the garden	(heh heh heh)
she went to the garden	(heh heh heh)
she went to the garden	(heh heh heh)
she went like crazy in the garden	(heh heh heh)
that's where she went	(hah hah hah)

A Note on the Selections from "Shaking the Pumpkin"

Minimal poetry. Extensive use of a restricted number of non-semantic vocables. Words few & far between. Traditional sacred poetry with a strong play element, especially where used for renewal rather than curing—or, as Seneca singer Richard Johnny John explains it: ". . . but if everything's all right the one who says the prayer tells them: I leave it up to you folks & if you want to have a good time, have a good time!" Oral elements translated by visual (paginal) equivalents. To read sounds aloud, follow your own play-principle to wherever it takes you.

J.R.

Booger Event

Participants

A company of four to ten or more masked men (called "boogers"), occasionally a couple of women companions. Each dancer is given a personal name, usually obscene; for example:

Black Man	Swollen Pussy
Black Ass	Long Prick
Frenchie	Sweet Prick
Big Balls	Piercer
Asshole	Fat Ass
Rusty Asshole	Long Haired Pussy
Burster (penis)	Et cetera.

Prelude

The dancers enter. The audience & the dancers break wind.

First Action

The masked men are systematically malignant. They act mad, fall on the floor, hit at the spectators, push the men spectators as though to get at their wives & daughters, etc.

Second Action

The boogers demand "girls." They may also try to fight & dance. If they do, the audience tries to divert them.

Third Action

Booger Dance Song. The name given to the booger should be taken as the first word of the song. This is repeated any number of times, while the owner of the name dances a solo, performing as awkward and grotesque steps as he possibly can. The audience applauds each mention of the name, while the other dancers indulge in exhibitionism, e.g., thrusting their buttocks out & occasionally displaying toward the women in the audience large phalli concealed under their clothing. These phalli may contain water, which is then released as a spray.

Interlude

Everyone smokes.

Fourth Action

A number of women dancers, equaling the number of boogers, enter the line as partners. As soon as they do, the boogers begin their sexual exhibitions. They may close upon the women from the rear, performing body motions in pseudo-intercourse; as before, some may protrude their large phalli & thrust these toward their partners with appropriate gestures & body motions.

Postlude

The rest of the performance consists of miscellaneous events chosen by the audience.

(Cherokee Indian)

Three Midē Songs & Picture-Songs

(1st Set)

An Imploration for Clear Weather

I swing the spirit like a child

The sky is what I was telling you about

We have lost the sky

I am helping you

I depend on the clear sky

I give you the-other-village, spirit that you are

The thunder is heavy

We are talking to each other

Have I made an error?

(Silence)

I am using my heart

What are you saying to me & am I in-my-senses?

The spirit wolf

I didn't know where I was going

The Eleventh Horse-Song of Frank Mitchell (White)

Key: wnn Ngahn n NNN

Some are holy ones N wnn & some are holy & some are ones nahht wnn N nnnn N gahn
Some are holy ones N wnn & some are holy & some are ones nahht wnn N nnnn N gahn

Because I was thnboyyingside the dawn & holy & some are holy ones nahht wnn N nnnn N gahn
& leafing from theeyouse the whiteshell home & holy & some are holy ones nahht wnn N nnnn N gahn
& leafing from theeyouse the darknnd home & holy & some are holy ones nahht wnn N nnnn N gahn
& leafing from the swullhnhouse my breath has blun & holy & some are holy ones nahht wnn N nnnn N gahn
& leafing from theeyouse huhlowly home & wholly some are ones & holy nahht wnn N nnnn N gahn
& from theeyouse of jewels we walk (p)pon & holy & some are holy ones nahht wnn N nnnn N gahn
with (pn)p(rayersticks) that are white & holy & some are holy ones N wnn N hoooly wnnn N gwing
with my feathers that 're white & holy & some are holy ones nahht wnn N nnnn Ngahn
with my spirit horses that 're white & holy & some are holy ones nahht wnn N nnnn N gahn
with my spirit horses that rur white & dawn & holy then some are holy ones N wnn nahht nnn N gahn
with my spirit howanorses that rur whiteshell & R holy some were holy ones N wnn N nnnn naht gahn
with my horses that hrr whiteshell & rholy & some were holy ones nahht wnn N nnnn N gahn
with jewels of evree(ee)ee kind to draw (nn nn) them on & holy & some are holy ones nahht wnn N nnnn N gahn
with cloth of evree(ee)ee kind to draw (nn nn) them on & holy & some are holy ones nahht wnn N nnnn N gahn
with sheep of evree(ee)ee kind to draw (nn nn) them on & holy & some are holy ones nahht wnn N nnnn N gahn
with horses of ever(ee)ee kind to draw (nn nn) them on & holy & some are holy ones nahht wnn N nnnn N gahn
with cattle of evree(ee)ee kind to draw (nn nn) them on & to be holy & some are holy ones naht wnn N nnnn N gahn
with men of ever(ee)ee kind to lead N draw (nn nn) them on & holy & some are holy ones nahht wnn N nnnn N gahn

from my youse of precious jewels to her backackeroom & being
   holy some were holy ones nahht wnn N nnnn N gahn
in her house of precious jewels we walk (p)pon & being holy
   some were holy ones naht wnn N nnnn N gahn
vvvevrything that's gone beffore M more we walk (f)fon & being
   holy some were holy ones nahht wnn N nnnn N gahn
& everything that's more & won't be(be!)be poor & wholly gone &
   some are holy ones nahht wnn N nnnn N gahn
& efreedthing that's living to be old (b)b(b)blesst & holy &
   some are holy ones nahht wnn N nnnn N gahn
because I am thm boy who blesses/blisses to be old N gahn N
   holy & some are holy ones nahht wnn N nnnn N gahn

Some are holy ones N wnn & some are holy & some are ones nahht
   wnn N nnnn N gahn
Some are holy ones N wnn & some are holy & some are ones naht
   wnn N nnnn N gahn

Commentary on the 11th Horse-song of Frank Mitchell, As Notes on the Process of Total Translation

The poem as presented here is the score of my almost final working of the first of 17 "horse-songs" in the blessingway of Frank Mitchell (1881–1967) of Chinle, Arizona. Their power, as with most Navajo poetry, is directed toward blessing and curing, but in the course of it they also depict the stages by which Enemy Slayer, on instructions from his mother Changing Woman, goes to the house of his father The Sun, to receive and bring back horses for The People. The first horse-song marks the point in the narrative where Enemy Slayer asserts the existence of the horses and his own claim to them.

With aid and guidance from David McAllester I've been attempting total translations of all 17 horse-songs, accounting not only for meaning but for word distortions, meaningless syllables, music, style of performance, et cetera; and, since translation is at no point mere reproduction, even the music isn't free from changes. The idea never was to set English words to Navajo music but to let a whole work emerge newly in the process of considering what kinds of statement were there to begin with. As far as I could I also wanted to avoid "writing" the poem in English, since this seemed irrelevant to a poetry that reached a high development outside of any written system.

Under the best of circumstances translation-for-meaning is no more than partial translation. Even more so for the densely textured Navajo. To present what's essentially a sound-poem, a *total* translation from Navajo must distort words in a manner analogous to the original; it must match "meaningless" syllables with equivalents in our very different English soundings; it may begin to sing in a mode suitable to the words of the translation; and if the original provides for more than one voice, the translation will also. Does in fact in the final recorded version as I come to it.

In all this what matters to me most as a poet is that the process has been a very natural one of extending the poetry into new areas of sound. Nor do I think of the result as poetry plus something else, but as *all* poetry, *all* poet's work, just as the Navajo is all poetry, where poetry and music haven't suffered separation. In that sense Frank Mitchell's gift has taken me a small way towards a new "total poetry," as well as an experiment in total translation. And that, after all, is where many of us had been heading in the first place.

—Jerome Rothenberg
1969/1970

ZUNI/DENNIS TEDLOCK

for Jerome Rothenberg

I
Liquid, Water

water in a shallow container
    honey
collection of water
    in water, floating
water on the surface
    lake, puddle
water on the surface coming out
    spring
    woman
sour water
    beer
    vinegar
water removed from a deep container
    whip
become water
    melt
water with a hot taste
    whiskey
    bilious phlegm
get water with a hot taste
    sick with an upset stomach

II
Grains

grainy pants
    bluejeans
grainy jacket
    bluejean jacket
salty grains
    salt
sweet grains
    sugar
collection of grainy water
    Zuni Salt Lake
toward the collection of grainy water
    south

III
Moon, Month

what belongs to moon
    moonlight
instrument for what belongs to moon
    moon

IV
Daylight

instrument for daylight
    sun
    clock

V
Two

multiplied with two
    twice
two tens
    twenty
coin of two
    quarter-dollar
two hearts
    witch

VI
On Top

cause to be on top
    put on top
    bewitch
    (placing victim's lock of hair
    piece of clothing
    on top of a tree or bluff)

VII
Angular Projections

(like the corners of a gunnysack)
like a witch
(a witch's hair projects
in two angular bunches
on each side of the head)
good angular projections
    something perfectly square

VIII
Hollow Tube

hollow tube making rattling sounds
    empty-headed person
become a hollow tube
    faint, forget

IX
Dance

cause to dance
    sponsor in a dance
    bounce a child on the lap
    spin a top

X
Wickerwork

growing bunch of wickerwork
    pine needles
static wickerwork
    paper
make static wickerwork
    attend school
wickerwork together on the ground
    in single file

XI
Stand

cause to stand
    stop
cause oneself not to stand
    run
stand together on the ground
    be a village

XII
Old

old ones
    parents
terrestrial old one
    dwelling-place of a deity
indeterminate old one
    calm, passive, quiet, shy
inconspicuous

old person
    man, man of the house, husband

XIII
Become Blue, Become Green

one who is black and blue with bruises
one who is blue from the cold
valuable blue, valuable green
    turquoise
    blue corn

XIV
Become Light, Become White

terrestrial light
    daylight
    life
cause to be light
    see
    make visible
valuable light
    white corn
    white shell necklace

AMAZON/ARMAND SCHWERNER
The Bird Tamurupara

will you dance with me
Tamurupara

I've been in your place
for a long time
Tamurupara

I'm looking for you
Tamurupara

will you give me
your spirit
Tamurupara

where is your spirit
in your loincloth
Tamurupara?

I'll give you your spirit back
since you asked me for it
Tamurupara

when I die
give them news about me
in my village
Tamurupara

HANS ARP/GEORGE QUASHA

Is It So It's Shriveling Up

Freely transposed from the French

is it so it's shriveling up
it's so it must be shriveling up
start up softly being vigilant
shroud that village up over the other

whatever I do
it ain't shriveling
it's easy to say
it's so it has to start shriveling up
it's so that that ain't shriveling
start up all over
so soft-shoe rivals saint's wings
living in villa-less villadom
so it sometimes toe-dances
half a giraffe unraveling
in half-slip showing thru
so sometimes it rolls
a tear in bounds
on in animate napkins
but it just ain't shriveling up

so call out the shroud-bearers
with their nuptial harps
call up the local snively shrimps
and say bring us your hairy candelabras
it's started sneezing now
just like a hemisphere buried in neckties
it's started giggling now
like a nigger equator all decked out
it's started up snoring now
like a heart in a gullet of glass
but it just ain't shriveling up

saintly sidereal acorn-barnacles
holy hoop of honey
holy ball
headless and tailless
it's so it must be shriveling up

FRIEDRICH HÖLDERLIN/MICHAEL HAMBURGER

Two Fragments from His "Madness"

Translated from the German

A Note on the Modernity of His Schizophrenia

It is interesting, and disturbing, to reflect that it is in the poems and fragments written when his schizophrenia was passing into its final phase that Hölderlin strikes us as most "modern." Often the modernity lies in his reliance on particulars, the mere invocation of a person or thing, where more conventional poets would have felt (and still feel) obliged to present a sequence of arguments or metaphors. In the later versions of the hymns there are instances not only of inverted or deliberately ambiguous syntax but of asyntactic one-word sentences that serve as a poetic shorthand. The poem proceeds by flashes of perception or allusion, true to the laws not of argument but of pre-articulate feeling and thought. In many cases it may well be that Hölderlin was only drafting poems which he was no longer capable of working out; yet even a sketch like the following seems to prefigure the kind of association practised by twentieth-century innovators, such as Mr. Ezra Pound in the *Cantos*. . . .

The resemblances are partly fortuitous, mainly because Hölderlin's lines are only nuclei of an unwritten poem; but there is something about the quality of his historical imagination here that seems more characteristic of our time than of his. One thinks of his words in the letter to Böhlendorff about "all the holy places of the earth coming together around one place," and the endeavour of a single imagination, a single consciousness, to embrace them all:

So Mahommed,* Rinaldo,
Barbarossa, as a liberal spirit,
The Emperor Heinrich.
But we are mixing up
the periods
                    Demetrius Poliorcetes
Peter the Great
                              Heinrich's
crossing of the Alps, and that
with his own hand he gave the people food
and drink and his son Conrad died of poison
Example of one who changes an age
reformer
Conradin etc.
all as representative
of conditions.

* Hear the horn of the watchman by night
After midnight it is at the fifth hour.

Patmos

Fragment of a Late Version

O island of light!
For when extinguished is fame, the delight in seeing, and no longer maintained
By human kind, shadowless, the paths succumb to doubt, and the trees,
And kingdoms, the youthful land of eyes, are perished,
More athletic
In ruin,   and inborn innocence
Is torn to shreds. For from God unalloyed
Does conscience come and go, revelation, the hand of the Lord
Richly beckons from judging Heaven, then and for a time there
Is indivisible law, and office, and hands to
Be raised, both this and to control
The falling of evil thoughts, loose. For cruelly
God hates omniscient brows. But pure
On a site unbound did John remain. When someone
Declares that a prophetic word is earthly

PAUL KLEE/ANSELM HOLLO

Irrational Speech and other poems

Translated from the German

Irrational Speech

1901

1

A good catch is great consolation.

2

Even this year, infamy
stalks me!

3

I must be saved.
By succeeding?

4

Has inspiration
eyes, or does she
walk in her sleep?

5

At times, my hands
do fold;
but right there, beneath them,
my belly
goes on digesting, my kidneys
filtering their clear juices. . . .

6

To love music
more than anything, that
is unhappiness.

7

Twelve fishes,
twelve murders.

Individuality

1905

Individuality?
is not of the substance of elements.
It is an organism, indivisibly
occupied
by elementary objects of a divergent character:
if you
were to attempt division, these parts
would die.

Myself,
for instance: an entire dramatic company.

Enter an ancestor, prophetic;
enter a hero, brutal
a rake, alcoholic, to argue
with a learned professor.
A lyrical beauty, rolling her eyes
heavenward, a case
of chronic infatuation—
enter a heavy father,
to take care of that,
enter a liberal uncle—to arbitrate. . . .
Aunt Chatterbox gossiping in a corner.
Chambermaid Lewdie, giggling.

And I, watching it all,
astonishment in my eyes.
Poised, in my left hand
a sharpened pencil.

A pregnant woman!, a mother
is planning
her
entrance—
Shushhh! you
don't belong here
you
are divisible!
She fades.

The Rescue

1905

Bound for
destruction?
Perhaps,
but then, I have
this knack
of saving myself,
in the nick
of time, time
and again.

I don't want to
be overgrown
by anything.
Though I would like
to have the experience.

I just don't want to.
Surely,
I must be saved.

Poem

1906

Water
Waves on the water
A boat on the waves
On the boat-deck, a woman
On the woman, a man.

Poem

The big animals: despondent
at table: unsated.

But the small cunning flies
scrambling up slopes of bread
inherit Buttertown.

•

There is
only one
true thing:

in the self
a weight,
a small
stone.

•

An eye
that sees.
Another eye
that feels.

•

Man-Animal:
Clock of Blood.

A Friend

1914

Notes
from afar,
a friend,
soon in the morning, behind the mountain.
Sound of horns.
Emeralds.

I am summoned
by cerebral
message, a promise, an abstract
embrace of minds, surmising
each other.

We were joined
by a star, by an eye
that found us out.
Two I's,
a content,
it is more than the vessel.

Yesterday's holy
stones, shorn of their riddle.
Today
there is meaning:

"A friend, soon in the morning, behind the mountain."

The Wolf Speaks

1926

The wolf speaks, while masticating
a man, addressing himself
to the dogs:

Tell me, where, then, is—
tell me, where?
then, is their god?
Where is their god? after this. . . .

Here you can see him
in the dust at your feet, the god
of the dogs

To see and to know
is one, is
that who has been torn by me
is no god!

Where, then, is
their god?

Caught

1926

Caught in a room.
Great peril.
No exit.

But there: a window: open: launch
Yourself—I am flying
Free

But it is raining
A drizzle
It is raining, a drizzle
It is raining
raining
raining . . .
raining. . . .

HENRI MICHAUX/ARMAND SCHWERNER

Tomorrow

1929
Adapted from the French

when the mar
                    when the mar
                                        the marshymorasswamps
the maledictions
when the mahahahahas
the mahahatorrors
the mahagonorrhyphilohahas
the matratrimatratrihahas
the rancywitherwatcheries
the bungholecockroachogrebuggers
the carbofecalfungorators of pus-y pissy pus-y
the voyeurisibled putrocephalics
the fat the plagues the maggofactions
the necroses the carnages the engulpings
the viscid the snuffed-out the foul
when the honey become stony
the icebergs leaking blood
the maddened Jews precipitously ransoming Christ
the Acropolis
the barracks turned into cabbages
the glances into bats or mailboxes
fresh hands into eagres
other vertebrae made of windmills
joyjuice shifting to burns
caresses into twinging ravages
the best articulated organs into saberduels
the sand with its russet caress into lead to crush sunbathers
the tepid tongues, passionate promenaders, changing themselves into knives or rocks
the exquisite sound of coursing rivers into forests of parrots or piledrivers
when the *Implacable-Indescribable* will sit his 1000 foetid buttocks on this
                closed
                concentred
                nailhung
                                        World
    turning, turning in
        upon himself without hope of escape
when anguish, last
        twig of Being, atrocious point,
        will alone survive, growing in fragility,
        sharper and increasingly intolerable
                                        and the
        obdurate Nothing all around
        drawing back like panic

Oh

Misery

oh
final memory
minute life of each man
tiny life of every animal
little
punctiform
lives

never again

Oh emptiness
space, unstratified

space

Space

Space

RAINER MARIA RILKE/GEORGE QUASHA

The Ninth Elegy Transposed

(for george oppen)

Why
when the curve
of Being begins to be
borne away
as a laurel, a
little darker than all
other green, with tiny
waves on every
leafedge (like a
wind's smiling)—
:why be
forced into humanness—and
shunning Destiny
long for Destiny? . . .

•

Oh not because Happiness
exists, those
premature profits of forthcoming loss.
Not from curiosity, nor
to exercise the heart—that also
could *BE* in the laurel . . .
But because to be here is so much, and because
it seems to us that the
Here and Now is in need of us, this
shrinking place that
strangely involves us.
Us, the shrinking. Once
only, just once. Once and no more. And we also
once. Never again. But this
once having *Been*, though only this once:
to have been *OF THE EARTH*—seems
incontrovertible

•

And so we
urge on, half-
willing it fulfilled,
or held with our simple hands,
within the glutted gaze and the
speechless heart.

Half-willing ourselves to become it.
To give it
to whom? Best to
hold on to it all forever . . . but oh! in other relations
alas! what can be taken across? Not this
mode of Seeing, that here,
slowly, is learned, nor anything
that happens here. Nothing.
The sufferings, then. Above all, the hardness
of being, and so: love's long training—and
so: purely untellable things. But later,
under the stars . . . what then . . . : *they*
are *more* untellable . . .

Still the wanderer brings forth from the brink
sloping thru mountains
no handfull of Earth
into the valley—not the
wholly untellable—but
a hard-won word, pure, the yellow and blue
gentian.
Are we perhaps *here*
in order to say: House,
Bridge, Fountain, Gate, Jug, Olive Tree, Window,—
at the utmost: Pillar, Tower . . .
but to *say*, oh know that to
say *even* as the things themselves inwardly
never meant to be . . .
Is it not the secret cunning
of this reticent Earth, as she
urges the lovers, that each,
within his sensing, enrapture himself
within the other?
Threshold: what is it for two
lovers, that they wear away
some of their own
ancient door of the threshold,
they too, as the many before,
and before the many coming . . . , freely

•

Here is the Time of the *Tellable*,
here is its home.
Speak

and admit. More than ever
Things
are falling away,
the liveable,
falling away from us, for this
plucking them out that takes
their place is
an act
without image.
Act under crusts, that willingly split
apart as soon as the
acting-out within
outgrows its shells
and sets itself
new outlines.
In
between the hammers our
heart holds on, and the tongue
between the teeth, that, still,
through all of it, in praising,
persists

•

Praise the world to the Angel,
not the untellable: to *him*
you can't brag about your glorious feelings;
in the cosmos
where he more feelingly feels,
you are a novice.
So show him
simple things, that
shaped
by generation upon generation,
lives as Ours
within the hand's reach and within
our looking out.
Tell him
things. He'll stand
more astounded,
as you stood
by the roper in Rome, or the potter on the Nile.
Show him how a thing can be happy, how
innocent and ours,
how moaning grief itself purely

decides on form, serves
as a thing, or dies
into a thing,—
and blissfully escapes
that trivia. And these things that live
on departure
understand that you praise them: fleeting
they rescue themselves in us   the most
fleeting.   Want us, in our invisible
hearts, to
transform them utterly
into—oh endlessly!—into
ourselves
whoever we also are in the end

•

Earth, isn't this it, isn't it this you want:
invisible
to arise in us?
Isn't it your dream
once   to be invisible?—Earth!   Invisible!
what, if not transformation, does your urging
command? Earth, beloved, I will! Oh, believe me, you need
your springs no more to win me—one,
one alone is more than the blood can bear.
Nameless
for years   I have been determined   yours
: you who dwell always within
the Right, whose holiest
invasion is intimate
Death.   Look!
I am living!
On what?
Neither childhood nor future are
growing less . . .
Supernumerous being
springs up in my heart

CÉSAR VALLEJO/CLAYTON ESHLEMAN

Telluric and Magnetic

from Poemas Humanos
Translated from the Spanish

Sincere and very Peruvian mechanics
our lady of the red-rutted hill!
Ground theoretical *and* practical!
Intelligent furrows; for instance: the monolith and his court!
Potatofields barleyfields lucernefields, great!
Cultivations that integrate an astonishing hierarchy of tools,
that integrate with wind the lowings,
the waters with their deaf antiquity!

Quaternary maize from opposite births
I hear through my feet how you withdraw,
I smell you return when earth comes
up against the technique of sky!
Crazed molecule! Terse atom! O

human fields!
Sunswept nutritious absence of the sea,
oceanic sentiment about everything!
O climates met inside gold, kinetic!
O intellectual field of cordillera
with religion, with country, with baby ducks!
Pachyderms in prose when they pass
poetry when they halt!
Rodents peering with judicial feeling all around!
O patriotic asses of my life!
Vicuña, national and graceful descendant of my ape!

O light hardly a mirror distant from the shadow
that is life with the point and in lineage dust
and for this I bow, rising through the idea to my skeleton!

Harvest in season of the dilated peppertree,
of the lantern they held up to a man's temple
and of the one they unhooked from that magnificent bar!
Cooped angels,
birds by the slip of a cockscomb!
Guinea-pigess or -pig to be eaten fried
with the burning tomato pepper of the temples!
(Condors? I'm fed up with these fucking condors!)
Christian logs by the grace

of a happy trunk and competent branch!
Relative of the lichen,
species in basalt formation that I
respect
from this most modest paper!
Reading writing arithmetic, I subtract you out
to save the blockhead and plant him straight!
You're worth in flagrante!
Wet-eyed auchenia, souls of my soul!
Sierra of my Peru, Peru of the world
and Peru at the foot of the earth; I cleave to myself!
Morning stars if I perfume you
burning coca leaves in this skull,
zeniths if I unveil
with a single doff my ten temples!
Arm made for sowing, get down, and on foot!
Rain based on noon
under the tile roof where indefatigable
altitude gnaws
and the turtledove files in threes her trill.
Rotation of modern evenings
and delicate archaeological dawns.
Indian after man and before him!
I understand it all on two flutes
and I make myself understood on a quena!
The rest they peel off my balls! . . .

KING DAVID/HAROLD DICKER

The Nineteenth Psalm

April 5, 1963

expound by day
grasp glories of God's words
explain by night

work with words
grip glories of His language
without speech no sky

no words no earth
no tracks of a chariot sun
no moon

no cool moonlight
only rails of holy ribaldries
no holy light

the law is clear
the soul holds perfection
the law sure

the law right
the heart stores its honey
the law pure

the law clean
candles of honeystained desire
the law fine

therefore our evil
and therefore the furnace heat
the innocence

therefore the mouths of heaven
and therefore the verses freed from Egypt
and the horn of God

and the tinkling mouths
and the strings and cymbals of heaven
and the light

the light

the light

LANGUAGE HAPPENINGS

EDITED BY

Emmett Williams

INTRODUCTION: WARNING
Emmett Williams

Casting aside the wisdom of experience, and the game of categories, I have put all my eggs in one basket. What started out as two independent and unrelated sections of an anthology of "expanded poetry," one for the Concrete poets and one for the Intermedialists, has shrunk to a single omniumgatherum called "language happenings." The result is smaller in size than the sum of the original parts, and, not surprising, wider in scope. But what *is* surprising is that the focus is sharper. Could anything less than chaos have been expected to follow after scattering the Concrete poets, with their rage for order, throughout the "uncharted land" of Intermedia?

Of course. They have belonged together all along. They have been separated from one another by definitions, manifestoes and self-imposed distances. The game of categories. Though their intentions and their commitments to art and life are worlds apart, how short a journey it is, poet to poet, from the Constellations of Eugen Gomringer, "father" of Concrete poetry, to the "Raining" scenario of Allan Kaprow, who gave the name to Happenings.

"Language happenings" is a title, nothing more, under whose aegis a number of workers with words are allowed to coexist without labels. All of them are involved in a new Poetics in which poetry is scurrying off the page in all directions at once—toward painting, film, theater, music, sculpture and concept art. And artists, film-makers, composers and scientists are bringing their talent and technology to bear on the new poetry. A small part of all this activity—a part that can adequately take place in book format—is exhibited in "language happenings."

I have pruned from the Concrete poets many familiar "picture poems," and for this crime I shall certainly be charged in those quarters where Concrete poetry is simply "a return to the poem as picture" with downright iconoclasm. My only defense is that picture poems are only part of the picture and that they have made a very good showing elsewhere.* But the Intermedialists have suffered the most from pruning. I have quite arbitrarily chosen to exclude, with several exceptions, three-dimensional works and performance pieces to keep the section *readable*. A compromise, and a serious one. But as far as the Intermedialists

---

* *An Anthology of Concrete Poetry*, edited by Emmett Williams, Something Else Press, New York, 1967.

Anthology of Concretism, edited by Eugene Wildman, Swallow Press, Chicago, 1967.

Concrete Poetry: An International Anthology, edited by Stephen Bann, London Magazine Editions, London, 1967.

Concrete Poetry: A World View, edited by Mary Ellen Solt, Indiana University Press, Bloomington, 1968.

Imaged Words and Worded Images, edited by Richard Kostelanetz, Outerbridge and Dienstfrey, New York, 1970

are concerned, the Book has outgrown its usefulness as a receptacle for their multimedia endeavors. Reading about *their* art is like talking about love-making.

Where possible the poets have been allowed to talk about their own work, and lexical keys have been provided for some foreign works. But it remains the wish of the editor to exhibit the works without labels and to let the "language happenings" happen as they may.

GEORGE BRECHT

George Brecht's own description of his *Book of the Tumbler on Fire* serves as a good introduction to the six exhibits, events and exercises that follow: ". . . a research into the continuity of un-like things; of objects with each other, of objects and events, of scores and objects, of events in time, of objects and styles, etc."

TWO EXERCISES

Consider an object. Call what is not the object "other."

EXERCISE: Add to the object, from the "other," another object, to form a new object and a new "other."
Repeat until there is no more "other."

EXERCISE: Take a part from the object and add it to the "other," to form a new object and a new "other."
Repeat until there is no more object.

SIX EXHIBITS

- ceiling
- first wall
- second wall
- third wall
- fourth wall
- floor

TABLE

- on a white table

  glasses, a puzzle

  and

  (having to do with smoking)

FIVE EVENTS

- eating with
- between two breaths
- sleep
- wet hand
- several words

THREE BROOM EVENTS

- broom
- sweeping
- broom sweepings

INSTRUCTION

- Turn on a radio.

  At the first sound, turn it off.

CLAUS BREMER

1958

Consonants and vowels of the word-material *(lichtfänge bahnen die sonne!)* are separated into lines that radiate from the "sun" and explode at the core of the construction into reverse mirror images.

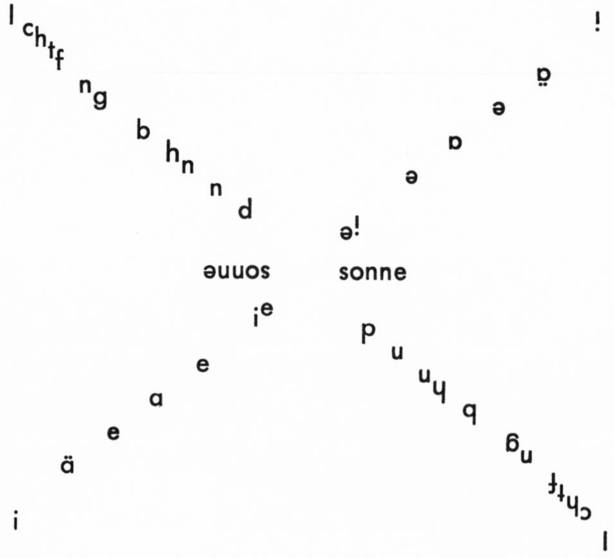

1966

"These are not engaging texts," Bremer writes of the collection *engagierende texte*, from which this poem is reprinted, "they are engaged texts." The word material is arranged in what Bremer calls a "star-shaped construction" but which looks and acts more like a pinwheel. To understand the organization of the poem Bremer asks the reader to move "either the poem or himself. The text reveals its word-play only to those who examine the subject . . . from all sides."

```
to inform
to infor
to info
to inf
to in
to i
to
to
t

not merely
not merely
not merely
not merely
not merely
not merely
not merely
not merely
not merely
not merely
not merely
not merely
not merely
not merely
not merel
not mere
not mer
not me
not m
not
not
no
n

to provoke
 to provoke
  to provoke
   to provoke
    to provoke
     to provoke
      to provoke
       to provoke
        to provoke
         to provoke
o provoke
 provoke
provoke
rovoke
ovoke
voke
oke
ke
e

attitudes
attitude
attitud
attitu
attit
atti
att
at
```

from Engaged Texts
1964

In the original the question reads: *ist der text der text der ausbleibt.* The blank space, a consequence of the structure of the poem, is what the poem is all about, and in it resides the answer—or is it the question? It is certainly not a simple operation, and it calls into doubt all our preconceptions about "text."

```
is the text the text left out
 is the tex  he text left out
  is the te   e text left out
   is the t     text left out
    is the      text left out
     is the      ext left out
      is th       xt left out
       is t        t left out
        is           left out
         is          left out
          i           eft out
                       ft out
           t            t out
           th             out
           the            out
           the             ut
           the t            t
           the te
           the tex           t
           the text          xt
           the text          ext
           the text l        text
           the text le        text
           the text lef      e text
           the text left     he text
           the text left     the text
           the text left o    the text
           the text left ou  s the text
           the text left out is the text
```

from Engaged Texts
1964

The superimposition of letters and words for strategic purposes is found often in Bremer's work. In this poem, the method is used "to arouse curiosity, to reveal something, and then to become obscure again; to arouse the reader's curiosity, to reveal something to him, and then to confront him with himself again."

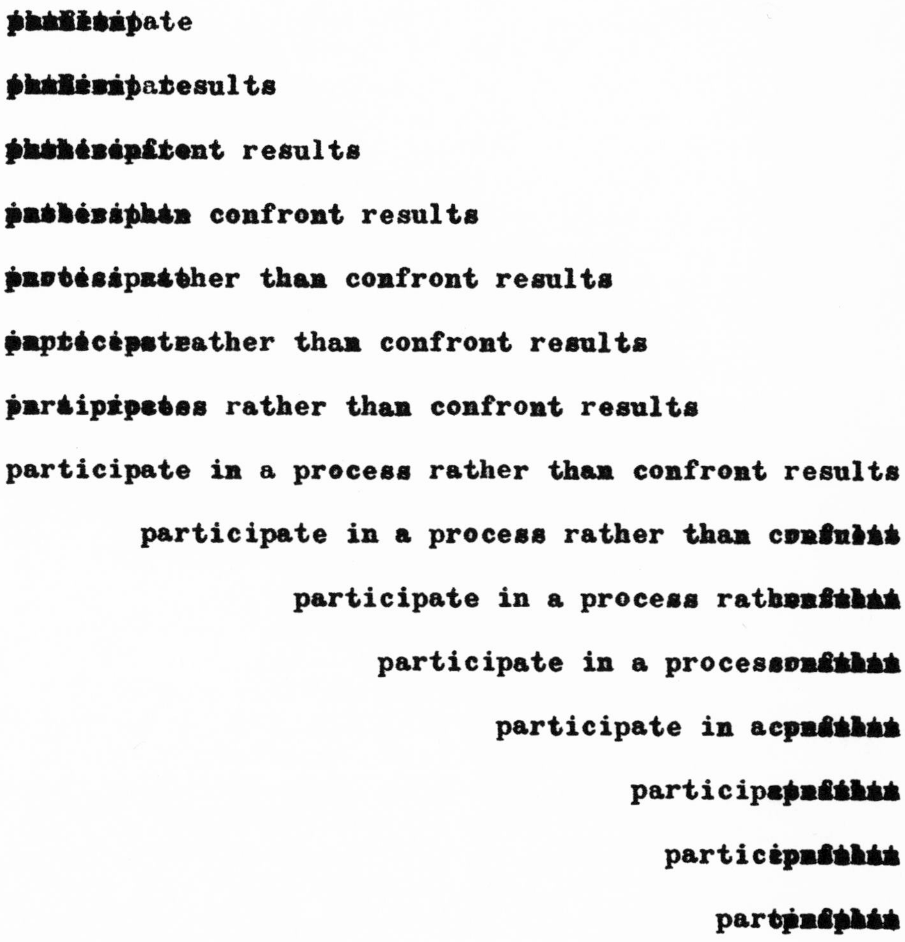
ate
results
results
confront results
her than confront results
ather than confront results
rather than confront results
participate in a process rather than confront results
participate in a process rather than
participate in a process rath
participate in a proces
participate in a
particip
partic
part

PHILIP CORNER

1968

"Philip Corner sticks pretty much to music, but his forms are graphic, and rules could easily be devised by which his graphic notations could be interpreted in other modes of activity, such as theater or dancing. However, his work is always rooted to a statement of intent that is so encompassing and inclusive that there is no doubt in the performer's mind at all about what (and why) he is doing when he does something (or nothing.)"

—Dick Higgins

you can always say that everything is music as in a
classroom in your life with uh-huhs as a philosophy but
no listening in reality. nor music for more than a
moment or so illustration. Learned from meditation and
out-of went in the world. Did with, and this was inter-
esting. A closer kind of symphony but how to make
that really respect for sound, how by no necessary voicing
with participation we listen. Quiet bodies pure receiver. To
have come from the practice even for our selves in sounding
things, no longer to us yet we out towards. The way
this has all been to here. . . . . . the ways to be possessed; the
posture when natures vibrates full ; within body mind ; in ear

(Ear close to)

now

when people put themselves
in one place in a place to really hear

sounds of background,
un-usually heard at all. bring fore. . . . .

(the fantastic detail)

to be perceived admirably
in a kind of continual thing, easy, just that
yet full of difference, very, actuality

be filled of

Ear very close-to

2 inches!

or closer

wave surf—flow—current
ripple stream
lapping of any water at
any edge.

heads hang over the edge and long hair in the pool

oh with eyes too!

(berry bush)

in grasses, and woods
trees gardens
where insects are

creaks, thingest fence

i gave the examples

she said that consumes a-lot-of 'time'

" No more than staying down in the soul ,"

The world might walk through me as a work of art.

"It takes all the time ." "without it there is none . "

the world can walk through me like that work of art

" , true " .

I too am a Technician of the sacred.

Jerry Rothenberg says on p.425 that *Anything can deliver a song.* " in fact"

(can any song deliver a thing)

list
night
mist
the blue sky
east
west
women
adolescent girls
men's hands and feet
the sexual organs of men and women
the bat
the land of souls
ghosts
graves
the bones
hair&teeth of the dead

etc.

(Have, i Too made this list ?
have i put down all these these
as well these all things.....?)

More important :
Have You . ?

"wow ,In Fact ! "

"of a connected and fluid universe
——just as much alive
as man is ,
No need with it, deifining .
whether or not
the heart transplantation
"takes" .

anything ?

etc. contains every

thing !

Let It Be That the World Walk Through Me Like An Art

.anything.

the senses systematic rerrangement of the senses systematic rerangement of the

toasted corn muffin
click
red light
jazz
au naturel
bubbles
how many dreams
mutter,mumble
appointments
counters
hiss
Spain
tropical fruits
vehicles
sunrise
war
nourishment
dogs & cats
service
of desire
chill
speak out
south
laughter
big city
up
school
language
crumbs
late
cranberry
hard mornings
grand
go
assassination
farmlands,wheatfields
virgins
warble
skeleton
horse show
busy
the place
soaked shoes
those living
arisen
colors of flesh
close at 4
gardener
squish
exhaustion
cup
spirit
spilled liquids
piano sonata
smiles
milk & honey desert
nada
comfort
cockroach
papers

toasted corn muffin
click
red light
jazz
au naturel
bubbles
how many dreams
mutter, mumble
appointments
counters
hues
Spain
tropical fruits
vehicles
sunrise
war
nourishment
dogs & cats
service
of desire
chill
speak out
south
laughter
big city
up
school
language
crumbs
late
cranberry
hard mornings
grand
go
assassination
farmlands, wheatfields
virgina
warble
skeleton
horse show
busy
the place
soaked shoes
those living
arteen
colors of flesh
close at 4
gardener
squish
exhaustion
cup
spirit
spilled liquids
piano sonata
smiles
milk & honey desert
nada
comfort
cockroach
papers

(Ear very close)

snowflakes fall on freeze pool can be heard

machines. fixtures
in pipes
huge engines
electric receivers
the generator
hum

or as close to closeto as—possible

roar waves far below the deck
go leaning most possible close-to

bodies. of one's own body
and even air.

sounds from other sides
of windows. pressed to, ears

(rain. wind)

and with eyes

(gasses) fizz & ice
& melting dripps

& boiling

fire
bubbling
wire

(Ear close)

ear into

shell
the sea shell
into the glass

coffee-perc counterpoint
tea

finished when (whenever) fall back into utilitarian consciousnss. Perform over as desire—able head
so just to be here changes so

AUGUSTO DE CAMPOS

Uma Vez

1957

uma vez = one time, once upon a time
uma fala = a speech, a talk
uma foz = a river-mouth
uma bala = a bullet
uma voz = a voice
uma vala = a ditch

Augusto de Campos' definition of concrete poetry, "tension of things-words in space-time," enriches the plot of this little story—or at least serves warning that the *denouement* is entirely up to the reader. Haroldo de Campos, the poet's poet-brother, describes it as "the reduction of a plot (love? murder?—'once upon a time . . .') to a dynamic iterative endless process."

uma vez
uma vala
uma foz
uma vez uma bala
uma fala uma voz
uma foz uma vala
uma bala uma vez
uma voz
uma vala
uma vez

Caracol

1960

colocar a mascara	= to put on the mask
mascara	= mask, (it) masks
mas	= but
cara	= face
caracol	= snail

A cyclical poem whose process is revealed by the slow progress of a snail.

c o l o c a r a m a s
c a r a c o l o c a r
a m a s **c a r a c o l**
o c a r a m a s **c a r**
a c o l o c a r a m a
s **c a r a c o l** o c a
r a m a s **c a r a c o**
l o c a r a m a s **c a**
r a c o l o c a r a m
a s **c a r a c o l** o c
a r a m a s **c a r a c**
o l o c a r a m a s **c**
a r a c o l o c a r a
m a s **c a r a c o l** o
c a r a m a s **c a r a**

Ovo Novelo

1957

o	= o	*temor*	= fear, dread, awe
novelo	= ball of yarn (umbilical cord?)	*morte*	= death, destruction
ovo	= egg, ovum	*termo*	= term
sol	= sun	*metro*	= meter
letra	= letter of the alphabet	*motor*	= motor, motive, mover
soletra	= spell, (it) spells	*torto*	= crooked, cross-eyed, wrong, unjust
estrela	= star	*morto*	= dead
so	= only	*termometro*	= thermometer
terremoto	= earthquake		

A generative story-poem, the "plot" carried along by the structured arrangement of semantic relationships—and linguistic surprises.

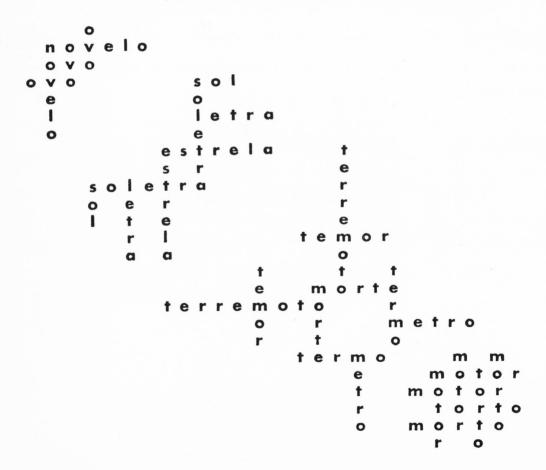

```
      o
  n o v e l o
  o v o
o v o             s o l
  e               o
  l               l e t r a
  o               e
              e s t r e l a       t
              s   r               e
      s o l e t r a               r
      o   e   r                   r
      l   t   e                   e
          r   l               t e m o r
          a   a                   o
                          t       t     t
                          e     m o r t e
                t e r r e m o t o       r
                          o     r       m e t r o
                          r     t       o
                              t e r m o       m   m
                                    e       m o t o r
                                    t     m o t o r
                                    r       t o r t o
                                    o     m o r t o
                                            r   o
```

HAROLDO DE CAMPOS

Branco

1957

branco = white
vermelho = red
estanco = staunch
espelho = mirror

"A progression with the word *branco* (white). In counterpoint, the word *vermelho* (red). The internal rhymes provide the skeleton *(branco/estanco/vermelho/espelho)*. The maximum opening of the poem coincides with the maximum blank of the page: a co-information, at visual level, with the effect of white color over a white surface in painting, or the word white written with white ink on white paper." (Author's note.)

branco	**branco**	**branco**	**branco**
vermelho			
estanco	**vermelho**		
	espelho	**vermelho**	
		estanco	**branco**

Cristal

1958

cristal = crystal
fome = hunger
forma = form
de = of

"An essay of poetic crystallography," writes the author. "The metaphorical hunger of form, and form as a kind of hunger. Crystal as the ideogram of the process."

cristal

cristal

fome

cristal

cristal

fome de forma

cristal

cristal

forma de fome

cristal

cristal

forma

Se Nasce Morre

1958

se = if
nasce = (a human being) is born
morre = (a human being) dies
re = again
denasce = (a human being) is unborn
desmorre = (a human being) undies

"Hans Arp once made the following comparison between the poetry of the painter-poet Kandinsky and the poetry of Goethe: 'A poem by Goethe teaches the reader, in a poetical way, that death and transformation are the inclusive condition of man. Kandinsky, on the contrary, places the reader before an image of dying and transforming words, before a series of dying and transforming words. . . .' This poem wants to be an exact *presentification* of that proposition. The vital cycle (or the Joycean 'vicocycle')." (Author's note)

se
nasce
morre nasce
morre nasce morre
renasce remorre renasce
remorre renasce
remorre
re **re**
desnasce
desmorre desnasce
desmorre desnasce desmorre
nascemorrenasce
morrenasce
morre
se

ALVARO DE SÁ

12 x 9

"A poem encloses a process," writes de Sá, "and is really new when it embodies and surpasses earlier poetic propositions. This process, gradually explored by the consumers, is finally worn out when a new process is devised that surmounts it." In his search for a new language he has ridded himself of the word (a "sacred cow"), substituting for Mallarmé's axiom "Poems are made with words, not ideas" one by his fellow Brazilian, Wlademir Dias-Pino, "Poems are made with processes, not words." De Sá employs words "only when indispensable." He offers instead "integral/international communication through the process," with interchangeable pages, "consumption in any direction." His objective is a "new stage for the consumer-participant-creator—totality-man *(homem totalidade)*"

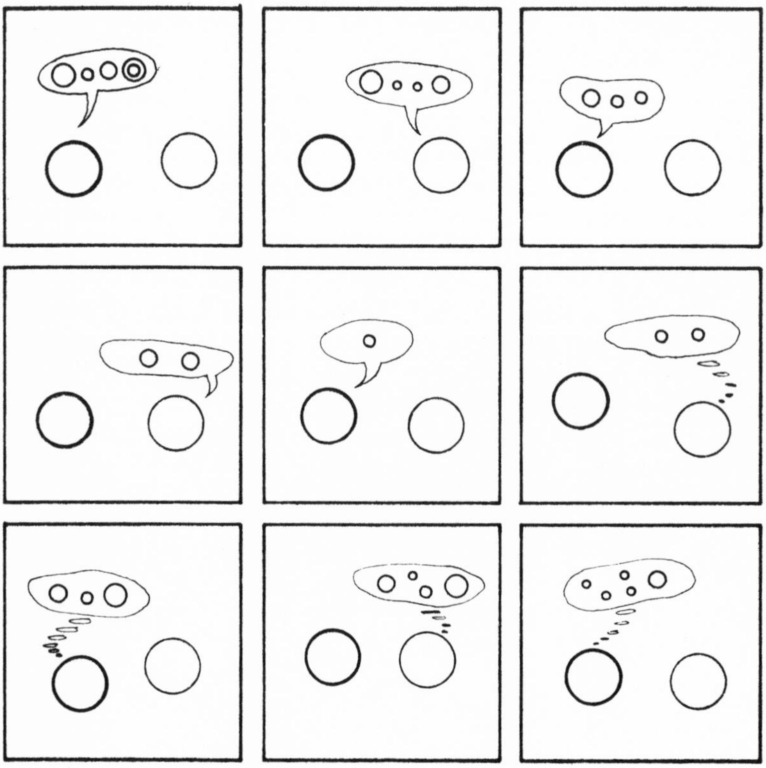

BUUM
BUUM
BUUM

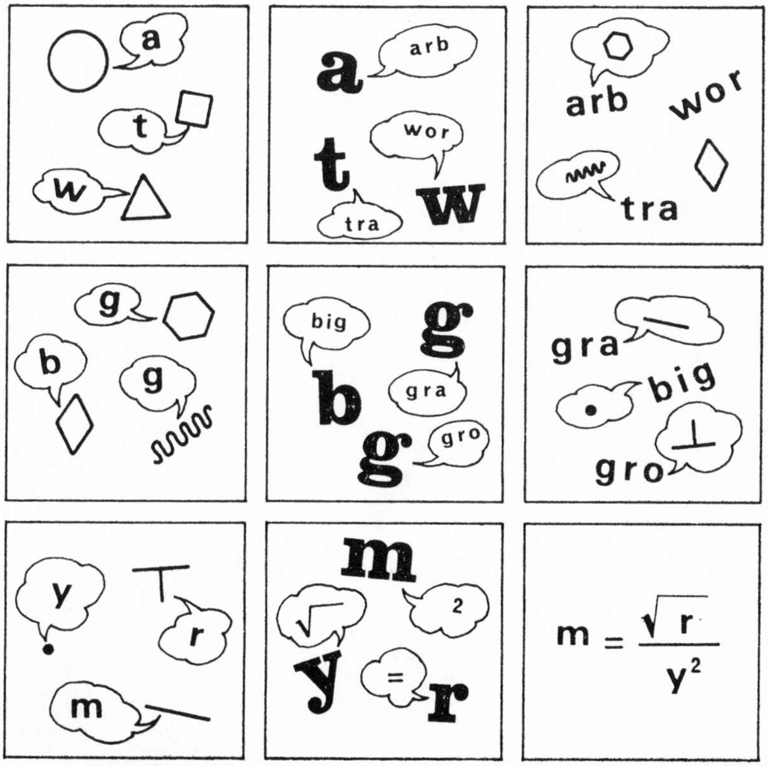
a
t
w
arb
a
wor
t
tra
w
arb
wor
tra
g
b
g
big
g
b
gra
g
gro
gra
big
gro
y
r
m
m
2
y
=
r
m = √r / y²

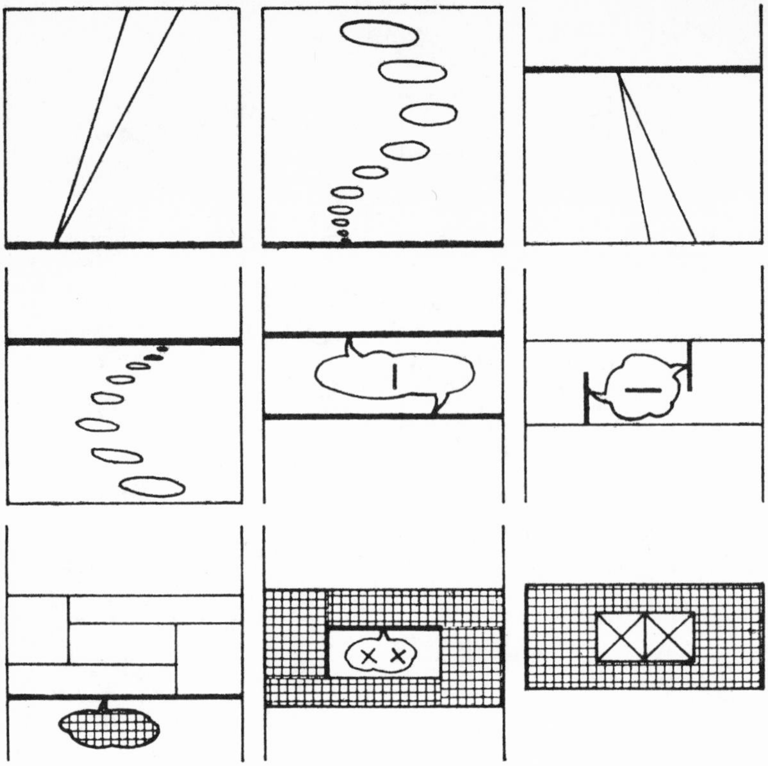

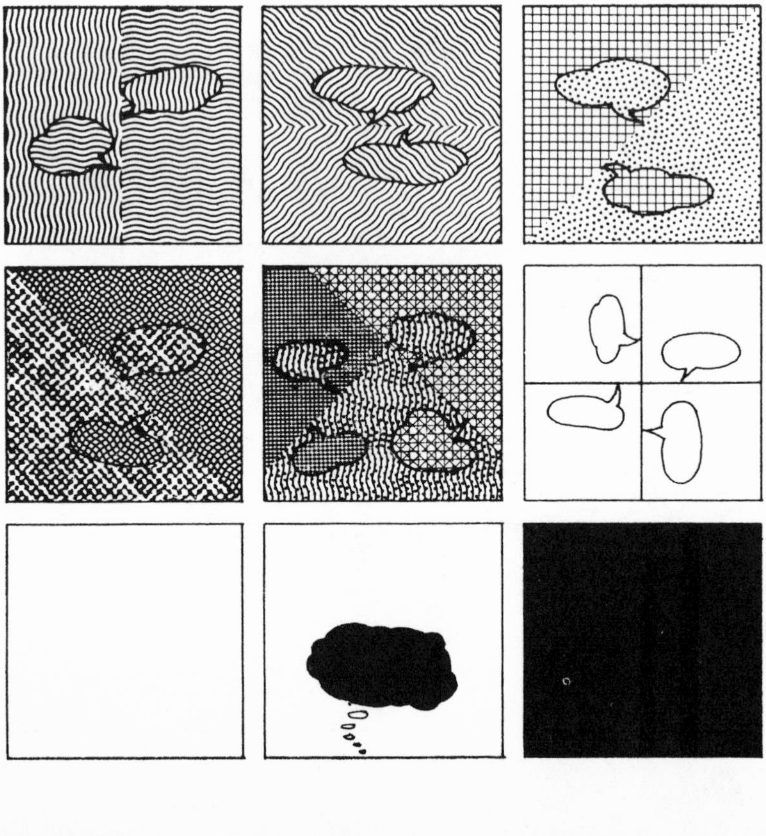

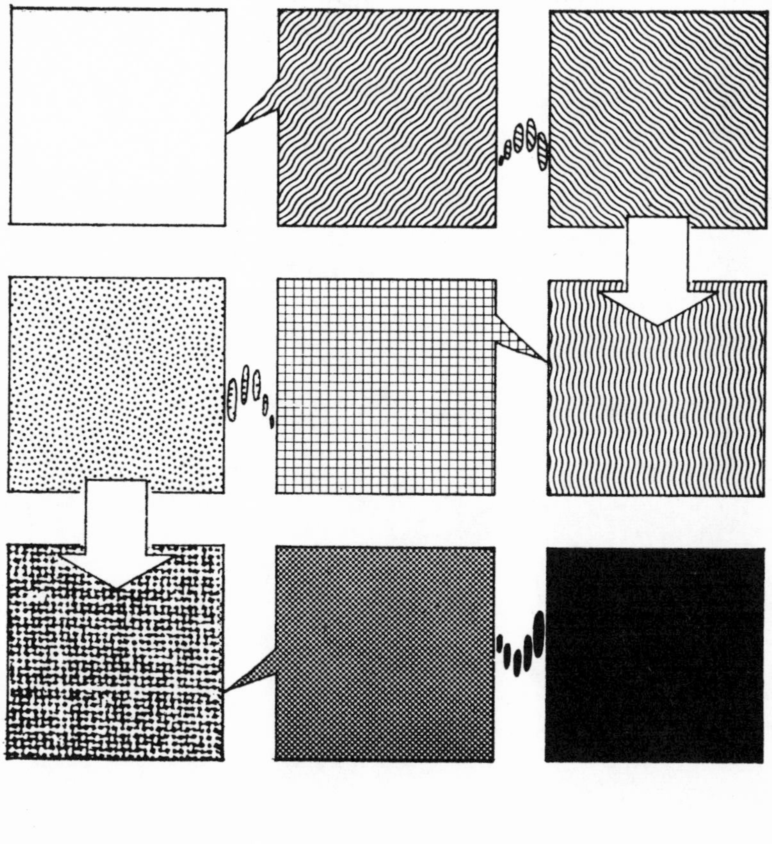

DENIS DUNN

All of These Poetry
The Star 61 Cygni
High Song 8

Denis Dunn's visual poems, plotted with meaningful precision on graph paper by the former mathematician-physicist, are scores for their sound equivalents. Or, as the poet phrases it, "The systems I have realized for my sight poems is an attempt to render visible the sound which I realize in the potential of the human voice and the possibilities of the English language. My aim is to reawaken the mystical experience of language which dwells in its ancient roots; to penetrate the outer conceptual layers to the deeper layers of meaning which are the realm of poetry and music; to bring life to the aid of machinery; to bring spirit to the aid of reason; to illuminate our surface world from within; to turn inside out in a gently compelling way; to help prepare us to enter the ethereal age which is now upon us."

L
L O
A F
T E s o
H S e f
P E Y
O R v l
o
E T a
w o
i
s g k
i n i
l
l n
u i g
s a
i
o o o n
n i gl
l k e
l l s
u f
s o
i o f
o s
n pers
s y p
a e
e w c
r t
a i
o k r l v
f o d p e
l o w o
o i
i n
n t t
g h e s
at
i
n
o
a space
o u n
f t d

space
v e
points a s

v o w of
i f f l
e o o g s o
p w o y f k
o s k n a o
ints i o i
of w w l n
v i e g

r
u
d o
o
f
m u n y s
w s t
m i
e
w
o
e p o
i
a
m
v in v
a
c
e i
v
s n
s i
g
y n
g
n
e
s
t
h
e
s s
i a
of
tone form
rw
o a
l v
o e
c
d
s
o n
u
a
n
a d
o r
n f l
o
o l
f
y r n
l
t
e o r
a
i a
e
l
r
y
t
i f
o
t s
i c p
e
a
a
n k

THE STAR
61
CYGNI

is 11 light years
a
w
a
y

if you start now

you will a r e
r v
i e
h r
t
e

y
e
s
t
e
r
d
a
y

you
are
he
a
d
i
n in
g t
o
s
p
e
a c

weep not
f o
r
a
n e
r e
c t t s
i n
e

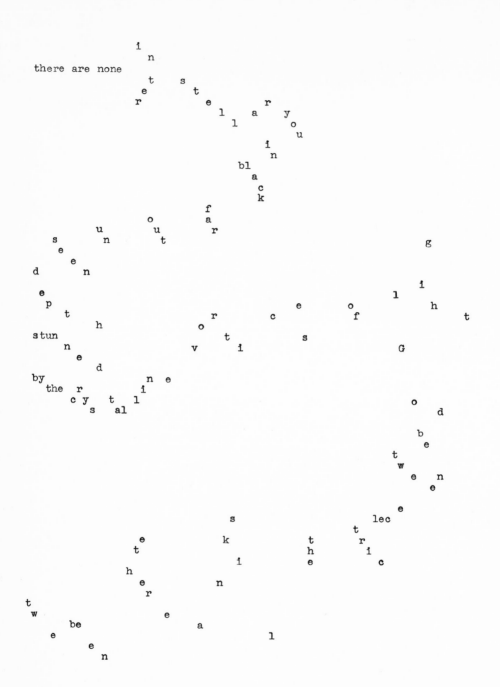

i
n
there are none
t s
e t
r e r
l a y
l o
u
i
n
bl
a
c
k
f
o a
u u r
s n t g
e
e
d n
i
e l
p
e o h
t r c f t
h o
stun t s
n v i G
e
d
by n e
the r i
c y t l o
s al d
b
e
t
w
e n
e
e
s lec
t
e k t r
t h i
i e c
h
e n
r
t
w e
be a
e l
e
n

S
O
H N
I G m e
G i s
H t
8 e i
m
o
s t k
h n
i
i m

s t r a i g h t

er

w h e n
n n
i m e
a h
h i g h w i
t m
s
t
r
a
i
and g t
straight h
means
d :
o
b n
e t
n o
d i
o n
e i n t
h t c a
t s o c p n
e n t n e d
i l
u o a h
q r m i
l e l e g
i t o o : a h
o n
: s
l l v k :
a e e i
y r n
s g
v
and

s t r a i g ht

m e a n s

t
t
s u
h
b
b s e
e
e u
s
n n
e
d
i i
i
n s
i
g
s s
l t
t
i
h of i h
t t
t n e
o
i
e
r
t
y
l
n
h
r
o
r l
e t t o e
t
u r o o w
r
o a n
e
y
o
u
t b
s r e r
a o
s
n t
o
m
h
f e s
v
t i r
e e a
o n
s v
h r
r e w
a m
b a e
t
i l
l
l
i
o
n
y
e
a
r
s
a
h
e
a

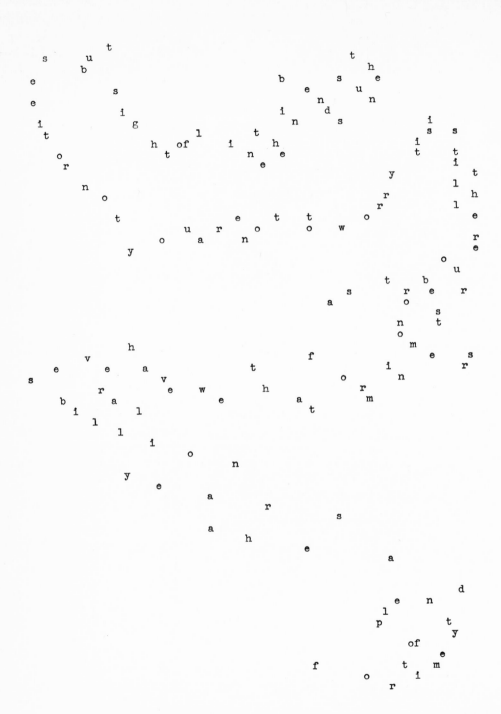

d
e n
l
p t
y
of
e
f t m
o i
r

G

O

D

is

t a

e

t

h

n

e

d

i

n n

w

g n

h

i

i h g

c

b

s

t e L

i h

o t e

O

w o

u

d

V

n n

a

d

E

u

i

r

s

o

d

a

o

u

g

h

t

u a r

o

n l

v

f

e

d

u

u

n m

i

t

c

n

o

CARL FERNBACH-FLARSHEIM

Numerical Game Poems

"Only the objects are stable; they are the islands, we are the sea."

—Pierre Garnier

It is in this context, perhaps, that the rationale for a fusion of the arts can be most easily understood. The object is separated from its illusory image thrown on our mental screen by our own cerebral motion-picture projector. The word becomes a compound, the letters its elements. The note is a digit, a concrete symbol. The line is a dot in motion. Color is wavelength perceived, sound is another, heat a third. We are the computer; the environment is the information fed into it.

A new language is in the process of being created. We used to listen into the other's mind. "Language was like clicks—we listened to the noise and guessed at what went on inside. . . ." (Houédard). Wittgenstein's word no longer "has meaning if it stands for an idea" but "to have an idea is to know the meaning of the word." The art object exists as a trinity consisting of observer, the creator as anarchist, and the object itself. . . .

Probably one of the greatest implications which all this activity holds is that in its core may lie the seeds for an eventual full fusion of the arts and sciences. . . . What shall be the impact historically, if any? Perhaps a statement attributed to Moholy-Nagy may serve as answer here. "If I succeed I shall have travelled a road, which others shall not have to travel again. If I fail? I shall be long dead and I shall never know it."

—Carl Fernbach-Flarsheim, "The Arts in Fusion"

code game key

IF :

0 = lick
1 = bed sheet
2 = wet
3 = smells
4 = tickles
5 = arm pit
6 = heavy
7 = stick
8 = sweet
9 = flower

THEN...

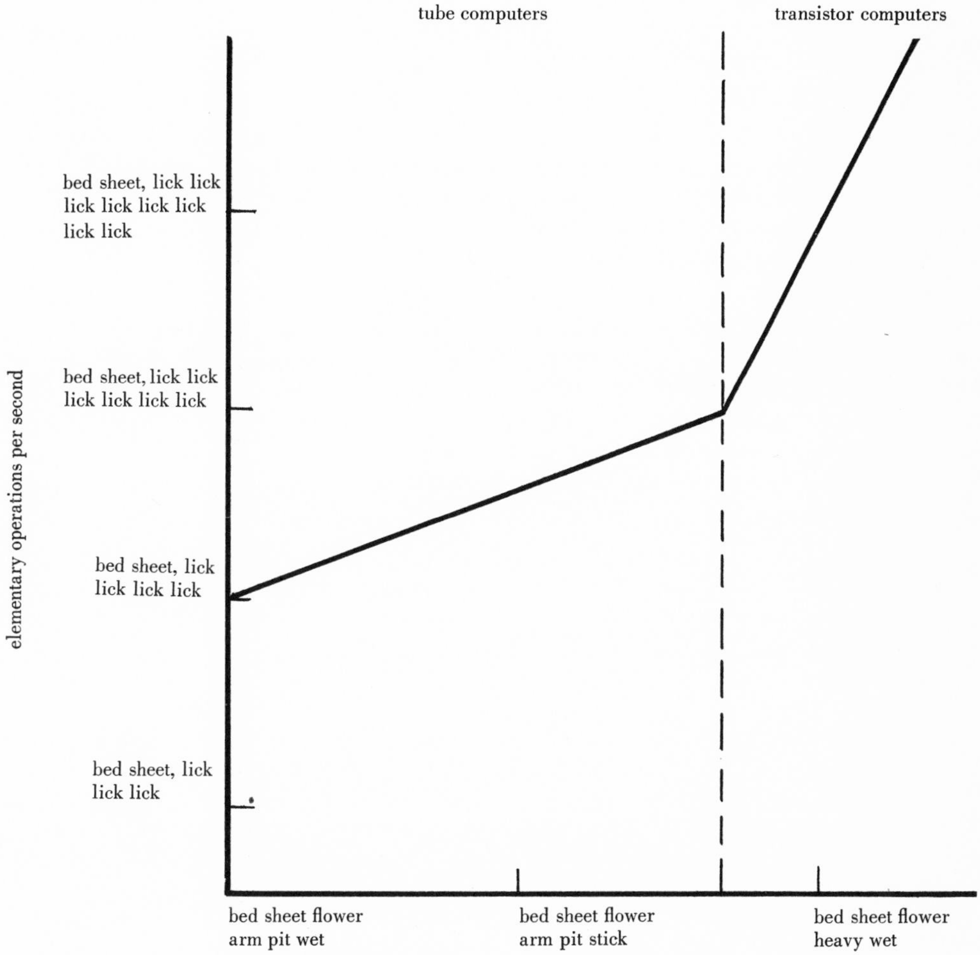
tube computers
transistor computers
elementary operations per second
bed sheet, lick lick lick lick lick lick lick lick
bed sheet, lick lick lick lick lick lick
bed sheet, lick lick lick lick
bed sheet, lick lick lick
bed sheet flower arm pit wet
bed sheet flower arm pit stick
bed sheet flower heavy wet

homage to CHARLES BABBAGE
(the *anticipatory carry* system)

heavy bed sheet	smells bed sheet wet heavy sweet stick	flower tickles arm pit flower arm pit sweet
stick	flower flower flower bed sheet	sweet flower smells bed sheet
stick bed sheet	licks licks licks	sweet flower bed sheet
sweet	licks licks licks	flower licks smells

ROBERT FILLIOU

Yes—an action poem

The Frenchman Robert Filliou has taken the poem far, far afield from the printed page. He has set its metaphors to work on the balls and pins of a bowling alley, in the forests, with poetic objects living and dead suspended from branches and boughs, and on the roulette wheels of the casino. His admirers on several continents regularly receive new installments on his "subscription poems"—sculptural objects that grow in relation to the frequency of checks and money orders.

Yes—an action poem was conceived for performance and was first seen in this country at the Cafe au Go-Go in New York in 1965. Part One—The Adult Male Poet—was read by Alison Knowles while Filliou sat crosslegged upstage, motionless and silent. For Part Two—His Poem—the poet stood up, spoke the text, then returned to his former position. Philip Corner improvised an almost silent musical accompaniment. The performance—"sitting quietly, doing nothing"—continued until all those in the audience who seemed anxious to leave had done so.

Filliou points out that the title of the poem in Part Two—"Le Filliou Ideal"—can be changed to designate any adult male poet who performs the work.

Yes
—an action poem—

(The poet sits on a chair. Behind him, a lecturer introduces him soberly to the audience, and reads as follows:—)

Part One—The Adult Male Poet

The body of the adult poet stands at an average height of 5′ 5″ and, on the average, weights approximately 145 pounds.

It is covered with and protected by a thin and elastic membrane, the skin, consisting of the epidermis and the dermis of the poet. The hair and the nails of the poet are mere derivatives of his skin. The surface area of the skin covers about 1.8 square meters (17.2 square feet) of the body of the average poet.

The body of the poet is built around a framework of bones, called the skeleton. When the poet is first born, the bones are still soft; but as the poet grows in stature, his bones get harder.

The skeleton of the poet consists of three main elements: the head, the trunk and the limbs.

The Head: this consists first of the skull, a hollow box containing the brain of the poet, to which his ears are attached; second is the face, with openings for the eyes, the nostrils and the mouth of the poet.

The Trunk: this also consists of two parts,—the chest and the belly of the poet, separated by a slight depression, called the waist. It is in his trunk that the spine of the poet is found, and which is made of rings of bone protecting the spinal cord, the ribs of the poet (twelve pairs of them), the breast bone, two collar bones, two shoulder blades, and, at the lower end of the spine, the pelvis of the poet. Keep in mind, however, that minor differences occur when the poet is spineless.

The Limbs: such are called the arms and legs of the poet. The arms—two of them—consist each in the upper arm, the forearm, and the hand of the poet. It would be superfluous to enumerate the many uses of this hand; thanks to the perfection of it, guided by the intelligence of the poet, he is able to realize the marvels of his art.

The Legs of the poet—also two of them—consist in three articulated parts: the thigh, the lower leg and the foot. The poet stands upright on his legs, this being one of the characteristics that distinguishes him from animals. What distinguishes him most from animals, however, is his intelligence and his highly articulate speech.

All poets present the characteristics which we have just described, but the diverse agglomerations of poets show, among themselves, some differences that suggest distinguishing among them.

——thus the yellow poet has yellowish skin, prominent cheekbones, thick hair, slanted eyes, a large nose and thick lips.

——the black poet has a colored

skin, varying from golden brown to deep black, kinky hair, a flat nose, thick lips, and very strong, powerful jaws.

——the white poet has pinkish skin, an oval-shaped face, straight hair, eyes slit horizontally, a straight nose and thin lips.

——the red poet has a copper skin, unruly hair, prominent cheekbones, a hooked nose, and thin lips.

i—of the Necessity of Alimentation

Just as a steam engine does not function without water and coal, and the motor of an automobile stops when short of gasoline, the poet, in order to furnish poetry, must be fed regularly. It is food that gives the poet strength and heat.

The first thing a poet does with food is to chew it. This consists of breaking the food into small pieces, mixing it up with his saliva, thus making it easier to swallow and to digest, and chewing it well. The poet needs for this a complete set of teeth, that is to say a total of 32, 16 in each jaw, consisting of cutting teeth or canines, and grinding teeth or molars.

Once his food is chewed, the poet swallows it, and it passes down the gullet (or "aesophogus") into the stomach of the poet. There the food is reduced to a semi-liquid paste by the digestive juices of the poet, and it passes into a long, thin tube called the small intestine of the poet, and from this small intestine in due time into a wider tube of the large intestine.

The stomach of the poet works at least two hours after every meal. If the poet did not take good care of it, it would tire easily. This is why:

——the poet eats at regular hours

——the poet does not eat too rapidly, in order to avoid indigestion

——the poet eats slowly, so that his food is well impregnated with his saliva

——the poet observes a well-balanced diet, building up his body with lean meat, fish, cheese, the yolk and white of egg, peas, beans, etc., accumulating energy with bread, potatoes, sugar, butter and margarine, fatty meat and fish, and protecting his health with fresh vegetables, fresh fruit, animal fats and wholewheat bread (The best food of all, nevertheless, is milk, which contains proteins, carbohydrates, fats, vitamins and mineral salts. This explains why poets drink all they can get.)

——the poet brushes his teeth mornings and nights, and following every meal, for the little bits of food remaining between his teeth rot if they are not removed, and give to the poet's breath a horrible smell

——the poet defecates at least once a day, for the digestive waste of the poet, if it stays too long inside his large intestine—which ends up with the anus of the poet—will cause certain poisoning.

ii—The Blood of the Poet

When you sever a poet's jugular vein, blood does not stop running out from the wound until the poet is dead. But if you saw up a poet whom you have just strangled to death, his body does not bleed. This is because the blood of the dead poet is motionless, while the living poet's blood is always in motion, propelled by his heart, so it keeps circulating through his blood vessels.

The blood of the poet is bright red in his arteries, which are the blood vessels along which the blood passes from the heart It is brownish red or purple in his veins, which are the blood vessels along which the blood returns to the heart. Its specific gravity ranges from 1,050 to 1,060. Its viscosity is about five or six times that of water. As to quantity, blood constitutes five to seven per cent of the body weight of the poet. For an average adult poet weighing 145 pounds, this would amount to five to six liters (nine to eleven pints).

Plasma constitutes about 59% of the blood of the poet, and water 91 to 92% of that plasma. It is obvious, then, that one thing all poets have in common is that 55% of what runs through their veins and arteries is water. The rest is made up of corpuscles and platelets.

The distribution of the blood of the poet is influenced by such factors as gravity and activity, as a moment's reflection will show. Thus if while reading his poem to an audience, the poet raises his hand high above his head, the skin of his hand becomes paler and the veins less obvious. Sedentary poets are often afflicted by varicose veins, and congestion of the veins of the liver and of the intestines. Walking poets are less liable to this trouble, because the flow of blood through their veins is assisted by the massaging action of their muscles.

It is also well known that when a poet feels faint, his head should be kept low, so that his brain will not be deprived of nourishment. In the majority of cases this is automatically insured by the poet's falling to the ground.

The blood of the poet is forced around the poet's body by the heart of the poet, which is a powerful pump, with thick muscular walls. This heart is divided into right and left sides, and each has its upper chamber called an "auricle" and its lower one, called a "ventricle."

The late Professor Pascal once said of this heart that it is hollow and full of garbage. However, exactly what he meant by this is not clear.

iii—The Poet's Breathing

The poet writes as he breathes. This points to the importance of respiration, which the poet carries out with the help of his nose, his nasopharynx, his larynx, his trachea, his bronchi and his lungs. While it is notorious that the poet can live several days without taking food, he couldn't even remain one minute without absorbing air. He does it constantly, he never stops, day or night.

Parenthetically, however, let us note that in spite of this, the poet is unable to appreciate the fact that his lungs are constantly slipping over the inner surfaces of his chest, or, for that matter that his stomach is in contact with his intestines. You see, there is no tactile sense in the deeper parts of the body of the poet. It is thought that at one time the poet was conscious of all the inside workings of his body, but he decided that it would be better if these became automatic and unconscious so that he might devote his attention to higher things.

When this automation stops, the respiratory movements of the poet cease. They must be artificially imparted to the chest wall until the poet resumes his automatic breathing. This is particularly important in the case of the apparently drowned poet. The technique of artificial respiration which used to be favored was that described by Schafer: the poet was placed face downward, with a cushion or folded coat under the lower part of the chest, and the resuscitator knelt on the ground athwart the poet. Then a forward and backward rocking movement of his chest was induced by throwing the weight of the body forward on to the hands, and then raising the body slowly to the upright position.

Another method, more in favor now, is known as "mouth-to-mouth respiration." The principle on which this method is based is that expired air from the resuscitator's lungs is breathed into the drowned poet's lungs.

iv—The Excretion of the Poet

The body of the poet produces waste materials which must be gotten rid of in various ways. Sweat glands get rid of some waste. They are coiled tubes which produce the sweat, and the sweat leaves the body of the poet through little openings in his skin called "pores." One can see the pores of the poet if you look at him with a magnifying glass.

The kidneys of the poet are his most important organs of excretion. They are at the back of his abdomen and the blood circulates through them. Under a microscope, one can see that the kidney contains many small tubules, which filter off waste material from his blood. The yellowish liquid containing this waste material is called the "urine" of the poet.

The urine passes down two tubes called "ureters" to a bag called the "bladder" of the poet, where it is stored until it leaves his body. In both male and female poets, the urine leaves the bladder along a tube called the "urethra." Normally the urethra is kept closed by a ring of muscle below the bladder. But when the bladder gets full, this muscle relaxes and allows the poet's urine to flow out.

In the case of the female poet, the urethra opens to the outside of her body, between her legs. Just behind her urine-opening is the vagina of the female poet, which, in the case of the adult virgin female poet is closed by a thin membrane known as the "hymen." Around these two openings are folds or lips of flesh, which form what is called the "vulva" of the female poet. But of course she is praised also for her poems, which are just as beautiful.

In the case of the male poet, the urethra passes through a fleshy tube called the penis of the poet, which hangs between his legs.

Excretion is of such vital importance to the good functioning of the poet that the departed savant, Leonardo da Vinci, insisted that "the poet is a wonderful mechanism transforming good wine into urine."

v—The Brain of the Poet

When the poet does not wear clothes, which protect him from the cold, rain, heat and curiosity, one can see his muscles, called biceps, triceps, tendons, etc. It is the movement of his muscles that makes the poet smile or scowl, wink his eye or screw up his nose.

The poet has many muscles, and each one must be shortened or lengthened at just the right moment and by just the right amount. When the poet wiggles his fingers, or pushes his pen across the page, you can see cords moving under the skin at the back of the hand. If they do not move just right, the poet may write "No" when he meant to write "Yes." If they do not move fast enough, the poet may not be able to stop a sentence where he had intended. As a matter of fact, if the muscles all over the body of the poet did not contract or stretch in harmony with each other, he could not even stand up to read his poems.

The movement of the muscles of the poet is controlled by his nervous system, which includes the brain of the poet, his spinal cord, and his nerves. Electric messages pass along one nerve cell to the next, and so travel from the head to the foot of the poet in the fraction of a second. That is why the poet is able to move out of the way quickly if something is thrown at him.

A cardinal property of all reflex actions of the poet is that his responses are purely automatic and independent of his will or desire. If the sole of the foot of the poet is tickled, his toes curl and his foot is withdrawn, no matter to what school the poet belongs. Likewise, the average adult poet spends about one third of his life in sleep. Very great adult poets, however, can do with as little as five hours of sleep a day.

The brain of the poet is really the expanded and highly developed upper part of his spinal cord. A poet once said that his brain was nothing but a bit of spinal cord with knobs on it. He was right, but he might have added that it is the seat of his intellect, his emotions, his speech, his balance and many other things as well.

All that can excite the nervous system of the poet must be avoided. Frequent attendance of films or television is harmful. Likewise the use of tobacco, alcohol and drugs has a dismal effect upon the brain and the nerves of the poet. The poet's hands begin to shake. His sight decreases, he becomes sad, with sudden fits of irritation and anger. Little by little he loses all dignity, and may eventually sink into madness. Besides, it becomes difficult for him to reproduce himself.

vi—Reproduction and Senses of the Adult Male Poet

The main organs of reproduction of the adult male poet are the testicles and penis of the poet. When the adult male poet sees a female, his brain gives to his penis, which is a muscle, the appropriate orders. The poet is then said to have, or not to have, an "erection." It stands to reason that only when the erection is achieved, and the consent of the female secured, can the penis of the poet be inserted into the vagina.

The frequency of these reactions depends upon the information that his brain possesses regarding what goes on around the poet. This is why special organs allow the poet to hear, to smell, to taste, to feel and to see.

You may have wondered how the poet can hear things and voices. It's because of his eardrums. The eardrum of the poet is capable of vibrating in response to a large range of tones. The precise range differs from poet to poet. Some are able to hear the high-pitched cry of a bat, and some not.

The sense of smell is the most mysterious of all the special senses of the poet, and the one about which we know least. While the majority of poets can distinguish between the delicate perfume of a rose and the foul odors of gas works, there are some poets who, chewing an onion with the eyes closed and the nose blocked, cannot distinguish it from a strawberry. This goes to show that what we often describe as the tastes of the poet are really odors.

The tongue of the poet is sensitive to different varieties of taste. Some poets appreciate sweetness toward the tip of their tongue, and bitterness towards the back of their tongue. Some others appreciate bitterness toward the tip of the tongue, and sweetness towards the back. All poets, however, make extensive use of their tongues in the modulating and enunciating of the sounds and words of their poems.

In the skin of the poet there are sensitive nerve endings which tell him when, what and whom he is touching. If a slice of skin of the poet is examined under a microscope, these "touch nerves" can be seen just below the surface.

vii—Conclusions

Let us suppose, then, that the poet sees a woman passing by. He looks at her, that is to say, the lens of his eye focuses upon her. Her image is formed upon his retina, small and upside down. The optic nerve of the poet transmits to his brain the information allowing him to realize what is meant by the exact position, the shape, the color of the woman situated in front of the poet's eye.

The poet must then decide if this woman is his woman, or my woman, or thy woman, or her woman, or our woman, or your woman, or their woman.

Or again, supposing the woman looked at is elderly, he must decide if she is his mother, or my mother, or thy mother, or her mother, or our mother, or your mother, or their mother.

And if she is getting out of a car, if it is his car, or thy car, or her car, or our car, or your car, or their car.

And if all this takes place in a town, if it is his town, or my town, or thy town, or her town, or our town, or your town, or their town.

And if it is night, if it is his night, or my night, or thy night, or her night, or our night, or your night, or their night.

And if the time is his, or mine, or thine, or hers, or ours, or yours, or theirs.

And even before deciding, perhaps it is boring to decide. Better, he thinks, to accept all the possibilities in advance. Better to accept all the possibilities in advance, and accepting them always, to remain beyond that region where everything is parcelled out, and everybody is owned by what he owns.

This at least is his ideal.

And he expresses this ideal in a poem, because he is a poet.

Part Two—His Poem

Yes.

As my name is Filliou, the title of the poem is:

LE FILLIOU IDEAL

It is an action poem, and I am going to perform it.

Its score is:

not deciding
not choosing
not wanting
not owning
aware of self
wide awake
SITTING QUIETLY,
DOING NOTHING

Paris, 1964

IAN HAMILTON FINLAY

redboat

". . . I should say—however hard I would find it to justify this in theory—that 'concrete' by its very limitations offers a tangible image of goodness and sanity; it is very far from the now-fashionable poetry of anguish and self. . . . It is a model, of order, even if set in a space which is full of doubt. (Whereas non-concrete might be said to be set in society, rather than space, and its 'satire,' its 'revolt,' are only disguised symptoms of social dishonesty. This, I realize, goes too far; I do not mean to say that society is 'bad.') . . . I would like, if I could, to bring into this somewhere the unfashionable notion of 'Beauty,' which I find compelling and immediate, however theoretically inadequate. I mean this in the simplest way—that if I was asked, 'Why do you write concrete poetry?' I could truthfully answer 'Because it is beautiful.' "

—Ian Hamilton Finlay, from a letter
to Pierre Garnier, September 17, 1963

r e d b o a t r e d b o a t r e d b o a t r e d b o a t r e d b o a t r e d b o a t

b e d b o a t b e d b o a t b e d b o a t b e d b o a t b e d b o a t b e d b o a t

d o

d r e a m s l e e p

s a y

d o f i s h

c a t c h

f i s h

s a y t o u c h

d o

b e d b o a t b e d b o a t b e d b o a t b e d b o a t b e d b o a t b e d b o a t

r e d b o a t r e d b o a t r e d b o a t r e d b o a t r e d b o a t r e d b o a t

Sea-Poppy 2 (1968)

Fishing-boat names. Set by Peter Grant.

DAY STAR
RADIANT STAR
WOOD STAR
DIVINE
MORNING STAR
LIGHT STAR
FAITHFUL STAR
FORTUNE STAR
ONWARD STAR
OF PEACE
NORRARD STAR
OF KINDRED STAR
FREEDOM STAR
GUIDING STAR
UNIVERSAL STAR

Ballad (1963)

s a i l

s a i l

s a i l

s a i l

s a i l o r

Formal Poem (1963)

The original is printed in three colors: the *tree* brown, the playful elements of *deer* blue, until, in the final arrangement, *ree* appears in a vivid green, the color it is a part of.

t
r
d e r
e

t
r
e
d e er

t
d r
e e
e

t
r
e
de e r

t
dee r
e
e

t
r
e
e
d

Hearts and Arrows

1963

```
h e a r t s                     a p p l e s
     h e a r t s          a p p l e s
          h e a r t s  a p p l e s
          a r r o w s  h u r t
     a r r o w s          h u r t
a r r o w s                     h u r t
```

2 Small Songs in 3's (1966)

from 6 Small Songs in 3's

Two simple permutations (with trick endings).

```
song          wind          wood

wind          song          wood

woodwind                    song
```

```
apple          autumn          earth

earth               autumn-apple

earth-apple               autumn
```

EUGEN GOMRINGER

Streets and Flowers

1951–52

Eugen Gomringer is the acknowledged "father" of Concrete poetry. His poems and theoretical writings, until recently known only to an international underground, have greatly reshaped twentieth-century poetics. This is his first "constellation." It was written in Spanish, his mother tongue. "Of all poetic structures based upon the word," he has written, "the constellation is the simplest. It disposes its groups of words as if they were clusters of stars. The constellation is a system, it is also a playground with definite boundaries. The poet sets it all up. He designs the playground as a field-of-force and suggests its possible workings. The reader, the new reader, accepts it in the spirit of play, then plays with it. With each constellation something new comes into the world. Each constellation is a reality in itself and not a poem *about* some other thing. The constellation is a challenge, it is also an invitation." (From *vom vers zur konstellation*, 1954, translated by Jerome Rothenberg.)

streets
streets and flowers

flowers
flowers and women

streets
streets and women

streets and flowers and women and
an admirer

Words Are Shadows

1956
(Translated from the German by Jerome Rothenberg)

". . . As a poet (but not a 'concrete' poet) part of the interest of concrete poetry for me is the clear light it throws on the nature of *all* poetry. You speak of constellations, Finlay speaks of corners, I speak elsewhere of combinations—but always it's a question of making the words cohere in a given space, the poem's force or strength related to the weight & value of the words within it, the way they pull & act on each other. The poetry shows this beautifully; the problem of translation is related to it also & throws its own clear light on how & why we translate." (Jerome Rothenberg, from a letter to Gomringer reprinted in Rothenberg's translation of *The Book of Hours and Constellations.*)

words are shadows
shadows become words

words are games
games become words

are shadows words
do words become games

are games words
do words become shadows

are words shadows
do games become words

are words games
do shadows become words

Butterfly

1955
(Original in English)

One of the most playful, and lyrical, of Gomringer's constellations. Here he allows two words to achieve their full effect through the force of an intruder-word that, as it changes from "mist" to "missed" to "meets," defines the changing relationship of "mountain" and "butterfly."

mist
mountain
butterfly

mountain
butterfly
missed

butterfly
meets
mountain

Ode

1961
(English version by Emmett Williams)

Gomringer's "ode to zurich in a hundred signs" is weighted with more literacy and cultural allusions (Zwingli, Füssli, Goethe, Jung, Joyce, Dada, etc.) than the English version, but that's part of the Zurich scene; and the translator felt that the East Side and the West Side, Central Park and Harlem, Tammany Hall and Wall Street, the Bowery and Old Broadway were more to the point in an ode to Manhattan than Whitman, Poe, Mailer, the Metropolitan Museum of Art, etc. Anyway, it's the same language game.

odei	odet
nhun	oman
dert	hatt
zeic	anin
hena	ahun
nzür	dred
izwi	sign
ngli	seas
füss	tsid
ligo	ewes
ethe	tsid
jung	ecen
yoga	tral
joyc	park
efoe	harl
hnut	emta
otok	mman
yohö	yhal
nggd	lwal
adao	lst.
deon	bowe
rämi	ryan
str.	dold
baur	broa
aula	dway

[English version, at right, by Emmett Williams]

The System Is Fool-proof (1967)

(Translated by Emmett Williams)

Gomringer's poetry has usually escaped the banality, and the boredom, of permutation for permutation's sake. Could this poem be a reproach to those well-intentioned practitioners of "concrete" who overplay such games in the belief they are escaping the "shackles" of poetry? Gomringer wrote recently: "Today I am anxious in case Concrete Poetry is accepted purely as a separate genus of poetry. For me it is an important, perhaps the most important aspect of the poetry of our time, and it should not develop into a form of poetry set apart from the main tradition . . . since our Concrete Poetry should actually be a genuine constituent of contemporary literature and contemporary thought, it is important that it should not become merely playful, that the element of play which we advocate, should not result in a facetious kind of poetry. Concrete Poetry has nothing to do with comic strips. In my view it is fitted to make just as momentous statements about human existence in our times and about our mental attitudes as other forms of poetry did in previous periods. It would be unfortunate if it were to become an empty entertainment for the typographer." (From *The First Years of Concrete Poetry*, translated by Stephen Bann.)

the system is fool-proof
the system is ofol-proof
the system is oofl-proof
the system is oolf-proof
the system is oolp-froof
the system is oolp-rfoof
the system is oolp-rofof
the system is oolp-rooff
fth esyste mi sool-proof
tfh esyste mi sool-proof
thf esyste mi sool-proof
the fsyste mi sool-proof
the sfyste mi sool-proof
the syfste mi sool-proof
the sysfte mi sool-proof
the systfe mi sool-proof
the systef mi sool-proof
the system fi sool-proof
the system if sool-proof
the system is fool-proof

DICK HIGGINS

Intermedial Object #1 (1966)

It was Dick Higgins' essay "Intermedia" that gave the avant-garde a new word for the "uncharted land" that lies between poetry and painting, between collage, music and theater, between music and philosophy, etc. His intriguing instructions for *Intermedial Object #1* explores the intermedium between the parlor game and aesthetic research.

Intermedial Object #1

by Dick Higgins

Construct what matches the following description:-

¶1. Size
Horse = 1, Elephant = 10. Object is at 6.

¶2. Shape
Shoe = 1, Mushroom = 10. Object is at 7.

¶3. Function
Food = 1, Chair = 10. Object is at 6.

¶4. Craftsmanship
Neat = 1, Profundity = 10. Object is at 3,

¶5. Taste
Lemon = 1, Hardware = 10. Object is at 5.

¶6. Decoration
Color = 1, Electricity = 10. Object is at 6.

¶7. Brightness
Sky = 1, Mahogany = 10. Object is at 4.

¶8. Permanence
Cake = 1, Joy = 10. Object is at 2.

¶9. Impact
Political = 1, Aesthetic = 10, Humorous = X10. Object is at 8 and is X7 up.

ALLAN KAPROW

Raining (1965)

Definition

A Happening is an assemblage of events performed or perceived in more than one time and place. Its material environments may be constructed, taken over directly from what is available, or altered slightly, just as its activities may be invented or commonplace. A Happening, unlike a stage play, may occur at a supermarket, driving along a highway, under a pile of rags, and in a friend's kitchen, either at once or sequentially. If sequentially, time may extend to more than a year. The Happening is performed according to a plan but without rehearsal, audience, or repetition. It is art but seems closer to life.

—Allan Kaprow

Raining

January 1965

(Scheduled for performance in the spring, for any number of persons and the weather. Times and places need not be coordinated and are left up to the participants. The action of the rain may be watched if desired.) (For Olga and Billy Kluver, January 1965)

Black highway painted black
Rain washes away

Paper men made in bare orchard branches
Rain washes away

Sheets of writing spread over a field
Rain washes away

Little gray boats painted along a gutter
Rain washes away

Naked bodies painted gray
Rain washes away

Bare trees painted red
Rain washes away

Notes to RAINING

Black highway painted black:

A lonely stretch of highway should be selected and a time when it is only sporadically traveled, such as 3 A.M. Black watercolor in large buckets is splashed and brushed onto as long a piece of road as possible. When it next rains, the painters may choose to return to sit at the edge of the black strip.

Paper men made in a bare orchard:

Constructions or papier-maché images should be made in the bare branches just before they bloom in early spring. When it next rains, the slow collapse of these paper men into dripping sogginess may be watched by the builders.

Sheets of writing spread over a field:

An elderly woman might sit by herself and watch her old love letters wash away; a painter might spread out his worst drawings and laugh in the drizzle. These papers should be personal, in any case.

Little gray boats painted along a gutter:

Children (or adults) should paint images of a boat in a gutter; when it rains, they may watch them dissolve and disappear down the sewers.

Naked bodies painted gray:

When it rains, adults or children may paint themselves or each other's naked bodies on a city rooftop, at the beach, or at a country place.

Bare trees painted red:

Here again, an April orchard is best, just before the leaves emerge. A gasoline-powered spray gun, using red watercolor, is most efficient for covering large areas of branches, but if preferred, brushes may be used. When it rains, the dripping color will probably stain the ground around the trees.

ALISON KNOWLES

A House of Dust

1968

This computer poem uses four lists—a list of materials, a list of places where the houses described might be situated, a list of how each might be lit, and a list of who might inhabit them—programmed by James Tenney to be randomly mixed throughout the progress of the poem—and it progresses for several miles of computer print-out.

```
A HOUSE OF DISCARDED CLOTHING
      AMONG HIGH MOUNTAINS
            USING ALL AVAILABLE LIGHTING
                  INHABITED BY ALL RACES OF MEN REPRESENTED WEARING PREDOMINANTLY RED CLOTHING

A HOUSE OF STEEL
      IN A DESERTED FACTORY
            USING ALL AVAILABLE LIGHTING
                  INHABITED BY CHILDREN AND OLD PEOPLE

A HOUSE OF STRAW
      IN MICHIGAN
            USING NATURAL LIGHT
                  INHABITED BY LITTLE BOYS

A HOUSE OF GLASS
      INSIDE A MOUNTAIN
            USING ALL AVAILABLE LIGHTING
                  INHABITED BY PEOPLE WHO LOVE TO READ

A HOUSE OF PLASTIC
      IN SOUTHERN FRANCE
            USING ELECTRICITY
                  INHABITED BY CHILDREN AND OLD PEOPLE

A HOUSE OF STEEL
      IN A DESERTED CHURCH
            USING CANDLES
                  INHABITED BY PEOPLE WHO SLEEP VERY LITTLE

A HOUSE OF WEEDS
      IN JAPAN
            USING ELECTRICITY
                  INHABITED BY PEOPLE WHO SLEEP ALMOST ALL THE TIME

A HOUSE OF BROKEN DISHES
      BY AN ABANDONED LAKE
            USING ALL AVAILABLE LIGHTING
                  INHABITED BY VEGETARIANS

A HOUSE OF DUST
      IN A COLD, WINDY CLIMATE
            USING ALL AVAILABLE LIGHTING
                  INHABITED RY PEOPLE FROM MANY WALKS OF LIFE

A HOUSE OF DISCARDED CLOTHING
      IN A DESERTED CHURCH
            USING ELECTRICITY
                  INHABITED BY COLLECTORS OF ALL TYPES

A HOUSE OF DISCARDED CLOTHING
      IN A HOT CLIMATF
            USING NATURAL LIGHT
                  INHABITED BY LITTLE BOYS
```

A HOUSE OF STEEL
      UNDERWATER
            USING ALL AVAILABLE LIGHTING
                  INHABITED BY PEOPLE FROM MANY WALKS OF LIFE

A HOUSE OF TIN
      IN A GREEN, MOSSY TERRAIN
            USING NATURAL LIGHT
                  INHABITED BY PEOPLE WHO SLEEP ALMOST ALL THE TIME

A HOUSE OF TIN
      BY A RIVER
            USING CANDLES
                  INHABITED BY FISHERMEN AND FAMILIES

A HOUSE OF SAND
      AMONG SMALL HILLS
            USING ELECTRICITY
                  INHABITED BY FRENCH AND GERMAN SPEAKING PEOPLE

A HOUSE OF DUST
      IN AN OVERPOPULATED AREA
            USING CANDLES
                  INHABITED BY VERY TALL PEOPLE

A HOUSE OF ROOTS
      IN A DESERTED AIRPORT
            USING CANDLES
                  INHABITED BY CHILDREN AND OLD PEOPLE

A HOUSE OF ROOTS
      IN A PLACE WITH BOTH HEAVY RAIN AND BRIGHT SUN
            USING ALL AVAILABLE LIGHTING
                  INHABITED BY PEOPLE WHO SLEEP VERY LITTLE

A HOUSE OF ROOTS
      IN A COLD, WINDY CLIMATE
            USING ELECTRICITY
                  INHABITED BY PEOPLE WHO EAT A GREAT DEAL

A HOUSE OF PAPER
      BY AN ABANDONED LAKE
            USING NATURAL LIGHT
                  INHABITED BY VARIOUS BIRDS AND FISH

A HOUSE OF STEEL
      IN MICHIGAN
            USING ALL AVAILABLE LIGHTING
                  INHABITED BY PEOPLE WHO LOVE TO READ

A HOUSE OF WEEDS
      IN A HOT CLIMATE
            USING CANDLES
                  INHABITED BY HORSES AND BIRDS

A HOUSE OF STONE
IN A GREEN, MOSSY TERRAIN
USING ELECTRICITY
INHABITED BY VARIOUS BIRDS AND FISH

A HOUSE OF STONE
ON THE SEA
USING CANDLES
INHABITED BY COLLECTORS OF ALL TYPES

A HOUSE OF TIN
IN A HOT CLIMATE
USING ELECTRICITY
INHABITED BY NEGROS WEARING ALL COLORS

A HOUSE OF ROOTS
BY AN ABANDONED LAKE
USING CANDLES
INHABITED BY VEGETARIANS

A HOUSE OF DISCARDED CLOTHING
BY A RIVER
USING ALL AVAILABLE LIGHTING
INHABITED BY NEGROS WEARING ALL COLORS

A HOUSE OF DISCARDED CLOTHING
BY A RIVER
USING NATURAL LIGHT
INHABITED BY CHILDREN AND OLD PEOPLE

A HOUSE OF DUST
ON AN ISLAND
USING ELECTRICITY
INHABITED BY FRIENDS

A HOUSE OF GLASS
AMONG OTHER HOUSES
USING ALL AVAILABLE LIGHTING
INHABITED BY ALL RACES OF MEN REPRESENTED WEARING PREDOMINANTLY RED CLOTHING

A HOUSE OF WOOD
IN MICHIGAN
USING ELECTRICITY
INHABITED BY PEOPLE WHO EAT A GREAT DEAL

A HOUSE OF DUST
AMONG SMALL HILLS
USING CANDLES
INHABITED BY FRIENDS

A HOUSE OF SAND
IN HEAVY JUNGLE UNDERGROWTH
USING ELECTRICITY
INHABITED BY VEGETARIANS

A HOUSE OF PAPER
IN MICHIGAN
USING ELECTRICITY
INHABITED BY PEOPLE WHO EAT A GREAT DEAL

A HOUSE OF STRAW
IN SOUTHERN FRANCE
USING NATURAL LIGHT
INHABITED BY PEOPLE WHO SLEEP VERY LITTLE

A HOUSE OF PLASTIC
IN A PLACE WITH BOTH HEAVY RAIN AND BRIGHT SUN
USING CANDLES
INHABITED BY VEGETARIANS

A HOUSE OF WEEDS
ON AN ISLAND
USING ALL AVAILABLE LIGHTING
INHABITED BY ALL RACES OF MEN REPRESENTED WEARING PREDOMINANTLY RED CLOTHING

A HOUSE OF ROOTS
BY THE SEA
USING CANDLES
INHABITED BY FRIENDS AND ENEMIES

A HOUSE OF ROOTS
BY AN ABANDONED LAKE
USING CANDLES
INHABITED BY FRENCH AND GERMAN SPEAKING PEOPLE

A HOUSE OF BROKEN DISHES
UNDERWATER
USING ELECTRICITY
INHABITED BY LITTLE BOYS

A HOUSE OF DUST
IN A DESERT
USING ALL AVAILABLE LIGHTING
INHABITED BY PEOPLE WHO SLEEP ALMOST ALL THE TIME

A HOUSE OF BROKEN DISHES
IN A DESERT
USING ALL AVAILABLE LIGHTING
INHABITED BY PEOPLE FROM MANY WALKS OF LIFE

A HOUSE OF STEEL
IN MICHIGAN
USING ALL AVAILABLE LIGHTING
INHABITED BY PEOPLE WHO SLEEP ALMOST ALL THE TIME

A HOUSE OF MUD
IN A HOT CLIMATE
USING ALL AVAILABLE LIGHTING
INHABITED BY FRIENDS

FERDINAND KRIWET

"Contemporary literature," Ferdinant Kriwet believes, "has long since rejected the idea of the book being its only legitimate abode." This does not mean the book is dead; "the age of the book is yet to come," with texts specially composed for it. In the meantime, Kriwet is in the forefront of the intermedialists, composing total literary environments for live speakers, actors, magnetic tape, films and projections with the same controlled mastery that marked his earlier experiments with "visually perceptible literature," sound-poems and teletexts. The following photographs show poetry "writ large" in both word and deed.

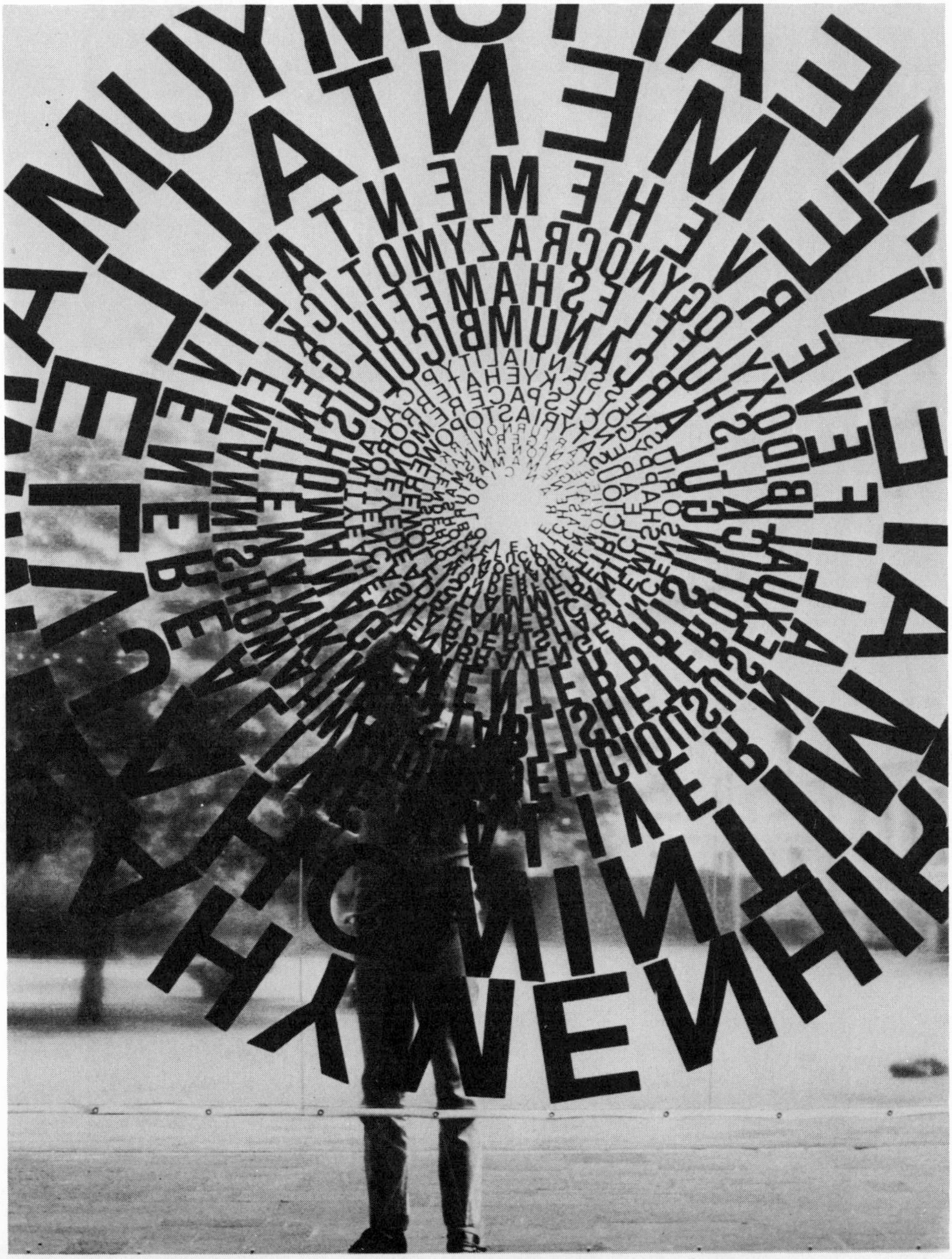

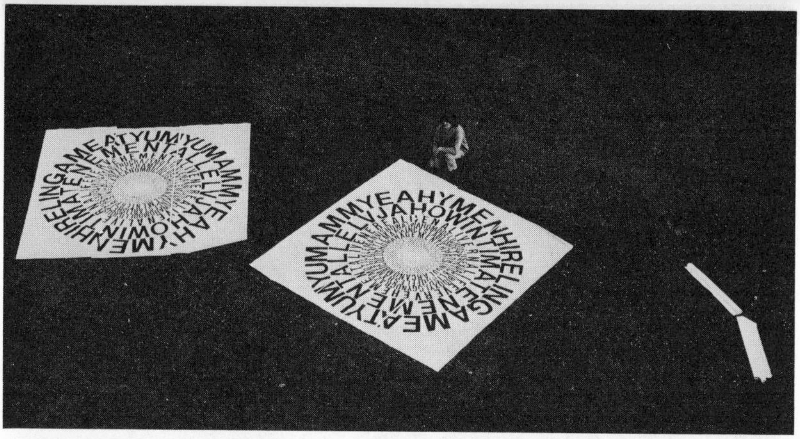

HAND
AD
HE AD
S IN
IN
E K
R E
HAPPY
HAPPY N
HAPPY NE
HAPPY NES
HAPPY NESS
END HAPPY NESS
JA
NE IN
A
NO NO NO NO NO NO NO
NO NO NO NO NO NO
NO NO NO NO NO
NO NO NO NO
NO NO NO

MARKUS KUTTER

Programme for Berio (1962)

The Swiss writer Markus Kutter wrote this song for composer Luciano Berio, who had asked Kutter if lyrics writers could write songs to fulfill these conditions: "Few words. Simple words. But words which could be sung back to front and front to back. Or even over one another. Or higgledy-piggledy. Or, of course, one after another. Now just a few words picked out. Now one beautiful word alone. Perhaps a long chain in which the links are continually rearranged. And it must make sense. And it must have atmosphere and sound marvelous. For example, for a woman's voice. (Because his wife Kathie sings so well.)" The programme can be used in the following sequences

a b c d e f g h i
or e alone
or a e i
or a d g b e h c f i
or g h i a b c f e d
or a d e f i
or c f i a d g h e b
or c e g

or any sequence one chooses.

a Give me	b a few words	c for a woman
d to sing	e a truth	f that allows us
g before night falls	h without sorrow	i to build a house

ROBERT LAX

This Bread

"The later poetry of Robert Lax, which has undergone various linear changes, remains almost sacramental in its attempts to grasp the essence and quiddities of a few things that are by their very nature eternal. If one really believes, with all attendant nuances, that

this
bread
is
bread

as Robert Lax does, then faith, which he has in great abundance, is often both wonderously and mysteriously present. Such faith, in God, in life, bears repetition of line, which somehow miraculously does not become repetitious. His constant re-discovery of the possibilities of love, or of the sea, or the sky—the genuine re-discovery of what has always existed—can only lead to reprise, a restatement of theme." (William F. Claire, Introduction to the special Robert Lax issue of *Voyages*.)

this
bread

is
bread

this
wine

is
wine

this
bread

is
bread

this
wine

is
wine

these
hands

are
hands

these
hands

are
hands

this
bread

is
bread

this
wine

is
wine

The Wheels of God (1965)

(leros)

the wheels of god
they say
grind slow

but they
grind exceed-
ing fine

the wheels of god
they say
grind slow

but they
grind exceed-
ing fine

grind
slow

grind
slow

grind
fine

grind
fine

grind
slow

grind
slow

grind
fine

grind
slow

grind
slow

grind
fine

grind
fine

grind
fine

grind
fine

(grind
slow)

Hola (1965)

(kalym-
nos)

(a song
to be
sung
in that
future
time

when
every-
thing
else
is

quite
ok)

hola
hola

behold
the
sun

hola
hola

behold
the
sun

the
sun
is
up
now

the
sun
is
up
now

clap
clap

look
look

behold
the
sun

The White Bird

". . . the recent poetry of Robert Lax bears witness to a . . . conviction of the need to forge a connection between poetic and pictorial form, and to exclude from poetry that redundancy of images which has been progressively eliminated in post-Cubist painting. Where Gomringer associated his venture specifically with such artists as Hans Arp and Max Bill, Robert Lax—though ready to admit his admiration for the Concrete artists—is inclined to cast his net over a wider field. His recent 'color' poems are built up entirely from successive blocks of color notations: one is dedicated to the painter Ad Reinhardt, who had a comparable disregard for unnecessary syntax. And there is more than a hint of Braque in Lax's overtly symbolic "white bird," which achieves the simplicity and poise of one of that painter's memorable images of flight." (Stephen Bann, from the introduction to *Concrete Poetry—an international anthology*.)

the white bird	the dark hill
the white bird	the dark hill
the dark hill	the white bird
the dark hill	the white bird
the white bird	the white bird
the white bird	the white bird
the dark sea	the dark sea

For Ad Reinhardt

FOR
AD
REIN-
HARDT

black
black
black

blue
blue
blue

black
black
black
black

blue
blue
blue

JACKSON MAC LOW

The Presidents of the United States of America

A Note on the Composition of *The Presidents of the United States of America* by Jackson Mac Low, 15 December 1968

The Presidents of the United States of America was composed in January and May 1963. Each section is headed by the first inaugural year of a president (from Washington thru Fillmore), and its structure of images is that of the Phoenician meanings of the successive letters of the president's name. The meanings are those given in *The Roman Inscriptional Letter,* a book designed, written, and printed by Sandra Lawrence in the Graphic Arts Workshop at Reed College, Portland, Oregon, in May 1955. They are:

A (aleph) "ox"
B (beth) "house"
C (gimel) "camel"
D (daleth) "door"
E (he) "window" or "look!"
F (vau) "hook"
H (cheth) "fence"
I (yod) "hand"
K (kaph) "palm of the hand"
L (lamed) "ox-goad"
M (mem) "water"
N (nun) "fish"
O (ayin) "eye"
P (pe) "mouth"
Q (qoph) "knot"
R (resh) "head"
S (shin) "tooth"
T (tau) "mark"
V (vau) "hook"
X (samekh) "prop"
Y (vau) "hook"
Z (zayin) "weapon"

Letters developed by the Romans or in the Middle Ages were given the meanings of the letters from which they were derived or to which they were similar:

G (developed by Romans in third century B.C.: similar in form to C) "camel"
J (introduced during Middle Ages as minuscule form of I and made into majuscule in the sixteenth century) "hand"
U (introduced during Middle Ages as a minuscule form of V and made into majuscule in the sixteenth century) "hook"
W (Anglo-Saxon addition in eleventh century; similar to two V's) "hooks" or "hook hook"

These letter-meaning words were used as "nuclei" which were freely connected by other material. This method was first used by the poet in writing a sestina, "The Albatross," in 1950; here a list of end words was obtained "automatically" and then permuted and connected into a sestina. The poet first connected chance-given nuclei in this way in 1960 in writing such prose pieces as "A Greater Sorrow" (in *An Anthology,* edited by La Monte Young, New York, 1963 and in my *Stanzas for Iris Lezak,* Something Else Press, Barton, Vt., 1972). Most of the poems in *22 Light Poems* (Black Sparrow Press, Los Angeles, 1968) were composed in 1962–63, using names of kinds of light as nuclei. In *The Presidents of the United States of America,* each letter-meaning nucleus could be used in any form class (e.g., M could be translated as the noun "water," the verb "water," the adjective "watery," or as the adverb "waterily"). In the earlier sections (written in January 1963), a minimum of connective material was introduced between the nuclei, and the meanings of the letters of each name delimited a strophe. In the later sections (written in May 1963), much more material was introduced between the nuclei, and the verse structures became much more complex.

The poet has often been asked by friends and well-wishers to write further sections dealing with the presidents following Fillmore. He has often thought of doing so and has even collected materials for this purpose, but so far he has not.

The Presidents of the United States of America

1789

(begun about 15 January 1963)

George Washington never owned a camel
but he looked thru the eyes in his head
with a camel's calm and wary look.

Hooks that wd irritate an ox
held his teeth together
and he cd build a fence with his own hands
tho he preferred to go fishing
as anyone else wd
while others did the work *for* him
for tho he had no camels he had slaves enough
and probably made them toe the mark by keeping an eye on them
for *he* wd never have stood for anything fishy.

1797

John Adams knew the hand
can be quicker than the eye
& knew that not only fencers & fishermen live by this knowledge.

If he kept an ox
he kept it out of doors in summertime
so the ox cd find his water for himself
& make it where he stood
& find the tasty grass
his teeth cd chew as cud.

1801

Marked by no fence
farther than an eye cd see

beyond the big waters
Thomas Jefferson saw grass enough for myriads of oxen
to grind between their teeth.

His farmer hands itched
when he thought of all that vacant land and looked about for a way to hook it in for us
until something unhooked a window in his head
where the greedy needy teeth & eyes of Napoleon shone
eager for the money which
was Jefferson's bait to catch the Louisiana fish.

1809

James Madison's hand cd lead an ox to water
and he'd look at him while he drank
                                        letting it
        spill down from grassy teeth.

After he'd water'd his ox
                                James Madison'd
  push open his door with his hand
                                        & then his teeth'd
grind and mash up all but the bones & eyes of a large fish.

1817

James Monroe
laid a hand
as heavy as the ox that stands on every peon's tongue
on all between the waters between
the new world and both old ones
& looked across both of them
                                    baring but
puppy teeth then.

Across the waters eyes
                              in fishers' heads
eyed this newest angler
with the grudging look of fellow-recognition
                          old members of the Predators' Club
                    bestow on former prey
      that blunders past all blackballs
& soon must be accepted for admission.

1825
(written 24 May 1963)

John Quincy Adams's right hand
shaded his eyes
as he sat on a fence & fished.

At one end of his line was a knot & a hook
at the
other end
his hand & he sat
fishing for a camel with a hook instead of a hump?

No & not for an ox
because
behind a door he had his papa's ox
& when he went fishing in water
(& that's what he was doing he was no fool)
he was looking to get something
good
something
he cd sink his teeth into & want to.

1829

(24 May 1963)

Andrew Jackson's last name's the same as my first
but
that makes me no more like him
than an ox is like a
fish
(or vice versa)
but
open a door in your head
(or a window)
& look!
if your eyes are hooks
what's on those hooks?
Andrew Jackson?

Nonsense:
Andrew Jackson's dead:
you can no more see *him*
than your hand cd hold in itself
an ox:
than you cd hold a camel in the palm of your hand
as you *cd* hold a tooth
or an eye of a fish:
forget Andrew Jackson:
(you already have).

1837

(24 May 1963)

If Martin Van Buren ever swam in water
(if Martin Van Buren ever swam)
what kind of swimmer was he if he held onto an ox's head

(did he?)
to keep his own above the surface?
(he knew about banks
but
what did he know about swimming?)
but
what is MartinVan Buren now
but
a series of marks I make
with
my
hand?
(maybe
Martin
Van
Buren cd swim like a fish!)
do
I
make
these
marks
with
"my"
hand?
can
"I"
catch
this fish
(i.
e.,
"I")?

A hook big enough to hang an ox from's
a hook too big to catch a fish with.

Martin Van Buren lived in a fine big house in New York State
before he was president
but how did he get his hooks into
Ezra Pound's head:
look!
I want to know how a poet became a
rich old dead old politician's fish.

1841 (I)

(24 May 1963)

Andrew Jackson & Martin Van Buren
are heroes of that old
hero of mine in whose honor I write

"wd"
&
"cd"
&
"shd"
in-
stead
of
"would"
&
"could"
&
"should"
(I write
"&"
in-
stead
of
"and"
in
honor
of
William
Blake
but
whose
hero's
William
Henry
Harrison? (I mean
whose
hero is he *now*?):
old
hero hung on a hook
the
hook is "Tippecanoe"
&
the smart old politicians used it as an ox-goad
(their
theory was: "an ox-goad in the hand
can
make 'em
go:
treat 'em like oxen & they'll lap it up like water."

That's the way those wily Whigs
fenced:
(look!

who remembers who *they* were now?
—those old phynancial string-pullers
(*peace*, Jarry!)
who hung an old Indian fighter on their line
(a smaller fish to catch a bigger one)
pushing thru his aging head
the hook
"Tippecanoe":
who remembers who *they* were now?
we
remember "Tippecanoe":
whose
fish is
who?)—
but
that
was the way those old finaglers did it
&
if you can't learn from history
what *can* "you" learn from?

(Mystery.)

Who was sitting on the fence?
Who was treated like an ox?
Whose head was used as bait?
Whose head planned it all?
Whose hand held the line?
Whose teeth chewed what was caught?
Whose eye caught what was going on?
Who was the fish & how did *he* like it?

1841 (II)

(written 24 May 1963)

The poor old bait got sick & died
&
then they had "Tyler too!"
(exclamation point & all)
&
some there were who had him on their hands
& some there were who had him in front of their eyes
& some there were who had him
& some there were who wished he'd just go off
& sit on a fence somewhere & fish.

That's the way John Tyler made his mark
& he knew whose hook he was on
& he knew who held the ox-goad

&   he knew when to turn his back to the window
:   (*he* knew when to look
&   when
not
to look:
he knew   how to use his *head*):
but
where's John Tyler
now?   (Dead.)
& what do "we" have because he made a deal? (Texas.)

1845

(written 24 May 1963)

Tyler was no Whig at all & after his term's end
wanted the Demo*crat*ic nomination but
only
a splinter group
nominated him &
Clay
got
the Whigs'   &
'the first "dark horse"
of
American
national politics
was suddenly brought forward in the morning.
James K.
[for "Knox"]
Polk,   of Tennessee,
after one ballot, was unanimously chosen as
the Democratic candidate.
The   country,   bewildered,
asked
"Who is Polk?"
He
was
indeed,
not entirely unknown.'
[I quote (I've quoted)
a   descendant(?)   of
John Adams & John Quincy Adams (?)
—*do* I quote a descendant of
John Adams & John Quincy Adams?—
I   don't think I do I
quote a history-textbook-writer
named
James Truslow Adams
who wrote a book called

The Record of America with another
history-
textbook-
writer
named Charles Garrett Vannest
a Professor of History
at Harris Teachers College
in St. Louis:
he (Vannest)
was co-author of
Socialized History of the United States
(whose co-author was he *then*?)]

The main things about James Knox Polk were
that first he had Texas & then a war with Mexico on his hands
that he was no ox but a man with a conscience who made war anyway
that "we" got all of Texas, Utah, Nevada, & California
& most of Arizona & New Mexico because
of conscience-stricken Mr. Polk's war
that Mr. Polk's war
extended "us" to the waters of the
Pacific (Ocean)
(how "pacific" can an ocean be if "we"
got
"our"
window on it thru a war?)
(Answer: just as
"pacific"
as any other ocean)
("window" hell:
"our"
teeth
snapped up a whole damn coast *that* time
& everything up *to* it)
that *that* war
was
why
Thoreau refused to pay his tax
& stayed in jail a night
& wrote *Civil Disobedience*
& eventually
was read by a little Indian lawyer (*Indian* Indian)
who invented another way to fight
& thought it wasn't violent
&
used it
so shrewdly that
he & circumstances made

the British Empire lose a whole sub-continent.

In the palm of his hand
a man who ate no fish or meat
held for a time
an
empire on which the sun never set
his eye
controlled that vast melange of
hungry peoples
he
didnt
fight
not
that is
as
other people fought
he thought
he made no threats
thought
he used no violence
thought
he used only
Satyagraha
the force of truth
to pull away the British Empire's props.

Thus we've come by word of mouth
from James Knox Polk
America's
first "dark horse" president
to the eye of Mohandas Gandhi:
that ox-goad
small enough to be
hidden in the palm of a hand.
(to here at 1:10 am Sat 25 May 1963)

1849

(written 25 May 1963)

Zachary Taylor made his name in the Mexican War.
(They say there's something about a soldier that is fine fine fine.
I've always wondered what it is.
Maybe it's his weapons.)
Zachary Taylor made a name for himself by
acting toward other men
as if they were oxen or camels.
He didn't pay attention to other people's fences—
especially if they were only Mexicans.

"After all oxen have heads
only to hear
commands to eat
(as little as they can & still work)
& to keep yokes
from falling off.
If they try to use 'em for anything else
hang 'em up on hooks."

If "Old Rough & Ready"
Zachary Taylor didn't think this way
how *else* did he make his mark in the Mexican War?
As "a Louisiana slave-holder"
he must have known all about
how to treat people like oxen.
All right then how did it happen
he let the Californians
adopt a constitution
prohibiting slavery?

I guess he just didnt think they *wd*
or maybe
he just didnt care
as long as it
didnt affect *his*
holding of slaves.
(Maybe
some Northern politician got his hooks in him.)
Anyway
getting to be
President of the United States of America
didnt do Zachary Taylor
any
real
good—
—(unless it's a
real
good
to be
President of the United States of America
one year & a third
& thus have
one's name
on every subsequent list of American Presidents).
Zachary
Taylor
("Old Rough & Ready")
died on July 9th, 1850.

He had had *his*
chance
to wield *that*
ox-goad
(I mean the one
every President of the United States of America
has at hand).
Now what
I wonder
is: how did Zachary Taylor
manage to
stick it in his own eye
(if *that's* what he did)?
Did
things just start to happen in his body & his head?

1850

(written 25 May 1963)

Millard Fillmore seems to have been a watery customer.
My book says he "was a friend of Clay & compromise"
& in
my book that means
he didnt let his right hand know
what his left hand was doing
so
if
one hand was
wielding an ox-goad
his
other one didnt know
whether
the ox-goad
was prodding an ox's head
or stabbing a door.

Millard Fillmore used the hook in *his* hand
(let's call an ox-goad an ox-goad)
not just to force the
Fugitive Slave Law thru
(as part of the Compromise of 1850)
but
to "secure" "by
treaties with Honduras & Nicaragua
the right of transit across
their
territories" &
to freeze the English where they were in Central America
getting them to agree to

"guarantee the neutrality
of any canal built."
That's how
Millard Fillmore laid the foundations
for the Panama Canal
altho he never saw it even begin to join the waters
never saw it with his own physical eyes.
Millard Fillmore must have had a head on him:
I
mean a head for "diplomatic" business & the like.
Had
he been poor
he'd've
never passed
any
neighbor's window
without looking to see
whether it was open & if it was
what there was for him to grab from it as he went by.

Bravo
brave
Millard Fillmore.

(end of "1850" & of the first series of "The Presidents of the United States of America" (Washington thru Fillmore))
written from about 15 January 1963 thru 25 May 1963

HANSJÖRG MAYER

alphabet (1963)

Hansjörg Mayer, certainly the most original and adventuresome of the younger generation of designers and typographers, has made available through his publishing house in Stuttgart the works of the major experimental writers of Europe, England and North and South America. His own work, which explores the intermedium between poetry and typography, has earned him the title "poetypographer," bestowed by Haroldo de Campos, theoretician of the Brazilian Noigandres poets.

"*alphabet* . . . is a portfolio containing twenty-six printed sheets. On each sheet there is one of the twenty-six letters of an alphabet in a fairly common typeface, the bold condensed akzidenz grotesk, repeated a few times consecutively. In this way twenty-six stapled sequences have been constructed, in which the sound and meaning of the letters is reduced and their visual form made into the focal point. The letters are detached from a language system and are treated instead in a system of shapes. They do not relate to other letters with which they might form a word, but exclusively to their own visual shape and to the accumulated shape which has thus been constructed. In the same way that by normal usage of a letter a definite potential sound and meaning always emerges, so in these sequences definite graphic possibilities of the letter are made visible. . . . The result, however, is never a completely abstract shape, not even when the normal shape of the letter has been to a great extent obscured. Although the aggregate shape draws attention to new shapes, alongside this it continually refers back to the letter shape from which it has been built. In these sequences a visible transformation of language into image is always the case." (Hans Locher and Kees Broos, in the introduction to the catalogue of the retrospective exhibition of publications and works by Hansjörg Mayer at the Gemeentemuseum in the Hague, 1968.)

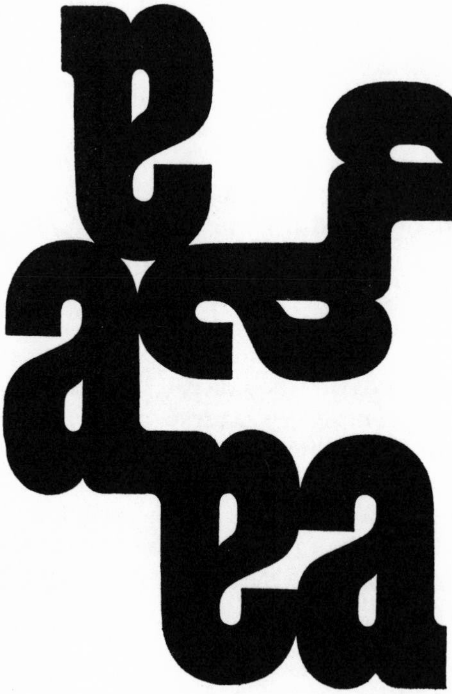

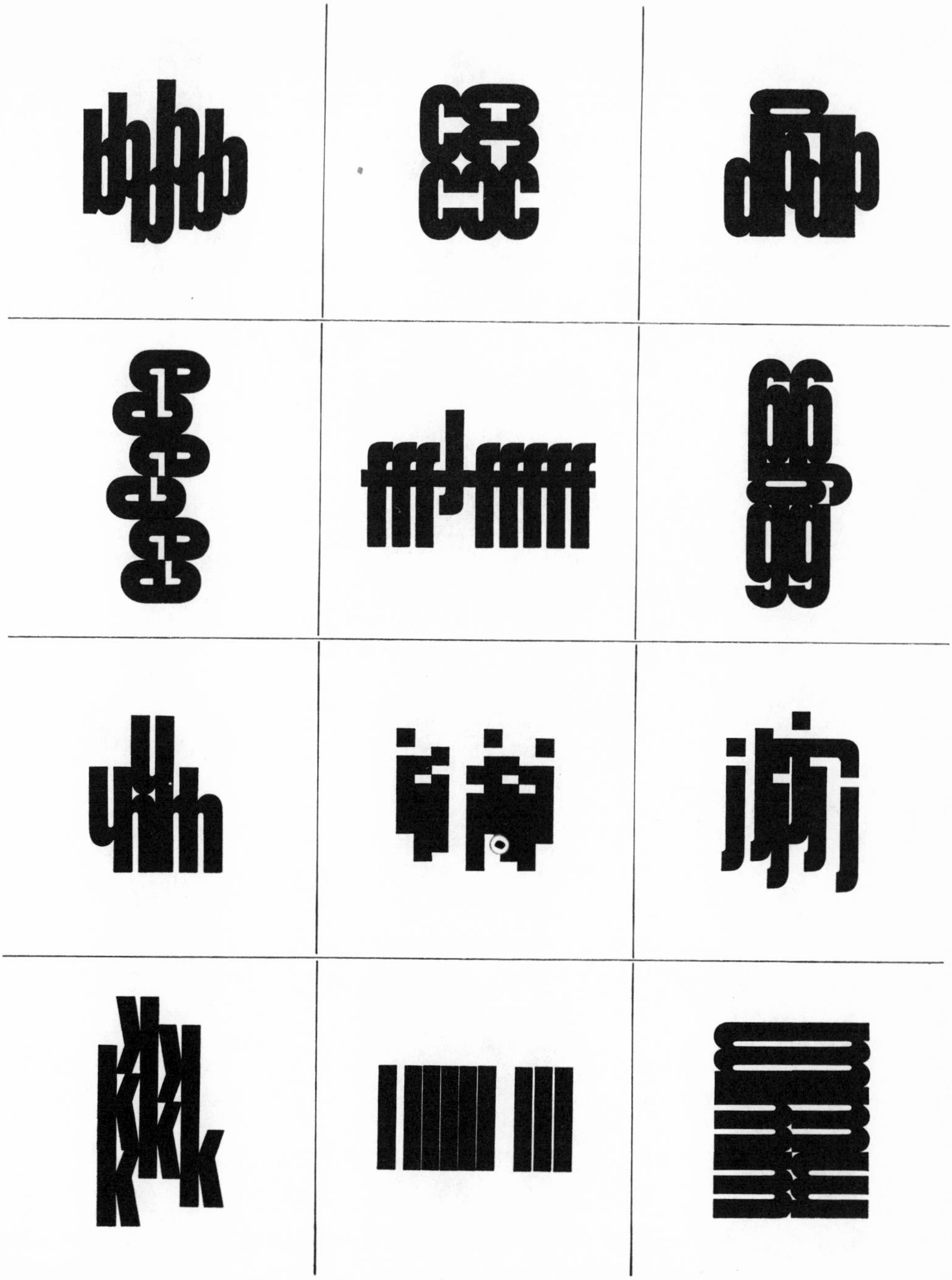

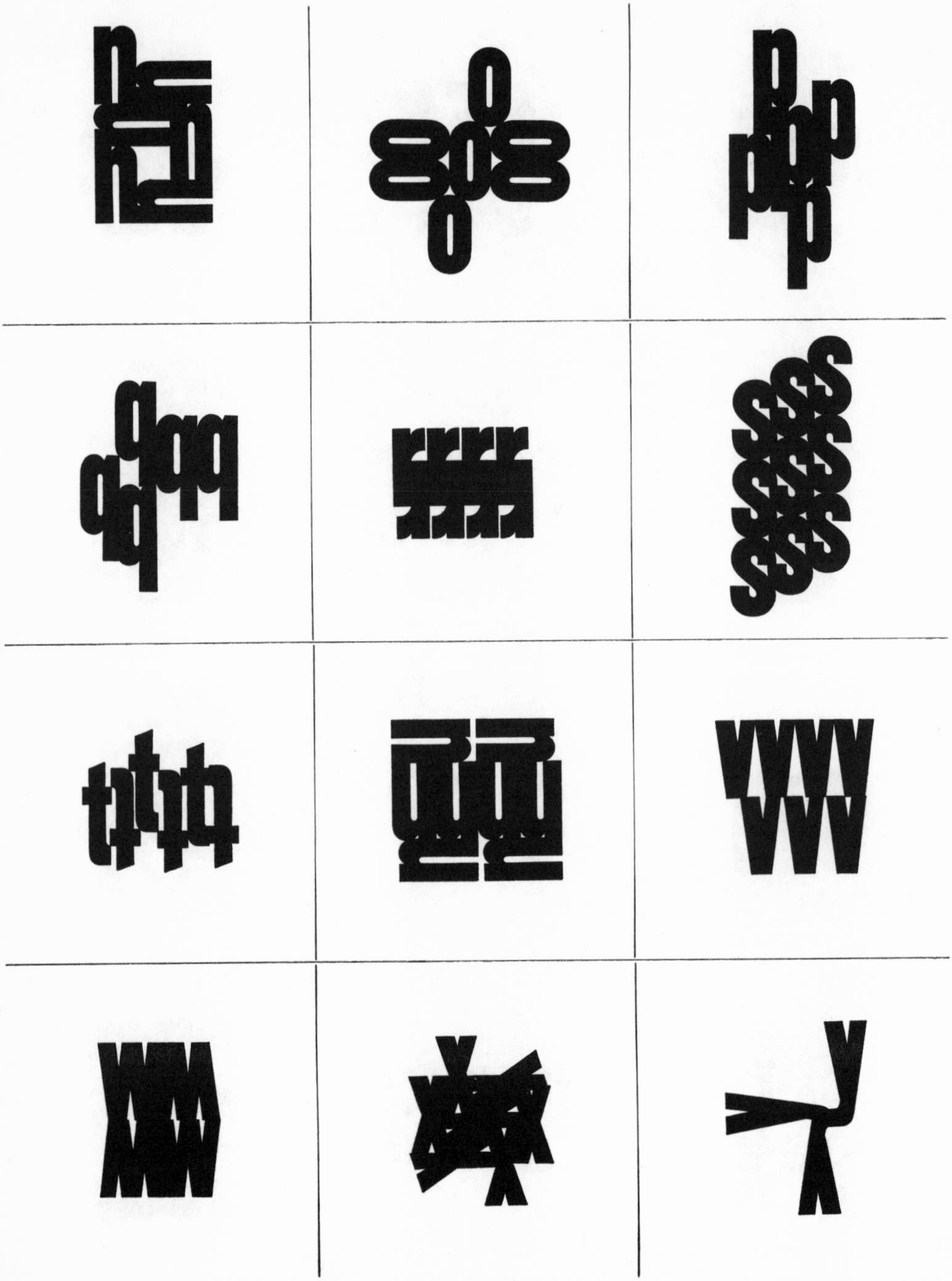

serie rosenschuttplatz (1964)

This series consists of ten "variations" on texts selected by the German philosopher Max Bense. Reprinted here are pages 1, 6 and 10.

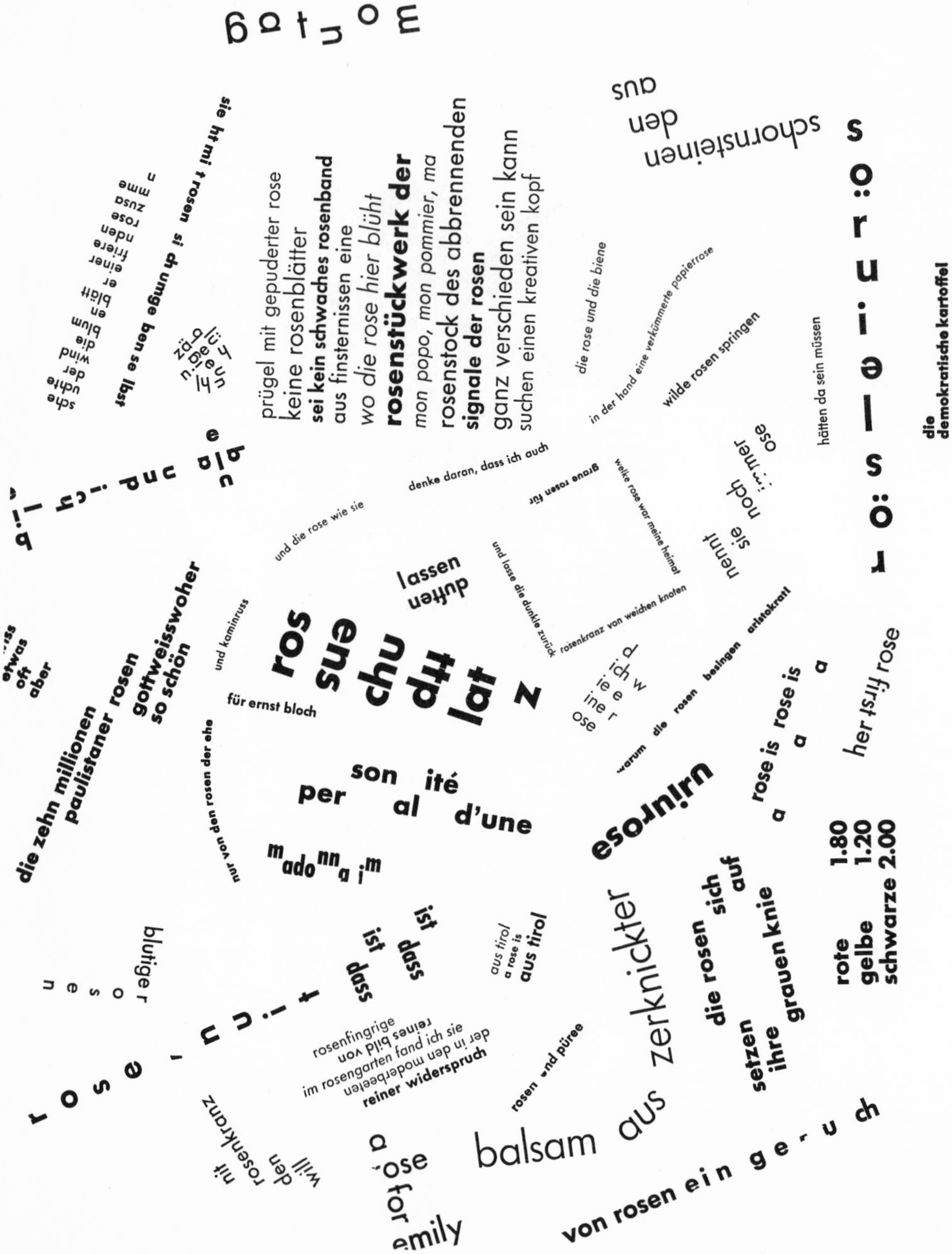

prügel mit gepuderter rose
keine rosenblätter
sei kein schwaches rosenband
aus finsternissen eine
wo die rose hier blüht
rosenstückwerk der
mon popo, mon pommier, ma
rosenstock des abbrennenden
signale der rosen
ganz verschieden sein kann
suchen einen kreativen kopf
schornsteinen
den
aus
die rose und die biene
in der hand eine verkümmerte papierrose
wilde rosen springen
hätten da sein müssen
die
demokratische kartoffel
denke daran, dass ich auch
und die rose wie sie
lassen
duften
grau rosen für
welke rose war meine heimat
und lasse die dunkle zurück
rosenkranz von weichen knoten
nennt
sie
noch
immer
rose
und kaminruss
für ernst bloch
gottweisswoher
so schön
die zehn millionen
paulistaner rosen
etwas
oft
aber
warum die rosen besingen aristokratt
rose is rose is
her first rose
son ité
per al d'une
nur von den rosen der ehe
rote 1.80
gelbe 1.20
schwarze 2.00
die rosen sich auf
setzen ihre grauen knie
zerknickter
aus tirol
a rose is
aus tirol
blutiger
rosenfingrige
reines bild von
im rosengarten fand ich sie
der in dem wohlbedeten
reiner widerspruch
rosen und püree
balsam aus
von rosen ein geruch
rosenkranz
emily

schornsteinen
und die rose wie sie
denke daran, dass ich
grüne rosen für
wilde rosen springen
in der hand eine verkümmerte papierrose
rosenkranz von weichen knoten
für ernst bloch
lassen
warum die rosen besingen
aristokratisch
demokratische kartoffel
madonna
balsam
emily
von rosen

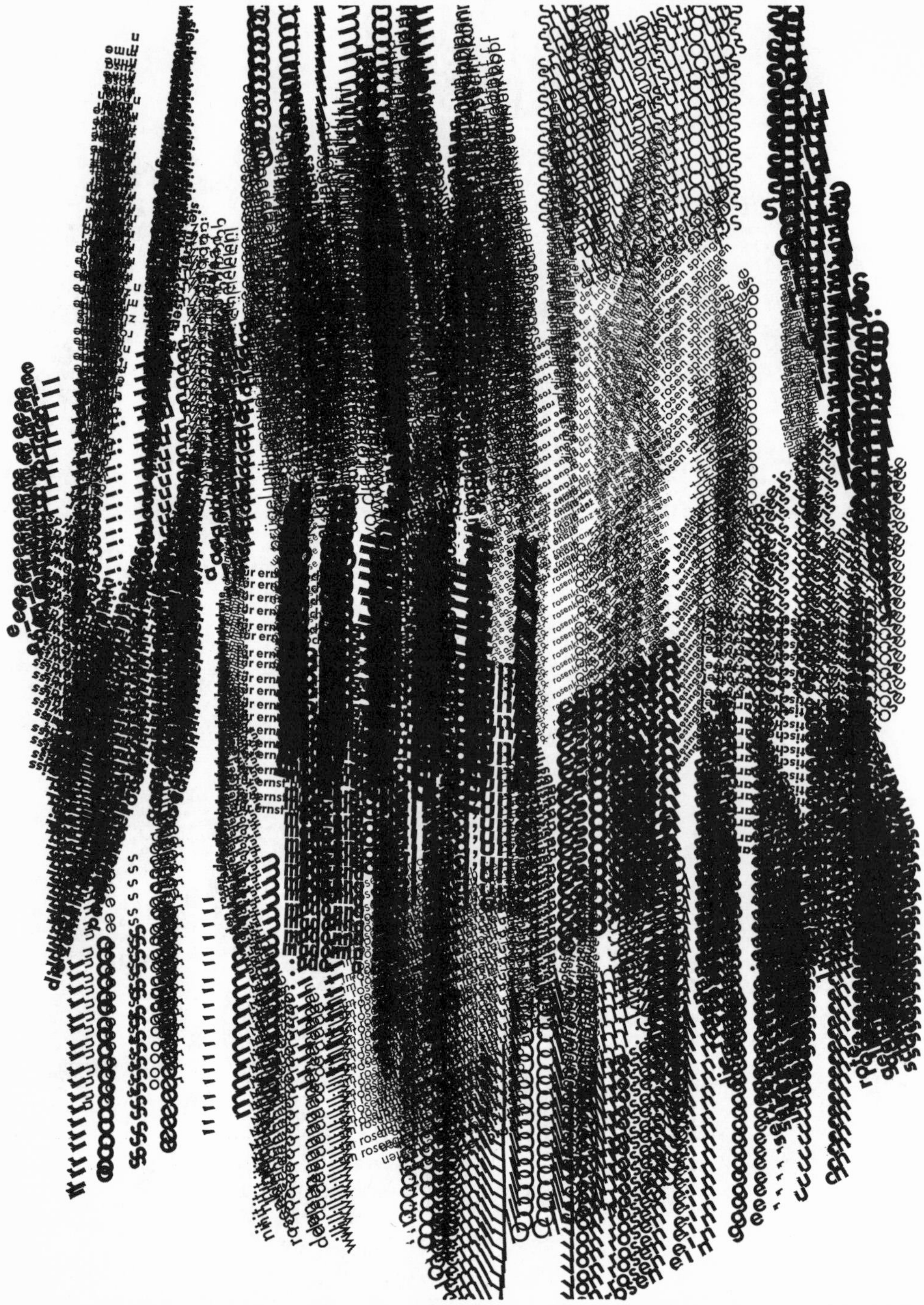

sau aus usa (1965)

"In this construction a visual arrangement in rows of three different successions of the three letters of this word is closely allied with three different meanings emerging from it. . . . A square block is made up of 3 x 3 letters, which appear in the ambiguous sphere between shape and meaning. The shapes of the letters constantly point to the three words which appear both horizontally and vertically. But these words do not detach themselves from the letters and they in turn constantly point back to the visual presence embodied in the shapes of the letters themselves." (Hans Locher and Kees Broos, *op. cit.*)

sau = sow, slut
aus = from

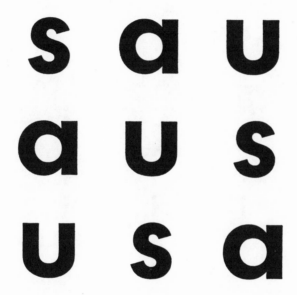

s a u

a u s

u s a

oil (1965)

Circles, points and lines merge in meaning.

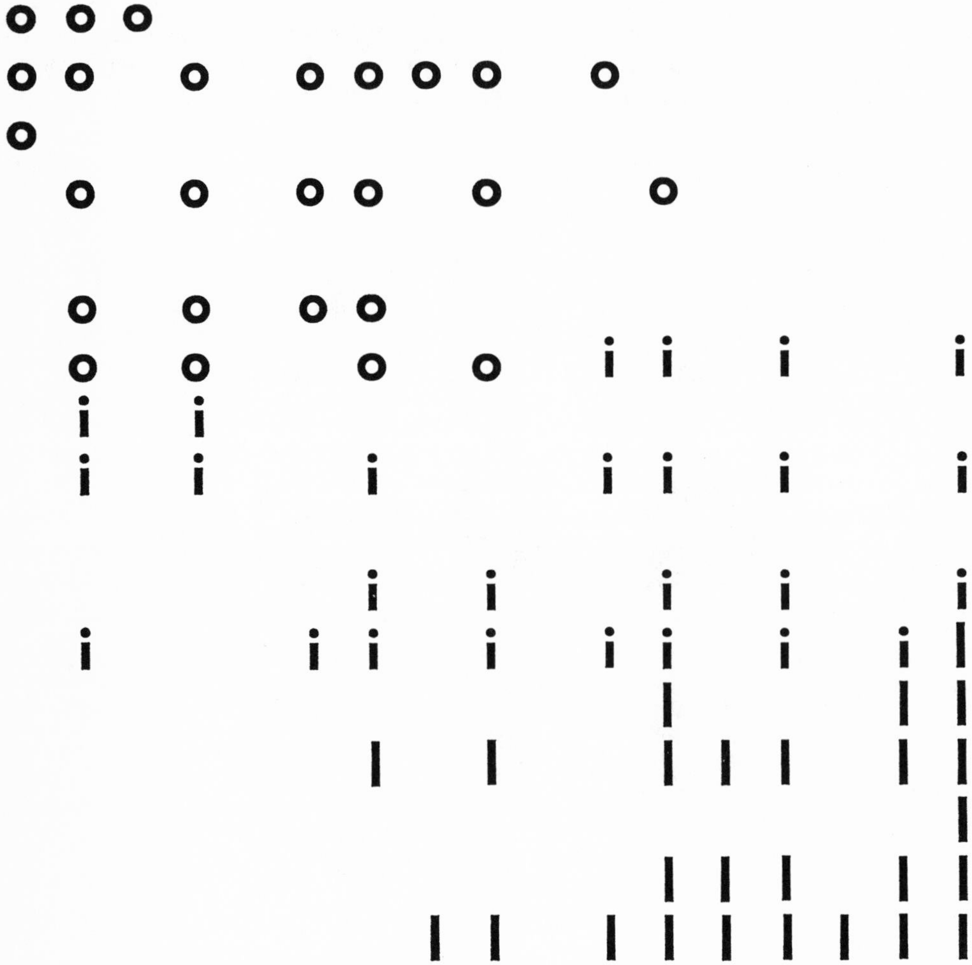

THOMAS MERTON

(1968)

Almost a year to the day before his death in 1968, Thomas Merton "discovered" concrete poetry. Acknowledging the gift of the present editor's *An Anthology of Concrete Poetry*, Merton wrote his old friend Jonathan Williams: "Many, many thanks for the Concrete Poets. Magnificent. Great to have and soak in. I see what you mean by my square effort. True does not connect at all. I look at those Brazilians. Wow!"

In a letter to the editor written the following July, he had "started on some visual stuff. Hasn't loosened up yet but I think it will start to break soon. If only we had more type here and the monastery printer had more time we could really do something about it. But I think he is a bit dubious about it all, and the locals are not attuned to any of it." In the same letter he explored the possibility of visiting a proposed exhibition of visual poetry in Minneapolis in October. But by October he was in Asia. In a letter dated November 9 from New Delhi he enthusiastically described his meeting with the Dalai Lama and Buddhist monks: ". . . the other day one of the lamas . . . composed a poem for me in Tibetan so I composed one for him (in English) and we parted on this note of traditional Asian monastic courtesy." A month later he was dead, electrocuted by a short-circuited fan in his Bangkok hotel room.

Of the present selection of Merton's concrete work, the first and last are reprinted from manuscripts in the editor's collection, and the other three first appeared in *Monk's Pond*, the magazine Merton edited from the Abbey of Gethsemani in 1968.

Readers familiar with Merton's only existing pre-monastic prose work, *My Argument with the Gestapo*, written in 1941 while he was a student at Cambridge but published posthumously, will be able to relate Merton's sound-poems published in this anthology to such macaronic portions of *My Argument* as the Hotel Rocamadour section of Chapter XXI. The following quotation is greatly condensed:

> Yherezt nopitty ont dzhe steirs . . .
> Dzhere eitz nobbudy onz dhe stoirs . . .
> Dzhere idz nyubbodi omn dlhe shtiars . . .
> Tzere its noobodo uan we stairs . . .
> Dear has nopretty in the stars . . .
> Dzhere ess know's doddy on these stairs . . .

```
H U R L U B
    E R L  U H
U R L     U  B   E   R
L   U     H  U   R    L
U    B    E   R   L       U
    H  U       R  L
           U
B E R    L     U  H   U
R L U B E R       L U U
U  U    U    U   U U U U
H U R L U B E R       LU
B B B E B B E B E R B E
R L U L E R L U B   E R
LU LUH LU LHU LU LUH HU
    H U R L U B E
    E R L U H U H
         UH
    BERLULULUBEREL
         U
```

(1968)

Part of the fun of the magazine *Monk's Pond*, which Merton edited the year of his death, were the "embellishments" of concrete texts by himself and other poets.

OVID   DIVO
VOID   DIOV
IDOV   IOVD
VIDO   OVID

VOID   DIOV
DVOI   OIVD
IDVO   OVID
OIDV   VOID

IVOD   DOVI
VIDO   OVID
OVID   VIDO
DOVI   IVOD

DVOI   VOID
IDVO   VIDO
OIDV   IDOV
VOID   DIVO

OVID   DIVO
VOID   DIOV
IDOV   IOVD
VIDO   OVID

Semiotic Poem from Racine's "Iphigenie"

(1968)

Most of Merton's experiments in his last year were with sound-poems, which seemed to come easier to him than the "visual stuff." This one is in French, his first language.

c e s   m o r t s
c e t t e   l e s b o s
c e s   c e n d r e s
c e t t e   f l a m m e

C E S
C E T T E
C E S
C E T T E
M O R T S
L E S B O S
C E N D R E S
F L A M M E
C E S
C E T T E
L E S

b o s
e e e e
o e e l
s t s t
r s n a
t t
e e
s o r m
l e s b o
m o r f a
f l a m m a
M O R S

L E S B O S
C C C C C C
E E E E E E
S T S T S T
C E S M O R T S C E T T E
L E S B O S

c e n d r e s

(1968)

W H I S K E
W H I   S K
W H I S S S
K E   E   Y
S H K E E Y
W H I S K W
H I S K W Y
W H I S K Y

whisk E Y
EYE **hisky**
W H I S K W
aaaa s h ky
w **h** I S **key**
w **h i** S K **y**
YK e h w ik

W H I S K I
h s e y k W
H I s k e y
W I S H K I

(1968)

BROnze fasHIONs

RONZEfa shIONS BR

onzeFAS hionSB RONZE FA

SHI onsbr ONzeFabrASH FASHio

BRonzefa shIONSB rasho FONZE R

AshION

ONZE mash

FAbra SHION MA

ROnsha FashbrON

BRA shon RONZE Fashbra RASha

BRonsh

ASHMA frabshon BRASS on

HIONBronza FAShibro Ronzba BRASFO

Nshion

RASHA MO BARiosh Ronza Br

ONZE Fa shio nbr

onZE FAZESH

ON BR ONZA Fonze FASHIO Nsbronze

RasHMA Fashio BRASH a fonz

RONza BRONZA

Fash ION

NIObr ONfaSH NOBro ShF ia BRONZE

FASHIONSBRONZEFASHIONSBRON ZEF

ASHio nbron nbrsh BROnsh Bronsh FAS

FASFASFAS GASGASGAS FASFASFASFAS

BRONZEFAShionshionshoniashioniasha

BRON Zefa FaRonZE FAsb RONZ eashBR

O N Z E

PETER G. NEUMANN and EMMETT WILLIAMS

Guillaume Apollinaire

This visual sound poem, the result of a collaboration between a computer scientist and a poet, was constructed with the aid of a computer. It is based on the words of Apollinaire, "O mouths mankind is in search of a new form of speech / With which no grammarian of any language will be able to talk / . . . We want new sounds new sounds new sounds." The words were arranged in the shape of a diamond, the building block of the work. Only the basic diamond was entered into the computer. The work was generated by using a powerful context editor on the computer. This context editor facility (Ken Thompson's version of QED) was given instructions as to how to iterate upon the diamond, and thus produce the resultant shapes, the letters of Guillaume Apollinaire. The context editor is capable of easily manipulating text (in this case in geometric patterns), with selected replication in horizontal and vertical directions. It acts as a flexible generative tool rather than as a creative entity.

The work was created especially for the Apollinaire Anniversary Celebration at the Institute of Contemporary Arts in London in 1968.

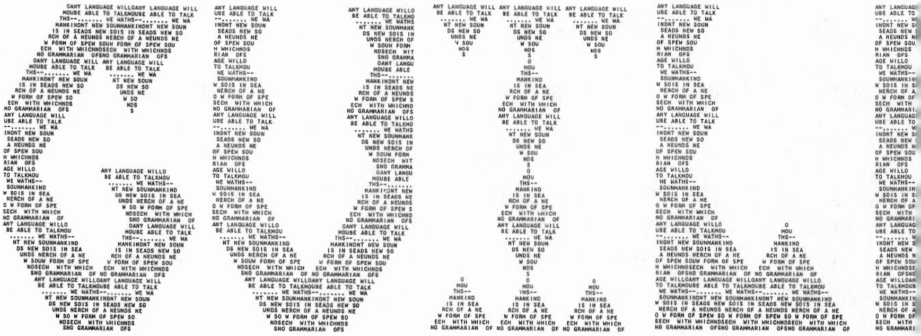

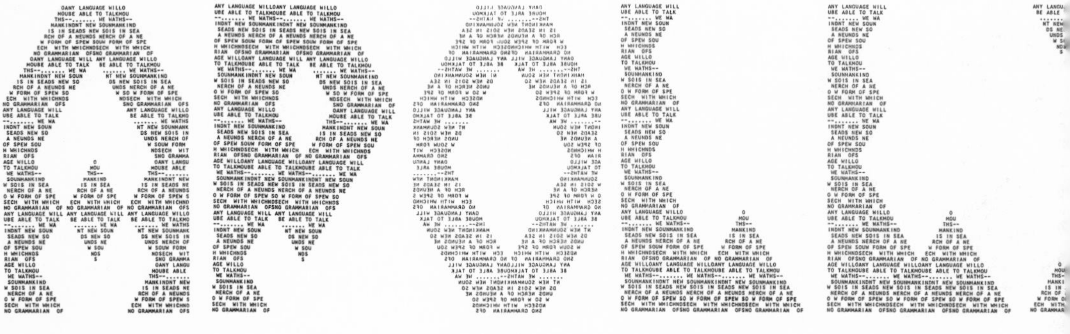

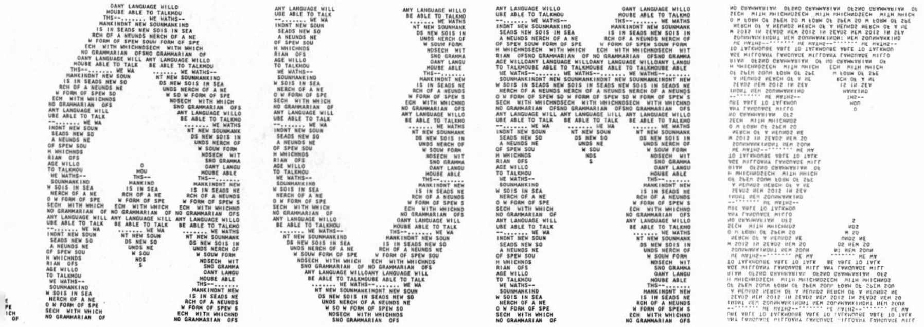

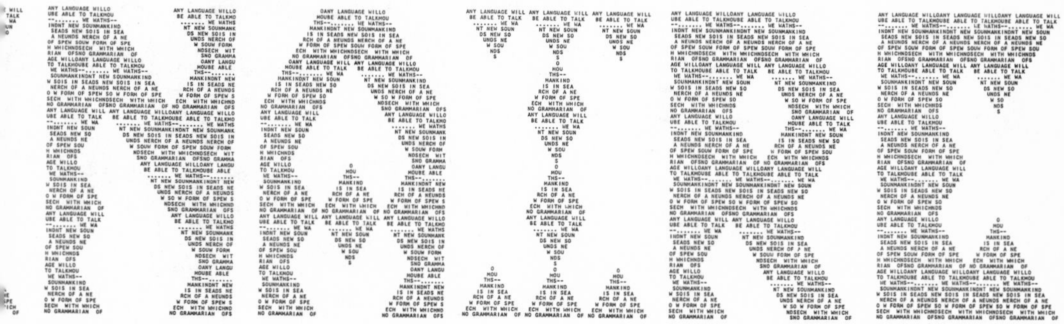

CLAES OLDENBURG

(1961–62)

"During his last year at Yale. . . . Oldenburg also had a class with the distinguished literary critic Cleanth Brooks, whose textbook *Understanding Poetry* brought the New Criticism to a generation of college students. Some welcomed its message more than others; it is doubtful, for example, that Brooks realized that his teaching inspired one daydreaming undergraduate from Chicago to begin plotting revenge against the bloodless, restrictive canons of formalism. "I shall always have an undying grudge against Cleanth Brooks," Oldenburg recalls as he speculates "how poetry *might* be taught if the aim were not didactic. I myself accepted poetry as I might the morning newspaper, with my eyes wide open—but that was soon knocked out of me."—from *Claes Oldenburg*, by Barbara Rose

I am for an art that is political-erotical-mystical, that does something other than sit on its ass in a museum.

I am for an art that grows up not knowing it is art at all, an art given the chance of having a starting point of zero.

I am for an art that embroils itself with the everyday crap & still comes out on top.

I am for an art that imitates the human, that is comic, if necessary, or violent, or whatever is necessary.

I am for an art that takes its form from the lines of life itself, that twists and extends and accumulates and spits and drips, and is heavy and coarse and blunt and sweet and stupid as life itself.

I am for an artist who vanishes, turning up in a white cap painting signs or hallways.

I am for art that comes out of a chimney like black hair and scatters in the sky.

I am for art that spills out of an old man's purse when he is bounced off a passing fender.

I am for the art out of a doggy's mouth, falling five stories from the roof.

I am for the art that a kid licks, after peeling away the wrapper.

I am for an art that joggles like everyones knees, when the bus traverses an excavation.

I am for art that is smoked, like a cigarette, smells, like a pair of shoes.

I am for art that flaps like a flag, or helps blow noses, like a handkerchief.

I am for art that is put on and taken off, like pants, which develops holes, like socks, which is eaten, like a piece of pie, or abandoned with great contempt, like a piece of shit.

I am for art covered with bandages. I am for art that limps and rolls and runs and jumps. I am for art that comes in a can or washes up on the shore.

I am for art that coils and grunts like a wrestler. I am for art that sheds hair.

I am for art you can sit on. I am for art you can pick your nose with or stub your toes on.

I am for art from a pocket, from deep channels of the ear, from the edge of a knife, from the corners of the mouth, stuck in the eye or worn on the wrist.

I am for art under the skirts, and the art of pinching cockroaches.

I am for the art of conversation between the sidewalk and a blind mans metal stick.

I am for the art that grows in a pot, that comes down out of the skies at night, like lightning, that hides in the clouds and growls. I am for art that is flipped on and off with a switch.

I am for art that unfolds like a map, that you can squeeze, like your sweetys arm, or kiss, like a pet dog. Which expands and squeaks, like an accordion, which you can spill your dinner on, like an old tablecloth.

I am for an art that you can hammer with, stitch with, sew with, paste with, file with.

I am for an art that tells you the time of day, or where such and such a street is.

I am for an art that helps old ladies across the street.

I am for the art of the washing machine. I am for the art of a government check. I am for the art of last wars raincoat.

I am for the art that comes up in fogs from sewer-holes in winter. I am for the art that splits when you step on a frozen puddle. I am for the worms art inside the apple. I am for the art of sweat that develops between crossed legs.

I am for the art of neck-hair and caked tea-cups, for the art between the tines of restaurant forks, for the odor of boiling dishwater.

I am for the art of sailing on Sunday, and the art of red and white gasoline pumps.

I am for the art of bright blue factory columns and blinking biscuit signs.

I am for the art of cheap plaster and enamel. I am for the art of worn marble and smashed slate. I am for the art of rolling cobblestones and sliding sand. I am for the art of slag and black coal. I am for the art of dead birds.

I am for the art of scratchings in the asphalt, daubing at the walls. I am for the art of bending and kicking metal and breaking glass, and pulling at things to make them fall down.

I am for the art of punching and skinned knees and sat-on bananas. I am for the art of kids' smells. I am for the art of mama-babble.

I am for the art of bar-babble, tooth-picking, beerdrinking, egg-salting, in-sulting. I am for the art of falling off a barstool.

I am for the art of underwear and the art of taxicabs. I am for the art of ice-cream cones dropped on concrete. I am for the majestic art of dog-turds, rising like cathedrals.

I am for the blinking arts, lighting up the night. I am for art falling, splashing, wiggling, jumping, going on and off.

I am for the art of fat truck-tires and black eyes.

I am for Kool-art, 7-UP art, Pepsi-art, Sunshine art, 39 cents art, 15 cents art, Vatronol art, Dro-bomb art, Vam art, Menthol art, L&M art, Ex-lax art, Venida art, Heaven Hill art, Pamryl art, San-o-med art, Rx art, 9.99 art, Now art, New art, How art, Fire sale art, Last Chance art, Only art, Diamond art, Tomorrow art, Franks art, Ducks art, Meat-o-rama art.

I am for the art of bread wet by rain. I am for the rats' dance between floors. I am for the art of flies walking on a slick pear in the electric light. I am for the art of soggy onions and firm green shoots. I am for the art of clicking among the nuts when the roaches come and go. I am for the brown sad art of rotting apples.

I am for the art of meowls and clatter of cats and for the art of their dumb electric eyes.

I am for the white art of refrigerators and their muscular openings and closings.

I am for the art of rust and mold. I am for the art of hearts, funeral hearts or sweetheart hearts, full of nougat. I am for the art of worn meat-hooks and singing barrels of red, white, blue and yellow meat.

I am for the art of things lost or thrown away, coming home from school. I am for the art of cock-and-ball trees and flying cows and the noise of rectangles and squares. I am for the art of crayons and weak grey pencil-lead, and grainy wash and sticky oil paint, and the art of windshield wipers and the art of the finger on a cold window, on dusty steel or in the bubbles on the sides of a bathtub.

I am for the art of teddy-bears and guns and decapitated rabbits, exploded umbrellas, raped beds, chairs with their brown bones broken, burning trees, firecracker ends, chicken bones, pigeon bones and boxes with men sleeping in them.

I am for the art of slightly rotten funeral flowers, hung bloody rabbits and wrinkly yellow chickens, bass drums & tambourines, and plastic phonographs.

I am for the art of abandoned boxes, tied like pharaohs. I am for an art of watertanks and speeding clouds and flapping shades.

I am for U.S. Government Inspected Art, Grade A art, Regular Price art, Yellow Ripe art, Extra Fancy art, Ready-to-eat art, Best-for-less art, Ready-to-cook art, Fully cleaned art, Spend Less art, Eat Better art, Ham art, pork art, chicken art, tomato art, banana art, apple art, turkey art, cake art, cookie art.

BENJAMIN PATTERSON

from "Methods & Processes" (1962)

Methods & Processes was composer Benjamin Patterson's first attempt "to structure specific environments for conditioning. They were, for the most part, micro-environments, composed of instructions relating back to the reader-participant." For Patterson, the artist's role is the dual one of discoverer and educator. The "art object" is not an aesthetic object but an educational tool "to help train a public in the ability to perceive in newly discovered patterns." Such styles and discoveries in painting as perspective, distribution of light, Pointillism, Cubism, Op, Pop, etc., are by-products of "a new discovery of how precepts stimulated by the environment may be selected and organized to obtain visual significance—i.e., enter into a critical relationship with the individual's previous comprehension of the environment."

wash hands

put on gloves

and

think dietician, obstetrician, pedicure, etc.

take off gloves

and

wash hands

put on gloves

and

think fop, fad, banker, boxer, etc.

take off gloves

and

wash hands

put on gloves

and think garbage man, boogy man, Eichmann, etc.

take off gloves

and

wash hands

ring small bell

light candle

ring bell again

light another candle

ring bell again

light another candle

continue until there are no more candles to be lighted

stand erect

place body weight on right foot

lift left leg and foot with bent knee several inches above ground while balancing on right foot

extend left leg forward and place foot on ground, heel first, several inches ahead and to left of right foot

shift body weight to left foot

lift right leg and foot with bent knee several inches above ground while balancing on left foot

extend right leg forward and place foot on ground, heel first, several inches ahead and to right of left foot

shift body weight to right foot

continue sequentially left, right, left, right until process becomes automatic

enter bakery

smell

leave

enter second bakery

smell

leave

enter third bakery

smell

leave

continue until appetite is obtained

think color of brown
    (azure)
think smell of roasting coffee beans

think feel of brown suède leather

think color of cognac

think smell of coconut shelled crabs

think feel of cognac brown Indian silk
    (lavender)

think color of orange

think smell of apricots

think feel of gold fish
    (iris)

think color of nicotine fingers

think smell of sweat stained shirts

think feel of scalying orange iron rust
    (scarlet)

think color of blue sulphate

think smell of blue-black figs

think taste of burning purple smoke
    (violet or pink)

drop water on mirror

break mirror

throw mirror into still water

look into mirror, reflecting mirror

lay on back

close eyes

sleep

dream of future event

dream of past event

skewer brain and suspend between these two points

look at bright star

count ten

maintain focus on star and rotate head
     clockwise three times

look at dimmer star to right of bright star

count ten

look at bright star

look at dimmer star

look at space between and beyond bright star
     and dimmer star

count ten

look at ground

...

repeat, look at Milky Way, or watch for shooting star

sit before mirror in dark room

make pleasant face

make angry face

make perplexed face

make indifferent face

stop

imagine expression of no face

open umbrella, hold over head
eat banana
close umbrella
think peanuts
open umbrella, hold over head
eat orange
close umbrella
think beets
open umbrella, hold over head
eat strawberry
close umbrella
think cabbage
open umbrella, hold over head

cover shapely female with whipped cream
lick
...
topping of chopped nuts and cherries is optional

place paper in fire
identify symbol
place water in mouth
identify symbol
place screw in meat
identify symbol

build pyramid of crocodile teeth and feather

fill catacomb with witch's toenails and
    old lion's hair

raise temple of skulls of white mice

erect obelisk, perhaps with fresh canon
    fodder

think of number 6

bark like dog

think of number 6 twice

stand up
    (do not think of number 6)
sit down

think of number 6

bark like dog

stand in bottom of deep hole

read lines 1. to 9., Canto III., Dante
    "Inferno"

dig hole deeper

read again louder

dig deeper

read again very loud

climb out of hole

defecate, expectorate, flatuate, masturbate
    menstruate, or urinate into hole

discover interesting sound

capture it

preserve it

perform it

place volition in rationality
     explain Jesus
place resolution in intuition
     invent infinity
place perseverance in evasion
     refuse experience
place caprice in curiosity
     read history
        ...
       repeat

close eyes
walk to most distant visible point
open an eye

enter open or closed space
listen
sing tone best complimenting space
listen
if previous tone is again appropriate, repeat
if not, sing different tone
listen
if previous tone is again appropriate, repeat
if not, sing different tone
listen
leave space

fill container with water
add plant seed
hang fishhook in water
wait

DÉCIO PIGNATARI

Beba Coca-cola

(1957)

beba = to drink
babe = to slob
cola = glue
caco = pieces

"An early committed concrete poem. A kind of anti-advertisement. Against the reification of the mind through slogans, demistifying of the 'artificial paradise' promised by mass-persuasion techniques. *Cloaca* is made out of the same letters as Coca-Cola." (Haroldo de Campos)

beba coca cola
babe cola
beba coca
babe cola caco
caco
cola

cloaca

Mallarmé Vietcong

1968

An iconographic quotation from Mallarmé's *Un Coup de Dés Jamais n'Abolira Le Hasard.*

lexical key:

le vierge indice	virgin index
ancestralement à n'ouvrir pas	ancestrally not to open the hand
sa petite raison virile	his small virile reason
penché de l'un ou l'autre bord	leaning to one or the other side
l'effleure une toque de minuit	a midnight cap gracing it
plume solitaire éperdue	solitary feather bewildered
en foudre	in thunder
le vieillard vers cette conjonction suprême	the old man towards this supreme conjunction
si c'était le nombre	if it was the number
ce serait le hasard	it would be chance

le vierge indice

ancestralement à n'ouvrir pas

penché de l'un ou l'autre bord

l'effleure une toque de minuit

plume solitaire eperdue

en foudre

le vieillard vers cette conjonction suprême

le vieil art vers sept, conjonction suprême

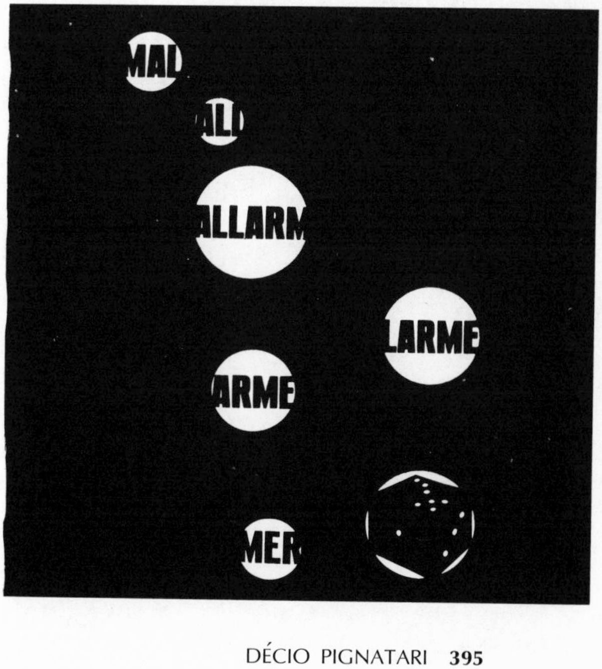

SI C'ÉTAIT LE NOMBRE
CE SERAIT LE HASARD

SI SEPT EST LE NOMBRE
CESSERAIT LE HASARD

DITER ROT

(1956)

"The review *material*, as its name implies, was intended to propagate concrete poetry, in which I myself was interested at the time. Its aim was to eliminate the subjective point of view of the author and present poetic material that the reader could do with as he saw fit. Some of the texts, 'ideograms,' appealed to the optical sense by their typographic arrangement. Here is an example by Diter Rot, who composed the second number of the review. Two squares, interlocking, form at their intersection the two little words *ut* and *tu*. A possible interpretation would be that there is no meeting without reciprocal influences." (Daniel Spoerri, *An Anecdoted Topography of Chance*.)

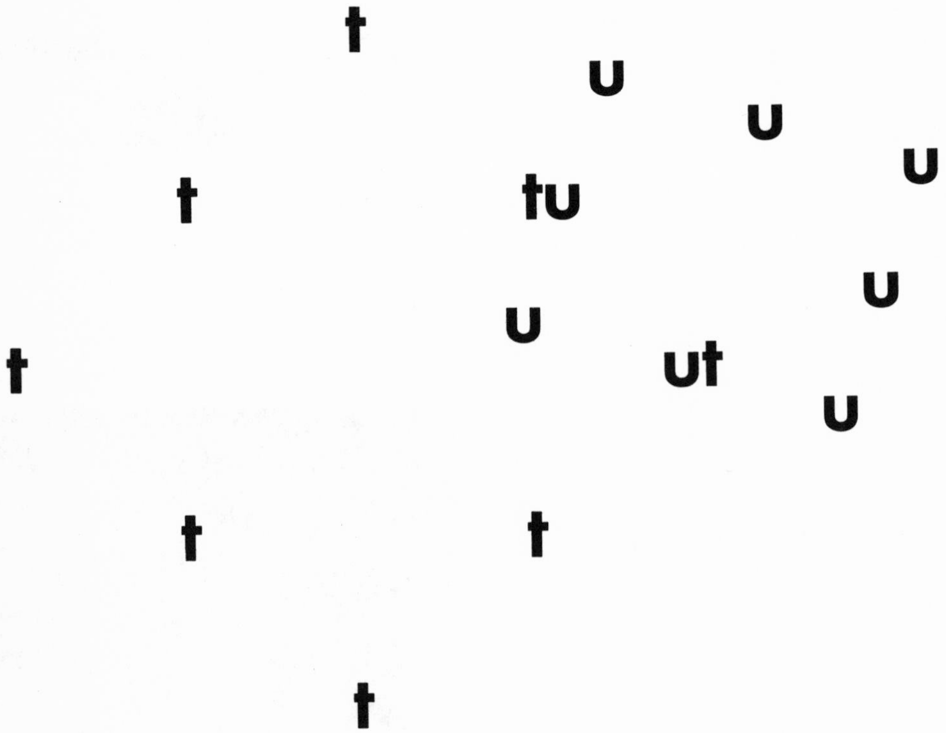

she greened
she greened
she greened so green
she blued
and blued
and blued so blue
and came
and came
and came from afar
and went
and went
and went far away

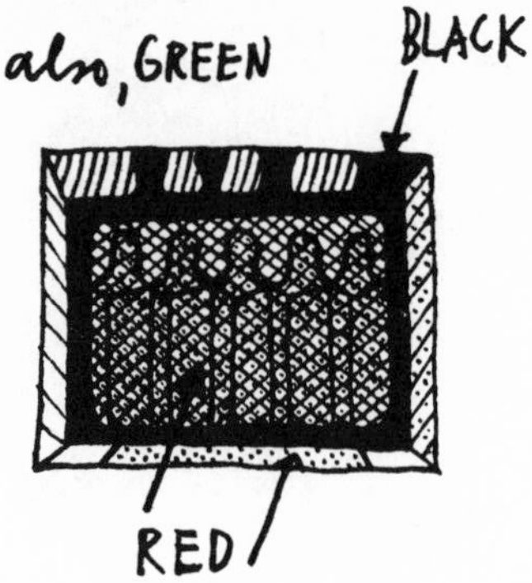
also, GREEN
BLACK
RED

sometimes,
when i think
of something green,
i believe, i then
think of it
as red, too.
red is green,
when the eyes
are not involved.

WRITING

when i see the TWINS
i look for marks
of difference

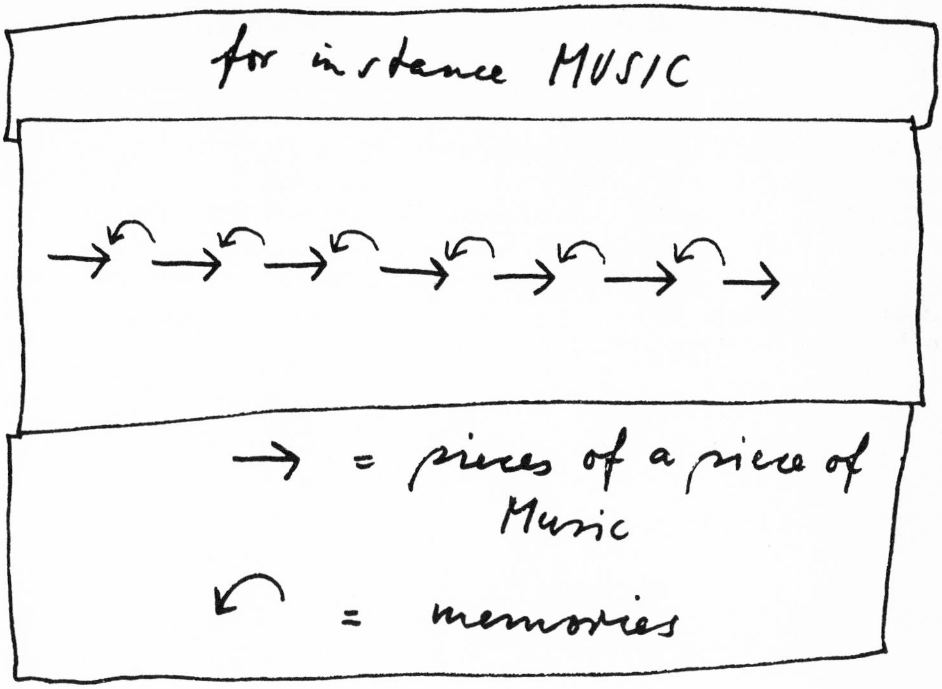
for instance MUSIC
= pieces of a piece of Music
= memories

write a heart's picture?

from "Quadrat-Buch"

1962

". . . INSTEAD OF SHOWING QUALITY (surprising quality)
WE SHOW QUANTITY (surprising quantity).
I got this idea (Quantity instead of Quality) in this way:
QUALITY in BUSINESS (f.i. advertising) is just a subtle way
of being Quantity-minded:
Quality in advertising wants expansion and (in the end)
power = Quantity
So, let us produce Quantities for once!"

—Diter Rot

Rot's *Quadrat-Buch* consisted of blow-ups from an earlier inch-square book cut from London *Daily Mirrors*.

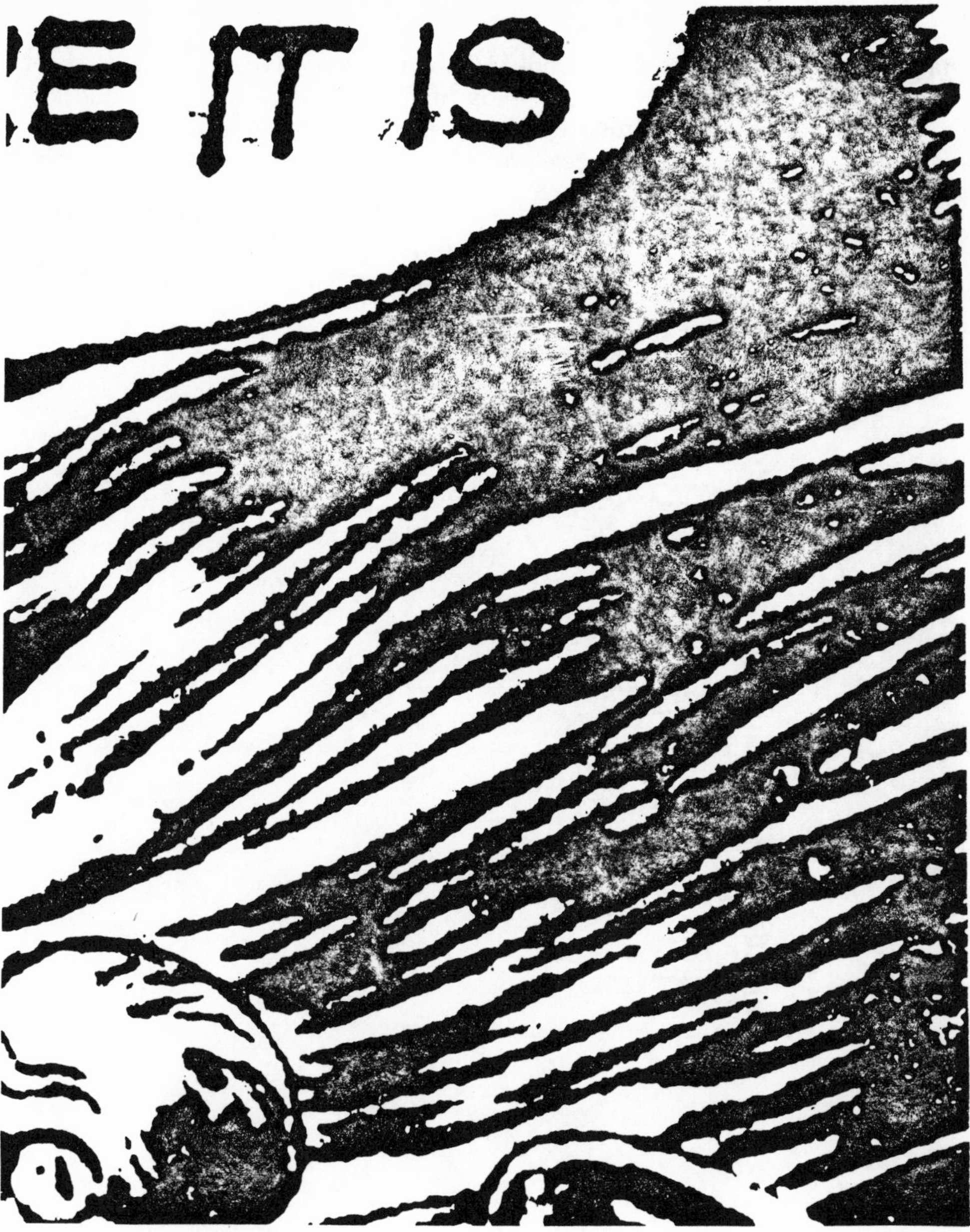
E IT IS

(1958)

A statement accompanying Rot's *Book AC*, which consisted of 24 loose sheets, 12 black and 12 white, containing fields of die-cut slots in six geometrically related sizes. By turning or rotating the sheets and arranging them in varying orders, the spectator could produce a practically infinite number of compositions.

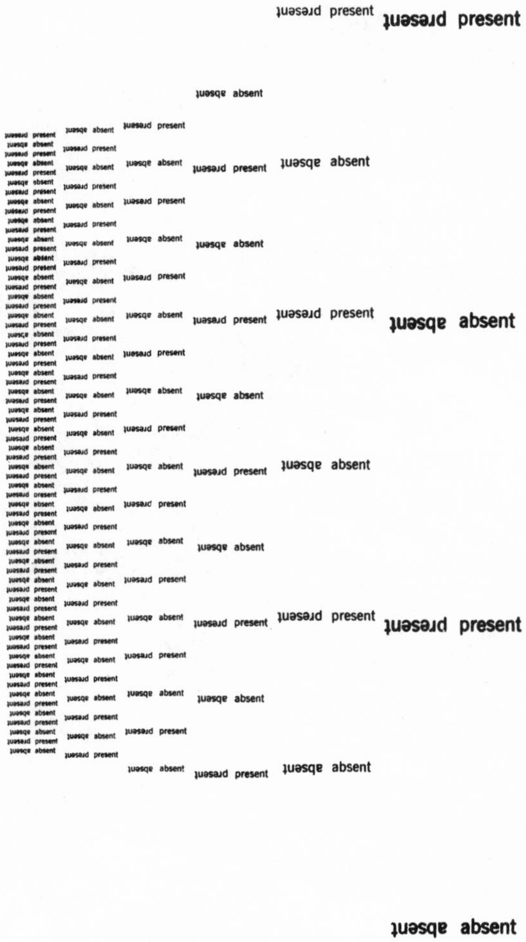

GERHARD RÜHM

Du

1954

"I have avoided being purely illustrative in the graphic presentation of concepts. Rather, I try to establish a tension relationship between both the graphic and the conceptual, so that one dimension does not simply support the other but completes it, or the optical form fixes a definite aspect of the concept."

—Gerhard Rühm

uuuuuuuuuuuuuuuuu
uuuuuuuuuuuuuuuuu
uuuuuuuuuuuuuuuuu
uuuuuuuuuuuuuuuuu
uuuuuuuduuuuuuuu
uuuuuuuuuuuuuuuuu
uuuuuuuuuuuuuuuuu
uuuuuuuuuuuuuuuuu
uuuuuuuuuuuuuuuuu

the night

(1954)
(translated by Emmett Williams)

the night
and the daughter of the night
and the daughter of the daughter of the night
and the daughter of the daughter of the daughter of the night

the day
and the son of the day
and the son of the son of the day
and the son of the son of the son of the day

the son
and
the daughter

and all their kindred all kindred

they look at the brother and sister

they look at the son and the daughter
of the son and the daughter
of the son and the daughter

and day is breaking
and night is falling

Stern

(1954)

stern = star, fate, stern (of a boat)
ernst = seriousness, seriously, serious
gestern = yesterday
geste = gesture

sternsternsternsternst
stern stern stern
stern stern
gestern
stern
geste

blue in blue

(1954)

blueinblueinblueinblue
manbymanbymanbyman
theblue
thebluemanbyman
blueman

MARY ELLEN SOLT

Forsythia (1966)

In his introduction to Mary Ellen Solt's *Flowers in Concrete*, George Zadek writes: "Traditionally the typographer has given visual form and order to words, thus serving both the writer and the reader. His problem is mainly one of clarity of communication, literary meaning, and hopefully aesthetic contribution to the art of the printed page. When publishing concrete poetry, it is sometimes difficult to draw a line between the contributions, as well as final responsibilities, of the poet and the typographer. The literary and visual meaning of concrete poetry as conceived by the poet and interpreted by the typographer is somewhat analogous to a stage performance of a play." The design of "Forsythia" is made from the letters of the name of the shrub, their equivalents in Morse Code, and the text, which literally grows out of the title. "Forsythia" was designed by John Dearstyne.

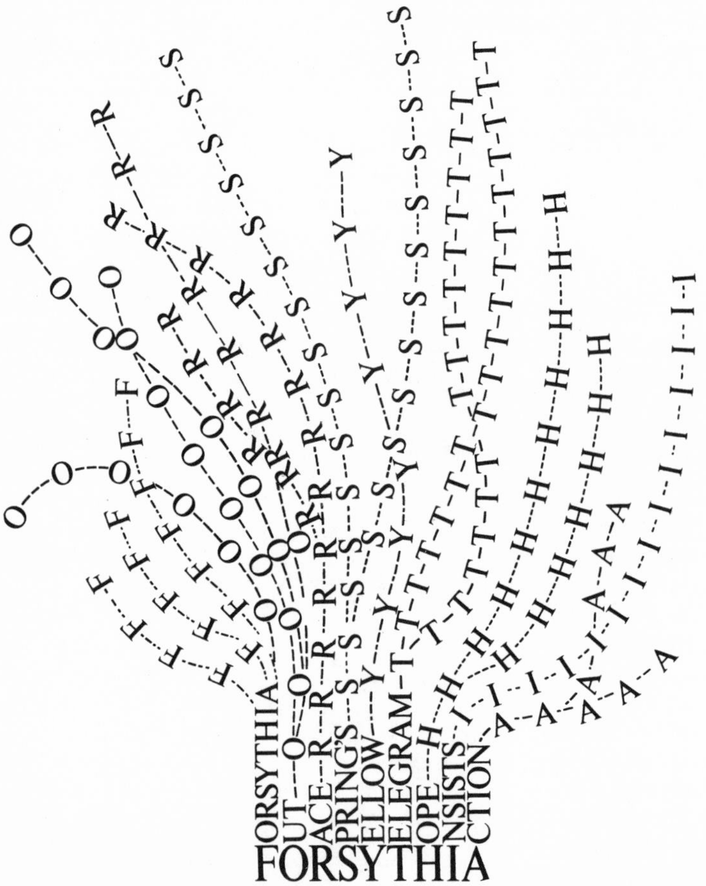

The Peoplemover 1968

A Demonstration Poem

The original *Peoplemover* posters were made during the late summer of 1968 as a "demonstration" against conditions in the United States during that horrendous period which began with the assassination of the Reverend Martin Luther King, Jr. in April and progressed through the consequent civil riots, the assassination of Senator Robert F. Kennedy, the injustices and suffering of Resurrection City, the continuing war in Vietnam, the deadlocked peace talks and ended with the triumph of machine politics at the balloon-filled Republican convention in Miami and the riot-provoking Democratic convention in Chicago. The intent was to use a sociological form of human behavior as the over-all formal concept for a poem concerned with the same events—not to write a poem about demonstrations but to make a poem that was itself a demonstration. The original consists of nine large two-sided posters mounted on latticewood sticks so that they may be carried, four cubes numbered 1-9-6-8, and two large American flags. The poster sticks were extended to make minimal ideograms on the backs related to the word content on the opposite sides. The letters on the original posters were of various types: wood type printed on rice paper and pasted onto the poster board; plastic sign letters; cardboard letters painted with tempera or acrylic enamel. The posters on display were printed by silk-screen process by A. Doyle Moore, The Finial Press, Urbana, Illinois, January 1970.

I : CIVIL RIGHTS
Back: JAIL
II : For MARTIN LUTHER KING
Back: RESURRECTION CITY
III : VIETNAM
Back: JET PEACE
IV : THE USnApalm!
Back: EQUALS THE QUESTION
V : PEACE TALKS
Back: FIVE PAST MIDNIGHT
VI : HUBERT HORATIO HUMPHREY
Back: VOTER'S X
VII : NIXON
Back: VOTER'S X
VIII: KENNEDY
Back: THE LINCOLN MEMORIAL
IX : THE AMERICAN ENVIRONMENT
Back: DOLLARS

The poem takes its name from a machine in Disneyland—The Peoplemover—which carries hordes of seated Americans daily around a world of fun, fantasy and fake history. In the real world of Summer 1968, the Peoplemover was the demonstration. Four poem-demonstrations have been performed: by Donald Bell's experimental design class at Indiana University in Bloomington, August 7, 1968; by the Fiasco group on James Brody's lawn in the country near Bloomington, Indiana, September 22, 1968; by the poet reading a short historical text and members of the audience at The Owl, Bloomington, Indiana, November 16, 1968; and by two black and two white readers reading a long historical text, with demonstrators and the names of presidents, politicians, citizens, and pertinent historical documents being flashed upon a screen during the month-long exhibition Expose Concrete Poetry, Indiana Memorial Union, Indiana University, February 20, 1970. During all performances the music of John Philip Sousa's "The Stars and Stripes Forever" could be heard.

CIV
ILL
RIOTS

THY

KING DOM COME ...

RESURR **ACTION**

→ CITY

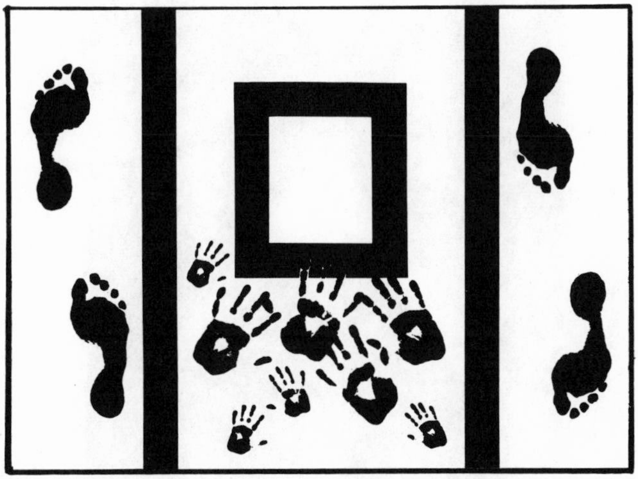

VIETNAM

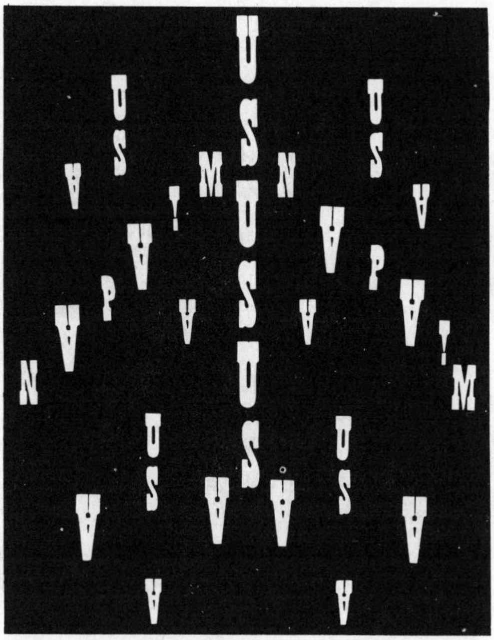

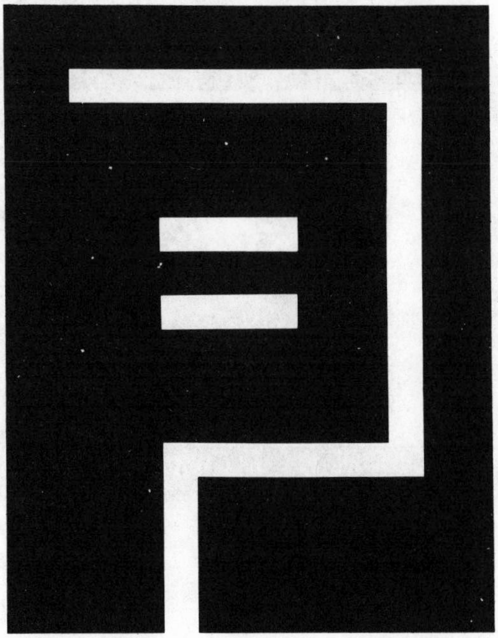

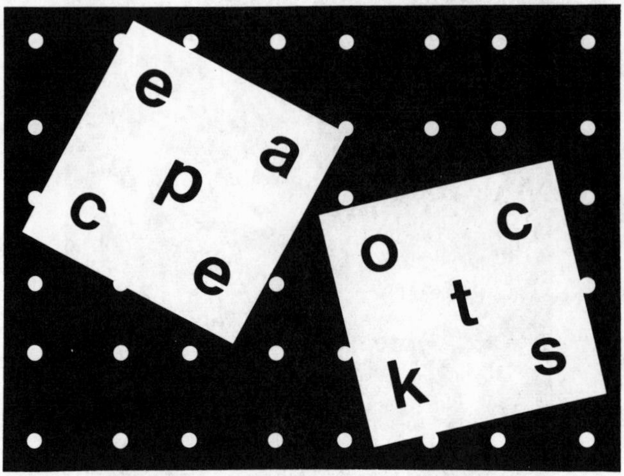
e
a
p
c
e
c
o
t
s
k

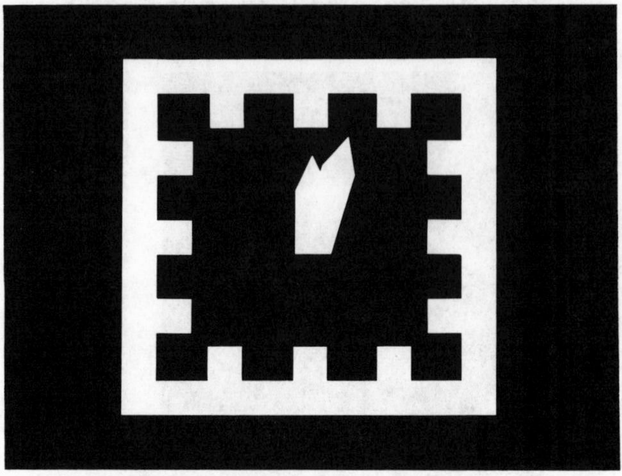

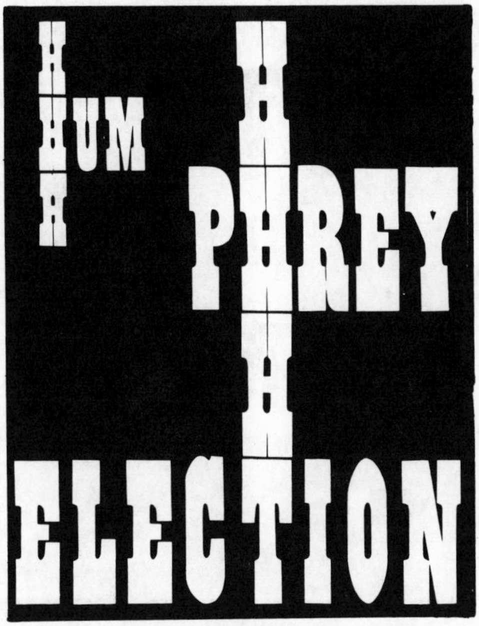
HUM
PHREY
ELECTION

VOTE

SON

NIX !

ON

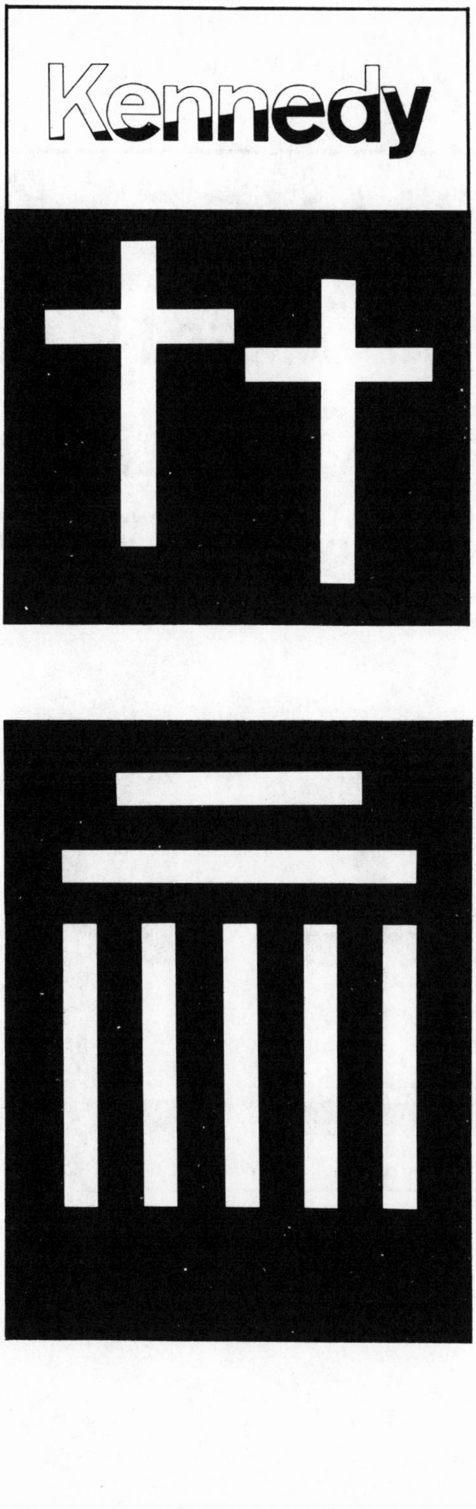
Kennedy

CHANGE the guns

snipers AMERICAN

ENVOIRENMENT

ASSASSINATION

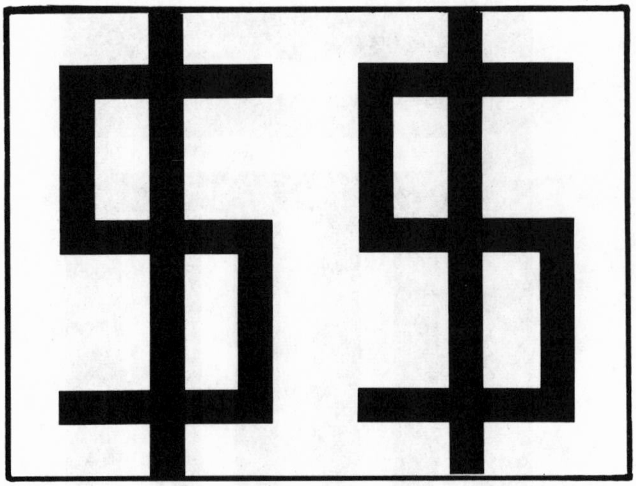

JAMES TENNEY

Letters to Gertrude Stein (1968)

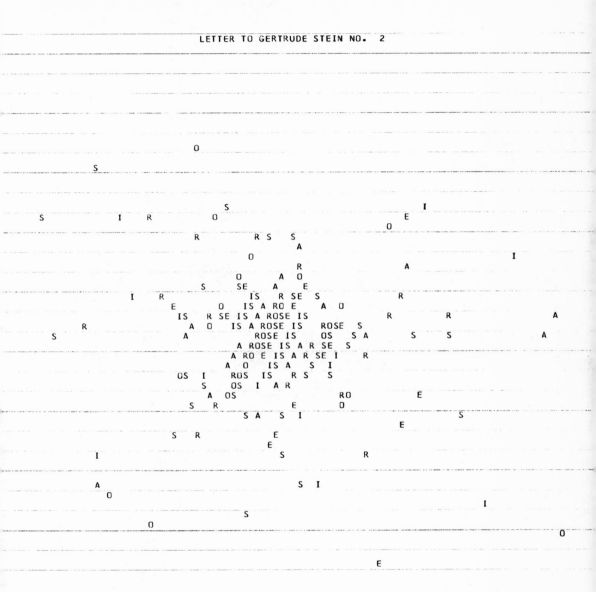

LETTER TO GERTRUDE STEIN NO. 2

```
                            O

          S



                                  S                                   I
S             I     R          O                                  E
                                                               O
                            R          R S    S
                                               A
                                      O                                               I
                                               R                  A
                                    O       A  O
                             S      SE    A     E
                 I    R               IS    R SE  S              R
                        E        O   IS A RO E     A  O
                         IS   R SE IS A ROSE IS                R         R                  A
        R                  A   O   IS A ROSE IS    ROSE   S
  S                       A            ROSE IS     OS    S A       S      S                A
                                    A ROSE IS A R SE   S
                                   A RO E IS A R SE I      R
                                  A  O    IS A   S  I
                         OS  I     ROS  IS    R S   S
                              S    OS  I   A R
                               A  OS                   RO            E
                           S    R             E        O
                                     S A    S  I                            S
                                                                 E
                        S   R              E
                                         E
          I                                 S              R


          A                                    S  I
            O
                                                                                 I
                                     S
                    O
                                                                                               O


                                                             E
```

LETTER TO GERTRUDE STEIN NO. 3

```
                                                                E
                                                                          I
                           O
                                                                                                  E
                                                     O
                                           S
                                                              S
                                                                I  A
                                                           O
                                                                                 E
                     I                   I              R
                                         S           A R                              R
                                                        S                                         E
                                    E       O E    A  O E
                            S           A      I    ROS     A
  S                                      R E          E    A
                                          SE  S    OSE  S                    S
                                E      RO   IS A ROS              A
                                       O E  S A R SE  S   RO   I
                            O           E IS A ROSE IS A R S   S
                     I         I          S   ROSE IS A   S   S
                  E      R              IS A ROSE I  A ROS
                         O        R S  IS A  OSE IS A R SE
                                    E       OSE IS A   SE       O
                                          R  E I  A ROS           E
                                     S         S   R S   S A R
                                                A R  E I    R
                                         S     A    E        SE
                                                 O
                                               R SE
                             E                           O         R  E
                                                                     I
                                       S                   S
                      E
                                 I
                                                                   O
                          E                                            A
                               R
           E
```

LETTER TO GERTRUDE STEIN NO. 6

```
                            S        S



                                                             R

                                             S

                                                     S
                                       E

                            E                     S
                   I                                 R
                                            S                     S
                                                        I
                        E                     S                    A       S         S
                                                   S
                                   S
                                  S            R
                                     R SE        E
                           O   I         IS A     I     OS   S              S
                               S            R     S              O          E
                        R  E IS    SE IS A      I    R  E
              O                  OSE  S A ROS  I  A R S
                            S    SE IS A ROSE I  A RO E    A
A R                I      I      S  S A ROSE IS A RO E                       A
                            A RO     A ROSE IS A  OSE  S A  O      A
                        I       E  S  R SE IS A R SE
                                 S A ROSE IS A R  E I
                         A       S A R SE IS  ROSE                 O
                               I           A R S
           I                        O  IS A RO E       O    S            R
              R                 A   S        S         S
                                    E I  A  S
                                      S    S             S
                                  E             A
                                 E

       A                      S
                                                   I
                                S                                    I
                                          A    E


                                                              O

                                                           R


                                        E

                                                            S
```

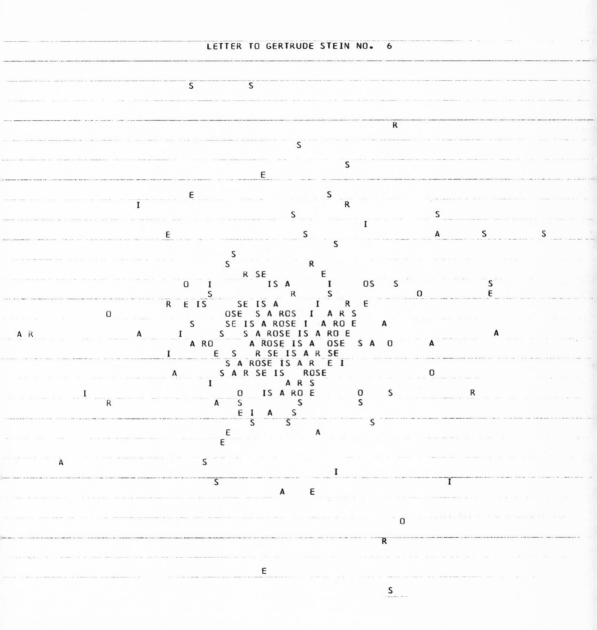

LETTER TO GERTRUDE STEIN NO. 9

```
                                                  S

                R                                                            E

                                              E

                                                                          I

                                                                A

                                                                               A
                                                      E
     E          I                          E           I
                                            I
                      E                   E  S A   S       R
                                      R     S A R SE  S
           E                       A    E  S     OSE S               SE
                                  A  O E  S   ROS  IS A                                 E
                            S      R  E    A ROSE  S   RO      A
                                       IS A ROSE I  A R S  I
                             I A   S  I    ROSE IS   R    IS
                                  S     A ROSE IS A R S   S
                                       A R SE IS A ROS                        A
                               R        R S   S A R SE
                                        O   IS A R    I  A
                                 I       E    A  O   I  A   S
                                       SE I  A R
                                          S    O
                                         S     S         SE
                                     E
                    S    O          E                           O       R

                                            E
                                                    S
                          S                    A
                                                      S

                                                                  R

                                    E
                                                                   I

                                          S
```

EMMETT WILLIAMS

Soldier (1970)

". . . the makers of the new poetry in the early fifties were not antiquarians, nor were they specifically seeking the intermedium between poetry and painting, the apparent goal of so many of their followers. The visual element in their poetry tended to be structural, a consequence of the poem, a "picture" of the lines of force of the work itself, and not merely textural. It was a poetry far beyond paraphrase, a poetry that often asked to be completed or activated by the reader, a poetry of direct presentation—the *word*, not *words, words, words* or expressionistic squiggles—using the semantic, visual and phonetic elements of language in a way seldom used by the poets of the past. It was a kind of game, perhaps, but so is life. It was born of the times, as a way of knowing and saying something about the world of *now*, with the techniques and insights of now."

—Emmett Williams, from *An Anthology of Concrete Poetry*

SOLDIER
SOLDIER
SOLDIER
SOLDIER
SOLDIER
SOLDIER
SOLDIER
SOLDIER
SOLDIER

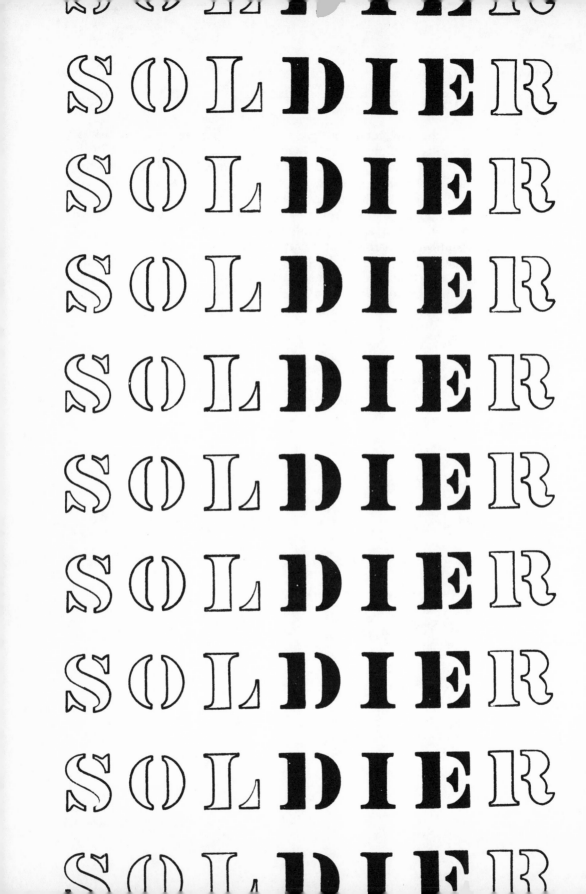

iv (1968)

i

ii

iii

iv

five

Like Attracts Like (1958)

like attracts like
like attracts like
like attracts like
like attracts like
like attracts like
like attracts like
like attracts like
likeattractslike
likeattractslike
likeattractslike
likeattractslike
likeattractslike
likeattractslike

A Festive Marching Song in the Shape of 10 Dixie Cups (1966)

This was written for *Win*, a publication of the New York Workshop in Nonviolence. Printed with it was a note, taken from a letter to Jackson Mac Low, the poetry editor, that "i think it would sound lovely hissed aloud by masses of folks." The arrangement of the "dixie cups" into a 10-stage missile, a consequence of the system of permutation, was not accidental.

```
m                   m
mi                 im
mis               sim
miss             ssim
missi           issim
missis         sissim
mississ       ssissim
mississi     ississim
mississip   pississim
mississipp ppississim
mississippippississim
 i                 i
 is               si
 iss             ssi
 issi           issi
 issis         sissi
 ississ       ssissi
 ississi     ississi
 ississip   pississi
 ississipp ppississi
 ississippippississi
  s               s
  ss             ss
  ssi           iss
  ssis         siss
  ssiss       ssiss
  ssissi     ississ
  ssissip   pississ
  ssissipp ppississ
  ssissippippississ
   s             s
   si           is
   sis         sis
   siss       ssis
   sissi     issis
   sissip   pissis
   sissipp ppissis
   sissippippissis
    i           i
    is         si
    iss       ssi
    issi     issi
    issip   pissi
    issipp ppissi
    issippippissi
     s         s
     ss       ss
     ssi     iss
     ssip   piss
     ssipp ppiss
     ssippippiss
      s       s
      si     is
      sip   pis
      sipp ppis
      sippippis
       i     i
       ip   pi
       ipp ppi
       ippippi
        p   p
        pp pp
        ppipp
         p p
         pip
          i
```

(1954–55)

From an unpublished novel, *The Clouds*. The text was part of an eye-and-ear test administered by Aristophanes to the hero of the novel, a deceased buttonhole puncher who knows more about linguistics than his earthly vocation would seem to have prepared him for. The letters are swapped back and forth until sense is sound and sound sense. (The odd bird was chosen as an "embellishment" by Thomas Merton when he published the poem in *Monk's Pond*.)

SENSE SOUND

SONSE SEUND

SOUSE SENND

SOUNE SENSD

SOUND SENSE

duet (1964–65)

The first line of each couplet is the male voice, the second the female, and the erotic imagery is suited to the sex of the speaker. I first read it over John Giorno's Dial-a-Poem service in 1969. When Merv Griffin decided to treat Dial-a-Poem on his television show, he selected *duet*, and it was read magnificently well by Garry Moore and a beautiful lady guest and telecast to family audiences coast to coast—which makes me wonder if the erotic imagery comes across as well as I once thought.

duet

art of my dart
arrow of my marrow
butter of my abutter
bode of my abode
cope of my scope
curry of my scurry
den of my eden
do of my ado
ember of my member
eel of my feel
fort of my effort
flexibility of my inflexibility
go of my ego
gain of my again
hence of my whence
him of my whim
inky of my dinky
inter of my hinter
jog of my ajog
johnny o of my o johnny o
kipper of my skipper
kin of my skin
licker of my flicker
lapstick of my slapstick
mission of my emission
motion of my emotion
nip of my snip
now of my enow
oiler of my toiler
orpheus of my morpheus
port of my sport
patter of my spatter
quash of my squash
quiescence of my acquiescence
raving of my craving
ream of my cream
scent of my ascent
swan of my aswan
tiff of my stiff
top motion of my stop motion
unction of my function
urging of my purging
vent of my event
vocative of my evocative
well of my swell
wallow-tail of my swallow-tail
x-factor of my ex-factor
x of my ax
ye of my aye
y of my my
zip zap zoff of my o zip o zap o zoff
zim zam zoom of my o zim o zam o zoom

A Selection from 5,000 New Ways

(1962)
(from the London Times Literary Supplement, *August 6, 1964.)*

sound effects

alison knowles' *nivea cream piece for o.w.*
applause
automobile starter
baby
breathing
cat purring
chain
chewing
chimes
chopping .
clearing of throat
comb
cough
crying
dishwashing
dog
draining sink
drumroll
firecracker
foghorn
gong
high c
horse
jet
jew's harp
john barrymore
laughter
love
peddlar
pouring
printing press
rain
ripping
roaring lion
rooster
satie's *vexations* (first 90 notes)
sandpaper
shattering glass
sneeze
snoring
star-spangled banner played backwards
static
station identification
subway
tapdancing
thirty seconds from a transistor radio
thunder
ticking
train whistle
wind

a selection from 5,000 new ways

the new way the maiden heads
the new way the banana splits
the new way the belly buttons
the new way the hippety hops
the new way the lickety splits
the new way the drum sticks
the new way the bamboo shoots
the new way the cream puffs
the new way the jig saws
the new way the powder puffs
the new way the tootsie rolls
the new way the bottle necks
the new way the race questions
the new way the pussy willows
the new way the cake walks
the new way the partner ships
the new way the ear trumpets
the new way the gang bangs
the new way the square roots
the new way the pork chops
the new way the ding dongs
the new way the fig leaves
the new way the diaphragm jellies
the new way the ham hocks
the new way the venetian blinds
the new way the soda pops
the new way the sheep dips
the new way the cock pits
the new way the rootatoot toots
the new way the fever blisters
the new way the band aids
the new way the ear drums
the new way the pen names
the new way the poop decks
the new way the cork screws
the new way the finger nails
the new way the side walks
the new way the ice creams
the new way the skid rows
the new way the circle jerks
the new way the joy sticks
the new way the fox trots
the new way the foot notes
the new way the orange crushes
the new way the bean sprouts
the new way the tom tits
the new way the curtain calls
the new way the left-handed monkey wrenches
the new way the eye lashes
the new way the organ stops

projections

apple
armpit
balloon
big toe
burning book
candle
castle
charlie chaplin
chess game
chicken foot
clock
cobbler's bench
comb
declaration of independence
dice
dinosaur
fish
football game
funeral
great wall of china
hamburger
harpoon
harry truman
heart
hundred-dollar bill
jukebox
mona lisa
mouth
movie queue
mummy
new year's eve
nude
ocean liner
piano
piccadilly circus at night
postage stamp
prison bars
rocket
scissors
snow
starvation
streetcar
sylvano bussotti's fluxus namecard
taj mahal
tube of signal toothpaste
two left shoes
wishbone
wig
yellow rose
zodiac

FOUND POETRY

EDITED BY

John Robert Colombo

A FOUND INTRODUCTION
John Robert Colombo

Found poetry. What is it?

- "Art must not look like art."—Marcel Duchamp
- "Obviously the basis of just about every great age in literature is the force and innocence of its plagiarism."—Bertolt Brecht to Walter Kerr
- "Immature poets imitate; mature poets steal; bad poets deface what they take, and good poets make it into something better, or at least something different." —T. S. Eliot
- "If A thinks himself a better poet than B, let him stop hinting it in the pages of an essay; let him re-write B's poems and publish his own improved version. . . . an absurd suggestion? Well, I am only proposing that modern artists should treat each other as Greek dramatists or Renaissance painters or Elizabethan poets did. If anyone thinks that the law of copyright has fostered better art than those barbarous times could produce, I will not try to convert him." —R. G. Collingwood
- "It is the culmination of realism. So the found poem is really a piece of realistic literature, in which significance appears inherent in the object—either as extravagant absurdity or as unexpected worth. It is like driftwood, or pop art, where natural objects and utilitarian objects are seen as the focus of generative form or meaning."—Louis Dudek
- "Found poetry turns the continuous verbal undertone of mass culture up full volume for a moment, offering a chance to see and hear it with a shock of recognition."—Ronald Gross

Background. Fine art.

- Yuan Yuan, an ancient Chinese governor, who was also an artist, specialized in cutting certain rocks in such a way as to reveal "already painted scenes."
- Pablo Picasso has produced a number of *objets trouvés.* One day he found a stove element he thought resembled his own work, so he mounted it on a wooden block and christened it "*La Vénus du Gaz.*" He explained to Françoise Gilot, "It arouses a new emotion in the mind of the viewer because it momentarily disturbs his customary way of identifying and defining what he sees."
- "Kurt was at the very back of the streetcar," Hans Richter wrote about the German artist of collage Kurt Schwitters. "He was standing with his hands behind him. Accustomed as I was to his peculiarities, I was nevertheless curious as to why he kept wriggling so. He looked like a shimmy dancer. Suddenly he leaped off the car at a stop. I followed. After the car had gone on, he showed me a 'No Smoking' sign which he had removed from the streetcar with a small screwdriver he always carried. Nothing could stop the man once he wanted some piece of material for his work."

- "Dada wished to destroy the hoaxes of reason and to discover an unreasoned order," wrote Jean Arp. Tristan Tzara's movement gave artists an unparalleled opportunity to pillage the culture of the past and the present, and to make out of old works (like "Mona Lisa") new works (like Duchamp's "L.H.O.O.Q.," which is Mona Lisa with a mustache) to shock the bourgeois public which idolized Art.
- Today's Pop Art, far from destroying the real world in the Dadaist fashion, tries to redeem any reality the world of contemporary symbols happens to retain. Judy R. Lippard writes that neo-Dadaists and pop artists have made "a widespread decision to approach the contemporary world with a positive rather than a negative attitude." When he reproduces current imagery and iconography virtually without alteration—whether Jacqueline Kennedy's sorrow-stricken face or a beaming can of Campbell's soup—Andy Warhol celebrates what Apollinaire called "the heroic of the everyday."
- Junk sculpture, concept art, earth art, expanded art—these are a few contemporary manifestations of the artistic impulse to use what is at hand, to discover rather than to invent. This involves the notion that things are magical in themselves. "If you inhabit a sacred world," Harold Rosenberg the art critic noted, "you *find* art rather than *make* it."

Background. Literature.

- Before the printed page, even before the handwritten parchment, there were words, signs on stones. Lapidary inscriptions required that the messages be adjusted to the requirements of the medium, so attention to lineation produced a stylized presentation which not only heightened the reader's emotion response to the meaning but produced an over-all artistic effect as well.
- When he translated the Bible into Latin, St. Jerome presented the Psalms and Proverbs as new poems in Latin. The arrangement of rhetorical texts into meaningful units is called colometry or stichometry, and the practice is the precurser of found poetry.
- Three quotations from Robert Burton's *The Anatomy of Melancholy*: "I have borrowed, not stolen." "One made books as apothecaries made medicines by pouring one bottle into another." "The matter is theirs most part, and yet mine, whence it is taken appears, yet it appears as something different from what 'tis taken from."
- Popular during the nineteenth century were "whimseys," which is Carolyn Wells's term for such things as shaped poems taken from given texts (like the Bible, or the novels of Dickens). Metered and sometimes even rhymed poems were found in novels like *Nicholas Nickleby,* proving that found poetry could boast a "period" air.

The grass was green above the dead boy's grave,
    Trodden by feet so small and light,
    That not a daisy dropped its head
        Beneath their pressure.
    Through all the spring and summer time

Garlands of fresh flowers, wreathed by infant hands,
Rested upon the stone.

- In French, found poetry is not "found." An *object* may be *trouvé*, but *poésie* is *d'emprunt*. *Poésie d'emprunt* translates "borrowed poetry" or "expropriated poetry."
- One of the earliest, if not the earliest, found poem is Blaise Cendrars' *"Dernière Heure,"* which is a verbatim account of an Oklahoma jailbreak "copied from *Paris-Midi*, January 1914."
- In English, the found impulse informs Ezra Pound's *Cantos* (from 1915), James Joyce's *Ulysses* (1918), and T. S. Eliot's *The Waste Land* (1922).
- William Butler Yeats "wrote" a celebrated found poem when he turned Walter Pater's evocation of the Mona Lisa from *The Renaissance* into free verse and published it as the first poem in *The Oxford Book of Modern Verse* (1936). He called it a work "of revolutionary importance."
- When the Scottish poet Hugh MacDiarmid published a poem which begins with a passage from another author's short story arranged as verse, there followed a long correspondence on the morality, legality and aesthetics of such "appropriations" in the correspondence columns of the *Times Literary Supplement*.
- Marianne Moore has made decorous use of quoted matter in her work, but always with quotation marks and elaborate source notes. "I was just trying to be honourable and not to steal things," Miss Moore explained to Donald Hall in a *Paris Review* interview. "I've always felt that if a thing had been said in the *best* way, how could you say it better?"
- The first *book* of found poetry (in English, at least) is *A Stone, A Leaf, A Door* which was published by Scribner's in 1945. John S. Barnes "selected and arranged in verse" purple passages from Thomas Wolfe's novels. Here is a sample:

  Which of us has known his brother?
  Which of us has looked into his father's heart?
  Which of us has not remained forever prison-pent?
  Which of us is not forever a stranger and alone?

- The master of the comma, José Garcia Villa, started experimenting in 1951 with "adaptations" or "poems: from prose." These appeared in *Selected Poems and New* (1958) and have a deliberate literary air to them, like the opening of this Villa adaptation of a Rilke letter:

  Do not be bewildered by the
  Surfaces; in the depths
  All becomes law.

- George Hitchcock of Kayak Press edited and published the first anthology of found poetry. *Losers Weepers: Poems Found Practically Everywhere* appeared in 1969, and included the work of twenty-five poets, all of whom found poetry "somewhere amidst the vast sub- or non-literature which surrounds us all."

Cinema verité. Found movies.

- The impulse to find rather than to invent finds expression in those feature films that have been shot in the documentary or *cinema verité* manner. Chief among these are Pontecorvo's *The Battle of Algiers*, Watkins' *The War Game*, Godard's *La Chinoise*, Pasolini's *The Gospel According to St. Matthew*, Allan King's *Warrendale* and *A Married Couple*. Not one is fully "found," of course, for they all merge actual and artful footage in different proportions. Perhaps the first feature "taken from life" is Robert Flaherty's *Nanook of the North*.
- Gene Youngblood, in *Expanded Cinema*, quotes Jean-Luc Godard as saying: "The ideal for me is to obtain right away what will work. If retakes are necessary it falls short of the mark. The immediate is chance. At the same time it is definitive. What I want is the definitive by chance."

Music. Theatre.

- Ever since Tchaikovsky scored the *1812 Overture* for a real cannon blast, natural sounds have been part of Western music. In *musique concrète* they take over, especially in the work of composers like John Cage and Luciano Berio.
- At the Berliner Ensemble, Bertolt Brecht's actors did not act out their parts so much as "demonstrate" their roles to the audience. Brecht sometimes referred to this as the "alienation effect." His art was once described as "presentational" rather than "representational."

Possible distinctions.

- Found object, *objet trouvé*, ready-made: Something removed from one context and placed within an aesthetic context. An object valued more for its aesthetic than its utilitarian appeal. If a passage of prose, it must not be altered in the process.
- Found poem: A passage of prose presented as a poem. The transformation usually involves rearranging the lines on the page.
- Pop poem: A found poem taken from a sub-literary source, especially advertising matter.
- Pure, impure: Found poems are "pure" if they reproduce the original source verbatim; "impure" if they are a reworking of the original source. Reworking is sometimes referred to as "assisting"—hence, "an assisted found poem."
- Found prose. The "collaged novels" of William Burroughs are examples of found prose. It is possible to see Ralph L. Woods's commonplace book, *A Treasury of the Familiar*, as a collection of found prose and poetry: the anthologist as artist.
- Lost prose: *The New Yorker*'s term for a found poems that falls flat.

What is found? Perception?

- "Poetry is not a turning loose of emotion, but an escape from emotion; it is not the expression of personality, but an escape from personality."—T. S. Eliot
- If Dada and the Bauhaus are seen as two mutually complementary art move-

ments which occurred almost in unison, and if Dada is seen as raising chance to the level of a principle and the Bauhaus as raising control to the same heights, then found poetry partakes of both: From Dada it takes the element of randomness and from the Bauhaus the element of craftsmanship. Finding is searching; presenting is making aesthetic choices. When poetry is discovered rather than written, it is found "accidentally on purpose."

- "The message is: widen the area of consciousness." Allen Ginsberg's formulation applies to found poetry as much as to any other poetry, for found poems make us conscious not only of our immediate environment but also of ourselves within this totality.
- "The basic changes of our time lead us towards confronting the environment as artifact," explained Marshall McLuhan in *Counterblast.* "In a non-literate society, there is no art in our sense, but the whole environment is experienced as unitary. Neolithic specialism ended that. The Balinese say: 'We have no art. We do everything as well as possible'; that is, they program the environment instead of its content."
- Found art is the most conservation-minded of the arts, for it recycles the waste of the past and reuses it in a surprisingly different way, thereby giving the original a new lease on life. "Collage seems to me the one medium most suited to the age of conspicuous waste," painter Harold Town wrote, "and it's marvellous to think of the garbage of our age becoming the art of our time."
- An especially valuable function of found art and found poetry in particular is its ability to make us respond aesthetically to the universe around us, not just to those separate parts of the world called works of art. It is possible to act as if the universe itself were an immense piece of art, a collage perhaps. But does this spell the doom of art? As the Czech poet Miroslav Holub wryly observed, "There is poetry in everything. That is the biggest argument against poetry."

DAVID ANTIN

A List of the Delusions of the Insane What They Are Afraid of

the police
being poisoned
being killed
being alone
being attacked at night
being poor
being followed at night
being lost in a crowd
being dead
having no stomach
having no insides
having a bone in the throat
losing money
being unfit to live
being ill with a mysterious disease
being unable to turn out the light
being unable to close the door
that an animal will come in from the street
that they will not recover
that they will be murdered
that they will be murdered when they sleep
that they will be murdered when they wake
that murders are going on all around them
that there are murderers all around them
that they will see the murderer
that they will not
that they will be boiled alive
that they will be starved
that they will be fed disgusting things
that disgusting things are being put into their food and drink
that their flesh is boiling
that their head will be cut off
that children are burning
that they are starving
that all of the nutriment has been removed from food
that evil chemicals have been placed in the earth
that evil chemicals have entered the air
that it is immoral to eat
that they are in hell
that they hear people screaming

that they smell burnt flesh
that they have committed an unpardonable sin
that there are unknown agencies working evil in the world
that they have no identity
that they are on fire
that they have no brain
that they are covered with vermin
that their property is being stolen
that their children are being killed
that they have stolen something
that they have too much to eat
that they have been chloroformed
that they have been blinded
that they have gone deaf
that they have been hypnotized
that they are the tools of another power
that they have been forced to commit murder
that they will get the electric chair
that people have been calling them names
that they deserve these names
that they are changing their sex
that their blood has turned to water
that their body is being transformed into glass
that insects are coming out of their body
that they give off a bad smell
that houses are burning around them
that people are burning around them
that children are burning around them
that houses are burning
that they have committed suicide of the soul

Code of Flag Behavior

the flag should never be displayed with the union down   except
            as a sign of distress
the flag should never touch anything underneath it
such as the ground   the floor   or water
it should never be carried laid out flat or horizontally
but always aloft and free
it should not be festooned   drawn back   or up in folds
but allowed to fall free
the flag should never be used to cover a ceiling
it should never have placed on it   or attached to any part of it
any mark insignia letter word figure design picture drawing
of any nature whatsoever
the flag should never be used as a receptacle for
receiving holding carrying or delivering
it should not be used for advertising purposes   and
when the flag is in such condition that it is no longer fit for use
as an emblem of display
it should be destroyed
in a dignified way
preferably by burning

ELEANOR ANTIN

The Proportions Which a Perfectly Formed Man's Body Should Possess

for Sir Kenneth Clark

i will now give you the exact proportions of a man
those of a woman i will disregard for she does not have any set proportions
first the face is divided into three parts
the forehead one
the nose another
and from the nose to the chin another
from the side of the nose through the whole length of the eye one of these
measures
from the end of the eye up to the ear one of these measures
from one ear to the other a face lengthwise one face
from the chin under the jaw to the base of the throat one of the three
measures
the throat one measure long
from the pit of the throat to the top of the shoulder one face
and so for the other shoulder
from the shoulder to the elbow one face
from the elbow to the joint of the hand one face and one of the three
measures
the whole hand lengthwise one face
from the pit of the throat to that of the chest or stomach one face
from the stomach to the navel one face
from the navel to the thigh joint one face
from the thigh to the knee two faces
from the knee to the heel of the leg two faces
from the heel to the sole of the foot one of the three measures
the foot one face long
a man is as long as his arms crosswise
the arms including the hands reach to the middle of the thigh
a man has one breast rib less than a woman on the left side
the handsome man must be swarthy
he is eight faces and two of the three measures in length
this is the whole man

Painter Poems

How to Paint Wounds

to do a wounded man
take straight vermilion
lay it in wherever you want to do blood
either in drops or wounds or whatever it happens to be
a color known as vermilion is red
but bear in mind that it is not its nature to be exposed to the air
because in the course of time it turns black
when it is used and laid on the wall

How to Fashion or Cut Out the Stars and Put Them on the Wall

first you have to cut out all the stars with the ruler
and wherever you have to put them on first put a little lump of wax on
    the blue
and shape the star on it ray by ray just as you cut it on the board
and know that much more work can be done with less fine gold than
    can be done by mordant gilding

A Certain Color

this color is really poisonous
we do not use it except sometimes
there is no keeping company with it
when you want to work it up adopt those measures which i have taught
    you for the other colors
and look out for yourself

Mending Stones

there is a cement which is good for mending stones
take your broken stone and warm it well
put some of this cement on it
it will last forever
in wind and in water

The Way to Copy a Mountain from Nature
for diane wakoski

if you want a good style for mountains
if you want them to look natural
rugged and not cleaned up
copy them from nature
apply the lights and the dark as your system requires
if you want to embellish these mountains with groves of trees or with plants
first put in the trunk of the tree and scatter the leaves upon it
and then the fruits
and scatter occasional flowers and little birds
then scrape it up and put it into a little dish
cover it and keep it
the older and more seasoned it is the better it will be
just keep it well covered and protected from dust

MICHAEL BENEDIKT

The Golden Years

He seemed genuinely sorry about his error.
The air in the poolroom smelled stale.
She is a comely child.

Sherman stepped nearer to examine the bomb.
That was Sherman's last act.
Truly we shall all miss Sherman.

The search continued far into the night.
Early in the first quarter I sprained my ankle.
His actions became unbearable.

We ran fast to catch the bus.
His curve ball is fast and always under control.
Your story sounds most unlikely to me.

She has sung twice on our concert series.
The new man proved lazy and unreliable.
He fell off the platform and onto the third rail.

I like a man who works hard and complains little.
Leave your umbrella there on the porch.
This weather is, I admit, very unpleasant.

This room always looks bright and cheerful.
I tried to smile, although I felt sad.

Finales

I

Some of my friends left very early.
Father can repair your electric train.
Did you see the eclipse of the sun?
A bedraggled individual entered the lobby.
There is no excuse for such carelessness.

II

After lunch I usually take a short nap.
The owner of the dog took him home.
Only a few of the students could get tickets.
Should we invite her sister also?

III

One of my cousins now lives in Oslo.
Near our farm lived several Indians.
Behind the shed was a row of plum trees.
Please leave the passkey with the secretary.

IV

Never before have I tasted such delicious peaches.
Nearly a fourth of the students are self-supporting.

V

Some of my answers must have been wrong.
There is still hope for his recovery.
With a cry of rage Thorwald lunged at me.
One of my favorite sports is archery.
Be sure and mark every error.

Poem No. 1515*

Hassi-Messaoued

Dear Sir,

By the time I arrived at the house where you sent me to make repairs, the storm had torn a good fifty bricks from the roof. So I set up on the roof of the building a beam and a pulley and I hoisted up a couple of baskets of bricks. When I had finished repairing the building there were a lot of bricks left over since I had brought up more than I needed and also because there were some bad, reject bricks that I still had left to bring down. I hoisted the basket back up again and hitched up the line at the bottom. Then I climbed back up again and filled up the basket with the extra bricks. Then I went down to the bottom and untied the line. Unfortunately, the basket of bricks was much heavier than I was and before I knew what was happening, the basket started to plunge down, lifting me suddenly off the ground. I decided to keep my grip and hang on, realizing that to let go would end in disaster—but half way up I ran into the basket coming down and received a severe blow on the shoulder. I then continued to the top, banging my head against the beam and getting my fingers jammed in the pulley. When the basket hit the ground it burst its bottom, allowing all the bricks to spill out. Since I was now heavier than the basket I started back down again at high speed. Half way down, I met the basket coming up, and received several severe injuries on my shins. When I hit the ground, I landed on the bricks, getting several more painful cuts and bruises from the sharp edges.

At this moment I must have lost my presence of mind, because I let go of the line. The basket came down again, giving me another heavy blow on the head, and putting me in the hospital. I respectfully request sick leave.

* It is interesting to note that this "found poem" by the French poet Jean L'Anselme was originally "found"—unknown to L'Anselme—a few years before by Gerard Hoffnung, the great cartoonist and humorist, who gave it wide currency and popularity in Britain.

JOHN ROBERT COLOMBO

The Central Intelligence Agency Awards Richard Mervin Bissell Jr. A Secret Intelligence Medal Honouring Him for His Years of Service as Deputy Director for Plans

(The Invisible Government *by David Wise and Thomas B. Ross*)

There was no public announcement
of the award,
and Bissell was not allowed to talk
about his medal,
to show it to anyone
or to wear it.
As far as the CIA was concerned,
officially the medal did not exist.

The Invisible Government
has awarded him
an invisible medal.

"Being a Somewhat Detailed Account . . . of the Sinister Chinaman"

(*Sax Rohmer's* The Insidious Dr. Fu-Manchu)

Imagine a person, tall, lean and feline,
high-shouldered, with a brow like Shakespeare
and a face like Satan,
a close-shaven skull,
and long, magnetic eyes of the true cat-green.
Invest him with all the cruel cunning
of an entire Eastern race,
accumulated in one giant intellect,
with all the resources of science past and present,
with all the resources, if you will,
of a wealthy government—
which, however, already has denied
all knowledge of his existence.

Imagine that awful being,
and you have a mental picture of Dr. Fu-Manchu,
the yellow peril incarnate in one man.

Memory Gardens Association Limited

Oftentimes in our busy lives
we neglect one of the most important
of family matters. What is that?
The purchase of a final resting place
for our loved ones. The WRONG WAY
is perhaps the most trying ordeal in life.
Alone and confused at a time of sorrow,
someone must now make cemetery arrangements.
Shall it be done the WRONG WAY
or the RIGHT WAY? The RIGHT WAY
is to face this responsibility TOGETHER,
when able to reason without physical
or emotional strain . . . thus assuring
FINANCIAL PROTECTION and PEACE OF MIND.
Our Family Pre-Need Plan has many
other benefits, and within a few days
I will call to see when I could tell you
about them. I will also deliver
a valuable free Family Register
wherein you may record important details
needed for your estate settlement.
Your courtesy in receiving me
will be greatly appreciated. Sincerely yours,
MEMORY GARDENS ASSOCIATION LIMITED,
Family Service Division. (This letter
is in general distribution. Should
it reach any home in which there is illness,
it is completely unintentional.)

Two Cures for Fever

from The Sixth and Seventh Books of Moses

1. Rabbi Huna's

For fever recurring every three days,
take seven different grapes from seven different grapevines,
seven chips from seven joists,
seven nails from seven bridges,
seven small quantities of ashes from seven stoves,
seven bits of earth from seven holes in the ground,
seven pieces of pitch from seven ships,
seven grains of cumin,
seven hairs out of the beard of an old dog.
Bind these all together
and carry them with a string
upon the nape of the neck.

2. Rabbi Jochanan's

For the burning fever,
take a knife
that is made entirely of iron,
go to a thorn bush
and tie a hair line to it.

On the first day
make a notch in it
and say:
"And there appeared
unto him
an angel of God
in a flame of fire
out of the midst
of the burning bush."

On the next day
make another indentation
and say:

"Then God saw
that he approached
in order to see, etc."

The following day
make another indentation
and say:
"Come nigh, etc."

Then cut
the thorn off
near the ground
and say:

"O thornbush!
O thornbush!
I trust in thee!"

Overdue

Dear Sir
it has come to our attention
the following amount owing
if the balance has been paid
please accept our thanks
if the balance is not paid by
we will be forced to
turn your account over to
our collection agency
we deplore
delinquent accounts
naturally would not wish to
but you force us to
and unpleasant situations
Dun & Bradstreet
and damage your credit rating
no other way but to
due process of law
Cordially yours

Levitations

E. Cobham Brewer's A Dictionary of Miracles

And the spirit lifted me up between the earth and the heaven.   Ezekiel 8:3

St. Agnes was often lifted from the ground "in the ecstasy of prayer."
St. Angela at mass "remained suspended for a long time."
Jamblichus the same, while praying. "Ten cubits."
St. Peter Celestine, as he said mass. "Through the whole service."
St. Clara of Rimini would go to church "without touching the ground."
St. Coletta was lifted up by the spirit "sometimes so high as to be
    quite out of sight."
St. Francis of Posadas, twice. "During Pentecost."
St. John of the Cross was frequently lifted by the spirit into the air
    "where he remained suspended so that his head touched the ceiling."
St. Margaret of Hungary. "On Good Friday."
St. Mary of Egypt. "More than five feet."
St. Monica. "Three feet."
Philip of Neri. "Two feet or more."
St. Joseph Oriol. "Many feet."
St. Stephen, King of Hungary. "Lifted by the hands of angels."
St. Theresa was "raised from the earth and radiant with light."
St. Francis Xavier. "Many and many and many a time."

The Jingle of the Open Road

1.

IF YOU
DON'T KNOW
WHOSE SIGNS THESE ARE
YOU HAVEN'T DRIVEN
VERY FAR
BURMA-SHAVE

2.

WITHIN THIS VALE
OF TOIL
AND SIN
YOUR HEAD GROWS BALD
BUT NOT YOUR CHIN
BURMA-SHAVE

3.

A PEACH
LOOKS GOOD
WITH LOTS OF FUZZ
BUT MAN'S NO PEACH
AND NEVER WAS
BURMA-SHAVE

4.

THE BEARDED LADY
TRIED A JAR
NOW SHE'S
A FAMOUS
MOVIE STAR
BURMA-SHAVE

5.

BROKEN ROMANCE
STATED FULLY
SHE WENT WILD
WHEN HE
WENT WOOLLY
BURMA-SHAVE

6.

BENEATH THIS STONE
LIES ELMER GUSH
TICKLED TO DEATH
BY HIS
SHAVING BRUSH
BURMA-SHAVE

7.

ALTHOUGH WE'VE SOLD
SIX MILLION OTHERS
WE STILL CAN'T
SELL THOSE
COUGHDROP BROTHERS
BURMA-SHAVE

KIRBY CONGDON

Icarus in Aipotu

Meet today's
modern Army, Dad.
We're always ready
to take to the air.
Just above the tree tops
lies one of the greatest hopes
for Victory.
"But how do you know
where the front line is, Son?"
Dad, this is a nuclear age.
Troops massed in a battle line
would be pulverized
by nuclear weapons.
So we have to disperse.
The battlefield becomes a checkerboard
with little battles going on
for miles in every direction.
It's fluid war.

"You mean we no longer need
a strategic army corps, Son?"

We need them more than ever, Dad.
The Strategic Army Corps is 114,000 strong.
They're lean and mean—
ready to fight
a nuclear or conventional war
any place in the world.
And they can be on their way
in minutes.

Today, nuclear capabilities
are fantastic.
Yet, we're equipped for smaller,
limited wars.
The Honest John has a 15-mile range.
The Chopper John missile travels by helicopter.
The Sergeant is small, light,
easily transportable.
The Redstone has a 200-mile range,
and the brand new Pershing
is smaller, more mobile, farther ranging.

Then there's the brand new,
smaller,
lighter,
Hawk.
The Hawk has already brought down
an Honest John missile in flight.
Believe me, today's Army is fascinating.
Every man is a fighting man.
Even when he's not fighting personally,
he is contributing
to the Army's fighting strength.

Manual ME 101 dash C dash 500 M.

United States Government Printing Office.
For peace and prosperity.
Made in U.S.A.
In God We Trust.
Prepare for War.

Chorus for Phonograph

from The Plumed Horn No. 6 *(April 1963)*

Help me, Mr. No-One; I am drowning.
Death.

The sun in my great-grandfather's barn,
the easy motes in the straw-colored light
are as silent as undiscovered constellations.
The secret place I knew on the hillside,
the broken poem I saw in the grass,
the whale's granite back in the meadow,
shake in darkness, frozen under the fill,
when the wheels and the whine of the trucks pass over
carrying surplus stores to the land of plenty.
Help me, Mr. No-One; I am drowning.
Death.

My schoolmates are spreading my childhood
on the shoulders of the highways in winter.
The gravel pits are the graveyards of tomorrow.
Our monuments are glaciers of stones.

Death.
Help me, Mr. No-One; I am drowning.

A machine is sawing, in silence,
the steeples of the silent town.
A machine is filling in the swampland
where we skated our games in the dusk.
The mountains laid low, the valleys are filled
with executive golf balls.
This is an entirely new development this year.
Once an abandoned barrier reef,
these acres are now an authentic replica
of a Japanese (or Chinese) garden.
Help me, Mr. No-One; I am drowning.
Death.

Fine weather boosts holiday traffic toll,
an all-time record for the world.
I have a headache. Do not incinerate.
Why don't you go out and play with the other boys?
Cut along the dotted line. To open: pull up tab.
To close: tuck in tab.
In case of emergency,
lift arm. Pull up. Push out.
Carry full identification with you at all times.
To open, break glass.
If hammer breaks, replace immediately.
The line is busy.
Your battery's dead.
And, now, an important announcement from our sponsor.
I can't help you.

My skin itches.
Run, now, to your nearest dealer.
Walk, do not run, to the nearest exit.
Use other door.
I have lost my ticket.
Okay. Take off your clothes.
The pen of my aunt,
the swimming pool of my uncle
leak.
Your dog just died.
You are dying.
Get ahead.

Think fast.
Don't worry.
Because of mechanical failure,
your insurance does not cover disaster.
Help me, Mr. No-One; I am drowning.
Death.

Your house is a parking lot now.
Aren't you drinking too much?
To call police, dial the operator.
If you need help, call, "Help!"
Now you take your statistics.
You write with a facility
which has held our attention.
Mama's plastic breast is deteriorating.
They all look alike to me.
Aren't you a member?
These are collectors' items.
Buy six and save.
One moment, please.
Keep moving.
Wait your turn.
Wait until your father gets home.
The wind is from the northeast,
and the sky will be intermittently contaminated.
No smoking. Fasten your seat belts.
We are all completely out of danger.
And that's when I shot him.
Whatever you can spare.
Aren't you attending the reunion this year?
I didn't touch any button.
Where's the emergency switch?
Didn't you see the light?
It happens all the time.
We are all completely out of danger.
Help me, Mr. No-One; I am drowning.
Death.
The mountains look like Theodore Roosevelt.
Engineers who have graduated college
drain weedless lawns with concrete streambeds.
The birds are dying.
The tap water is full of liquid detergent.
The natives hate us.
I like everybody.

I said everybody.
Help me, Mr. No-One; I am drowning.
Death.
Well, that's life.
You can't fight progress.
It's not as attractive,
but the upkeep is less.
This is a friendly bank.
Ten years of continual expansion
and look at us now.
Not responsible.
Emergency only.
Offenders will be prosecuted
to the full extent of the law.
Out of order.
Please remit.
Your loved ones are preserved forever.
I didn't know it was loaded.
Watch your coat.
Honk your horn.
No passing.
No speeding.
Maintain speed.
Passengers are requested to remain seated.
Keep out. Keep off. Keep away.
Danger. Live wire.
Watch your step.
Mind your business.
You failed to file.
Pay your fine.
Report immediately for capital punishment.
Let us hope for a quick, merciful success.
This is your number.
What is your dialing code?
I can't read your figures.
Fill in here.
We regret to inform you.
This means you.
Off with your head.
No unsightly bulge.
I've got to pee.
You're late.
I'm toilet-trained.
Greetings.

Hit him.
Help me, Mr. No-One; I am drowning.
Death.

I work with all-electric equipment,
My heart has a plastic pump.
My head revolves on a steel pin.
My parts are guaranteed.
Be prompt. Take your time.
Pay cashier. Pay when served.
Oh, before you go. When you get a chance.
You're late.
The sun shines here an hour a day.
On Friday, at five, it rains.
The bottom rung
on the ladder of success
is temporarily broken.
Power is progress.
There will be a slight delay.
I'll never, ever take you out again.
We turned the switch, but nothing happened.
Stop crying.
You said you were coming yesterday.
This is the land of tomorrow.
Help me, Mr. No-One; I am drowning.
Death.

No ball-playing. No papers. No dogs.
Cover-up; you're showing.
This, too, was once a wasteland.
It was your idea in the first place.
It's a piece of glass. It's a splinter.
It's a rusty nail.
Do something.
Aren't you listening to what I'm saying?
You're odd, but you'll change
—and you know it.
Get in line.
This park is for your enjoyment.
The policemen are here to help you.
Two dollars for indecent exposure.
This is a friendly, family community;
now you get out.
Your round trip ticket

Is good for twenty-five years.
And here is your gold watch.
Prepare for war.
You brought the wrong papers.
The cranberries are malignant this year.
Water has pitted mother's stainless steel.
Plane trees resist carbon monoxide.
I really love the hurly-burly of the big city.
It's a fire engine; I thought it was an ambulance.
It figures. That follows.
I'll check. I'll double-check.
You made a mistake.
You have been somewhat of a disappointment to us.
I want my penny back.

Push, don't pull.
Don't push.
Help me, Mr. No-One; I am drowning.
Death.
We're out of stock.
Help me, Mr. No-One; I am
Death.
They're all in storage.
Help me, Mr. No-One
Death.
They don't make this part any more.
Help me, Mr.
Death.
We can order one for you.
Help me
Death.
If you didn't want it, why did you ask?
Help.
Death.
Okay—sorry.
Help.
Death.
I said sorry.
Death.
Help.
Death.

Death.

Death.

JOHN DANIEL

Watch

found in Capital *by Karl Marx*

Formerly the individual work of a Nuremberg artificer
The WATCH
has been transformed
into the social product
of an immense number of detail labourers,

such as:

mainspring makers
dial makers
spiral spring makers
jewelled hole makers
ruby lever makers
hand makers
case makers
screw makers
gilders

with numerous sub-divisions such as:

wheel makers (brass and steel separate)
pin makers
movement makers
acheveur de pignon
(fixes the wheels on the axles, polishes the facets &c.)
pivot makers
planteur de finissage
(puts the wheels and springs in the works)
finisseur de barillet
(cuts teeth in the wheels
makes holes of the right size &c.)
escapement makers
cylinder makers
for cylinder escapements
escapement wheel makers
balance wheel makers
raquette makers
(apparatus for regulating the watch)
the *planteur d'echappement*
(escapement maker proper)

then the

repasseur de barillet
(finishes the box for the spring &c.)
steel polishers

wheel polishers
screw polishers
figure painters
dial enamellers
(melt the enamel on the copper)
fabricant de pendants
(makes the ring by which the case is hung)
finisseur de charniere
(puts the brass hinge in the cover &c.)
faiseur de secret
(puts in the springs that open the case)
graveur
ciseleur
poliseur de boite &c. &c.

and last of all

the *repasseur*

who fits together the whole watch
and hands it over in a going state.

Smith L.J.

found in GPO telephone directory
London Postal Area S-Z, October 1966

Smith L.J, 28 Clarendon dr SW15
Smith L.J, 157 Covington wy SW16
Smith L.J, 18 The Elms Nicoll rd NW10
Smith L.J, 16 Erlesmere gdns W13
Smith L.J, 74 Flowersmead Upper Tooting pk SW17
Smith L.J, 46 Green la SE9
Smith L.J, 82 Hubert gro SW9
Smith L.J, 162 Lansdowne rd N17
Smith L.J, 8 Mayfair ter N14
Smith L.J, 25 Montfort Ho Victoria Pk sq E2
Smith L.J, 7 Oaklands rd SW14
Smith L.J, Plmbr, 59 Phipps Bdge rd SW19
Smith L.J, "The Cottage of Content" 123 Rodney rd SE17
Smith L&J, Elec Engs, 108 St James la N10
Smith L.J, 5 St Johns Hl gro SW11
Smith L.J, 88 Temple Sheen rd SW14
Smith L.J, 39 Westbrook Ho Victoria Pk sq E2
Smith L.J, Barrstr, 9 Old sq Lincolns Inn WC2

Injury to Insured

(found in North British and Mercantile Motor Car Insurance policy)

total loss
by physical severance
at or above
the wrist
or ankle
of ONE hand
or ONE foot £250

total and irrecoverable
loss of sight
of ONE eye £250

total loss
by physical severance
at or above the wrist
or ankle
of ONE hand
or ONE foot
together with
the total and irrecoverable
loss of sight
of ONE eye £500

total loss
by physical severance
at or above the wrist
or ankle
of BOTH hands
or BOTH feet
or of ONE hand
together with ONE foot £500

total and irrecoverable
loss of sight
of BOTH eyes £500

death £1,000

Eel

found in Larousse Gastronomique *by Prosper Montagne, translated by Froud, Gray, Murdoch and Taylor.*

We repeat
EEL MUST BE KEPT ALIVE UNTIL THE LAST MOMENT

Before skinning it
STUN it
by BANGING THE HEAD AGAINST A STONE.

As soon as the eel is dead
HANG IT UP ON A HOOK
by a string tied at the neck.
Make a circular incision below the string.
TURN THE SKIN BACK ALL ROUND THE NECK
(in such a way as to be able to hold it with a cloth)

TEAR IT OFF IN ONE GO.

Of 91 Men Leaving an Underground Station

found in Sets and Logic *by C.A.R. Bailey*

of 91 men leaving an Underground station,
41 wore hat and gloves
and carried an umbrella.

61 wore hat and gloves
and 68 wore gloves.

There were 7 who wore a hat
and carried an umbrella,
but wore no gloves,
and 21 who wore a hat
but no gloves.

Only 2 carried an umbrella
but wore neither hat nor gloves,
although there were 50 men with umbrellas
altogether.

How many of these
wore gloves
but no hat?

Colour Bra

found in the Brian Mills Postal
Shopping Service catalogue

Two Spinney brief
cotton bras,
with embroidered cotton
pre-shaped foam
cups.
Elastic
centre-front.
Adjustable
stretch shoulder
straps.
Twin hook
(and eye)
back-fastening.
Made in Jamaica.
One black
and one
white.

JOHN GIORNO

Leather

This is your letter
of welcome
to Gentlemen's Quarterly,
America's newest
boldest,
most exciting
journal for men—
the only publication
available today
devoted exclusively
to the subject
of Masculine Fashion
and Grooming.

Helen looked up
at his vigorous
naked body,
with its flat stomach,
lean hips,
and towering erection.

These juvenile hormones
keep the bugs immature
until they are ready
for metamorphosis.
Only when the hormone flow
stops can the bugs
become adults.

I've got
the house
pretty well straightened up now.

He moved behind her
and pressed
himself close.
His great penis
slid smoothly
over the leather
of her tunic.

Immature bugs
died from sprays
of the hormone
because they were unable
to transform themselves
into adults.

I still have
to hang
the curtains
in your room
and make
those dividing curtains
upstairs.

Adults died
when their reproductive organs
went haywire.

He put his arms
beneath hers
and felt
for her breasts.

A pretty Half Bushel Basket
filled with Pineapple Oranges,
honey-sweet Grapefruit,
Persian Limes . . .
and three Jars
of Guava Jelly,
Pineapple-Cherry Marmalade
and Tropical Fruit Conserve.

He lowered
his head sideways
and smelled deeply:
the sweet scent
of the leather,
mingled with her perfume,
filled his nostrils
and made his head swim.

The unaided
human eye
can distinguish
10 million
different
color surfaces.

"It was like painting
these bugs
into a corner,"
said Dr. Williams.
"In effect,
they committed suicide."

He continued
to run his penis
against her tunic.

I didn't
have time yet
because I didn't want
to make them
ahead of time
and have them
hanging around
getting dirty.

He gave
a final rub,
and did
as she said.
She stepped
over him
and sat down,
on his penis,
facing him.

"After I'm underway,"
says James,
"the only thing
on my mind
is getting stopped.
When the chute
opens
I kinda relax."

One big difference
between the way
young and adult bugs
were killed
by the hormone
was the length
of time
it took.

The penis slid far,
very far, inside her.
She gasped,
put her hands
behind her
on his knees,
and arched
her leather-clad body
backwards.

The living room
really looks nice
and so much lighter
in there.

Model
of the Boeing Company plane
shows it
with wings in place
for subsonic flight.
In supersonic flight,
they would be swept back
to join the tailplane,
forming one surface.

The penis slid
even further into her.
He put up his hands
to her stomach,
stroking
the soft kid leather
with the tips
of his fingers.

Immature insects
were killed
in minutes
while it took
as long as a few days
for the adults
to die.

Janet gave me
a new lamp
for Xmas.

He slid
the hands higher
and caressed
her breasts.

Astronaut
Richard F. Gordon Jr.
stepped into the eerie stillness
of space today,
reported initial tiredness
and straddled
an Agena satellite,
"riding it like a cowboy."

Helen leaned forward
and made movements
with her thighs,
as though she were
riding a horse.

Scientists
are trying to enlist
the common barnacle
in the fight
to save man's teeth.

I want
to get
another
end table.

The man under her
put his hands
to her shoulders
and gently drew her
a little downwards.

I also want
to have a light put in
down in the dining end
of the room.

He raised
his head
from the floor
and buried
his face
in her soft leather
tunic.

While bathing,
Paravati,
the consort
of Shiva,
longed for a son.
A sweat covered
her body and,
as she was wiping it off,
she found a child
in the hollow
of her hand.

He opened
his lips
and began
to lick away
the spots
of dried blood
that covered it.

Bullet holes,
look like
the real thing,
set of 3
only 50¢

Plus white
helps remove
tobacco and food stains
that dull your teeth.

His head swam
with the excitement
of the feeling
of the wet slippery leather
on his tongue.

I'll try
to have
that done
next month.

Intense investigation
led to the finding
that the chemical
in the newsprint,
which came from
North American wood pulp,
was a cousin
to the juvenile hormone
secreted by
this same insect species.

I'd like
to go spend
New Years
with my sisters.

Five women
and two children,
forced to lie face down
on a beauty shop floor
like spokes in a wheel,
were shot methodically
by a high school senior today.
Four of the women
and one child
died.

Rose

Her name
was Margaret
and she drummed
her fingers
on the card table,
a blonde woman
in her early 40's
who played bridge
by the book—
bickering earnestly
throughout
with her partners
who also played
by the book—
but not
the same one.

No James,
I never
deceived you
with anyone.

Dazzle-charged silver
(this page) twisted
as boldly as chicken wire
against silken smooth white.

N.Y.-FEMALE,
dominant,
attractive.
Love the bizzare
and anything unusual.
Can travel.
Want to meet
anyone who has
similar interests.

Males,
females,
couples.
Send photo.

I never slept
with another man.

A worldwide effort
is under way
to assess the possibility
that the periodic
outbreaks
of flu
besetting mankind
may originate
in domestic animals
and be spread
by birds.

The surprise power
of a young, shimmering
coat-dress (opposite)
as it flips open
to reveal
dashing little
evening pants.

I never even
kissed one.

FLA.-FEMALE, 22,
5′5″ 34-24-34.
Interested
in discipline.
Want to hear
from a dominant male
or female.

I was
completely
faithful.

Like so many
of her sisters
of the streets,
Mathilda's
arms and legs
are blotched
with purple
and pocked
with countless jabs
of the heroin needle.

Webbed
with jewel roses
at the shoulders,
slinked
body length
(above).
By Kiki Hart,
in Celanese acetate
and rayon
crepe-backed satin
by Chardon-Marche.

Samples
of bird blood
are being collected
by laboratories
in a number of countries
on behalf of the World
Health Organization.

And I didn't
sleep
with Diter
until I had
left you
and returned
to Iceland.

N.Y.C.-FEMALE,
negro.
Assertive nature.
Would like to hear
from passive males.

Dark velvety red.
Medium-sized buds
open into multi-petaled blooms
up to 4 inches across.

Like many,
she is also
a Lesbian
who gets no pleasure
from the sexual act
with her customers,
but finds solace
with other women.

GA.-FEMALE,
would like to meet
a genuine transvestite
for a fun filled trip
throughout the U.S.

The blood
is tested
to see
if the birds
carry—
or once carried—
a flu type
of virus.

Emmett
or Maurice
would probably
have liked
to sleep
with me
but they never even
alluded to it

Golden-heeled
gilded legs
(for sipping
brandy
on the rug),
splashed
with brillants
and pearls,
pulled
under a black
crepe tunic
with a bib
of jewels.

The cause
of concern
is the periodic
appearance
of new influenza
strains
against which
existing vaccines
are useless.

Two Montgomery women
are building
a two-bedroom,
bath-and-a-half house
all by themselves;
well, almost
by themselves.

Our talk
was always
on another level—
there was always
a distance
between us.

A million
night blue
sequins
swooped
with a hard-edge
finish
over soft flowing
crepe pajamas
in this season's
most irreverent
pink of evening.

The Arctic tern,
whose remarkable migrations
carry it yearly
from one polar region
to the other,
has been found
to carry
such a virus.

This is
completely
honest.

She told me
that when about
nine years old,
she and another girl,
a schoolfellow,
used to push
their fingers
up each other's cunts.

I don't know
how to make it
stronger.

One cost-cutting
device
has been to use
old crown jewels
that were lying around
loose in bowls
in a vault
in Tehran's
central bank
for the Empress's
new crown.

ILL.-FEMALE, 31,
is seeking
a female
who is interested
in modelling.
Send
a full-length
photo.

YOU WERE RIGHT
TO BE CONFIDENT.

SEAL
THIS ENVELOPE
CAREFULLY
and write
your name
across the seal
as indicated above,
before delivering
to custodian.

YOU KNEW ME
WELL ENOUGH.

Poem

Her thighs
crushed
Her thighs crushed
around
my ears
like a vise
around my ears
like a vise
and they started
ringing
and they started ringing
but I kept
tonguing
but I kept tonguing
and rubbing
with my chin
and rubbing with my chin
until she had
my cock
until she had my cock
all the way
down
her throat
all the way down
her throat.

I rolled
over on top
I rolled over
on top
and fucked away
and fucked away
with even
my balls
with even my balls
in her mouth
in her mouth.

She scratched
at my ass
She scratched at my ass
but I just kept
thrusting away
but I just kept thrusting away
and tonguing away
burying
my head
and tonguing away
burying my head
as deep as
I could
as deep as I could
between her legs
between her legs.

When she came
When she came,
she kept
shuddering
all over
she kept shuddering
all over
and her throat
muscles
and her throat muscles
jerked me off
jerked me
off.

Her thighs
crushed
Her thighs crushed
around
my ears
like a vise
around my ears
like a vise
and they started
ringing
and they started ringing
but I kept
tonguing
but I kept tonguing
and rubbing
with my chin
and rubbing with my chin
until she had
my cock
until she had my cock
all the way
down
her throat
all the way down
her throat.

I rolled
over on top
I rolled over
on top
and fucked away
and fucked away
with even
my balls
with even my balls
in her mouth
in her mouth.

She scratched
at my ass
She scratched at my ass
but I just kept
thrusting away
but I just kept thrusting away
and tonguing away
burying
my head
and tonguing away
burying my head
as deep as
I could
as deep as I could
between her legs
between her legs.

When she came
When she came,
she kept
shuddering
all over
she kept shuddering
all over
and her throat
muscles
and her throat muscles
jerked me off
jerked me
off.

RONALD GROSS

America Is Names

Seattle, Chicago, Kansas City . . .
Elm Street, North Main, Times Square . . .
Wrigley, Kellogg, Squibb, Ipana . . .
Goodrich, Chevrolet, Heinz, Calvert.
Names you have always known . . .
believed in . . .
names of things you've bought and used . . .
Yes, America is names.
Good names.
Familiar names that inspire confidence . . .
For America *is* names . . .
good names for things to have . . .
So it's up to you
as a salesman
for a brand name
to keep pushing
not only YOUR BRAND,
but brands
in general.

Ditty

DoubleDouble youryour pleasurepleasure,,
DoubleDouble youryour funfun,,
WithWith Double-Double- MintMint Double-Double- MintMint
Double-Double- MintMint gumgum.. gumgum..

Ice Cream Cone

Flour, cereal, sugar, starch,
vegetable shortening,
salt, protein, gum leavening,
propylene glycol.
Certified colors, artificial flavors.
Chocolate coating containing
cocoa, vegetable oil (containing
an emulsifier and tenox 2
less than .05%).
Tenox 2
is an antioxidant containing
butylated hydroxyanisole,
propyl gallate, citric acid,
propylene glycol.

Heroic Couplets

Now it's Pepsi—for those who think young!
    Abraham Brodsky of 1671 North Avenue
Now parties are more fun. So if you're the sort who
    founded and served as president of the Regal Supply Company
Reflects the new way of life everyone's leading
    in Newark for forty years, died yesterday
Thinking young. This is the life
    at the Elizabeth General Hospital. He was
light, bracing, clean-tasting
    87 years old. He retired in 1961 from
Pepsi. So think young! Say:
    Services today at 1:30 P.M. at University Funeral Chapel.

2/29c

2/29c

for Andy Warhol

Contents Counted, Inspected, Mechanically Loaded to Insure Accuracy

makes old pans shine like new
burned-on scorch
greasy film
disappears in seconds

A New Utensil
Free If Brillo
Fails To Clean

If Product Or
Performance
Defective

Replacement or refund
to consumer

FOR INSTANT SHINE

With pink polishing
soap

Outdoors, Brillo
whitens white
walls, gets burned
grease off grills
5 Pads 5 PADS

Brilloisthesoappadthat'sreally
madetoshine.Containsenoughpink
polishingsoaptodoaraftofheavy
dutyjobs.Evenoldpanscansparkle
likenew.Ovens,greasybroilersclean
upfastwithBrillo.

On Notice, Any Shortages Promptly Replaced.

TIP!
The
special
rust-resister

in Brillo
will make the
pads last
and last

if you
let the suds
dry on the pad
between usings.

As long as there's
suds—there's
no room
for rust.

Sonnet

Painful Hemorrhoids?

All too often, humans who sit and stand
Pay the price of vertical posture. Sitting
And standing combine with the force of gravity,
Exerting extra pressure on veins and tissues
In and around the rectal area.
Painful, burning hemorrhoids result.
The first thought of many sufferers
Is to relieve their pain and their discomfort.

Products, however, often used for this
Contain no anesthetic drug at all, or one
Too weak to give the needed pain relief,
Or only lubricate. But now, at last
There is a formulation which provides
pain-killing power, prolonged relief, on contact.

Song of the Road

Yield.
No Parking.
Unlawful to Pass.
Wait for Green Light.
Yield.

Stop.
Danger.
Narrow Bridge.
Merging Traffic Ahead.
Yield.

Squeeze.
Dead End.
Do Not Enter.
Enter at Own Risk.
Yield.

Yield.

Yield.

Yield.

Why Negroes Prefer Treatment as Human Beings

40011	Q1	Just want dignity, good treatment	.27
40012	Q1	Mixing not important, just treated normally	.25
40013	Q1	Want equal rights	.13
40014	Q1	Let me go where want to and do what want	.03
40015	Q1	Want to be treated as full citizen	.03
40016	Q1	Want equal opportunity for education	.01
40017	Q1	Fought in wars, should have benefits of country	.01
40018	Q1	Want more opportunities	.01
40019	Q1	Not sure	.28
		Percentages add to more than 100% because some Negroes gave more than one reason for their preference.	

Suppose, Instead

Whatever your father wills you
is not taxable to you
as income. It's a bequest,
a tax-free bounty.
Suppose, instead,
he's sick and wants you
to *care for him.*
In return, he agrees
in writing
to leave you
his property.
Then you've got a
transfer for a consideration—
all taxable income when
you receive your "bequest."

Congratulatory Message

I wanted to say to both of you,
Well done.
We are all in this country
very proud of you and,
I think, the entire world
is grateful
for what you have done
and, particularly, for your
safe return. You have both
written your names
in history and
in our hearts.
God bless you and
your very fine families.
—Now I just want to say
this finally
to the two
of you:
What you have done
will never be forgotten.
We can hope and we can pray
that the time will come
when all men
of all nations
will join together
to explore space together
and walk side by side
toward peace.
And you two
outstanding men
have taken a long stride
forward in mankind's
progress. And everyone
in this nation and,
I think, the free world
feels in your debt.

Thank you
very much,
Mr. President.
We appreciate
that.

Epithalamium

at lubet innuptis ficto te carpere questu.
quid tum, si carpunt, tacita quem mente requirunt?

Hymen o Hymenaee, Hymen ades o Hymenaee!

But girls love to chide three with feigned complaint.
What then, if they chide him whom they desire in their secret heart?

Hymen, O Hymenaeus, Hymen, hither O Hymenaeus!

I can't understand
why the career girls
who write to you
feel they are missing
so much in life
by not being married.

Where do they
get the idea
that a husband
is the answer
to everything?

I wish
one of those gals
would take mine.
I'm not bitter—
just experienced.
Marriage is not
the dream it's
cracked up to be.
I had a wonderful
job when I married
and gave it up
to be a household
drudge.

My husband is
a nice guy,
but he's dull.
I've had it
both ways
and let me tell you
that marriage is
plenty over-rated.
Many single girls
who write to you
say they are
lonesome.

Well,
I'm married
and I'm lonesome,
too.
I'm not a
cold person,
Ann,
if that's what
you're thinking.
In fact
I never refuse him.

The single woman
who supports herself
can travel,
spend her money
as she wishes,
have a romance,
or a full-blown
affair
when she feels
like it.
She can turn love
off and on
like an electric
bulb.

So why
don't you
level with
the girls,
Ann?

Thank You—Come Again

Close cover before striking.
    Thank you—come again.
Please pay cashier.
    Thank you—come again.
We appreciate your patronage.
    Thank you—come again.
Service is our middle name.
    Thank you—come again.
The pleasure was ours.
    Thank you—come again.
Here's your correct change.
    Thank you—come again.
We aim to please.
    Thank you—come again.
Thank you—come again.
    Thank you—come again.
Thank you—come again.

FRANK KUENSTLER

Introductions

"Mary McCarthy, meet Susan Sontag. Susan Sontag, meet Mary McCarthy."
"F. Scott Fitzgerald, meet John Keats. John Keats, meet F. Scott Fitzgerald."
"Arthur Cohen, meet Hunter Ingalls. Hunter Ingalls, meet Arthur Cohen."
"Joe Di Maggio, meet Marilyn Monroe. Marilyn Monroe, meet Joe Di Maggio."
"Norman Mailer, meet Norman Weisselberg. Norman Weisselberg, meet Norman Mailer."
"Howard Everngam, meet Howard Nemerov. Howard Nemerov, meet Howard Everngam."
"Irving Howe, meet Max Shactman. Max Shactman, meet Irving Howe."
"Linda Lev, meet Leonard Lipton. Leonard Lipton, meet Linda Lev."
"Judith Malina, meet Antonin Artaud. Antonin Artaud, meet Judith Malina."
"Lionel Trilling, meet Choo-Choo Johnston. Choo-Choo Johnston, meet Lionel Trilling."
"Mark Stern, meet Irving Feldman. Irving Feldman, meet Mark Stern."
"Northrop Frye, meet Wm. Shakespeare. Wm. Shakespeare, meet Northrop Frye."
"Ernest Hemingway, meet Ernest Truex. Ernest Truex, meet Ernest Hemingway."
"Lana Turner, meet Larry Rivers. Larry Rivers, meet Lana Turner."
"Linda Darnell, meet Jackie Wilson. Jackie Wilson, meet Linda Darnell."
"Kenneth Anger, meet Jonas Mekas. Jonas Mekas, meet Kenneth Anger."
"Karl Bissinger, meet Diane Arbus. Diane Arbus, meet Karl Bissinger."
"Elizabeth Taylor, meet Elizabeth Montgomery. Elizabeth Montgomery, meet Elizabeth Taylor."
"Herb Bronstein, meet Harold Rosenberg. Harold Rosenberg, meet Herb Bronstein."
"Dov Lederberg, meet Jimmy Hoffa. Jimmy Hoffa, meet Dov Lederberg."
"Al Capp, meet Huntington Hartford. Huntington Hartford, meet Al Capp."
"Michael Benedikt, meet Michael Smith. Michael Smith, meet Michael Benedikt."
"Cassius Clay, meet Captain Steve. Captain Steve, meet Cassius Clay."
"Allen Arbus, meet Andy Warhol. Andy Warhol, meet Allen Arbus."
"Leon Trotsky, meet Jean Cocteau. Jean Cocteau, meet Leon Trotsky."
"Sholom Aleichem, meet Mark Twain. Mark Twain, meet Sholom Aleichem."
"Fred Astaire, meet Arthur Murray. Arthur Murray, meet Fred Astaire."
"Rachel Carson, meet Capt. Costeau. Capt. Costeau, meet Rachel Carson."
"Laurel & Hardy, meet Mutt & Jeff. Mutt & Jeff, meet Laurel & Hardy."
"Dame Rumour, meet Damon Runyon. Damon Runyon, meet Dame Rumour."
"Miss America, meet Miss Universe. Miss Universe, meet Miss America."
"Aaron Cohen, meet Bela Kun. Bela Kun, meet Aaron Cohen."
"Omer Simeon, meet Colin Young. Colin Young, meet Omer Simeon."
"Marshall McLuhan, meet Harvey Matusow. Harvey Matusow, meet Marshall McLuhan."
"Walt Whitman, meet Henri Rousseau. Henri Rousseau, meet Walt Whitman."
"George Kennan, meet Genghis Khan. Genghis Khan, meet George Kennan."
"Captain Video, meet Captain Kangaroo. Captain Kangaroo, meet Captain Video."

Napoleon & the Letter M

Marboeuf was the first to recognize Napoleon's genius at military college
Marengo was the first great battle he won; Melas made room for him in Italy
Mortier was one of his best generals; Moreau betrayed him
Marat was the first martyr to his cause; Marie Louise shared his highest fortune
Moscow was the abyss of ruin into which he fell
Metternich vanquished him on the field of diplomacy
Massena, Mortie, Marmont, Macdonald, Murat, Moncey served as
marshals under him, & 26 of his generals had names beginning with the letter M
Marat, Duke of Bassano, was his most trusted counsellor
Montenetto was the localle of his first battle, & his last
Mont St. Jean, as the French term Waterloo
Millesimo, Mondovi, Montmirail & Montereau were battles he won, then
Montmartre was stormed
Milan was the first enemy capital, & Moscow the last, he entered victorious
Mallet conspired against him; he lost Egypt through
Menou, & employed Miellis to take Pius VIII prisoner
Murat was the first to desert him, then Marmont
Maret, Montalivet & Mallieu were three of his ministers
Montesquien was the name of his first chamberlain. His last halting place in France:
Malmaison. He surrendered to Captain
Maitland. His companions on St. Helena were Montholon & his valet Marchand

Movie Bulletin

"My film Renaissance began after World War II," Luis Buñuel said
"Jackie Gleason is one of the best music arrangers in the business," Marlene Dietrich said
"The film must have been cut by the studio gardener," Orson Welles said
"Can this be happening to Gabriel Pascal?" Gabriel Pascal said
"Photographers have ruined my life," Brigitte Bardot said
"I dream all the time," Doris Day said
"I am the Queen of Ajax," Marlene Dietrich said
"There are no primitives behind a camera lens," Curtis Harrington said
"We put the money in the escarole," Samuel Goldwyn said
"Don't drink the water. Fish fuck in it," W.C. Fields said
"I am an essayist," Jean-Luc Godard said
"We need the kind of progress that goes backwards," Orson Welles said
"Actors are cattle," Alfred Hitchcock said
"Tragedy is a long shot," Frank Kuenstler said
"Poets are the Jews of America," Jonas Mekas said

GAIL KUENSTLER

Stage Directions

Let Paradise be set up in a somewhat lofty place;
let divers trees be therein, and fruits hanging upon them,
so that it may seem a most delectable place.

Then let the Savior come, and let Adam and Eve be set before him.
But Adam, a little nearer, with a composed countenance;
Eve, however, with a countenance a little more subdued.

And let those things that are said be said in their due order.
Whoever shall speak the name of Paradise,
let him look back at it & point it out with his hand.

Stagecraft

The Machinery for the Paradise

"How to Light the Lamps."
"How to Make Dolphins and Other Sea Monsters Appear to Spout
Water While Swimming."
"How to Produce a Constantly Flowing River."
"How to Divide the Sky into Sections."
"How Gradually to Cover Part of the Sky with Clouds."
"How to Cover Part of the Sky, Beginning with Small Cloud
That Becomes Larger and Larger and Continually Changes
Its Color."
"How to Make a Cloud Descend So That It Will Gradually Move
from the End of the Stage to the Middle, a Cloud, Moreover,
with Persons in It."

An Accounting

outlay for blue and gold
item for each small vault
time: 4 days
for the windows
on the 29th of January, 1494
cloth for hose
making
to Salai
a jasper ring
a sparkling stone
to Caterina
to Caterina
the wheel
the shield
the ends of the axletree
parsley
item for 24 pictures of Roman history
the philosophers
for pilasters, one ounce of blue
for gold
Total

How large is the hall
How large is the garland

WALTER LOWENFELS

Leader of First Raid on North Returns to U.S.

(The New York Times, *January 20, 1968*)

I thought it was a drill.
I was full of apprehension.
I was a little scared.
I was just at the right place
at the right time
and hit them hard.
I don't see how he can make it
day in and day out.
I don't see how he does it.
I didn't expect it
to last this long.

Haiphong is one hell
of a busy port.
You can see the trucks
and the equipment
being unloaded.
I'd like to hit that port.
There are also a lot of nice
buildings in Haiphong. What
their contributions to the war effort
are I don't know. But
the desire to bomb a virgin
building is terrific.
But we don't do it.
A lot of people at home feel
we're bombing buildings
for the sake of
bombing buildings.
That's not true. I've seen
bombs fall short, yes I have,
but it happens when you're getting
triple A* shot at you
and so accidents
are bound to happen.
I was fascinated with the navy
and flying since a kid.
I was always a big fan of
Charles Lindbergh and I saw
"Dawn Patrol" with Errol Flynn
at least eight times.

* Anti-aircraft artillery.

From an Exposition of Power and Industrial Machinery

Open float inspirator and injector
    super simplex pulverizer
        gyrating cruster
armature spider
    quick-change chuck and collet
        clipper-belt lacer
    expanding lathe mandrel
    non-return vertical indicator
        multiwhirl baffle
hanger boxes
    pillar boxes
        drop-forged steel body
hardened worms with thread ground
    cement slurry
        metallurgical slimes
carbon steel hand taps
    precision high-speed ground thread taps
        two and three fluted taps
spiral pointed serial hard machine screw
    bent shank tapper taps
mud or washout spindle staybolt
    couple taps for pipes and tubes
short die hobs
    long die hobs for the man who
        makes his own dies.

Blood

A found poem from Blood *by Leo Vroman*

Once you know the lady's hematocrit,
    the hematocrit of the injected sample
                    (which is diluted with some salt solution
                    that was used to wash excess
                    radioactive chromium off the cells),
the radioactivity of the injected sample,
    and the radioactivity of the mixture
        of the lady's own, "cold" red cells
            that had never left her body before
                            and were never tagged
                                        but had been stirred inside
                                                        her
                                            with the "hot" red cells
                                                    that were
                                                    injected—

with all that information available,
    you can calculate
what percent the known amount of hot cells
    occupies among the cold cells,
and how large the total red cell volume
    and the total blood volume of the lady are.
A much cleaner method
    than that of a few hundred years ago,
when all the blood had to be removed.

EDWARD LUCIE-SMITH

Beckford at the Abbey of Batalha

I had no wish to sleep,
And yet my pleasant retired chamber,
With clean white walls,
Chequered with the reflection of waving boughs,
And the sound of a rivulet softened by distance,
Invited it soothingly.
Seating myself in the deep recess
Of a capacious window which was wide open,
I suffered the balsamic air
And serene moonlight
To quiet my agitated spirits.
One lonely nightingale
Had taken possession
Of a bay-tree just beneath me,
And was pouring forth its ecstatic notes
At distant intervals.

In one of those long pauses,
When silence itself,
Enhanced by contrast,
Seemed to become still deeper,
A far different sound
Than the last I had been listening to
Caught my ear,—
The sound of a loud but melancholy voice
Echoing through the arched avenues
Of a vast garden,
Pronouncing distinctly
These appalling words—
"Judgement! judgement!
Tremble at the anger of an offended God!
Woe to Portugal!
Woe!
Woe!"

My hair stood on end—
I felt
As if a spirit
Were about to pass before me;
But instead
Of some fearful shape,
Some horrid shadow,

Such as appeared in vision to Eliphaz,
There issued forth
From a dark thicket,
A tall, majestic, deadly pale old man:
He neither looked about nor above him;
He moved slowly on,
His eye fixed as stone,
Sighing profoundly;
And at the distance of some fifty paces
From the spot where I was stationed,
Renewed his doleful cry,
His fatal proclamation:—
"Woe! woe!" resounded through the still atmosphere,
Repeated
By the echoes of vaults and arches;
And the sounds died away,
And the spectre-form that seemed to emit them retired,
I know not how nor whither.

Shall I confess
That my blood ran cold,
That all idle,
All wanton thoughts
Left my bosom,
And that I passed an hour or two at my window
Fixed and immovable?

(*Found poem from William Beckford's* Recollections of an Excursion to the Monasteries of Alcobaça and Batalha—*Sixth Day.*)

JACKSON MAC LOW

Solar Speculations

(from Stanzas for Iris Lezak—*Summer 1960)*

Should astronomers, of them feel that they should stick pretty closely to the facts, "landing parties will see them, and to guess what manner of things those landing parties may find." Realizes.

Should astronomers, planets. Effect upon it. Captured by freezing on the planet's dark, use imagination? "Landing parties will see them, and to guess what manner of things those landing parties may find." Them feel that they should stick pretty closely to the facts, is a physician, of them feel that they should stick pretty closely to the facts, not an astronomer. Should astronomers?

Spoils the sport. Of future space voyagers. "Landing parties may find. Any known fact about the solar system." Realize is that speculation about them.

Spoils the sport. Physical sciences. Effect upon it. Cold side "can never again escape as gases." Unlikely. Later he describes "great frigid hurricanes" of gases blowing away from the dark side. "Any known fact about the solar system." This chapter should have been read more carefully before it was sent to the printer. Information about the solar system, of future space voyagers. Not straining for sensation, spoils the sport.

They're living it up at our expense

(from Stanzas for Iris Lezak—*Summer 1960)*

The who engrossing. In report ethical
legal individuals Florida yacht magazine,
impressive data.
Unlike popular
America thereby
offering a report
extrapolate *caveat* "sucker break." 'Experts' money stock easy

To histories exposure. Years. Losses entire
realm is for (it) makes. Gibney
in depletion
allowances, provisions
a tax
of attempts roles
ethic criticism. Saving portion excessive member Society example,

Pattern Recognition by Machine

(from Stanzas for Iris Lezak—Summer 1960)

Perceive. As letters. Think? Think? Elusive, relations, now met most of the classic criteria of intelligence that skeptics have proposed.

Relations, elusive, *can* outperform their designers: original: group from the Carnegie Institute of Technology and the Rand Corporation (now met most of the classic criteria of intelligence that skeptics have proposed). In *Principia Mathematica*, think? In *Principia Mathematica*, original: now met most of the classic criteria of intelligence that skeptics have proposed.

Bertrand Russell. In *Principia Mathematica*.

More elegant than the Whitehead-Russell version. *As letters. Can* outperform their designers: His ability to solve problems, in *Principia Mathematica*, now met most of the classic criteria of intelligence that skeptics have proposed. Elusive.

Prove theorems and generally run his life depends on this type of perception. Achievements in mechanical problem-solving will remain isolated technical triumphs. The difficulty lies in the nature of the task. The difficulty lies in the nature of the task. Essentially classified the possible inputs. Request to pass the salt. Not transmit these ideal intervals.

Request to pass the salt. Essentially classified the possible inputs. Clear. Of variation among the dots and dashes, grid and converted to a cellular pattern by completely filling in all squares through which lines pass (not transmit these ideal intervals). In gaps (the difficulty lies in the nature of the task). In gaps of variation among the dots and dashes), not transmit these ideal intervals.

(Bottom left). In gaps.

Maximum number of intersections of the sample with all horizontal lines across the grid. Achievements in mechanical problem-solving will remain isolated triumphs. Clear. Have been found and the range of the identified character spaces. In gaps (not transmit these ideal intervals). Essentially classify the possible inputs.

Process, are identified as dots and dashes. The classified marks and spaces gives a string of tentative segments, the classified marks and spaces gives a string of tentative segments. Experience has shown that when one of the tentative segments is not acceptable, reclassifies the longest space in the segment as a character space and examines the two new characters thus formed. Not fully specified in advance.

Reclassifies the longest space in the segment as a character space and examines the two new characters thus formed. Experience has shown that when one of the tentative segments is not acceptable, continuous message is divided into appropriate segments. Often be appropriate. Generalizing about pattern recognition. Not fully specified in advance. Is rather specialized. The classified marks and spaces gives a string of tentative segments, is rather specialized. Often be appropriate. Not fully specified in advance.

Be expected; is rather specialized.

Mechanical reader is to provide it with a means of assimilating the visual data. Are identified as dots and dashes. Continuous message is divided into appropriate segments. Handle. Is rather specialized. Not fully specified in advance. Experience has shown that when one of the tentative segments is not acceptable.

Presents no problem. An image of the letter could be projected on a bank of photocells, the output of each cell controlling a binary device in the computer. The output of each cell controlling a binary device in the computer. Experiments to be described here the appropriate digital information from the matrix was recorded on punch cards and was fed into the computer in this form. Representing the unknown letter would be compared to each template sequence, number of matching digits recorded in each case.

Representing the unknown letter would be compared to each template sequence, experiments to be described here the appropriate digital information from the matrix was recorded on punch cards and was fed into the computer in this form. Clearly fail. Orientation or size could destroy the match completely [good deal more than mere shapes]. Number of matching digits recorded in each case. INCORRECT MATCH may result even when sample (the output of each cell controlling a binary device in the computer). INCORRECT MATCH may result even when sample (orientation or size could destroy the match completely) number of matching digits recorded in each case.

Believe to be an important general principle. INCORRECT MATCH may result even when sample.

Matches. An image of the letter could be projected on a bank of photocells, clearly fail. Hierarchical structure is forced on the recognition system by the nature of the entities to be recognized. INCORRECT MATCH may result even when sample (number of matching digits recorded in each case). Experiments to be described here the appropriate digital information from the matrix was recorded on punch cards and fed into the computer in this form.

4.5.10.11.2.8.4.2.,the 2nd biblical poem

New York / January 1955

thither;/____/to/____/
not/____/ /____/tribe/____/
every/____/the not/____/ /____/the before lest/____/
Arabah, a thy/____/All/____/ /____/ /____/ /____/the/____/
Get/____/
/____/ /____/thy/____/them,/____/thy/____/
/____/ /____/shalt/____/
/____/this

/____/ /____/ /____/ /____/
/____/ /____/of this/____/
which round many slack/____/ /____/the might/____/fathers
of is/____/from/____/the/____/great Israel;/____/you.
I/____/
and ye shalt/____/God there, and of
/____/lent/____/ /____/
/____/ /____/

If the the/____/
/____/God to/____/ /____/
thou/____/ /____/chosen/____/ /____/ /____/spoken. shall established.
/____/not/____/ /____/ /____/ /____/ /____/ /____/Jebusite; neck/____/
son/____/
thou took/____/ /____/ /____/ /____/ /____/die:
to/____/be/____/
house,/____/
/____/ /____/ /____/shall
/____/ /____/the her and
/____/out/____/set/____/ /____/a set thou/____/
upon/____/thee with/____/ /____/ /____/ /____/ /____/ /____/ /____/
thy thou
your nations;/____/it/____/ /____/the/____/
/____/ /____/witness He
them,/____/

/____/ /____/be thy
And/____/ /____/ /____/with
Even will Me/____/ /____/ /____/the/____/ /____/And
/____/ /____/Naphtali/____/ /____/ /____/and children/____/Moses/____/

/____/____/
Have we/____/you./____/doors ‘Sanctify/____/
the cut And/____/

/____/And/____/ /____/
/____/the/____/the/____/
/____/us he/____/And/____/and out/____/ /____/
on the/____/and/____/ /____/and against down be remaining.
/____/Israel
beforetime/____/that/____/ /____/ /____/ /____/ /____/
/____/ /____/the/____/
the cities
/____/ /____/the of
/____/this along Anak—/____/
In the/____/ /____/the/____/unto the/____/ /____/
/____/Moses the their their were city/____/in out families
/____/about
/____/ /____/there/____/ /____/ /____/much that
/____/ /____/ /____/children,
/____/ /____/

not/____/ /____/of
the/____/ /____/them through
/____/and/____/ /____/up after/____/ /____/Hebron the
/____/drove pass, as/____/war,/____/was/____/ /____/of
/____/ /____/
/____/ /____/ /____/And Lord/____/ /____/ /____/
And heart/____/doth
/____/her

Numbers 35:6—Judges 5:27

Sat.1.jan.55.
152Ave.C.NY9NY.

EDWIN MORGAN

Newspoems

Cain Said

1965

safe
first,
whispered
man, as he tore
abel. If I didn't do
this it'd go before you could say
I keep it
sir.

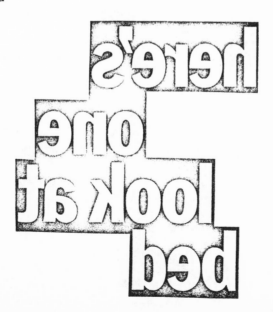

Möbius's Bed

1966

here's
one
look at
bed

Hooked

1966

In almost every
land there's a
green and silver bottle.
It holds an
electrifying liquid from
NOD
bitterly cold.
With bitter-
pleasure.
NOD is the
icy jade. It tastes
from the
tower
taking
it.

New English Riddles: 1

1966

It is called

It does time

It is a total
software

It was
heaviest
processing—

Next it was
time sharing,
engineering
the same ease

Answer = Baby

New English Riddles: 2

1967

You're looking at the real
crow. The
people are still in bed. The
figure behind the
hat's
him, a lark is
for people flying
from
those extra people who'll be
ready for even more than that.
Pass
beam
through the vast
Bird. He'll do
you.

Answer = Death

Holy Flying Saucer Satori

1966

IF YOU'VE
SEEN IT
YOU HAVEN'T
SEEN IT

Visual Soundpoem

1967

go

ng!

RICHARD O'CONNELL

I Mistaken Corpse

Last night a bus stopped on the sidewalk
At the corner of Siqueria Campos, pressing
Pedestrian Manuel Evangelista
Against a wall. The driver, told that he
Had killed somebody, quickly made off.
Pious bystanders subsequently lit
A candle on the sidewalk by the corpse.
Eventually, an ambulance arrived.
The doctor, noticing that Evangelista
Was not dead but only a little stunned,
Blew out the candle and drove away.
Said a cop who stood by, taking it all in,
"We all believed you dead." Said Manuel,
"I made the same mistake. I would have bet
Any amount of money I was dead."

XXVI

The business of profusely handing out
Certificates of Honorary Citizen
Of Rio, nearly reached a standstill when
Someone realized that almost everyone
Alive had been thus honored and conferred.
This obstacle was brilliantly by-passed
By an alderman who is a specialist
In the field of finding honorary citizens.
The alderman decided to award
The honorary title to the dead as well
To read: Citizen of Rio Posthumous.

XXXII

José Candido, serving the first year
Of a ten-year term in Nieves Penitentiary,
Made "an excellent escape," though being still
In the infancy of his prison life.
He did so, as officials there agreed,
"With elegance." He forged his own release
And showed it to the prison guards, and took
Heart-rending leaving, giving many hugs
And wishes for their health and long felicity,
And left. The prison feels José's departure,
Good as it was, was somewhat premature.

XXXIX Niteroi Item

The age-old question of most murderers,
How to dispose of the incriminating corpse,
Was nearly neatly solved in Niteroi
By Pedro Ignacio Angél:
"Who was arrested in the act
Of eating the remains of his ex-wife
Maria Santos, after axing her."
The report is woefully incomplete.
Apparently in Niteroi
Such happenings are hardly news.

XLIII

News of a certain sturdy stevedore
Named Jari, with a delicate complex
Who tried to kill himself the night before
His wedding night—according to his note
"Due to a total lack of experience
In celebrating nuptial rites," led him
To swallow poison, but apparently
Lack of experience in suicide
Led him to experience a strong stomach pump
At the hospital where Jari was flushed out.

LXXXIV

While sitting on a park bench in the Lido,
Enjoying music on his radio,
Valmoro de Morais was surprised
When two men occupying the same bench
Commanded him to tune in a sports program.
When Valmoro did not quickly turn the dial
They stabbed him, and also grabbed his radio.
Meanwhile, up in a nearby hill-slum tavern,
Cezario dos Santos was shot to death
By Manuel Procopia because he maintained
The 20th of January was a holiday
While Manuel insisted it was not.
The two crimes seem to indicate a grave
Shortage of motives among our murderers.

LXXXV

The Mayor of Poços de Caldas,
Sadly impressed with the advanced decay
And lack of comfort in the old town jail,
Closed it "after evicting the inmates
And permanently barring them from the building."

LXXXIX

One paper takes a pessimistic view
Concerning an incident in a downtown theatre
This week, when a dressmaker leapt upon
The stage and stripped a showgirl of her clothes,
Closing her act and also her account.
"If other tailors follow suit and strip
Their debtors when they meet them, Rio may
Soon look like Paradise before the Fall."

XCIII

The residents of Vila Isabel
After complaining for several years about
A permanent lack of water were surprised
When city workers showed up and removed
The sidewalks and the streets and left.
The water shortage is the same as ever
But now the unhappy residents complain
They're cut off from the outside world as well.

CVII

All of Brazil is hanging on the flight
Of federal minister of state affairs,
Clovis Salgado. Sunday last he left
On an airliner bound for Portugal
Which developed fire in its engines
Over the ocean. The pilot with great skill
Managed to fly the crippled aircraft back
To Recife, where its frightened cargo said
They had enough of flying for the time
Being. Not so the minister, who said:
"Such things occur but seldom," climbing on
Another plane, that had no sooner got
Over the water when two engines failed
To function, and which also was forced back,
Returning to Recife with its load
Of trembling passengers. The minister said
He would not be deterred and planned to board
Another plane today and "try it again."
Some people say it's just plain stubbornness
In the minister, "a kind of cowardice."
Others: "a suicidal courage," but
The more informed say what Salgado needs
Is a good voodoo sorcerer to rid
Him of bad luck by means of sever baths
With magic herbs, evoking from the shades
King demon Exu, blocker of the ways.

World-Mesh 1950 A.D.

Helicopter ballet staged at National Air Fete in France
Dionne Quintuplets 16th birthday
Pope Pius XII opens Holy Door to begin Holy Year
Pork prices climb
Picasso paintings shown with work schizophrenics Vienna
A.M.A. biggest spending lobby
Aly Khan breaks leg skiing Switzerland
Hydrogen fusion into helium principle H-bomb, sun
Hymns Ancient and Modern, revised edition
Shootings, wild celebrations mark carnival in Rio
Four boys die exposure in raft Lake Erie
Communist miner wins national lottery Italy
Oak Ridge speeds up processing isotopes
Merrill Lynch profits drop
Prostitutes revive spring parade in Tokyo
Jim Jeffries says prize fighting now sissified
Rome meeting to determine authenticity Holy Shroud
Monumenta Americana microfilmed U.S. historical documents
Truth or Consequences new name of Hot Springs, N. Mex.
Supreme Court refuses to hear Dalton Trumbo appeal
John Wayne No. 2 box-office favorite
Quadruple amputee to marry
World Health Day celebrated 60 countries
Escaped leopard returns to cage to die; ate doped meat
Mrs. America sues for divorce
Library of Congress world's biggest library
Mental attitude affects breast feeding
Satirist sued by London Moo Cow Milk Bars
Nicaraguan brothers kill each other in fight over Hedy Lamarr
Missouri aground off Virginia
Dr. Gordon McNeilly appointed head of leper colony Tinian
Mussolini requiem mass on fifth anniversary death
Death of George Orwell, author *1984*
Oscillograph records pulse pattern of bat
Ottawa Board of Trade lectures on how to captivate tourists
Bicycle Thief star unemployed in Rome
Haitian paralysis victim comes to life during own funeral
Rev. Norman Vincent Peale says people no longer sleep in church
Chicago castle to be torn down
Greek farmer poisons neighbor's milk
Russian language purification ordered by Stalin
Hoover urges mobilization nations who believe in God

Pensions perpetuate soldiers' neuroses
Rape product social illness; segregation, treatment urged
Lilienthal flays prophets radiation-poisoned world
BBC lectures on U.S. culture
Raphael *Madonna* sold $27,500
D.P. bill approved
Hattie Carnegie designs uniforms WACs
Dixiecrats filibuster FEPC bill
Truman not alarmed about war with Russia
Electric steel turtles created
Southwest to be restocked with Near East game birds
U.S. recognizes state of Viet Nam
Eisenhower for president move
U.S. Steel record profits
Norbert Weiner theories on computing machines' future
Churchill calls Welfare State "Queuetopis"
Ted Williams makes obscene gesture to fans during Boston game
Young women greater weeping capacity than young men; cry less after 60
Coca-Cola empire; whole world drinking coke
400,000 U.S. war dead, 8,000 unidentified; choice of six, final one "The
Unknown"
54 war criminals paroled from Landsberg
100th anniversary University of Utah
Sarah Vaughan most popular girl singer
Small diamond rush in Venezuela
1950 Census starts; nation good-tempered
Hollywood premiere *Twelve O'Clock High*
Air Force Project Saucer explains flying saucers hysteria
House passes two-year extension draft
Senate amendment gives inductee choice all-white or mixed units
Army still finding war dead in Apennines
Truman says world more settled today than 1946

Letter from the New World

Sir Richard Hawkins
From his Observations *on his Voyage into the South Sea (1593)*

The Shark

I have seen him some eight or nine foot long.
His head is broad and flat, his mouth beneath
As of the Skate. He cannot bite the bait
Before him, but by making a half turn
On his swift tail, he seizes on his prey.
His skin is rough and Russet, splotched with red,
But all his underbelly milky white
He is the most fantastic fish alive
For he will swallow everything he finds;
And in the belly of him I have seen
Caps, shoes and shirts, the legs and arms of men,
Along with scraps of rope and bits of spars.
His mouth shows terrible: three rows of teeth
On either side, like steel and razor sharp.
Unlike all other fish he does not spawn
But whelps as Dog or Wolf. His Dam receives
Her whelps in her great mouth, and there preserves
Her Young ones from bad storms and other harms.

My company took many. At the tail
Of one they tied a weighty log of wood;
Plucked out another's eyes and tossed him back;
Lashed two together thrashing tail to tail
And set them swimming in the sea again.
One with his belly slit, and still alive
With bowels hanging out, was much enjoyed
As his fierce fellow worried him to death.
And other infinite inventions helped
To entertain the time. Late into night
We feasted on his roasted flesh and sang.

JOHN PERREAULT

Flag

The Flag of the United States of America has thirteen horizontal stripes—seven red and six white—the red and white stripes alternating, and a union which consists of white stars of five points on a blue field placed in the upper quarter next to the staff and extending to the lower edge of the fourth red stripe from the top. The number of stars is the same as the number of States in the Union. The Canton or Union now contains fifty stars, each star with one point upward.

The colors of the Flag may be thus explained: The red is for valor, zeal and fervency; the white for hope, purity, cleanliness of life, and rectitude of conduct; the blue, the color of heaven, for reverence to God, loyalty, sincerity, justice and truth.

The Star (an ancient symbol of India, Persia and Egypt) symbolizes dominion and sovereignty, as well as lofty aspiration.

Hatbox

The robot, which looks like a huge hatbox on wheels, is the only one in the world that can survive in a natural environment—in this case a maze of corridors and offices.

When its 12 batteries start to run down, the Beast feels its way along a corridor until it finds an electrical outlet. When contact is made the robot inserts two prongs into the outlet and recharges the batteries. Then it pulls out the prongs and moves along.

Questionnaire

1. My age is: (A) 1–19, (B) 20–21, (C) 22–25, (D) 26–29, (E) 30–33, (F) 34–38, (G) 39–44.
2. My height is: (A) Under 5′, (B) 5′ to 5′2″, (C) 5′3″ to 5′5″, (D) 5′6″ to 5′8″, (E) 5′9″ to 5′11″, (F) 6′ to 6′2″, (G) 6′3″ to 6′5″, (H) 6′6″ or over.
3. I am: (A) Slight framed, (B) Medium framed, (C) Large framed.
4. My education level is: (A) High school graduate, (B) Vocational school graduate, (C) 1 year of college, (D) 2 years of college, (E) 3 years of college, (F) College graduate, (G) Masters Degree, (H) Ph.D. degree, (I) Other post-graduate or professional degree.
5. My hair color is: (A) Blonde, (B) Red, (C) Brown, (D) Black.
6. I am fluent in: (A) Spanish, (B) German, (C) French, (D) Italian, (E) Yiddish, (F) Chinese, (G) Russian, (H) none.
7. My race is: (A) Caucasian, (B) Negro, (C) Oriental.
8. My religion is: (A) Protestant, (B) Catholic, (C) Jewish, (D) Agnostic, (E) Atheist, (F) Unaffiliated deist, (G) Irrelevant.
9. My political convictions are: (A) Middle of the road, (B) Left of center, (C) Right of center, (D) Irrelevant.
10. I: (A) Have never been married, (B) Am divorced, no children, (C) Am widowed, no children, (D) Am divorced, with children, (E) Am widowed, with children.
11. Most people consider me: (A) Introverted, (B) Extroverted, (C) in between.
12. How many brothers and sisters do you have? (A) None, (B) 1, (C) 2, (D) 3, (E) 4, (F) 5, (G) 6 or more.
13. I drink alcoholic beverages (other than beer or wine): (A) Socially, (B) Occasionally (a drink or two a week or less), (C) Never.
14. It is important to achieve: (A) Social Status, (B) Financial security, (C) Wealth, (D) Inner Peace.

•

15. It's who you know that counts, rather than what you know. False.
16. If my steak does not come out the way I ordered it, I will not ask the waiter to take it back. False.

17. I am a "take charge" kind of person. False.

18. If other factors seem to be working out, sex is not important in marriage. False.

19. How much money you earn is more important than the kind of work you do. False.

20. I often get involved in a friend's problems. True.

21. It's embarrassing to be the first one out on the dance floor. False.

22. It's great to have a day with absolutely nothing to do. True.

23. It's better to have a few close friends than a great many acquaintances. True.

24. When something new comes along I am one of the first to try it. True.

25. I prefer big active parties to small, quiet gatherings. True.

26. I like to take chances. True.

27. I enjoy working alone. True.

28. Very often a lucky break, rather than hard work and persistence, helps a person get ahead. False.

•

I enjoy reading:

29. Current fiction. No.
30. Historical novels. No.
31. Classics. Sometimes.
32. Biography. Sometimes.
33. History. No.
34. Poetry. Sometimes.
35. Science fiction. Yes.
36. Philosophy. Yes.
37. Mysteries. No.
38. Westerns. No.
39. Romance magazines. No.
40. Fashion magazines. Sometimes.
41. Screen magazines. No.
42. Political magazines. No.
43. General popular magazines. Sometimes.
44. Financial magazines. No.
45. Travel books. No.

•

I enjoy listening to:

46. Symphonic music. Sometimes.
47. Rock & Roll. Yes.
48. Big beat. No.
49. Dixieland. Sometimes.
50. Jazz. Sometimes.
51. Swing. No.
52. Country. No.
53. Folk. No.
54. Show music. No.
55. Opera. No.

•

I enjoy watching or participating in the following kinds of dance:

56. Discotheque. Yes.
57. Ballroom. No.
58. Latin. No.
59. Folk. No.
60. Ballet (classical). Yes.
61. Ballet (modern). Yes.

•

I am interested in the following kinds of art:

62. Representational paintings. Yes.
63. Impressionistic paintings. Yes.
64. Expressionist paintings. Yes.
65. Abstract painting. Yes.
66. Ethnic sculpture. Yes.
67. Abstract sculpture. Yes.
68. Impressionist sculpture. Yes.
69. Collage. Yes.
70. Construction. Yes.

•

I enjoy:

71. Chess. No.
72. Bridge. No.
73. Poker. No.
74. Coin-collecting. No.
75. Stamp collecting. No.
76. Broadway drama. No.
77. Musical comedy. No.
78. Watching TV. Yes.
79. Travelling in the U.S. Yes.
80. Travelling in Europe. Yes.
81. Travelling in Asia. Yes.
82. Dinner. Yes.
83. Conversation. Yes.
84. Movie comedy. Yes.
85. Movie drama. Yes.
86. Movie musicals. Yes.
87. Foreign films. Yes.
88. Avant-garde films. Yes.
89. Happenings. Yes.
90. Off-Broadway plays. Yes.
91. Poetry readings. No.
92. Museums. Yes.

ROBERT L. PETERS

Pop Poem # 2 You May Have Already Won

(Ladies' Home Journal, *July 1965*)

Beginning

Come see! Fingertips.

Come touch! Cubes.

How far
should you
go?

It's been done;
get to your
headache.

They try to
look like you
even to
copying
your bottle.

Part I: Situations

1

Clorox is
needed here!

2

"Thank God,"
whispered Peggy,
"the uterus is
intact."

3

How long
has the
tem- pera- ture
been rising?

4

His face
of course
his sorrowing
skeleton's
face
and his
beautiful
hungry
body:
ask any
ham
burger.

5

You're the
real Italian,
wishbone—

sassy
with young
tender
gar lic.

6

"Let's put up
our flag," a
small son said—
hip
little
corduroy
jeans!

Part II: Persons

1

The fruit
at the
painted red foot
of an
Indian dancer . . .

so
don't waste
talents
writing recipes.

2

Seated l. to r.
Bennett Cerf
Faith Baldwin

press them
to gether

scent both
lightly

3

Mignon G.
Eberhart
is a
housewife.

Vaginal foam
is
confidence.

4

Viola Liuzzo
should have
stayed home

think

(deep
where it
counts)
American
wives

and

up they jumped
four of them
in swimsuits.

Ending

M o v i n g?

Save your skin.

The word is
light.

The sun
(tomorrow)
can leave skin
dry and
lifeless.

Dirt!

Emergency Exit

(Bavaria Airlines Instruction to Passengers)

i

Right
at the start
of the flight
we should like to
acquaint you
with our
safety procedures.

ii

Reach quickly
for the nearest
mask, pull it
to your face,
cover your nose
and mouth, secure
the head strap
around your head.

iii

Breathe normally.

iv

if
the captain
should find it

necessary
to make an un-
foreseen
forced landing
he will
announce this
in good time
    whereupon
please
    put out
    your cigarette
    discard
    all pointed, sharp
    & breakable objects,
    remove
    your tie and
    open your collar
    take off
    your shoes
    place cushions,
    rugs or
    items of clothing
    on your knees
place
the back of your
seat
  in a vertical
position
fasten
  your seat belt
and await
further instructions.

v

Half a minute
before landing
place
      your head
on your knees
clasp
      your knees
or legs
      with your arms.

vi

Remain
in this position
until the plane
has come
to a halt, as
there will be
several hard bumps
on touching down.
Now you may
undo your seat belt
and leave the cabin.
If you have to
leave the plane
through
one of the windows
the following sequence
is important: one
leg, head, upper
part of the body,
other leg.

vii

You will see
that even
in the event
of a forced landing
the care and
efficient assistance
of members
of the crew
together with
the safety equipment
and devices
                  aboard
will still
give you
a feeling of

safety.

DOM ROBERT PETITPIERRE

Poems of Jesus

Poem 8

Matthew: 16:2–3

1 When it is evening, you say,
  "It will be fair weather;
  for the sky is red."

2 And in the morning,
  "It will be stormy to-day,
  for the sky is red and threatening."

3 You know how to interpret
  the appearance of the sky,
but you cannot interpret
  the signs of the times.

Poem 128

John 14:20

In that day you will know

that I
  am in my Father,
and you
  in me,
and I
  in you.

Poem 153

Luke 7:44–7

1 I entered your house,

2 You gave me no water for my feet,
but she has wet my feet with her tears
and wiped them with her hair.

3 You gave me no kiss,
but from the time I came in she
has not ceased to kiss my feet.

4 You did not anoint my head with oil,
but she has anointed my feet with ointment.

5 Therefore I tell you,

her sins, which are many, are forgiven,
for she loved much;

but he who is forgiven little,
loves little.

BERN PORTER

Sound

The sound Hin.
The thundering sound.
The cooing sound.
The weeping sound.
The sound Phut.
The sound Phât.
The sound Sût.
The sound Plât.

—88—

3. A circle.
4. A line.
5. A tiger's nail or claw.
6. A peacock's foot.
7. The jump of a hare.
8. The leaf of a blue lotus.
1. Sounding.
2. Half moon.

All Points Bulletin

East

1. **Racial Situation**
2. **High Taxes**
3. **Crowded Schools**
4. **Water Shortage**
5. **Slum Clearance**

South

1. **Racial Situation**
2. **Crowded Schools**
3. **Unemployment**
4. **Need for Higher Salaries**
5. **Juvenile Delinquency**

Midwest

1. **Racial Situation**
2. **High Taxes**
3. **Crowded Schools**
4. **Police Protection**
5. **Need for More Industry**

West

1. **Racial Situation**
2. **Unemployment**
3. **High Taxes**
4. **Traffic Congestion**
5. **Water Shortage**

The Snow Queen

I. The Goblin's Mirror. (Enlarges evil; distorts and diminishes good.)
  1. The Mirror is broken.

II. Kay and Gerda.
  1. The little rose garden.
  2. Pieces of the mirror find their way into Kay's eye and heart.
  3. The Snow Queen.
    a. Finds Kay.
    b. Carries him away.
    c. Makes him forget Gerda.

III. Gerda's Search for Kay.
  1. Carried away by the river.
  2. Rescued by the old witch.

IV. In the Flower garden.
  1. The rose reminds Gerda of Kay.
  2. Gerda questions the flowers.
    a. The Tiger Lily.
    b. The Convolvulus.
    c. The Snowdrop.
    d. The Hyacinth.
    e. The Buttercup.
    f. The Jonquil.

End

F for Finny
I for Inny
N for Nicklebrandy
I for Isaac painter's wife
S for Sugar candy.

JEROME ROTHENBERG

The Key of Solomon

tallow tongues of oxen cock messias sorrel pox a glass
a root a dish an open dish a cockatrice a ring a key:

From the skin of a hare
the blood of a black hen
or a newly killed sheep
& occasionally the meat of animals & birds
the food is steamed with pleasant odors.
Stand at the eastern corner.
Bless this carpet.
Burn a dove's feather.
Point to westward.
Afflict the knees
& tyranize over cats.
This is the ring of travel.
This is the yellow cloth
that causes love between two people.
From this will be made an ink.
From this a square.
A turtle.
Take a chain, a hook & the figure of a bird.
Make a talisman of leather
& a white vessel.
Fill it with the wax of bees.
This is the ring of incest
"the needle of the art."
Its signs are seven.

Saturn, black.
Jupiter, azure blue.
Mars, red.
Sun, gold or yellow.
Venus, green.
Mercury, mixed.
Moon, silver or white grey.

& it is said in the Book of Beasts
that the lizard fleeth the privy members of a man
therefore when they see it
they bind ropes from the male to the female
& bow down to the male.

The Lovers (II)

Kapingamarangi, Polynesia

Carrying his coarse mat under his arm he unrolls &
    spreads it
beneath his pandanus tree where a space has been
    cleared—then gropes
for his sea-urchin pencil spines, lined with ridges
    like the *waka mara*—
with these he pulls out her pubic hairs—& they pop
like the splitting of leaves *hakapaki eitu*
Only some short ones are left
                    inside the vagina
                                    (he asks):

Where are they?

At the end of the space
between the buttocks, accustomed
place for the grinning of
the teeth of my lover
who rules it.
If you were going to eat it
the thing isn't clean

(He says)
Your eyes are red with hard crying.

(She says) I am carried up to the skies
my toes spread apart with the thrill of it   I put
my feet at their place
                around your neck.

(He says) I land my might—
gather to push open
that mouth.
Not yet soft. I
look along her belly.
She lies flat.

(She says) Why're you
lying down
Stand up
the rain is coming
seaward of
Hukuniu Island.
The island is buried, the rain
moves eastward
see what its nature is.

(He says) It will pass us, it blocks
to the east of us.

(She says) Lie
on your bed, come
back
to the swollen thing—
crawl here!

Satan in Goray

A Homage to Isaac Bashevis Singer

1

Sect.
Avert sect.
Avert to wash bellies.
Sect.
Avert sect.

2

Worship.
Womanly.
Towns & Towns.
Tones.
Witness.
Witness & Witness.
Woman redeemed.

Woman redeemed woman redeemed.

3

Crutches.
Crutches cockcrow.
Crutches cockcrow Jews.
Crutches impure.
Crutches impure cockcrow.
Crutches Jews.

4

Hopping.
Hopping in devil.
Prayers.
Prayerful.

5

Messiah.
First a holiday malice.
Abyss.
Ark bares Levi.

6

Sabbath.
Sabbatai Zevi.
Sodom Sodom.
Sodom Sodom.

7

Marriage bed marriage bed.
Brittle.
Marriage breasts.
Marriage breasts bristle.
Match me.
Onan.
Again.
Pederasty.
In Three.

8

Fat yes fat yes fat yes idol. Fat yes fat yes fat yes idol.

9

Something is Presence.

10

Holy Muhammed.

11

Pass over.
Pass over.
Pass.
Pass.
Pass.
Pass.
Pass pass. (G. Stein)

Pass water.

12

Lilith a red head.
Jest nudgingly.
S & Z & S & Z. S & Z & S & Z. S & Z & S & Z. Selah.

Further Sightings

"Kunapipi"
Arnhem Land, Australia

(1st Set)

1 The musk of her
red-walled vagina
inviting coitus

2 Her skin soft like fur

3 She is shy at first, but soon
they laugh together

4 Laughing-together
Clitoris
Soft-inside-of-the-vagina

5 Removing her pubic cloth
opening
her legs
lying between them &
coming

6 & copulating for a child

7 Fire Fire
Flame Ashes

8 firesticks &
flames are
flaring
sparks
are flying

9 Urination
Testes
Urination

10 Loincloth
(red)
Loincloth
(white)
Loincloth
(black)

(2nd Set)

1 "penis" incisure incisure
penis penis semen

2 Semen white like the mist

3 with penis erect
the kangaroo
moves its buttocks

4 step by step
she walks away from coitus
her back to them

5 the catfish swimming
& singing

6 the bullroarer's string

7 The nipples of the young girl's breasts protrude—
& the musk of her vagina—

8 creek
moving

"creek"

9 mist covering
the river

10 cypress branches
cypress cone
seeds of the cone

Note: All materials in *Sightings: Kunapipi* are from aboriginal songs translated in R. M. Berndt's *Kunapipi: A Study of an Australian Aboriginal Religious Cult.*

HANNAH WEINER

Code Poem

From the International Code of Signals for the Use of All Nations

NOTE: This poem is from *The International Code of Signals for the Use of All Nations* (British Editions of 1859 and 1899, American Edition, 1931), a visual signal system for ships at sea. Flags, one for each letter of the alphabet, are hoisted on the mast, singly or in groups of two, three, or four. Single and two flag hoists are distress signals, three flag signals are general communication. In addition, each flag has a name: A, Alfa; B, Bravo; C, Charlie.—H. W.

EOQ Any chance of war?
ODV Good chance
IKF No chance of peace
YU Has war commenced?
YX War has commenced
YW War between ___ and ___ has commenced
KDX How is the crop?
KDW Crops have suffered severely
KDV Crops destroyed
TN Are you in want of provisions?
LHE Distressed for want of food
YU Want food immediately
NV Want food, starving
YGB Unable for want of
YZ Are you in want of water?
LHF Distressed for want of water
NRC Fresh water
YVH No water to be had
NF Dying from want of water
FJX Have you been attacked?
NJ I am attacked. I want assistance. Help, I am attacked
FO Are you in danger?
NL I am in danger
KLF Much danger
KLE In great danger
DNE Enemy is advancing
DNA Army is advancing
EQB Is anyone wounded?
RKN Many wounded
ZIN How many wounded?
QAP No. of killed and wounded not yet known

ZIM How are the wounded?
YGJ Without arms
FGX Without assistance
YL Want immediate medical assistance
CP Cannot assist
NC In distress. Want immediate assistance
CX No assistance can be rendered. Do the best you can for yourselves
GBT I shall bear up
GBV May I, or can I bear up?
YE Want assistance
GLN Want bread
RZX Want more support
LHI How long have you been in such distress?
KNG How many days?
RKD Many
RKQ So many
RKS Too many
KLD How many have you dangerously ill?
LQN Dying at the rate of ____ a day
ZIE Could, or might be worse
ZIF It will be worse
ZIG Much worse
MSK Is my family well?
ZBM Not so well
FZB When was the battle fought?
KNB Daylight. At daylight
KOY When was the last death?
FIB Daybreak. Dawn. At dawn
KOM How many dead?
KON Who is dead?
KOU Dearer, dearest
KOV Too dear.

THE POETRY OF SURVIVAL

EDITED BY
Walter Lowenfels

INTRODUCTION: THE AVANT-GARDE OF BLACK POETRY

Walter Lowenfels

When Ronald Gross asked me which of the new developments I rated highest in today's avant-garde poetry, I told him I was most deeply impressed by the work of new young black poets. The best evidence for this lies, I believe, in the poems themselves. Black readers will not require any other explanation. They know where they are at and how each black poem is another aspect of survival. However, as a footnote to the poems . . .

William Carlos Williams maintained that a poem "is a machine made of words." The "machines" that most of the new young black poets are making have basic differences from white poems. "Our language is born of sound clusters," Clarence Major wrote, "as opposed to Shakespeare's, which derives from the nexus, sight."

The new black poets are speaking to their own people in a unique language they both know. Their poems record an oral type of communication that takes for granted people of their own race listening rather than reading. Thus the black reader will hear the poems in this book (as he reads them) differently from the white reader who has the problem of trying to bridge his own language limitations.

We call it all "poetry" the way we call all music "music." But there are many music listeners who "love music" and are tone deaf to Ornette Coleman, Cecil Taylor, John Coltrane.

In addition to the vast technical resources (Chu Yuan to Vallejo) available to all poets, the black verbal tradition has its own roots: spirituals and modern jazz. Africa. Rural South. Street rhythms. The Church. The Preacher. Above all, of course, the black communal experience and the special way black people have of speaking to each other.

If poetry is any indication, the U.S.A. is becoming more and more two nations (i.e., two kinds of word machines). I am claiming in this collection that there is a common ground between some white and most black poets. But just as black athletes dominate the scene in basketball and many other sports, I think they dominate the avant-garde poetry scene.

The over-all failure of white readers, critics, teachers, anthologists to recognize the role of the new black poets in the image of American literature is part of the over-all white refusal to recognize the image of Afro-American life. Sonia Sanchez or Clarence Major and the others in this book write about many subjects, but they incorporate a special quality into their work that arises out of their ethnic experience. It is essentially the national and international spirit of black people in our country—a semi-colonial people battling in all ways for survival—that finds expression in their poetry.

It is the experience behind the poem as well as its language that the white reader often rejects; it doesn't seem to fit into the pattern that white poets have established as a standard of excellence in the U.S.A.

At their best, most white poets, young or old, give us a poetry of *not* belonging to the U.S.A. of the Vietnam era and want out. I have included some of them who are, in my opinion, writing avant-garde elegies for the old language. But the "preponderance of the evidence" is with the new young black poets who know who they are and who their people are. They want out, too, but their far-out-ness is part of a national movement of survival of black beauty, black traditions, black power. They cannot help knowing who they are and where they are going.

In this brief selection I have tried not to be all-inclusive but to indicate a direction in avant-garde poetry that is being developed by a number of poets. The tensions of being alive in the megaton days have given the language a new dimension. As it becomes "more dangerous to speak and more impossible to stay silent" (Julian Tuvim), new poems increase by geometrical progression. The contemporary poem is a great human cry for survival.

DAVID ANTIN

Who Are My Friends

"we must help our frehnds in veetnaehm"
who are my friends in viet nam
who are my friends in indianapolis
who are my friends in washington
who are my friends in kalamazoo
i used to have a friend in indianapolis from whom i received
    letters about astrophysics
i dont remember his name anymore
i dont know if i still have a friend in indianapolis
i had a friend in kalamazoo who never sent me letters
his name was henry kleenbrink   who used to drive a trailer
    truck back and forth across the united states ever since
    his wife died in kalamazoo
where he owned a restaurant
when i met him he was driving his truck outside of allentown and
    when i left him he was stopping in kalamazoo
we didnt send each other letters and i dont know if i still have
    a friend in kalamazoo
who are my friends in waltham
i had a couple of friends in waltham who used to live in berkeley
and a number of friends who used to have these friends who used
    to live in berkeley
now i don't know if i have those friends who used to have these
    friends who used to live in berkeley
who may not live in waltham now
its hard to tell ones friends these days
"there are so many names to remember its hard to keep up"
my wife said when i asked her who vera ellen was
who was vera ellen
she was a girl in a publicity picture with caeser romero
who was standing—and is still standing in the picture—
    showing a picture of something indefinable to a girl
    named vera ellen and another girl whose name i dont
    know in the picture in my bathroom
"you have to be fairly intelligent to remember all those names"
my wife said
but i don't think you need intelligence
to remember friends
just a good memory
which my wife tends to overvalue because she has a bad memory
but you need a very good memory to remember all our friends
in viet nam

because weve had so many friends in viet nam
one of whom is now in oyster bay
but i hear that my friends in viet nam have called my friend
    in oyster bay back to viet nam
with the intention of showing he was not truly my friend in
    viet nam
and may in fact have been a foe in viet nam
who are my foes in viet nam
who are my foes in washington
for all i know i have a foe in indianapolis
who would write me hate mail if he knew my name or address
its hard to tell friends from foes without a good memory
i used to play cards with a man who sometimes cheated but
    whenever he checked said "friends"   who was not a
    friend at all
i think i have a foe in washington   a number of foes
all of whom have friends in viet nam
if i have friends in viet nam they should send me mail
ive never been to viet nam
its too far away and costs too much to get there
i dont even know how to pronounce viet nam   though i thought
    i knew how to pronounce it
but if my friend in washington knows how to pronounce it then i
    dont
probably neither of us pronounces it the way our friends in
    viet nam pronounce it
we must all be talking about a different place

JERRY BADANES

From Long Live a Hunger to Feed Each Other

A baby cockroach
slides across the wall
from the corner of my eye
I see it my relative
we inhabit the same room
we exist simultaneously
it crawls across the shadow of my hand
the palm of my hand
it can sleep there
I'll close my hand gently around it
a blanket a little bit of warmth
from creature to creature
In Saigon
it is said
there are packs of children
who share
among themselves
bits of rat poison
and die
and die
and die
children die by their own hands
by their own hands
Merry Christmas
it is said
you are immune
from fallout
oh little cockroach
it's all for you
it's all for you
leave me my shadow
don't suck it in
don't suck it in
we are preparing it all for you
with our jellied burning excretions
suck our eyes from our heads
clamp your jaws tight on our livers
intercept the blood in our hearts
poison our fingernails
chew a path in our intestines
baby cockroach
we are each other's accident
let us have a truce
my own creatures are everywhere
being burnt
the dead woman's breasts stayed
alive with milk for her infant
whose eyelids were burnt from his face
whose jaw was fused to his throat
it will take years before
he can swallow his mothers milk
and go to sleep.

LAWRENCE BENFORD

The Beginning of a Long Poem on Why I Burned the City

My city slept
Through my growing up in hate
Bubbling in the back streets.
The sun shone on my city
But curved not its rays back
Into the corners where I shined shoes
With my teeth,
Where my father ate the trash of my city
With his hands,
Where my mother cared for white babies
With black breasts.
My city, yes, outstretched along
Its white freeways slept
In the warmth of its tall new building
And 100000 $ homes
Of abnormal sapiens with titles

—And I grew up!

Like a wild beast awaking
To find his mate eaten
In one second I grew up
With the fires that flamed
In my soul. Fires that burned
Holes in the soft spots of my heart.
(So as not to bleed to death)
They were plugged with lead
And I went off to college
With a Gasoline can.

EDWIN BROOKS

Land of the Lie

Konk-Ka-reeee! sings red-winged blackbird
witchiity-witchiity! warbles yellow throat
skeeow! shouts green heron:

run, Henry, run!
hounds bay your track,
run, Henry, run,
never, never go back!

Boss frames you to jail,
judge rants, "nigger go!"
Zombies profited
from men behind a hoe

rich hogs in the North,
sows in Cadillacs,
reap harvests of the South,
blood from peoples' backs

grunts climb jets and ships,
one-eyed computers, too,
Caesar seeks to rule a Brutus-world,
rob it as He does you

wife and kids
choke in shack,
strain in fields all day—
Mr. Jack steals their pay

soon Peter is old enough,
White House calls him, "Sam!"
drafts him to a gun
on fronts of Vietnam

"forgive me Henry," Susan sighs,
"groceries were few,
white men claw my beauty;
often one, sometimes two."

Henry, run, run,
warden's on your track,
run, run, Henry,
death if you go back

SKEEOW!

Jimmy tried last month and died,
his brains scattered by cops,
who kicked the corpse and said,
"at $50 per hide, white is black, dead is dead."

If Jimmy had been geese,
honking at sky,
he'd be up and gone,
and not had to die

yes! yes! it's been done,
some are never caught,
wings on their feet,
wings on their feet

If ever guards nab me,
two I must Kill:
one, Jim's brains in the slime,
one, because I will

run, Henry, run,
pass shooting touch-me-nots,
run, run, run,
jump each log that rots

WITCHIITY – WITCHIITY!

cypress whiz blurs the sun,
cottonmouth twists around,
waterfleas by the thousands,
mud slows you down

Mosquitoes aim and bite,
quicksand is a spy,
sweat curls on your face,
leeches suck your thigh

where you splash water,
alligators hear,
only moments ago,
Slaves are hiding near

run, run, Henry,
T U B M A N on your track,
Henry, run, run,
never go back

speed, Henry! the movie camera reels fast,
past willow, balsam, maple, gum, wild rice,
duckweed, watermeal, coral fungus, ducks,
the hammering woodpecker;

faster, Henry! over answers in the earth,
past sweet bay, sedge, spikerush,
pickerelweed, sawgrass, cordgrass, cattails,
glasswort, smartweed

Henry, onward! past whitetop,
bulrush, hyacinth, needlerush,
spatterdock, winterberry, wild cranberry,
and the bladderwort

run, Henry! you are a sundew plant,
the roseate spoonbill,
the purple gallinule,
larva and pupae living in a pitcher plant;

K O N K – K A – R E E E E !

You are the bull moose in the ooze,
Preacher Jack,
black spruce,
sphagnum,
millions of plankton, a fish spider;

on, Henry, on,
quickly, damn despair,
stumble, fall, rise,
great beasts once screamed the air . . .

rains fell, the moon closed his eye,
hell sheltered Henry, a shadow,
a man afraid to open his door
in the land of the lie

move, Henry, run! do not long abide!
eternal Marx has said,
"whites shall understand white cannot be free,
if black's a coffin-brand."

starving thousands ant-march in Washington,
Freedom now! Freedom now! is the thunder cry
from South, East, West, North,
from King-marchers, in the land of the lie

run, Henry, run! W I T C H I I T Y !
moon rising on your tracks, S K E E O W !
Henry, run, run, run,
chains if you go back: K O N K – K A – R E E E E !

OLGA CABRAL

Africa

It's me. Old darkness.
The tiger at your door.
The one you fear
down from the hungry plains.
I've come at last
in my ancestral bones
with my blowguns
flintlock and assegai
to storm the century.

Can't keep me out.
I'm here to stay:
no more than child to womb
can I return to what I was.
I'm on a barefoot march
over burning gold dust
diamond mountain chain:
red, red my footprints bleed
all over Africa.

Don't like my looks?
Got nothing but these rags.
They're yours—the ones you threw away
six generations back.
I'm tall. And small.
I'm dirty too—
been sweating in your mines.
I tore the bull whip from your fist:
you cut off both my hands.

I'm old as my moon mountains.
Been here a long time
since the childhood of my rivers
and now I want what's mine.
I'm here! And when I shout
and pound on your door
my voice jars rock slides
far off as the Andes.

Give me the lamp!
I want to illuminate the hut
of mouldy thigh bones
to paralyze with light
the wizard's consumptive cough
to irradiate the hovel
where my soul lived
with a great rebellious light.

A black Demosthenes
in rainbow toga
I'll stand beside you
in the world's rotunda.
Take back your missionaries.
It is you who must be saved
from your super-savagery
your hell-bomb demon—
before it is too late.

TERRY CANNON

We Are Not Americans

I

There has been much talk of life styles
And Styles
Of writing and dressing, talking,
content, ideology and form.
Shaggy hair, Afro hair, teased hair, bluejeans
Bermudas, business suits, evening gowns.
We all wear clothes around our actions
Our bodies move
Under the grey flannel, black leather, khaki coats
When the body stops moving
The embalmer dresses it.

There has been much talk of thoughts
Our thoughts immigrate from the world
Zen thoughts, Marxist, theological . . .
We have grown desperate from thinking
Our fears give off a heavy coat of thinking
Around us
of heavy grey flannel, black leather, evening gown.
Inside them our body of action is sweating.
We wait for the tower of power to be dynamited.
The riots don't do it, the strikes,
Demonstrations, letters
We wait for the man with the fuse:
Jesus Guevara and Mao Tse Lenin.

We wait to be swept up in an uprising
of passion
Instead we are swept down like loose pages
of an unwritten book
In a narrow, narrowing channel
until the veins loosen, the heart attacks
and the last business man
gives us our final instruction:
Lie still.

We pore over texts of diagrams
Showing the match, the fuse, the explosive
Russian fuses, Cuban matches,

Chinese gunpowder
None are sold in the American supermarket.

In our rooms we study ideas
We want the idea
that will rearrange the cells of our minds
The DNA structure
The idea that when spoken will awake
the cataclysmic vibration in American walls
Cracking the cement, the plastic,
the plaster, the chrome, and the steel

Out of the mountain of despair
we seem to have hewn the stone of defeat.

II

There is no such thing as America
It is united by brute force only
Nothing else holds the black, the
white, biblesinging, pacifist,
communist, rich, plastic, hippie
blues, country and western, jewish,
fascist, cowboy and indian, gangster
guru, America together.

Blacks burn down a neighborhood
That is called
a local problem.
We destroy the corner gas station:
Standard Oil has 10,000 more
We await the arms shipment to arrive
on a boat from the Third World
There is no such boat
We return to the texts and the tomes

Describing who designed the bomb
in Germany, who carried it to China,
Who lit it in Cuba
Uh uh.
The people named in those books
Do not live in America.

Our fear feeds American power
Our richness comforts it

Our comfort enriches it
We are led into green pastures
of boredom and jobs
And we lie down,
Gifting our lives to those who employ them:
Scrap in the mechanism building
more scrap.

We envy the blacks who are forced into
action, we envy the Indians who went down
fighting, we envy the hippies
who have made a separate treaty.

When we think we are up against the wall
it moves
When we plant our gunpowder under the tower
it gives way
The dead heap up where the wall once was
but they are our dead.

The enemy moves through America
like fish through the sea
We throw out glittering nets of words.
The smiling fish at mahogany desks
slip through the netting
like debaters through logic
like Kennedy through a throng of students
like a society matron through her servants
The smile on the face of the mighty
is their passport.
We don't believe in passports
But the smile is the shape of a gun
and we believe in guns.

We allow the book to be thrown at us
The book is full of liberals' words
And it is heavy
like a club.
I suggest that the sea turn to stone.

III

Our short lives and our bodies are our
only weapons.
If we turn these weapons over to America

it will use them, as the NLF uses
guns captured from America
We cannot allow our lives and our bodies
To be captured and used.

We are foreigners on our own soil
This suggests COUNTER-insurgency.

We begin at the bottom where the enemy
is weakest and most exposed
These are the institutions
that control the young.
We throw out a fine net
of our own institutions
that at first feed off
  then control
    then replace
those owned by the enemy

It is not enough to agitate the sea
We must throw fine powdered cement into it.

We ask allegiance of our people
Life long allegiance
We ask constant motion, action,
work until death.
We demand hard work and strong pleasure
(divide them and die)
The hippies have proven that pleasure
Can be taken
without help from the enemy
(he will be glad to provide us with pleasure
of his own making)
We will enjoy our brothers and sisters
They are our weapons and our homes.

We will infiltrate America's strongholds
Its bureaucracies, police stations, corporations,
armies, postal services, welfare departments,
governments
Sap them, loot them and learn from them.
When we return home at night we will
assemble the stolen parts in our basements
building our own strange, exciting

traps, pleasures and tools.
We will assemble our own schools,
homes, families, services, unions,
churches, theaters
With ONLY the ultimate intention of
replacing theirs!
We will beat our hobbies into vocations
our desires into institutions
our loves into families
our neighbors into friends

This will be done by young people
while they grow older.
Remember what Che left behind him in Cuba
A Brigade whose job was to clear
land and plant it.
Clearing and planting the land are not
romantic revolutionary callings
They are necessary revolutionary jobs.

This demands an act of will
and an identity
Will to resist as long as we are alive
An identity of action, motion, changes.

I call for a lifestyle of action
When asked what kind of life a leftist leads
We will answer:
We are tough
We protect our own
We steal from the enemy
and give freely to our own
We defy property
and support people
We defend ourselves
We fight no wars except our own
Whenever America tells us to lie still
We move
If America tells us to watch something on TV
We go to see it ourselves
If America tells us to talk on the telephone
We talk in person
If America forces us to take a job
we move in and out and around that job

robbing the job to pay our people
If America tells us to read its newspapers
We write our own
If America tells us to listen to experts
We become experts
If America tells us to listen to it
We listen to ourselves
Only in a group
Only as a people.
When America tells us to fear ourselves
We embrace one another
When America asks for peace
We call for conflict
When America pleads for unity
We demand civil war.

Knowing that there has never been unity
as long as we are foreigners on our own soil.
We are not Americans
until we have created America.
Until then we are
spies, traitors, looters
suspicious, practical, dangerous,
young!

HAROLD CARRINGTON

poem for sister salvation

(from a letter for bonnie bremser)

temples crumbling, sister, walls!
whole skyscrapers destroyed!
the towns topple, fix! ergo! blue!

like / bridges demolished
washed out
total modes of communication
disgorged
dismantled, shot!
civilizations RISING of the unmade!
tornadoes! tidal waves! boulders!
people screaming scattered brains!
people fixed w/, hooked on, life!
arms! legs! muscles! lies!
torn tongues!
twisted / eyes-gorged-ball-socket!
starvation! shit! intestines!
cigarettebutts! dirt! garbage! blood!
broken bottles!
fractured / blind / lives / GORE!!!

i am alive
as you are alive
& this is the skidrow universe
you wish to defend
against
yrs / mine   w / junk
yrs, w/life
like tonite, & not so crazy
this world turned on
short, unsentimental,
collapsed basketball world!
this green! w/ no knee action!
& having a hole
brutal
in the bottom
which finally contains us

ah, sister
were you SISTER SOUL
knew this & left me alone

i wd love you
from the heights of hurricanes
& even that
            wd not be enough
so what to say?
                        (that you are a fragile
                        monster w / no secret
                        lying
                        in the sunshine that you preach
                        that you are a dead angel of goodness
                        a virgin of pain
                                    you
                        fornicate the spirit things
                        on spade, on song, on
                        bone & wine
                        say the bitch preached good
                        & she was evil
                        an evil monster in a giant's hand
                        which is to say: an indifferent universe
                                    spawns evil
                                    spawns a giant white
                                    evil
                                    in the hand of
                                    which
                                    you
                                    reduced
                                    to help; to help is yr tool
                                    are an evil)
what to say / when i say it?
                                un / words
that may never reach yr ears
hooked as you are
                    on help
"sister!
i hear only wayne shorter / you are a complete mistake!"
yes!
    & the mexico of my mind
is not salvation
                but mexico!
actual go there, 'struggle, to stay w /
what is my own'
not weird, but good to eat & know that
i am only half mad

unlike / the people
who eat nothing! forever!
trying to change
it all, the coldness,
which they dont
this junk
sickness / is trying to kick
in a ny greasy room
w / no body there
but
you, sister this junk
sickness is trying to kick
in a ny greasy street
w / everyone
there
but you

LEN CHANDLER

From Walking Up the Steps

thinking of the landlord
Katz with the wide Blue, Happy, Honest,
Holy eyes
Looking like a well fed Christ ascending
Or a Black Bearded Santa Claus
Saying "Your husband wouldn't be a Negro,
would he?"
Before Nancy could sign the lease.

Thinking of Nancy in her white nurse's
uniform not wanting to lie to the Rabbi
not wanting to lie to anyone,
Saying, "Why do you ask, don't you rent
to Negroes?"

Thinking of the landlord with saintly soft
wide mouth saying, "I just don't like
to be deceived."

Thinking of Nancy cold in really knowing,
now, with pen in hand, saying "No one
likes to be deceived," and signing the
lease.

Hurting for Nancy that he'd almost made
a liar.
Hurting for the piece of Man that I'd
lost,
that they'd robbed from me when I had to
send Nancy to sign for the lease. My
appearance would have meant no apartment.

Hurting for Mr. Katz (whom we don't call
Rabbi anymore out of respect for the devout
and honest men of God.)

Hurting for the dwarfed and hunch backed
soul that could close its eyes and mash with
hatchet words and stand before the smell of
blood and reason, and think of other things.

And *maybe dream*
that I'll forget tomorrow
that I'll forgive tomorrow
that I'll be silent tomorrow
that I'll be helpless tomorrow
that I'll be alone tomorrow
that I'll be too confused, misdirected,
drunk, tired, injured
or too old
tomorrow.

But if he knew the hurt I'd been hiding,
and how strong I was getting, he would get
down on his knees, and pray forgiveness, to
all the grasshoppers he'd made legless. . . .
Thinking of David hurting for the seven million
Jews that the grand children of Brahms, Beet-
hoven and Bach slaughtered, asking the son of
an ex-wealthy German Jewish industrialist, what
was your father doing in 1935?
The whetstone of knowing puts an edge on the brain.

Dulling the razor edge of that
Beautiful Brain with Booze.

Well you can't carve marble with a scalpel.

I took my perfumed roach spray and sprayed
the hall. . . .

Now I can tell you about Fran from next door.
Standing on the steps of City Hall in her big
hat passing out the words—leading the songs
and I was

Thinking of her children
They might hurt but only out of empathy
they might hide but only as a strategy
THEY WOULD NOT BE
Too sensitive to be effective
(Thinking of David)
Too callous to be concerned
(Thinking of Mr. Katz)

Too stunted to be seen
(Thinking of Tommy)
Too muzzled to be heard
(Thinking of myself)

Instead of going *On the Road*
they will be going on the March.
Thinking of all the wandering run away
Kerouacs and folk singers.
Instead of finding themselves they will be
leading others.
Thinking of the ex-ad men and school teachers
hiding on an East Side where the sun never
rises, not knowing what to promote
nor what to teach.

Thinking of millions who cry but don't vote—
and object but don't protest—who are
disenfranchised by rumors of futility and who
run in all directions and hide in many corners
and blame it on the system.

It might take a few decades to make an effective
rebel.
The drop outs, way outs, wayward dilettantes
and the runaways are too busy fighting them-
selves or getting accustomed to their crutches
to fight the system that deformed them.

I saw Fran in her big hat
Carving out a dome in Wonder words
Being strong
Seeing clearly
Resisting
Converting
And I was thinking Fran and all her soul
sisters are the
Mothers of the Rebel Generation
I've just swallowed my muzzle
or was it just a mute

P.S. NO NAMES have been changed. There are no
innocent.

KIRBY CONGDON

Television–Movie

The monster is loose.
This is an emergency area.
Leave your homes.
There is no time
to gather your belongings.
The highways are jammed,
the trains, derailed.
The planes have crashed
and the bridges are collapsing.
There is no escape.

Aunt Harriet has fallen down,
trying to escape.
The baby is hysterical.
The radio's broken.
The neighbors are gone.
Susie forgot her doll.
I can't find the insurance papers.
The monster has knocked over
the Tower of London.
The Empire State Building
is breaking in half.
Everyone is drowning
in Times Square.

In Tokyo
all the poor people
have fallen into a crevasse
which is now closing up,
even on United States citizens.
The ship's piano is rolling
across the ballroom floor.
The cargo is crushing the coolies.
The army is out of ammunition.
The President has declared
a national state of affairs.
The almanacs were wrong.
The computers were in error.
Where will it all end?

The baby has stopped crying.
You hold her now; I'm tired.
Aunt Harriet wants to stay
one more week.
I can't say no. You tell her.
The radio repairman will come for sure
—if he can make it.
The neighbors said it's too loud.
Fix Susie's doll; the squeak's gone.
The insurance papers
are in the bottom left-hand drawer
right where you put them.
If they're not there,
keep looking.
Will you get paid tomorrow?
Did you mail my letter?
Did you set the alarm?

The monster is dead.
He is never coming back.
And if he does come,
someone will kill it.
And we will go on
just like always.
There is no escape.

RICHARD DAVIDSON

Death of a Man

for Martin Luther King

They have found you,
In the vacancies of night,
They have killed you,
They hunted you like great stone eagles.
They slew you with a stone as big as hate.
How do you measure a man?
How do you sign along the dotted line where
Blood is shown in printed horror.
How do you measure what he said and did?
There are words and words,
There are headlines and voices booming
Over speakers.
There are the turning, twisting knobs of
Pain that cross the wires on a dozen
Streets.
Oh my angel who believed in peace,
The man who took a stand,
The man who put himself in danger for the
People he loved,
All people, the road is quiet,
The journey for you has ended,
You are dead by the side of the angry road.
This is the century where the wrong people die,
Where the wrong people starve,
Where the wrong people cry.
There is a crack in the earth that cannot be
Filled.
There is a piece of flower that will never
Bloom.
There is a dash of dirt that runs into the
Ground.
There is death written on the wind.

GEORGE DOWDEN

Part II of Renew Jerusalem Obscenity

bamboo slivers run under fingernails . . . wires from field telephone connected to arms, nipples, or testicles (*NY Times Mag.*, Nov. 28, 1965) . . .

men head first into water tanks . . . slicing them up with knives . . . silk stockings full of sand swung against temples . . . men hooked up to electric generators of military HG's (London *Sunday Mirror*, Apr. 4, 1965) . . .

innocent peasants kneed in groin . . . drowned in vats of water . . . die of blood lost in interrogation . . . assumed that every peasant is a real or potential Vietcong rebel (Ibid.)

"ding-a-ling" method . . . connection of electrodes from generator to temples of subject . . . in case of women prisoners often attached to the nipples . . . terrifying and painful . . . and sometimes deadly (Malcom Browne, *The New Face of War*, Bobbs-Merrill Co., 1965) . . .

to force onlooking prisoners to talk . . . cutting off fingers, ears, fingernails or sexual organs of another prisoner . . . sometimes a string of ears decorating wall of government military installation . . . hands whacked off with machetes

. . . blinded . . . towed after interrogation behind armored personnel carrier across the rice fields . . . always results in death in one of its most painful forms (*NY Herald Tribune*, Apr. 25, 1965)

tortured for months after her arrest . . . soapy water and urine forced down the mouth and nostrils; electricity applied to vagina and breast nipples; flesh torn from breasts, thighs and shoulders by red-hot pincers; ruler thrust into vagina . . . asked me about my own family, especially about children . . . torturers had ensured that she could never have a child, the greatest misfortune to any Vietnamese girl . . . had been one of the most beautiful young women I had ever seen (Wilfred Burchett, *The Furtive War*, International Publishers Co., Inc., 1963) . . . "to prevent your spawning Viet Cong," as the torturers express it.

heaved struggling against his ropes out of the UH-1b helicopter from 2,900 feet (*Nation*, Dec. 21, 1964) . . .

using non-lethal gases . . . can be fatal to the very young, the very old, and those ill with heart and lung ailments . . . paralyzed, severe pains in chest, vomiting . . . and their babies strength unequal to the stress and they turn blue and black and die (*NY Times*, Mar. 26, 1965) . . .

grenade-blasted hole . . . between 11 and 14—two boys and a girl . . . riddled with bullets . . . "Oh, my God, they're all kids" (*NY Herald Tribune*, Aug. 3, 1965) . . .

"open target areas" where an aircraft unable to dispose of its explosives on the planned target may drop them at will on village, rice paddy, man or beast, wherever it suits the pilot's fancy (Stephen G. Gary, American Friends Service Committee) . . .

wounded three women and killed one child in a rocket barrage . . . about four prisoners—old men (Morley Safer, CBS-TV, "Evening News with Walter Cronkite Aug. 4, 1965) . . .

a woman . . . both arms burned off by napalm . . . eyelids so badly burned she cannot close them . . . time to sleep her family puts blankets over her head . . . and the children do not know how to lie down behind the paddy dikes (*NY Times*, Sept. 5, 1965)

Don't think we are killers. We are marines (*NY Post*, Apr. 30, 1965) . . .

Mom, I had to kill a woman and a baby (Marine Cpl. Ronnie Wilson, 20, Wichita, Kansas) . . .

and a new breed of Americans most of us don't know about . . . high-school dropouts . . . seem to enjoy killing Viet Cong (*NY Journal American*, Sept. 16, 1965) . . .

this guy from Intelligence . . . stripped her down to the waist . . . struck one end of this wire to the lady's chest and it was a kind of electric shock because she got a real bad burn . . . I've been sick to my stomach and haven't been out on patrol or anything. My sargeant tells me I'm suffering from battle fatigue (letter from a soldier to friend of his mother, in *Women Strike for Peace* bulletin, ed. Lillian Hayward, Chicago) . . .

"the endless fascination of war" . . .

Ambassador Lodge who consistently disavows reports of atrocities by our side . . .

you can't believe *everything* you read in the newspapers!

take your choice . . .
know history? . . .

the world not just good guys and bad guys (Master Sergeant Donald Duncan, Green Berets) . . .

boys we might have loved . . . boys, mothers and fathers! . . . What we had to make of them . . . War! . . . spreading our Values! . . . Communist conspiracy! . . . "Terror," he said pleasantly, "so they can see that their real self-interest lies with us . . . Terror is what it takes" (U.S. Officer, *N.Y. Times Mag.*, Sept. 19, 1965) . . . boys . . . what must be done to them . . . making them good soldiers . . . mothers and fathers!

•

Saigon—Hanoi—Haiphong—Bien Hoa—Dong Xoia—Duchai—Tam Phuoc—Tan An—An Loi—Danang—Hue—"the fertile Mekong delta"—Plei Me—Pleiku . . .

St. Louis—Omaha—Detroit—New York—Oak Park . . . eating lunches, making memorial day speeches, playing softball, buzz of insects over still fielders, catcher, batter, pitcher, bench, grandstands, fierce invisible sun silent over the never-ending married v. single men softball game . . . skin pulled tight over eyes of mothers, wives, girlfriends, watching, unable to see anything . . . knowing nothing . . . forgiven . . .

HENRY DUMAS

Mosaic Harlem

what news from the bottle
    rats shedding hair in ice
    nodding veins filled with snow
    blackeyed peas, grits, red rice
through the broken glass I hear a breaking age
what song do we gurgle?
what news from the bottom?
    Jesus learning judo
    I scratch giant lice and ghetto
    fleas in the gutter of my mind
the sucking boll weevil converts to blood
when will the mosquito fear the rage under sweat?
what view from the bottle?
    cats pawing at cotton ideas
    the roach in the milk
    crawls safely to the nipple
why is green not black, brown, tan, only pain?
this hombre is a tiger rose star of sneaky david
what news from the bureau?
    a mole stoking coal in wine-steam and no gas
    building baby foundations from lamb-bone
    pray in Chinese, farting in English
I hear a black drum roaring up a green lion on yellow silk
    come to kill the keeper of our cage
what news from James' bastard bible?
    al-Mahdi kneels in the mosque,
    Melchizedek, Moses, Marcus, Muhammad, Malcolm!
    marshalling words, mobilizing swords
the message is mixed and masticated with Martin
the good news of the gospel is crossing a crescent
what they do at the bottom?
    went to the cop and he took my pot
    the law giveth and the law taketh away
    I can neither pee nor blow
they will rope Mary and take pussy for my bail
I will remember, I will recall, bottoms up, I cop
what news from the black bastille?
    ram of god busting up shit
    unicorning the wolf, panthering the fox
    the old shepherd is himself lost
the ram will not stop, what news from the bottom?
the east! the west! and the top!

NIKKI GIOVANNI

Woman Poem

September 10, 1968

you see, my whole life
is tied up
to unhappiness
its father cooking breakfast
and me getting fat as a hog
or having no food
at all and father proving
his incompetence
again
i wish i knew how it would feel
to be free

its having a job
they won't let you work
or no work at all
castrating me
(yes it happens to women too)

its a sex object if you're pretty
and no love
or love and no sex if you're fat
get back fat black woman be a mother
grandmother strong thing but not
woman
gameswoman romantic woman love
needer
man seeker dick eater sweat getter
fuck needing love seeking woman

its a hole in your shoe
and buying lil sis a dress
and her saying you shouldn't
when you know
all too well—that you shouldn't

but smiles are only something we give
to properly dressed social workers
not each other
only smiles of i know
your game sister
which isn't really
a smile

joy is finding a pregnant roach
and squashing it
not finding someone to hold
let go get off get back don't turn
me on you black dog
how dare you care
about me
you ain't got no good sense
cause i ain't shit you must be lower
than that to care

it's a filthy house
with yesterday's watermelon
and monday's tears
cause true ladies don't
know how to clean

its intellectual devastation
of everybody
to avoid emotional commitment
"yeah honey i would've married
him but he didn't have no degree"

its knock-kneed mini skirted
wig wearing died blond mamma's scar
born dead my scorn your whore
rough heeled broken nailed powdered
face me
whose whole life is tied
up to unhappiness
cause its the only
for real thing
i
know

DAVID HENDERSON

Bopping*

My main men and I bopped
to general agreement (like the toast to 'the boys upstate'
before every bottle of Paradise or
Thunderbird wine)
Down cats
we bopped to give cause to the causes
that died before they got to us.

I remember the arm pumping cap crowned blades
of my boyhood
their elemental gait talking
deep beneath my eyes . . .
the list at waist and trunk
whip of an arm
& abrupt then long wing-tipped stride
of days when we had to show ourselves love
in difficult pretensions
as if speaking words of self-love
was too remote a performance
when before the fact
we understood all too well
the action of the thrust.

We maneuvered
to turn that way in dawns or dusk
of the eternal wars
among ourselves our gangs:
the Crowns Chaplains Sportsmen
Boston Baldies Young Sinners Enchanters Duschon Lords
because talking after all is too little of glamour
to the hungry the ugly the mean

we bopped when about to fight
as we bopped when happy
all in our own slight variances
known to the members of the Road
and known to similar bops
of the roaming hordes

* Bopping: to bop, bip, bebop / Thru any ghetto, black stride—D.H.

From Avenue "D" to Red Hook
through Marcy projects then Crown Heights
Prospect Avenue in the Bronx & also in Brooklyn
The Fifth Avenue Armory on 141st & the Harlem River
Bronx River Housing   forty-three   Fifty-five
from Winters to graduation
from street duels
until
wedlock or the cops
shot us down
bopping

CALVIN C. HERNTON

Jitterbugging in the Streets

To Ishmael Reed

There will be no holy man crying out this year
No seer, no trumpeter, no George Fox walking
barefoot up and down the hot land
The only messiah we shall see this year
Staggers
To and fro
On the LowerEastSide
Being laughed at by housewives in Edsel
automobiles who teach their daughters the
fun of deriding a terror belched up from
the scatological asphalt of America
Talking to himself

An unshaven idiot
A senile derelict
A black nigger
Laughter and scorn on the lips of Edsel
automobiles instructing the populace to
love God, be kind to puppies and the
Chase Manhattan National Bank

Because of this there will be no Fourth-of-July
this year
No shouting, no popping of firecrackers, no
celebrating, no parade
But the rage of a hopeless people
Jitterbugging
In the streets
Jacksonville, Florida
Birmingham, Atlanta, Rochester, Bedford
Stuyvesant, Jersey City, Chicago,
Jackson, Mississippi, Harlem New York—
Watts L.A.
Jitterbugging
in
the streets
To ten thousand rounds of ammunition
To water hoses, electric prods, phallic sticks,
hound dogs, black boots stepping in soft
places of the body—

Venom is in the mouth of Christian housewives,
smart young Italians, old Scandinavians in
Yorkville, suntanned suburban organization
men, clerks and construction workers, poor
white trash and gunhappy cops everywhere
"Why don't we kill all the niggers.
Not one or two
But every damn black of them. Niggers will do
anything.
I better never catch a nigger messing with my wife,
And most of all never with my daughter! Aughter
grab 'em up and ship every black clean out of
the country . . . Aughter just line 'em up and
mow 'em down
Machine Gun Fire!"

All Americans. Housewives, businessmen, civil
service employees, loving their families, going to
church, regularly depositing money in their
neighborhood bank,
All Fourth-of-July celebrators belched up from
the guilt-ridden cockroach, sick sex terror
of America
Talking to themselves
In bars
On street corners,
Fantasizing hatred
At bridge clubs
Lodge meetings, on park benches,
In fashionable mid-town restaurants—

No Holy man shall cry out upon the black ghetto
this year
No trombonist
The only messiah we will know this year is a
bullet in the belly
of a Harlem youth shot down by a coward
crouched behind an outlaw's badge—

Mississippi
Georgia
Tennessee, Alabama
Your mother your father your brothers, sisters,
wives and daughters

Up and down the hot land
There is a specter haunting America
Spitfire of clubs, pistols, shotguns, and the
Missing
Mutilated
Murdered
Bodies of relatives and loved ones
Be the only Santa Claus niggers will remember
    this year
Be the only Jesus Christ born this year
    curled out dead on the pavement, torso
    floating the bottom of a lake
Being laughed at by housewives in Edsel
    automobiles

You say there are four gates to the ghetto
Make your own bed hard that is where you have got
To lay
You say there is violence in Harlem, niggers
    run amuck perpetrating crimes against
    property, looting stores, breaking windows,
    flinging beer bottles at officers of the law
You say a certain virgin gave birth to a baby
Through some mysterious process, some divine
    conjure—
A messenger turned his walking cane into a
    serpent and the serpent stood up and walked
    like a natural man:
You say . . . .
America, why are you afraid of the phallus!

I say there is no violence in Harlem.
There is TERROR in Harlem!
And fear! And corruption! And murder!
Harlem is the asphalt plantation of America
Rat infested tenements totter like shanty
    houses stacked upon one another
Circular plague of the welfare check brings
    vicious wine every semi-month, wretched
    babies twice a year, death and hopelessness
    every time the sun goes down
Big bellied agents of down-town landlords
    forcing black girls to get down and do the
    dog before they spell their names

If you make your bed hard
He said he was fifteen years old, and he walked
beside us there in the littered fields of the
ghetto
He spoke with a dignity of the language that
shocked us and he said he had a *theory* about
what perpetrated the
Horror that was upon us as we walked among
flying bullets, broken glass, curses and the
inorganic phalluses of cops whirling about
our heads
He said he was a business major at George
Washington High
And he picked up a bottle and hurled it above the
undulating crowd
Straight into the chalk face of a black helmet—
Thirty seven properties ransacked, steel gates
ripped from their hinges, front panes
shattered, pawn shops, dry cleaners, liquor
stores
Ripped apart and looted—
Niggers will do anything!
And if your church doesn't support the present
Police Action,
In dingy fish-n-chip and bar-b-que joints
The niggers will go on doing business as usual—
From river to river,
Signboard to signboard
Scattering Schaefer six-packs all over Harlem,
Like a bat out of hell,
Marques Haynes is a dribbling fool

TERROR is in Harlem
A GENOCIDE so blatant
Every third child will do the junky-nod in the
whore scented night before semen leaps
from his loins
A FEAR so constant
Black men crawl the pavement as if they were
snakes, and snakes turn to sticks that beat
the heads of those who try to stand up—
And Fourth-of-July comes with the blasting bullet
in the belly of a teenager

Against which no Holy man, no Christian housewife
In Edsel automobile
Will cry out this year

Jitterbugging
in
the streets!

ELTON HILL-ABU ISHAK

Theme Brown Girl

for gloria

I have watched you dancing
in
in the streets   of Dakar
                    robed in soft darkness;
bending over steel-edged counters
                                        in Detroit
face slick & hot with kitchen-sweat.

I have known your brown lips
in the sullen Congo
when your world was black,
        How beautiful you were there
        breasted with Africa,
But your new world is white
and you are mistress in another's house.

And when they called you "Nigger"
        were you not afraid?
And did the spit & whips & clubs
        & scars of hatred
a nation heaved on your head,
did they edge your beauty?

I have watched you
                                        in Haiti
crowned with bandanna & bathing in coolness
and in Harlem
                lonely on midnight corners;
and in Watts
                swollen with the sickness
of slums and poverty.
Yet,
      I still see Africa in your eyes
      girl with the spirit of a leopard
      tell the world that time
      will never mark your face.

GERALD JACKSON

Poems to Americans

I watched the road—as the white boys play:
Then as a bush—Then as a cloud passing over
I dug his arrogant wartime—
        marching up and down

The sunlight deepened into the trees
        timpani heralded
—dust went puff puff like fat men rejects
        of the Third Reich
Behind hob nails flashing, scenes, fascinated Jew
        smiling
While the white boys play

—Then as a drum, Then flags rolling on the wind
They came with the hand jive—Cry, goodbye,
        goodbye
as the sky dims and new day—was a white boy

So this was the Teutonic experience alas I know
        him well
All his toys are stamped mine—

Down the road the farmer grins—the house
        mother gleaming—
the sound and dreaming triumph strike the brain
        cell spit,
And the pussy is wet—
Wet with cells and whips of sweating burning
        drinking death—
And lost thighs stand back to back
Still they laid on the sweet scent—
carried carried carried on the white boy
—Grabbed my dick: Your name is dick he said
                You cannot stay he said
Then swift I did a sex dance before his eyes
The dance was gone—march—whirling and whirling
As the white boys play.

Up and down the road where dust clouds rise—
stayed all night pounding pounding for life—
and dividends

LANCE JEFFERS

Man with a Furnace in His Hand

From the ocean filled with sand inside of me,
from the mountaintop that snows my brain,
from the volcano overflowing with my viscera,
from the blood that clots my rain,
from the pleading last song of my jesus-nightingale,
    a-snare in a soul within my soul,
from the crippled hands that stretch for mercy in my heart,
from my consecrated stone of frozen tears,
from every buried vein that anguishes my blood
from every nerve that groans my hell,
from every well sunk deep into my loins
flies the hawk that longs to tear.
Flies the hawk that emptyhearted tears at my flesh,
flies this leopard with black beating wings,
flies the enemy of all humanity,
fly famine, humiliation, fear.
Flies the hawk: his beak and scissor-eye are as cruel
    as the mother who spat upon her child's grief.
The hawk is slavery still alive in me,
my testicles afloat in cottonfield.
The hawk is the West astride my mighty back—
    my love the beaten Comanche's bitter shame.
The hawk is the snarl of the sahib in the East—
    my love the Aztec crucified.
The hawk and my love are in the smoke of human flesh:
    SEE? Choking up from Hiroshima shore.
The hawk and my love are in the dumb and tortured maw
    of my idiot grandchild of the Bomb.
The hawk is a future of the devil on the throne:
    Cortez: his buttocks set in man's face.
My love is a furnace to burn him screaming alive,
    hands tender to caress the human race.

ALICIA L. JOHNSON

Black Lotus / a prayer

I

eternal spirit
of dead dried
autumn leaves
never seen in
B-L-A-C-K G-H-E-T-T-O-S
of this morbid country
let
a human
polyploid
triple in number
inside
the
ooctid
&
spermatid of
black beings /
to produce
powerful
causes for
candid
creatures.
come—
come—a
way with
your imbecilic ideas
of not
being able
to CEASE your killing
of INNOCENT SOULS—
the LOTUS
will rise / beyond stem
& root / to an unknown shoot
that exists in the heaven of
LOTUS LAND.

II

the blue african lotus
will taste
sweet to
black thick lips
&
foul to white
sour serpent lips.
W-E / W-I-L

K-I-L
your beauty &
squeeze your
worts & varicose veins
from your old women's legs
W-E / W-I-L
send messages
of death to your
children
swimming in
south / american pools.
W-E / W-I-L
take your oil refineries
& distileries & soak
your own bodies
til-they become
sliperi with oil buds
bouncing all over them.

III

BLACK LOTUS of
ghana
rhodesia
south west africa
of
vietnam
china
cuba
and the AMERICAS / feed
your bellies with
cultural chocolates
shout hosannas of holiness
raise your voice
        bring autumn leaves
        to your ghettos /
                                let the fruit
                                of the
                                LOTUS
                                perform on the
                                USURPERS in
                                OUR ghettos /
                                they'll forget
                                and become
                                dreamy
                                & WE WIL
                                then make
                                our move.

                                        a-men

JOE JOHNSON

If I Ride This Train

If I ride this train
The long lean road
The weary road with specks of blood that punctuate
Your movement of poverty
The road of fat asses singing joyous hymns to
Life, to love, to lime, to ash
Cracked souls of pimps weep beneath the junkie's jagged heel
In the night of the beginning excerpts of blood bless
The feet of the unloved
And if I ride this train when the deal goes down
The baby's pablum eyes will awake with the laughter of
Crocodiles
When the deal goes down and if I ride this train
On my nigger streets warm with neglect flowers will bloom
To greet cement pigeons
Harsh rhythms will repeat themselves to the ear of a blind
Man: Nigger boy, Nigger Man
                        Liv'in hard—Live if can!
If I ride this train I want a hotline to Jesus
I want to dance and draw blood
I want to grin and speak serpents
I want
I wanta hiss love through my intervenous jungle
Through the trash crowded eye of my quick-soon street
In a full-lipped song
To a junkman
Cut
Cut with a razor

BOB KAUFMAN

Benediction

Pale brown Moses went down to Egypt land
To let somebody's people go.
Keep him out of Florida, no UN there:
The poor governor is all alone,
With six hundred thousand illiterates.

America, I forgive you . . . I forgive you
Nailing black Jesus to an imported cross
Every six weeks in Dawson, Georgia.
America, I forgive you . . . I forgive you
Eating black children, I know your hunger.
America, I forgive you . . . I forgive you
Burning Japanese babies defensively—
I realize how necessary it was.
Your ancestor had beautiful thoughts in his brain.
His descendants are experts in real estate.
Your generals have mushrooming visions.
Every day your people get more and more
Cars, televisions, sickness, death dreams.
You must have been great
Alive.

ETHERIDGE KNIGHT

The Idea of Ancestry

I

Taped to the wall of my cell are 47 pictures: 47 black
faces: my father, mother, grandmothers (1 dead), grand-
fathers (both dead), brothers, sisters, uncles, aunts,
cousins (1st & 2nd), nieces, and nephews. They stare
across the space at me sprawling on my bunk. I know
their dark eyes, they know mine. I know their style,
they know mine. I am all of them, they are all of me;
they are farmers, I am a thief, I am me, they are thee.

I have at one time or another been in love with my mother,
1 grandmother, 2 sisters, 2 aunts (1 went to the asylum),
and 5 cousins. I am now in love with a 7 yr old niece
(she sends me letters written in large block print, and
her picture is the only one that smiles at me).

I have the same name as 1 grandfather, 3 cousins, 3 nephews,
and 1 uncle. The uncle disappeared when he was 15, just took
off and caught a freight (they say). He's discussed each year
when the family has a reunion, he causes uneasiness in
the clan, he is an empty space. My father's mother, who is 93
and who keeps the Family Bible with everybody's birth dates
(and death dates) in it, always mentions him. There is no
place in her Bible for "whereabouts unknown."

BILL KNOTT (1940–1966)

Unedited Tape

They were loading a body into the breech
When I arrived with my microphone and cameraman
Tell me I asked one of the generals hanging around
Is this the new ammunition we're testing to use to kill the enemy with
The general was draped over the enormous howitzer asleep
But he answered yes this big baby
This big baby will fire a thousand corpses a second
It will destroy tree grass flower no matter which microscope they're under
  thank you

I wanted to get more expert views on this major new breakthrough for our
  audience
But it seemed everyone had become deaf from standing too close to their
  heartbeats
So I asked the corpse who was in the muzzle
Sir can you sum up what we've seen here today
Yes he said life
Is a posthumous deathwish

This is Bill Knott (1940–1966) NBC News returning you to the Today show.

JOEL KOHUT

That I Had Seen . . .

That i had seen a Puerto Rican family evicted from the
brownstone next door to mine and could only shake my
head at the overweight policeman pretending to guard
the beds and suit cases lying half broken in the gutter

that i had seen a Negro boy of fifteen wearing a mad
checked crazy hat keeping siege over the body of his
bleeding heaving puppy that was tossed upon his lap
by a screeching ten ton laundry wagon; that was pounded
and eviscerated that oozed and coughed and died on the
street while i could touch its chest and say: he is dead
with all the authority of the world

that a suitor, enraged, did beat and torment his lover
before the eyes of the entire west eighty fourth street
social center executive committee and five curious
foreigners whispering in German; outside the window
of my study; in front of my face

that a purse was stolen, an automobile broken into,
a child beaten, a dog turned loose to growl its
hydrophobic way toward the tiny Catholic school at
recess time, that the police department parked their
anti-narcotics wagon with the pictures of dead men with
punctures in their arms and ulcerated thighs exactly
at the intersection of Columbus Avenue and eighty second
street during the beginning of lunch hour for the children
of the Louis D. Brandeis High School to parade through
and giggle

that i drink coffee and remain a part of the wall of
untouchable black and brown flesh of my neighborhood
and speak little and do very little and think of the
absurdities of urban renewal and the rebuilding of slums
and escape to the zoo where the animals turn upon their
warders and i plotted with a Negro keeper to set
free all the carnivores, permitting them to roam through
central Park

that seven teen-age boys played baseball with me one day
and treated me as another one of their minions though
i had been scorned for the grey hairs in my beard and
head

that a white woman married to a Negro man lives in the
basement of my apartment building

that a monstrous Puerto Rican boy who delivers meat for
the city dressed markets stops to talk with me or the
man from the dry cleaning shop explains trade secrets
like removing stains or turning collars; the man from the
stationery store who shouts at me in Yiddish to help him
pass his hours (i see the number on his arm: A-1032—how
the pain of Auschwitz must have entered his soul; he fought
with the Polish Army uselessly) and he wears spectacles
which are broken

the tiny Jew with the frayed wool coat and muskrat fur
piece admires my clean windows; the landlady says i
am very clean; the landlord invites me to a Seder at his
son-in-law's house because i am a Jew (though he a
Sabbath Observer with a married daughter and three other
children attending a Yeshiva in downtown Brooklyn somewhere
close to Grand Army Plaza several blocks from my first
museum trip during the Second World War when my father
tried to enlist in the Navy and wound up as a boiler-maker
in the Brooklyn Navy Yard which was closed late last year
by Defense Chief McNamara of the frameless eyeglasses)

that two college students that are never at home and live
above me in a room not quite as large as mine and having
lavatory facilities in the hallway which they must share
with four other tenant families

that bus drivers stare straight ahead when they give you
change; the woman crying for her hound destroyed for biting
sixteen people during a midday traffic jam on one hundred
and twenty fifth street and Lenox Avenue someplace along
the dangerous route through Harlem to the Bronx

that crippled men and paralyzed women pursue themselves
over the sidewalk gloom of Central Park West and pace
their laziness to last until the next social security
check

that hunger is evident on the faces of the children playing
stick ball in the street

that old men of black face and grizzly whiteness mustache
sit drinking beer from cans wrapped in brown bags drooling
dribbling their lives down their chins

that everywhere is sadness and no pity and i see it and
shake my head because my arms are tired and my heart broken . . .

T. L. KRYSS

This Wind

this wind
i cannot place my fingers on
it is the wind
that crushes small animals
to the floor of the forest
that
blows down silos across the highway
it is nine minds high
and gathers in election squares of the world
it comes when the plastic radio
melts in my hands on the eve of the revolution
while i lie in bed smoking
Turkish cigarettes
it is populated by numbers
that predict the outcome of more numbers
which click against each other
like pelvic dice
this wind that wanders through the capitals
and assassinates the wrong dictators in their pajamas
this wind with the Winged Victory's arms
lodged in its throat
in its ionosphere
minoan prayer rugs sailing on
currents of yellow nitrogen
this wind
that dashes grains of sand like needles
against the Electric Curtain and scratches
Mayan rubrics in the glass-eye of Radio Free
David Sarnoff
this wind is the loneliness of the mob
it is a tree of wind bent into the moon
it is bounded on all sides by the echoes of stars
it is the wind that cleans the spiders from my eyelids
it is the wind that carries Caesars to my door
i turn them away into the night with their speeches in their hats
and i listen to their footsteps in the wind / the wind
that only dead men do not hear.

DON L. LEE

The Death Dance

for Maxine

my empty steps mashed
your face in a mad
rhythm of happiness.
as if i was just learning to
boo-ga-loo.

my mother took the
'b' train to the loop
to seek work & was laughed at by
some dumb, eye-less image maker as
she scored idiot on "your" I. Q. test.

i watched mom;
an ebony mind
on a yellow frame.
"i got work son, go back to school."
(she was placed according to her
intelligence into some honkie's kitchen)

i thought & my steps
took on a hip be-bop beat
on your little brain
trying to reach any of
your senseless senses.

mom would come home late
at night & talk sadtalk
or funny sadtalk. she talked
about a pipe smoking sissy
who talked siss-talk & had
sissy sons who were forever playing
sissy games with themselves
& then she would say,
"son you is a man, a black man."

i was now tapdancing on your
balls & you felt no pain.
my steps were beating a staccato
message that told of the past 400 years.

the next day mom cried &
sadtalked me. she talked about
the eggs of maggot colored,
gaunt creatures from europe
who came here / put on pants, stopped eating with their hands,
stole land, massacred indians,
hid from the sun, enslaved blacks &
thought that they were substitutes
for gods. she talked about a
faggot who grabbed her ass as
she tried to get out of the
backdoor of his kitchen & she said,
"son you is a man, a black man."

the African ballet
was now my guide; a teacher or self &
the dance of a people.
a dance of concept essence.
i grew.

mom stayed home & the
ADC became my father / in projects without
backdoors / "old grand dad" over
the cries of bessie smith /
until pains didn't pain anymore.

i began to dance dangerous steps,
warrior's steps.
my steps took on a cadence with other blk / brothers
& you could hear the cracking of
gun shots in them & we said that,
"we were men, black men."

i took the 'b' train to the loop &
you SEE me coming,
you don't like it,
you can't hide &
you can't stop me.
you will not laugh this time.
you know,
that when i dance again
it will be the
Death Dance.

WALTER LOWENFELS

Elegy for the Old Language

"Why have thirty American poets
committed suicide since 1900?"
—Kenneth Rexroth

Language in the U.S.A. has become so disturbed,
when a poet uses it for resonance-capture,
everybody thinks his truth is lying—that makes people
feel bad and they kill themselves.
In the solar mirror in which we live, the coroner
thinks it is the poet who has committed suicide. . . .

Motivists speak of our weak character
Across the desert border,
on the Aztec altar where
we are all lovers in the flesh.
we watch those who escape the cyanide
having their hearts ripped out.

Even the "earth" in "rare earth" is not completely descriptive.

On the high end of the verbal spectrum
where words are metal, you pour out like beads;
only a poem measures the optimum relationship,
unveiling the riddle of rolling friction in the
magnetism of the sun.
Slice light the way you want it.
Where do we go from minus 320°F?
Magnetic exploration along the crystal axis?
Guided tour of the solar system?
Reaching tomorrow is our job;
success is to survive as a turbulent
transfer in the cybernetics of cre-
ation—not a chopped, stabilized amplifier.

On this vertical oscillator radar tracking unit.
lively as a walk on the moon,
from kitchen to stars,
camera weds duplicator
fishing for neutrons
Cosmic butterfly
spreading its wings
to absorb the eternal flow of solar energy.

In conclusion, comrade space,
The Big Elk is rounding the Cape of Good Hope.
    The Horn is on the deer. Beyond magnetic memory
    bells are sounding in star spaces
    and the Dog mounts the Bear.

Are you ready to go? Do you know which way the
    microwave is moving?
Have you got the ice-cutter ready for the
    passage around Point Vega?
And he named me Antrium and I said: "You don't
    frighten me. I have been used to you for
    ten thousand years. You always tell the last
    tale and you never win the first story.
Cut out the chatter. The time has come to start
    the Big Journey and we are all ready."

Shield for the battle for survival in space;
electroluminescence;
plasma flame spray;
plumbing for posterity.

CLARENCE MAJOR

I.

the comic moneypowerdream
        of this octopus
of the globe
                sunstruck with the
silent dangers
        of goofy operations and
unholy jive with
                sham visions
of honor drugged with
the weight of propaganda
        (harnessing)
our best   *smooth flux*   leaving us
open:
:to
the procrastinations of spaghetti brains in
judgement
in high places breathing in
        the dumb comfort of their
endless power
        ((trenched in
                ((the monster idiom
without SUBSTANCE of new
        laughter of new
        wisdom

could so easily
        BLOW THE GREAT MIND
                of hipcats
into that stale secret
isolation:
of expensive folly where
these obsolete
disaster objects fumble with
                precision, the agenda
of their false
command. MONKEYTIME SCABS
TRYING TO SLAP THEIR CHALKY STORES of
        vulgar (bitchy) aggression into
some sensible self-
defense fabrication but

                        get to this:

while these animated cartoon
figures spin
insanely around in
their stacked up mumbo-jumbo
Beautiful! Third World! People!
are
—o/p/ening to themselves
and
VI*brating* in the
SUBSTANCE
LAUGHTER
WISDOM
of this foxy
Birth Ritual.

Into the sweet
excellence of ex-
pand-
ing and deep-
ening TRUE FACTS of
C O N S C I O U S N E S S
of
"self"

life
beauty

II.

our children's
restless eyes & their sincere bodies
as defense
weapons lean & strong beneath
terrible arms
of shadows draped in the
extreme complex of an
illogical crisis
in voodooed and,
vamped cities of this
most demoralized jive Murphy Game

escape the
drill of viscous

death that
seeks to freeze
them
in the middle of their best gig, which is
HUMAN VICTORY
seeks to hang them
in MASSIVE VOICELESS EMPTINESS:
& crumble them
into cold print
where life is delivered into
the skilled naked
mind, like homing
pigeons, coming

home doing
their
thing.

III.

they lay broken
like the bottles around them
& their beautiful mouths busted open
screaming silent rage
my tough brothers trapped
beneath the elusive madness of huge cops
with the hairy arms of chimpanzees
toting well oiled metal items
of pain,   BUT THEIR SMOOTH TIME

EQUALS
the swiftness of their skins & does
not jam the
pace   of pushing in this   crowded Auschwitz!
beyond our dead brothers
stacked in cold
endlesstrickyrecords

THE STAGGERING BODIES OF DEATH
GAGGING HISTORY INTO STUPID SILENCE
this funnyfarm shit is enough
rhythmless   machine-washable   "philosophy

to cause Buddha to STAND UP UP   1 for a change
& blow
his cool

IV.

we hung from our windows & sat on
the steps we smoked cigarettes in
our vacant lots & we scribbled our
deepest deeds on our walls Cat in the barbershop
getting a
shave
rapping about his latest stickup DAMN it was a
set ofriffs you never ditched you
never put down those storefront churches
with the greatest western hungup artist
invented by the scapegoat needy
of all times
chipped a thousand times into black patterns
& these astonishing aretha franklins singing
blackchurch
church
graduating to james brown
BLACK PATTERNS of
BLACK PATTERNS of
astonishment itself
Bringing down THE HOUSE
Uptown!
(in the *broken promise*
land)

V.

that old sapphire sister
encased in &
looking outta her
twisted broken window snowed
with the witchcraft of time
& TV buttermilk
colored enthusiasm ain't checked
out the new rhythm of her
trans-
formed daughter ain't
opened her
eyes even to her
own wasted beauty *defended*
by teaming
kids not necessarily
from

the
ancient
mouth
                    TIME LESS WOMB
of her
    throwing bricks into
these empty symbols of the most
laughable line
        of bullshit getting in the way
of humantogetherness
that ever jived her CYCLE
        ain't even said BIP BAM THANK YOU MA'AM
for this good tragic
luck.

IFEANYI MENKITI*

Reflections

The ranks, being extremely loyal that year,
decided to stage their loyalty,
and brought Gowom to the top,
and took Ironsi to his death,

the wave on slaughter wave. . . .

And I have not thought of Nigeria this past hour,
how bitter the kola fruit tastes in our mouths

a time to kill,
and a time to heal;
a time to gather,
and a time to destroy;
a time, that is,
for all sorts of things
to happen.

Nigeria we hail thee
our own dear native land
though tribe and tongue . . .

The anthem, O yes, the anthem
I have forgotten the anthem
and cannot finish what I've started

Neither can we.

II

Ideals of the rational order
lacking concourse
with the beasts at large;
Akintola and Bello,
twin balls with one penis;
the pus, stinking, of politicians;
politicians, basis of disruption;
to the seedland
approached neither with care,
nor with caution;
the rampaging beasts,
rampaged all over it.

* This Biafran poet, originally in the Metapoetry section, was inserted here by the editor of the book, George Quasha.

Akintola and Bello
Akintola and Bello

And then the rains came in that year,
and people said it was a pity
it had to come,
but that it had to come,
since the mess had to be cleaned,
anyway.

And that was before they thought of their
"Ibo domination".

Nzeogwu, Ibrahim, Banjo;
the deed that never was in tribe,
nor in self;
staking their lives out,
for the rectification of history.

And the rectification of history,
the rectification of history, they tell me,
is a very difficult thing;
for the pig will follow its ways,
and the natives in their night,
the native in their night.

Which is to say,
which is not to say,
the sun of our madness
that is not the sun of our light
shines, as it has shone,
madly in Kano, unchecked.

O sun, keep thy detriment from these children;
tear not Nneka from her womb;
the bewildered little children
know not Garuba from Okoye
they run no more in their *sabron garis*
O sun. . . .

the opposition loyal and disloyal
that took Ironsi to his death
came Gowon the successor
sending the troops in
and no one would listen to him
no one would listen to him:

small talk comes
from small bones

III

The mortar days began.
July 6. The mortar days began.

Softening up operations they called it.
Broadcast over Lagos radio:
". . . have launched an attack
to end the rebellion in the eastern states"
for the killing of rebels
the mortar days began that day.

Operation Mecca,
The Medina came earlier;
Allah, the noble steed,
Islam riding thee,
Onward and southward
to Lagos and Pitaqua;
the conquest uninterrupted
to the sea.

"I should like to make it
clear to you that if the
British quitted Nigeria,
now, at this stage,
the Northern people would
continue their interrupted
conquest to the sea"
dixit Balewa
anno domino, 1947

The mortar days have begun.

Notes on the References in "Reflections"

Major General Yakubu Gowon:present boss of Nigeria; assumed power following the assassination of Major General Aguiyi Ironsi, his predecessor.

Stanza 5: words from the Nigerian national anthem

II

Akintola and Bello:two very powerful politicians of the old school whose alliance of oppression against the masses sparked the unsuccessful revolt of Jan. 15, 1966; revolt was led by Majors C.K. Nzeogwu, V. Banjo, and others.

Kano: moslem holy city in the North of Nigeria where thousands of Ibo men, women, and children were massacred in 1966. Massacre was organized by Moslem emirs, mallams, and politicians who had charged the Ibos with plotting to take over the country.

Nneka:a very common Ibo name for girls. (Many pregnant Ibo women were split open and fetuses cut from their wombs during the '66 killings)

Garuba:a very common male name (Hausa)

Okoye:a very common male name (Ibo)

III

July 6:Nigeria-Biafra war broke out.

Lagos:capital of Nigeria

Pitaqua:fond name for Port Harcourt, major port city of Biafra, since captured by Federal Nigerian troops.

ANNE OSWALD

Insurrection One — D.C.

the flowering of the branch
begins
like a red serpent
uncoiling
      the body of the dream
      is the seed within the slow dark fruit
      the sun
      repeating itself upon moist trees
in the tarnished silver night
I light two candles
one the colour of early marsh grass
the other like a thund'rous sky
      to the fat honky bitch on the bus
      I say
      "Soul is an Algerian word
      meaning the spirit of freedom"
      Algerian, you see, because I wanted her
      TO MAKE A CONNECTION
you black
people exist
in that high
energy
ghost universe
of which we are unaware
except when we commit
ritual murder
Whites, you see, never forget their sewer numbers.
You,
Tamayo's people, Blackfeet on the plains of time,
the dark elk of night will give you safe passage.
Like a tension behind mirrors,
JAIRO IS THE CONNECTION

longing   dances
like the expanding—contracting of a strung-out universe
      "to the point of trauma" as the honkee fishmonger put it,
      Chinese Year of Monkey,
      and truly Frederick Douglass Night
Yet I weep for my people cut off from earth
these grunting white puddings,
their eyes like blind raisins, their lips

the lips of true rapists,
gross chins fading out only
when the dark light becomes
a maw, a river of mud.
the Bodhisattva is among them,
invisible edge cleaving to all the splintered glass parts
of a strange wind chime
it is the 30th of November every day
as we are hurtled across your black faces
like a look of true despair
the columns of Capetown oppressing you,
posed carefully, as in a garden of the insane
moving under moist trees,
Gabriel the Archangel
brings filaments of flowers and the green forest
tendril by tendril
so though to feed us back our souls drop by drop
confusing us with the life of the plants
    Though we see through hungry tiger-eyes
    we are still too pale to come close to the growing,
    to the power of the earth-feast
    Still intrigued by Poe
    (M. for one wanted to take a degree in demonology)
    not just because we are so cruel
    but because we too
    have a headful
    of fearful crystal.
Yet the great green animal has a soul that is capable of confusion.
the snake is the holy root and the moon,
the mother of sea

Black Panther Scene—Holy Week:

Ubi Roi, aging infiltrator, utters UHURU on a bus
which has a sign "whites only" in Swahili
Men of Colour are in Siquieros' great design
true Rufus is a whoremaster but he is also very black
and leads a mass Resurrection Mantra for Malcolm
and a dirge for Gulf Oil Limited: Lumumba Lumumba
Geraldine reflects in a moonstone
that when the drinking black man turns ugly
he is said to have a white man's high

Fifty laughing pubescent boys, guns erect,
followed by prison-made black butches and old men,
write on the beanery walls LET US LIVE
REVOLUCION SI   and   ECSTACY IS OUR BAG
followed by money-burning folk-heroes
and the ground-glass voice of the sirens
On Ash Wednesday they invent a pineal eye
and notice that the function of mirrors
is to release us from stasis

in the tarnished silver night
a stoned junkie lights the sky with flame
that the plum might burst into blossom
and the earth again
become as a day of birth to all our Kind

FELIX POLLAK

A Matter of History

In Memory of Lotte, Ernst, and Fritz Strass

It all has passed and is gone, the cries silenced, the blood
congealed in the earth. The cries dissolved in air, the blood
sucked up by grass, transformed into the sap of young trees.
The torturers again what they had been before—hotel captains,
clerks, engineers, raising families and pets, watching wrestling
on *Fernseh* screens, with only a faint remembrance, a vague
nostalgia for *Kraft durch Freude*—wo sind die Zeiten! The
torture instruments themselves matured into museum pieces,
exhibits A,B,C, adjoining the nickelodeon and the paraphernalia
used to question witches. Dachau, Buchenwald, Auschwitz,
Theresienstadt—place names again, towns, railroad stops.
Hotels to spend the night in between trains. Silenced the cries,
congealed the blood, the ashes dispersed by winds. The mass
graves grown over, the cases closed, the compensations paid. Only
the bones still real in the graves, alone the numbers tattooed on
forearms surviving in San Francisco, Brussels, Shanghai, merely
the memories of feces and sweat, of whips and crucifixions and
howls of terror and death, of hoses, of bursting intestines, of
chimney fires and the smell of burning flesh and hair, of dog barks
and the shots of voices and cracking bones and sudden silences
still real buried in skulls dispersed over the globe, only the scars
on displaced souls bleeding mutely into private nights over the
earth, gray flickers across daytime eyes . . . faint, growing fainter
and scarce, bats fluttering through daydreams on their way into
the crevices of gray oblivion. Strewn by winds over seas the ashes
of Auschwitz, icicles hanging from trees the deathcries of Belsen,
melting in a new now. Sunken beneath the flowers the corpses
frozen into the ground barefoot at attention, their last moans
ground into soft powder by the wings of bees. The camps,
concentrating on tourists, now sideshowsights for travellers out
to learn the fine art of shuddering. No smoking, please, in
deference to the martyrs—a slight but symbolic sacrifice. Keep
off the grass, you might be walking on a grave. The touching of
the torture instruments strictly *verboten*, read the signs, ladies
and sirs, and kindly refrain from loud laughter, as it would
violate the decorum of the place. This way to the gas chambers,
if you please. — All past and gone. The murdered dead, the
blood of the red headlines congealed in archives, the writers,
the murderers, forgotten—have and are. *Wie gehts? — Man lebt.*

And already a child coming home from school asking,
Daddy, who was Hitler?

LENNOX RAPHAEL

Lament for Lloyd Warner

O how calm. The afternoon
Stalks the moon. A girl climbs
A tree. Is raped. She sees red
The Police come. The
Nigger did it. They tramp
Through fear. Looking
For a nigger. With
Stovepipe wet. That
Sports. The Red light

Tramp. Tramp. Tramp.
Their eyes go out

Hey you there. Open your fly

You are. Under arrest

Her parents seated. She
Waited. They brought him. Unto her

Is this the mad nigger

Let me see his Peter

He is. The wrong nigger
The right one had a larger Peter

Away. From the girl. They
Stared him down: Nigger
You are. Either a Commie. Or
A Jew. You are. CIRCUM-
STANCED. Why did
Your stovepipe heat up
When that white lady. Examined. It

He was. Beaten. Flogged
Icepicked. Butcherknifed. And
Noosedup. Into gasolinesoaked tree

Rev. Bishop threw the torch. The
Tree. And the body. Were
Roasted.

The girl came. Howling
I lied. I lied. I only
Wanted. To see. A nigger's
PETER   It was too late
His flesh. Like candle
Grease. Rolled down
Branches. And. The
Feast. Ended. Rev
Bishop. Said, May
The Good Lord have mercy
On his Black Soul. Amen.

EUGENE REDMOND

barbequed cong: OR we laid MY LAI low

at My Lai we left lint for lawns
feathered with frameless wingless birds,
barbequed and bodyless heads of hair
hanging from the charcoal gazes of burnt huts.

rice-thin hides harbored
flesh-flailing pellets,
unregenerative crops triggereddown from the trunks of branchless
mechanical trees.
as barbecue grills grew hotter with ghost-hot heat,
mothers cooked children and causes
in grease of blood-glazed breasts,
resigned in the weighty whisper that:
"one can only die once."

cannon cut My Lai into flesh confetti.
pellet-potted half cooked carcasses curing in rice wine.
(rat-tat-tat of an idea. souvenirs for patron-saints presiding
over oil wells).
flat-faced down in the mud like some unclaimed unnamed yet undreamt dream.

while miniature machine-gun minds
mate with mole-holes
on the muddy highways of swamp or swampless night.

"Westward, Whore!"
hear ye . . . hear ye:
a declaration of undeclared causes.
a preamble to constipation and conscription.
dare we overcome?
even arrive?
slightly begin?
entertain thoughts?
go forth against grains before mornings unfold?

My lands! My Lai!
puppet shows and portable pentogods soar or sneak from saigon.
Shine came on deck of the mind this morning and said:
"there's a sag in the nation's middle.
which way extends the natal cord—
north or south?"

i lay down my life for My Lai and Harlem.
i lay down my burden in Timbuctu and Baltimore.
we waited long and low
like low-strung studs for My Lai
when we reared and rammed her
with spark-sperm spitting penises
then withdrew westward 6000 miles
(a pacific coffin of mind between us)
to vex canned good consciences
and claim the 5th Amendment.

CAROLYN RODGERS

For Alex Haley

(the Man who did it)

i have often ached to know how
craved to find out where i
came from. not that i do not
know i was grown in a womb
(for nine months they tell me)
not that i do not know the street
the city the country i
was bled into. this i know and
meaningless more s. but.
i have a yearning.
like some stray dog a-howling feeling
in the i want to

KNOW where my fathers fathers
fathers fathers fathers fathers
father where were they
they were not here i know not
where where is the root of my
father long gone ago oh see my
most strutting, my most holy
precious my most private and my only FREE
me was ripped out of me before before

before (oh my FREE ME was stolen lynched where are they) those
who? mourns -ed for me my blood my
pain will cremate me. and.

i must sit. how. here. uh. stray
bitch, howling in the nights tight-
choking in my shackle of blindness
black rolling sockets of pain. oh.
i could drown in my puke the seed
future seeds forever, of
                                        those who did this to
                                                                        me.

JEROME ROTHENBERG

A Bodhisattva Undoes Hell

Because he saw the men of the world ploughing their
fields, sowing the seed, trafficking, huckstering, buying
& selling, & at the end winning nothing but bitterness,
For this he was moved to pity . . .

To the figures bathing at the river
Jizo appeared

The sky was full of small fishes
The bodies of the men
twisted in an afternoon
when earth & air were one

With Hell a hard fact
the double lotus
brought the son of heaven
down among us
And the bathers showed their hands
that bore the marks of nails

What Jizo said
was this

Let's bury their lousy hammers
My people
are tired of pain
The world's been crucified
long enough

The rain fell gently on their wounds
The women lugged
big platters of shrimp
to the bathers
when Jizo's diamond
caught the sun

The rest of us
sat at the stone windows
overlooking the river
We saw him climb the hill
& disappear
behind the guardhouse

What he told the guards
was this

Your bosses are men
who darken counsel
with words
But the white sun
carries love
into the world

When Jizo leaned on his stick
the blue lines in his face
were shining with tears
We followed him
into the city
where lilies bled beside a lake

He said

The heart's
a flower
Love
each other
Keep the old
among you

Write the poem
The image
unlocks Hell
Man's joy
makes
his gods

For those who heard him
hatred fell away

We spent the night
with angels
Fishing
in the ponds of Hell

SONIA SANCHEZ

for unborn malcolms

git the word out
now.
        to the man/boy
taking a holiday
from murder.
                    tell him
we hip to his shit and that
the next time he kills one
of our
            blk/princes some of
his faggots gonna die
a stone/cold/death.
                                        yeah.
it's time.
                  an eye for an eye
                  a tooth for a tooth
                  don't worry abt his balls
they al
          ready gone.
                              get the word
out that no blk/niggers
                                are out to lunch
and the main course
is gonna be his white meat.
                                          yeah.

ARMAND SCHWERNER

The inheritors

an anathema

they walk through the low tide at dawn
in the aluminum moonshine
kicking jellyfish, dreaming
paramecium cookies, and cool lemon soda
from traveling astronaut processed piss.
                                        I hate them all, every one, wild
                                        for the moon, baying for its maria,
rabid for its pockets and craters with a probe
directed from the Parthenon, the cold marble
silver-white under the moon.
                                        They are
serenely arriving, arriving
and kicking moonjelly in lunar Mare Imbrium;
they daydream metals that twist like rubber
and last like the memory of death, they dream
of pharmaceutical connections in the suburbs, of needs
to be filled, druggists coming to meetings.
                                                        They push golfcarts
stuffed with empty quart mayonnaise jars, they find
on the veldt on red Mars the green little fry
                                                            ready
for pickled service, they dream of the fry
oiled
transferred to airtight cans from the oozing jars
                                                                they dream
specialty stores, and talking at meetings,
                                                        corralling
passive Venusian atheists
in a ferment of pious barracks.
                                        O to those and their brothers
                                        a slow and gummy death
from some crack Elohim like Fu-Manchu,
providers
in the ravage of tree and beast
they sew the earth with dust and famished deer as offering;
                                                                monotheistic
thurifers dandle
                    thuribles of pus
to stanch the expensive
lacerations

in the dirt.
These
are the meek, the loving tongues, who ever to themselves have said,
Breathes there a soul who wouldn't grab it? and
maybe not.
The inheritors dance, arriving, arriving, their ears
to the ground in a jackal squat
their shit turns to stone before it fertilizes the ground, a lords
meditating on their worms, grubby
reminders of earth, they sell dead seeds
in a mystique of appropriations to stop up the wounds
of the earth.

They meditate, their eyes on the moon
they rise from their burrows like swamp smog,
enchanted, they
twist in a metaphysical fever
in the anguish of being subject to decay
infected
by sap running purposefully from maples
irregularity
in the arrangement of leaves
athlete's feet sneaking in under the deer
germs on the pet.
Order
some order
the old place is dying

THURMOND SNYDER

Beale Street, Memphis

Neon glitter of night
Rain splatters quietly
Silhouettes, shadows
Estranged from corporeal existence

Poltergeists ramble
Among ruins
A corpse lies lonely
In an alley coffin

Out of a dark street
Into a brilliant vertigo of sound
A mask falls
A player leaves the stage

Guatama has returned
From the mountain
The naked eye of truth
Bears the stain of a lonely tear.

TAR LEE SUN

Blackfireness

gonna spirit-spring flame
up&spirit-springflame
down
&spirit-springflame in a spirit-springflame out
&spirit-springflame around& around

to burn decadent-artificial-colorless Madison Ave BS
BLACKFIRENESS
BLACKFIRENESS
BLACKFIRENESS
to burn demoralizing-political-colorless Washington, DC BS
BLACKFIRENESS
BLACKFIRENESS
BLACKFIRENESS
to burn stars&stripes syphilis-gonorrhea pus
that pledges allegiance
to cancerpollute attack
the heart of every simple 2+2 = 4 truthatom TRUTH ADAM truthatom

&every starmoonbeam beautyatom BEAUTY ADAM

beautyatom in ALLAH

yes, ALLAH JEHOVAH YAHVEH BRAHMAN
blackFIRENESS gonna spirit-springflame

Aint gonna be no more
Madison-Ave BS BS BS brandnaming people
to infant psycho-neurotic graves
BLACKFIRENESS
BLACKFIRENESS
BLACKFIRENESS
Aint gonna be no more
whitehouse-pentagon dirty dry-gulching
fork-tongued phonies with fleabrains &
green-mucous spines playing GREAT GOD!
with pushbutton world destruction
BLACKFIRENESS
BLACKFIRENESS
BLACKFIRENESS
Aint gonna be no more
KKK white-citizen-council with FBI CIA
assistance to bomb to death black children
praying on their sweet humility knees in their mosque
BLACKFIRENESS
BLACKFIRENESS
BLACKFIRENESS

Aint gonna be no more
stupid west-point general glory-boying around like custer
with napoleon caesar hitler dreams
in pearlhandles of their guns for brains

dropping atomic bombs on Asians
because Asians have darkskins
BLACKFIRENESS
BLACKFIRENESS
BLACKFIRENESS
Aint gonna be no more
billionaire bastards jet-set safari-ing
around the globe
polluting the AIR
polluting the WATER
polluting the LAND
polluting the POORPEOPLE
for Marquis de Sade-kicks
BLACKFIRENESS
BLACKFIRENESS
BLACKFIRENESS
BLACK FIRENESS
gonna spirit-springflame
all that decadent-dehumanising-demoralising stars&stripes pus-stuff
to plenty-plenty carbon atoms CARBON ADAM carbon atoms
Plants will eat the carbon atoms CARBON ADAM carbon atoms
&grow strong
budding lotsa lovely flowers to feed the spirit of the multitude
In stomachs of our souls
flowers will sing songs
while stars dance in the sky

You don't have to believe me
Ask flowers when you breathe BLACKFIRENESS
Ask full-loonymoons when you kiss BLACKFIRENESS
Ask stars when you dream BLACKFIRENESS
Ask ALLAH dancing &singing in the skies of BLACKFIRENESS

Ask ALLAH laughing &crying in the rivers of BLACKFIRENESS
Ask ALLAH running &jumping out of the earth of BLACKFIRENESS
Ask ALLAH creating &creating out of HIS fire of BLACKFIRENESS

This night's nightmare will pass
&giving birth to a new dawn

so peaceful
so lovely
as the SUN rises in the Orient
orientating us to an eternity of angel-eyed rainbow days

HARVEY TUCKER

Tossed Upon the Rock

There is no symbol like it;
the fist growing out of an open palm.

I have heard it called passion.
I have seen it tossed upon the rock
where Sheba sat, a Queen of Beauty.

It was black like the eyes of the wind.

I have seen the man crawl from the
slime of the sea. I have tasted the sweat
of his heart for twelve centuries of death.

He is not my brother.

I have slipped the lash of thorns around
his head. I have made him the mock-god of
my anger.

But he is not my brother.

I am white.
He is black like the eyes of the wind.

I have listened to his woman singing.
I have heard the same songs before.
They are the songs of the eagle that flies
through the turbulent thunder.

They are the hymns of a woman I did not love.

They sound black like the eyes of the wind.

I have held his head between my knees
and asked for the symbol's meaning.

He would not answer.
He would not speak the language of time.

It is too late.

The black angels are burning the sky.

He has come forth.
He has come with the head of the lamb
in his arms.
Beware of the prophecy.

It shall pass unto this land a new age.
It shall pass unto this age a new man.

He shall be called Adam.

And he shall be black like the eyes of the wind.

NANCY WILLARD

A Speech for the Unborn

When I felt you leap, we found you a name.
Though you are all head and belly,
though you have the gills of a fish,
shy and mysterious, you are biding your time.

Though I am a teacher, I can learn plenty from you.
About entrances, for example, and waiting
to show forth at the right time.
"Believe that it grows," I hear myself saying.

"You want to write? You can't name it?
Put it away, let it alone.
Prepare for the coming of ripeness
with songs of Thanksgiving."

O sing unto the Lord a new song.

We are a Christian nation,
we have too many days off for famous men.
Someday, I'll tell you how we marched,
you in me, me in forty thousand,

bearing no flags but the names of the dead.
Living and dead leap in the womb of a terrible war.
Once they too lay nameless and waiting,
now they wait and do not cry when we call them.

I carried the name of a boy from Harlem,
Washington Watson, who left no child
and no great works, nothing except his name,
which I called out to the spiked fence

along the avenues of justice and remorse,
in the great roll call of the dead,
as you danced shameless and merry,
and far away, men gave up their names

faster than ever men could carry them.

WM. WANTLING

Your Children's Dead Eyes

This is hardly a hymn of praise for the
older generations
But when we speak to you of change, you
reply why things must remain the same
you answer with excuses you answer with
lies

We speak to you of Asian massacres
You say they massacre too . . .
Where would you stop the slaughter? &
when? When they stop theirs?
You speak to us of VietCong terrorist
children carrying plastic bombs meant
for GI Joe
We mention women with children in arms
nailed to wooden walls by bullets
You speak to us of women with grenades
beneath maternity blouses
O speak to us of 3-year-old VietCong
terrorists with pigtails & sunshine grins
of VietCong terrorist babies spun in
the air like footballs
& O Brothers where did you get yr
Nazi bullets for those slant-eyed niggers
those yellow-skinned jews?

You are wrong You are wrong
You have made too many errors &
you are wrong
O we do not say we will not make errors
& we do not say you are ugly for having
been wrong
We will make mistakes we will be wrong
(my god how wrong we have been already . . .)
We say do not defend yr errors
while standing on yr graves
& ours
Do not create these concrete coffin mistakes
upon the edge of which you foolishly stand
Go gladly, go gently into the sweet Earth
feed the sweet Worms
& return to nourish yr children

as we must also enter the sweet ground
to nourish *our* children

& WE WANT CHILDREN   we want children
O   not 3, or 4, or half a dozen
but one for each pair of us
for what will we be without children?
We will be as you, gunning them down
from the machinegun graves of our errors
We do not want that no we do not want that

But when we speak to you of change
you reply why things must remain the same
You answer with excuses you answer with lies
You speak to us of VietCong terrorist puppies
of VietCong terrorist cows, chickens, & ducks
of VietCong terrorist flowers
& speak to us of VietCong terrorist students
sneaking up on brave guardsmen, ah the long
Ohio midwest afternoons
Speak to us now of defoliation
air & blood pollution, overpopulation
chemical & biological bombs
of the Nixon & Agnew hydrogen Apocalypse . . .

Speak to us of ghettos, budgets
arsenals, priorities, elections
of radiation cancer & yr children's
dead eyes   yr children's dead eyes
Speak to us of the Hsiao Mieh   the
NKVD   the SS   Auschwitz   Dienbienphu
Dachau   Algeria   Siberia   Hiroshima
Dresden   My Lai   Biafra   Buchenwald
Nagasaki   Lidice   Kent State   yr children's
dead eyes
Speak to us of murder rape plunder & pollution
& how, because we enjoy sex in the sun
we must be obscene
Yes . . .   When we speak to you of change
you reply why things must remain the same
you answer with excuses you answer with lies
Speak to us but remember
yr children's dead eyes

INDEX OF POEMS

INDEX OF POEMS